LAKELAND **FELLRANGER**

THE **FAR EASTERN** FELLS

by Mark Richards

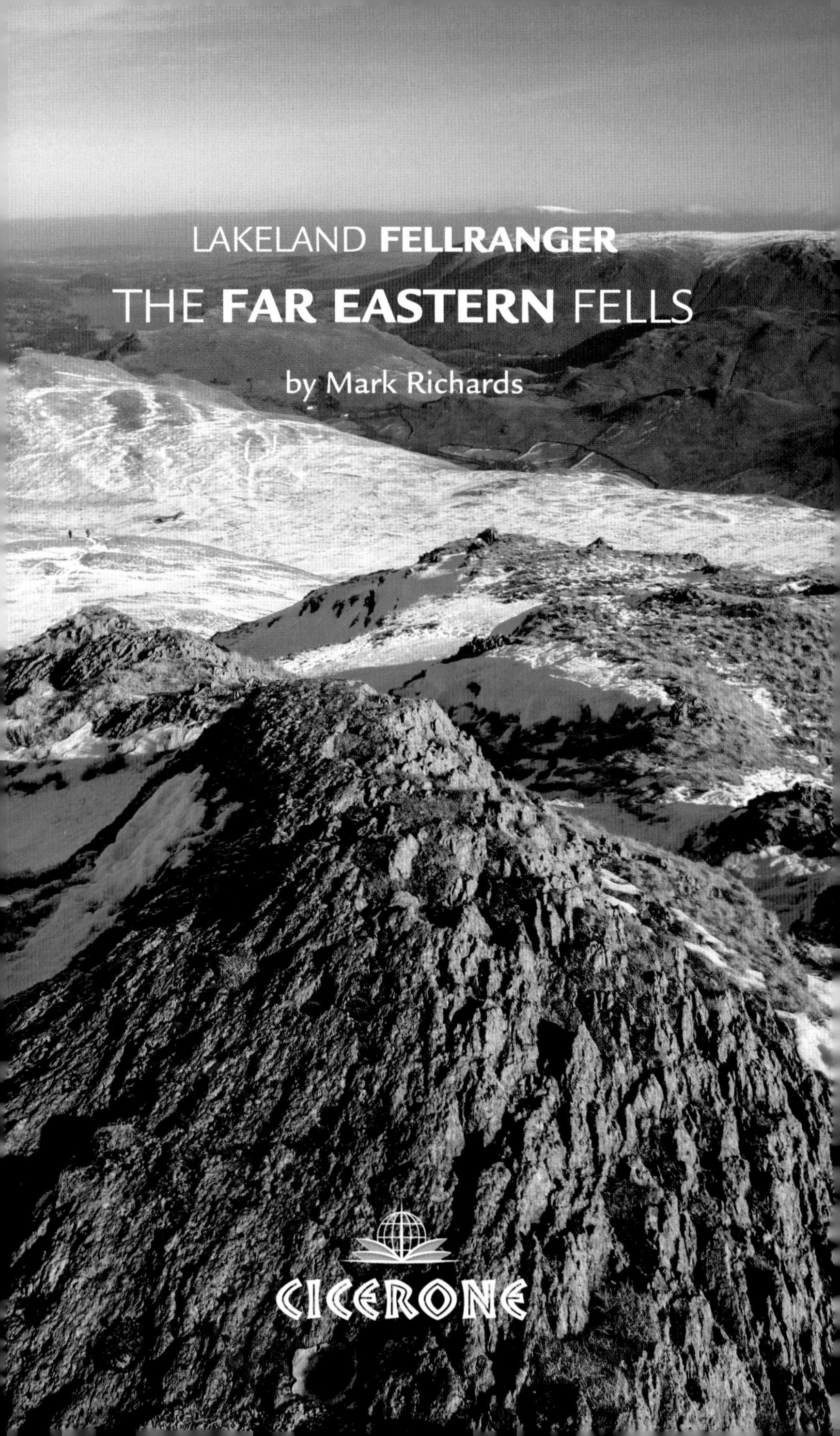

CICERONE

First edition 2013
ISBN: 978 1 85284 547 6

Printed by KHL Printing, Singapore

A catalogue record for this book is available from the British Library.

Artwork and photographs by the author.

Maps are reproduced with permission from HARVEY Maps, www.harveymaps.co.uk.

To the Friends of the Lake District, for 80 years watchful guardians of the integrity of this amazing mountain landscape, and of which, for half that time, I have been an appreciative member.

ADVICE TO READERS

While every effort is made by our authors to ensure the accuracy of guidebooks as they go to print, changes can occur during the lifetime of an edition. If we know of any, there will be an Updates tab on this book's page on the Cicerone website (www.cicerone.co.uk), so please check before planning your trip. We also advise that you check information about such things as transport, accommodation and shops locally. Even rights of way can be altered over time. We are always grateful for information about any discrepancies between a guidebook and the facts on the ground, sent by email to info@cicerone.co.uk or by post to Cicerone, 2 Police Square, Milnthorpe LA7 7PY, United Kingdom.

Front cover: Upper Kentmere valley (Chapters 8, 16, 33)
Title page: Looking north from Hart Crag on the descent from Place Fell (Chapter 21)

CONTENTS

ABOUT THE AUTHOR

The Cumbrian fells have held a lifetime's attraction for me. Brought up in the far-flung west Oxfordshire countryside, the romance of the high fells tugged at my emotions from my youth. In 2001 my wife and I were able to up sticks and make a permanent home within sight of the Lakeland mountains. The move was triggered by a commission to research and prepare the Lakeland Fellranger series, which has now found its natural Cumbrian home with Cicerone Press.

My early experience of walking in fell country came in two guises. My mother's cousin was a farm manager on a fell estate near Kirkby Lonsdale. Hence summer holidays were spent gathering sheep and tending cattle. Although busman's holidays from my stockman's life in Oxfordshire, these were great experiences, developing my awareness of the magic of fell country.

By my late teens the lure of mountains for recreation had taken a real hold, and shortly after joining a mountaineering club I met, and became a regular house-guest of, Alfred Wainwright. Just being with such a gifted artist and writer was very special. We shared a delight in drawing and in poring over maps and walking-guide ideas. He quickly saw my own appetite for pen and ink and my passion for the countryside, the fells in particular, and he encouraged me to consider creating my own illustrated guides.

Completion of this final volume is but the first step in a shared journey. The high plateau of personal fulfillment is tempered by a realisation, that while the series may have come of age, only now can its intended purpose meaningfully take root… After 14 years, 227 fells have been thoroughly explored in all weathers and seasons, backed up with many thousands of hours pinned to the desk with keyboard or pen in hand. With eBooks and downloads complementing the in-the-hand guides, only now can the series truly be seen as a complete guide for walkers and explorers of the Lakeland Fells.

To know the fells is a privilege: cherish your precious time in their company. Breathe deeply the wild fell domain. Respect all who you meet, especially those for whom this is a working landscape.

Mark Richards 2013

FROM FIRESIDE TO FELLSIDE

Free time spent out on the fell is always the very best of time. You may sit at home poring over maps and consulting guides, letting the imagination run riot, but nothing beats the fun and thrill of actually being out there. To wander by lonely becks and over rough fellsides, to climb to high cairned summits, to sense the freedom, space and sheer beauty of it all is a transforming experience beyond poetic words and pictorial expression. Walkers notice the contrasts of seasons and time of day, the play of light and shadow, the mischievous antics of mist and cloud. They cope with wind and rain, snow and ice in an environment that they come to know by stints and stages. The form and character of each fell become recognisable, like friends from childhood – reliable, and happy in reunion whatever the time span since last in their acquaintance. The walker harbours memories of times past with these companions and relishes new days in their company. How grateful we are for their existence, these magical fells.

THIS SERIES

Begun in 1989 while I was still living in Oxfordshire, Lakeland Fellranger owes its inspirational roots to my mentor, Alfred Wainwright, who encouraged me to believe that I too could learn to craft practical, inspirational guides to the best of walking landscapes way back in the early 1970s. This self-belief grew over the years and has been an ever-present part of my life. My upbringing and destiny seemed entirely wedded to farming and the land. But at 40 I took the plunge and turned, almost full time, to my

↑ Summit of Rough Crag (Chapter 15)

Walkers on the Patterdale path from Sandwick (Chapter 21)

first love of preparing walking guides. A passion for pen and ink drawing and a pleasure in exploring combined to give me opportunities to fashion guidebooks to inspiring places for many years, principally for Cicerone Press. Ultimately, the magical draw of the fells could be resisted no longer and this series was born. It was first published by HarperCollins and later Cicerone stepped in and gave new life and vigour to my work. My faithful readers are now rewarded for their patience with the full reference set of eight guides. Modern publishing enables regular revisions, and I look forward to future opportunities to wander these fabulous fells to ensure that the series remains accurate and up to date.

THIS GUIDE

This volume examines the lovely tract of fell country east of Ullswater, which has its high connection with the Near Eastern Fells upon Kirkstone Pass. This body of fells has a strong north–south spine traced by the Roman 'High Street', with a lattice of ridges embedding secretive dales, so many of exquisite beauty and charm. There are

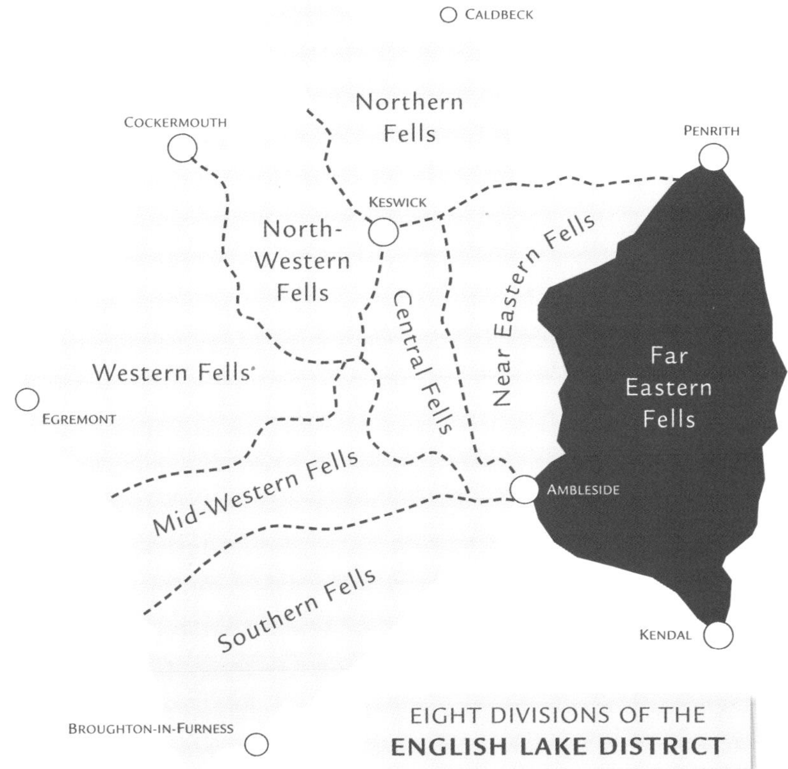

EIGHT DIVISIONS OF THE
ENGLISH LAKE DISTRICT

Harter Crag from the Gatescarth track (Chapter 12)

several notable reservoir 'lakes' and a handful of high-set tarns. The valleys, entered by quiet country roads, are every bit a part of the appeal of this area, as this is indeed a walkers' world. There are some really fine fells (some with a hint of mountainhood), steep climbs and gentle slopes, and several fabulous skyline horseshoe walks to whet your appetite for dedicated fellwalking holidays in the area.

The original National Park took the A6 as its eastern boundary. Plans are in train to extend that line towards the M6 to embrace the shy beauties of Bretherdale and Borrowdale – hence their inclusion on 'The Far Eastern Fells' projection graphic (see page 13). The flanking ridges of Whinash and Whinfell are not described in this guide, as they would make over-long expeditions. Downloadable descriptions of walks on the Whinash and Whinfell ridges can be found among the series prepared by the author on the Cumbria County Council website (www.cumbria.gov.uk) – click on 'Roads and travel' > 'Open Access in Cumbria' > 'Open Access walks in Cumbria'.

For ease of reference the 33 fell chapters are arranged in alphabetical order. Each chapter begins with a customised HARVEY map that illustrates the routes of ascent described in the guide, and shows ridge connections to neighbouring fells to assist in the planning of extended walks. The corresponding text describes routes up the fell from given valley starting points, identified on the map by a number (shown in a blue box). The starting points are listed in the 'Starting Points' table on page 18, and are also given in blue (in brackets) after the ascent route headings in the walks. In many

KEY TO FELL MAPS

 Route as a defined path

 Route as an intermittent or undefined path

 Fell summit

 Starting point

 Route number

For other symbols see HARVEY map key p14.

instances there is also a diagram that shows the routes from a particular perspective to assist visualisation.

The primary routes to the summit are described, with optional variations given, up to their natural point of connection with the more common route. Where a route follows a defined path this is shown on the map and diagram in red dashes, and where the recommended route follows an intermittent path (or there is no path on the ground at all) this is shown in green dashes. Where a route follows a road it is not picked out by dashed lines. Being aware of the safest lines of descent is important, and advice is given on these for nearly all fells. There are far more paths on the fells than are shown on a conventional HARVEY map, and for clarity this guide only shows the paths and routes that are described here.

As a good guide should also be a revelation, a full panorama is provided for each fell summit or better nearby viewpoint. This names the principal fells and picks out key features in their midst, with some more distant features beyond the national park to intrigue. When undertaking the walks in the guide, you are advised to take a map and compass with you (and know how to use them). The map can enhance your day by showing additional landscape features and setting your walk in its wider context, as well as being useful for your own safety. And remember that representation of a route in this guide, in whatever form, does not imply safe passage for all, at any time. The onus is on each individual to weigh up their own capabilities and the prevailing conditions. In fellwalking, as in any mountain travel, knowing when to retreat is often the greater part of valour. The author has taken care to follow time-honoured routes and has kept within bounds of access, yet cannot guarantee rights of way in all cases.

FIX THE FELLS

While we all relish a 'fix of the fells', our collective passing has, over time, brought about a need to secure the worn hill ways. Elsewhere in this series the work of the Fix the Fells project and its landscape restoration of the most seriously damaged fell paths has been consistently highlighted. The process has been a great learning curve, and the more recent pitching is superb, ensuring a flat foot-fall where possible and being easy to use in ascent and descent. The trails are not universally pleasant underfoot, but the process represents a huge step forward for the fell environment.

However, invariably these trails are not rights of way and are therefore beyond the statutory responsibility of the highway authority. Hence this partnership of the

National Park Authority, National Trust and Natural England, with additional financial support from the Friends of the Lake District, has worked to make good the hill paths. The whole effort has been made possible by third-party match-funding from the Heritage Lottery Fund.

Just as the fells have no respite from walkers, so the need to make good the paths has no end point, and neither does the pre-emptive repair work to stop paths from washing out in the first place, 'a pitch in time'. The local business-oriented environmental charity Nurture Lakeland also contributes significantly to this work, but with a metre of path costing up to £150 there is every good reason to cultivate the involvement of fellwalkers in a cause that must be dear to their hearts... and soles! Should we not all become fell champions? Make a beeline for www.fixthefells.co.uk to mark your commitment by giving a personal donation.

Clearly the occasional gift is welcome, but this is still only a tiny injection. If it were the culture for fellwalkers to make regular donations, so much the better – this would indeed be the making of a fell champion. If every pint purchased in Lakeland pubs included a 10p donation (made unless drinkers chose to opt out), imagine the cash that would generate. For me a new stile, signpost or length of restored path signals hope and optimism for the future. It means that walkers will come again to enjoy afresh the liberty of our cherished countryside and wild places – and you can be part of the future by giving a little and often. In exemplary manner Fellranger's author and publisher contribute a sum from their royalties and sales to support Fix the Fells.

ACCESS

May 2005 saw the implementation of the Countryside and Rights of Way (CROW) Act in Cumbria, from which time most rough open country became conditionally

Walkers in Martindale (Chapter 3)

accessible to walkers. The so-called 'right to roam' legislation is in truth something of a sledge hammer to crack a nut. Quite the majority of fellwalkers only feel at ease when striding upon a clear path, especially one that has a time-honoured sense of purpose, while the roving instinct, a broad-brush freedom to randomly explore trackless country, appeals to a narrow band of walkers. I love the liberty of exploring open country with a map, but being wedded to the preparation of practical guides, my liberty is tempered by the need to properly reflect regular routes and, where inventive, to be discerning.

SAFETY

Being constantly alive to, and aware, of the potential dangers of walking in high fell country is essential for everyone, and most especially those who come new to this activity. Fell craft, the intuition to know when to proceed and when to retreat, is an important skill to learn. The National Park Authority provides practical, up-to-date advice ranging from daily weather checks (Weatherline 0844 846 2444, 24hr fell forecast) to guided walks aimed at absolute beginners. As a first recourse obtain a copy of their leaflet 'Safety on the Fells' and consult their website (www.lake-district.gov.uk). A further important source of advice is the website of the Mountain Rescue organisation for England and Wales (www.mountain.rescue.org.uk).

ADVISORY NOTE

The National Park has prepared a short advisory note for conscientious walkers.

- Place your feet thoughtfully – every single footstep causes wear and tear on the environment. The slow-growing plants that can survive on mountains are particularly vulnerable.
- Keep to the path surface – do not walk along the vegetation at the edge of the path.
- Do not build or add to cairns – paths need stones more than cairns do.
- Do not take shortcuts – water will soon follow your tracks and an erosion scar will develop. Remember, there may be only one of you, but there are another 12 million pairs of feet treading Lake District paths every year.

FELL REVIEW

Visit www.markrichards.info to find the Fell Review, within the Lakeland Fellranger section. This contains dedicated fell galleries showing a more thorough pictorial record of the author's research of each fell. More importantly there are also downloadable PDFs of each fell's summit panorama – handy to print out and take to the fell-top. Readers can also follow the author on Twitter @fellranger1.

River Sprint at Cleft Ghyll (Chapter 28)

THE **FAR EASTERN** FELLS

four graphic projections of the range

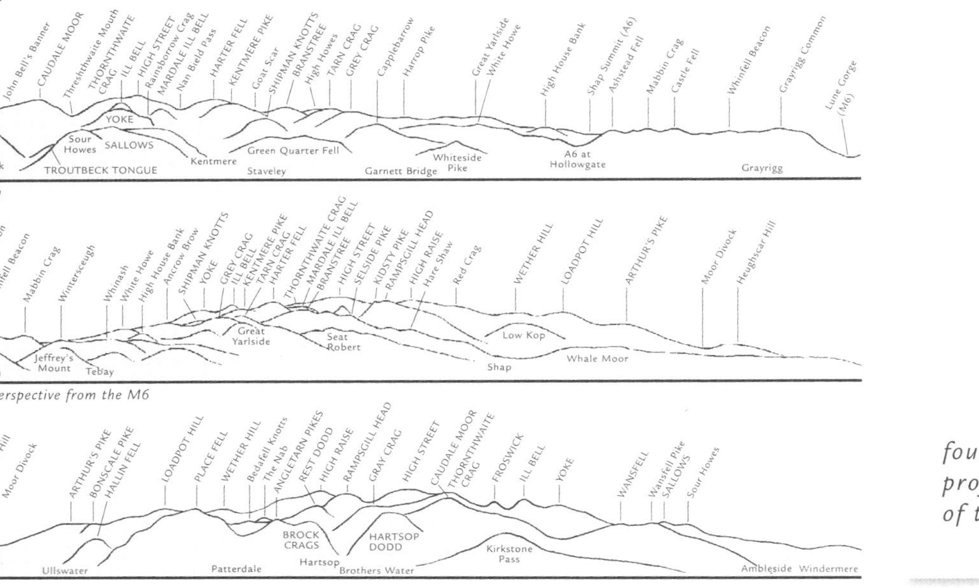

HARVEY MAP KEY

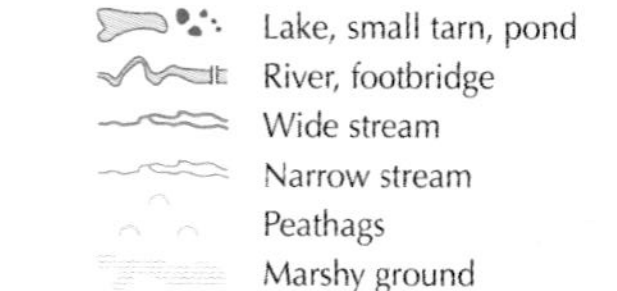

- Lake, small tarn, pond
- River, footbridge
- Wide stream
- Narrow stream
- Peathags
- Marshy ground

- Contour (15m interval)
- Index contour (75m interval)
- Auxiliary contour
- Scree, spoil heap
- Boulder field
- Scattered rock and boulders
- Predominantly rocky ground
- Major crag, large boulder
- O.S. trig pillar, large cairn
- Spot height (from air survey)

Contours change from brown to grey where the ground is predominantly rocky outcrops, small crags and other bare rock.

- Farmland
- Fell or moorland
- Open forest or woodland
- Dense forest or woodland
- Felled or new plantation
- Forest ride or firebreak
- Settlement
- Boundary, maintained
- Boundary, remains

On moorland, walls, ruined walls and fences are shown. For farmland, only the outer boundary wall or fence is shown.

SCALE 1 : 40,000

- Dual carriageway
- Main road (fenced)
- Minor road (unfenced)
- Track or forest road
- Footpath or old track
- Intermittent path
- Powerline, pipeline
- Building, ruin or sheepfold, shaft
- Pike — Fell summits that feature as chapters in this guidebook.

The representation of a road, track or footpath is no evidence of the existence of a right of way.

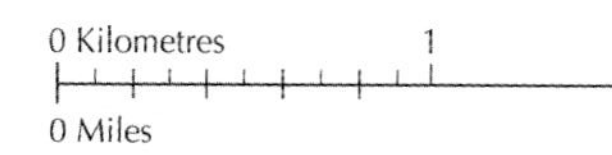

THE **FAR EASTERN** FELLS

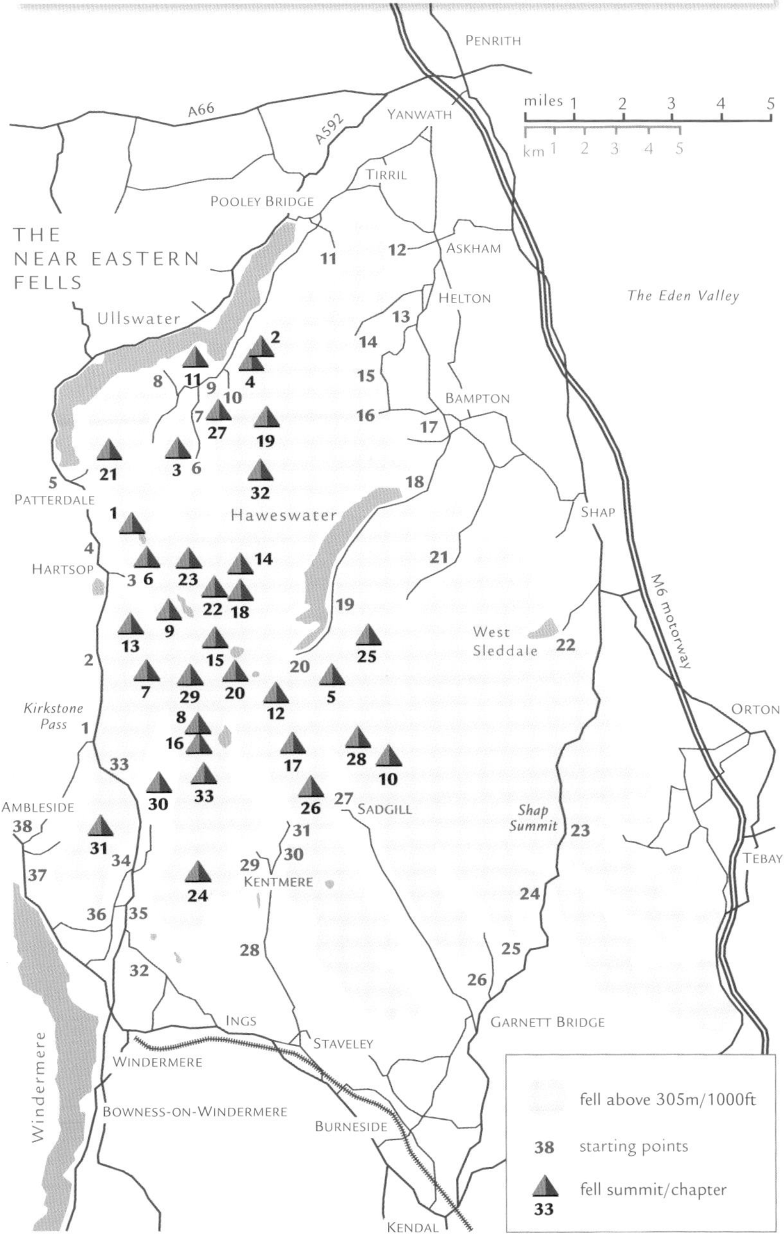

PENRITH
A66
A592
YANWATH
TIRRIL
POOLEY BRIDGE
ASKHAM
HELTON
BAMPTON
THE NEAR EASTERN FELLS
Ullswater
The Eden Valley
PATTERDALE
Haweswater
SHAP
HARTSOP
M6 motorway
West Sleddale
Kirkstone Pass
ORTON
AMBLESIDE
SADGILL
Shap Summit
TEBAY
KENTMERE
INGS
STAVELEY
GARNETT BRIDGE
WINDERMERE
Windermere
BOWNESS-ON-WINDERMERE
BURNESIDE
KENDAL

miles 1 2 3 4 5
km 1 2 3 4 5

fell above 305m/1000ft
38 starting points
33 fell summit/chapter

Gully at the head of the Kentmere valley looking to the Ill Bell range (Chapter 29)

FELL MOSAIC

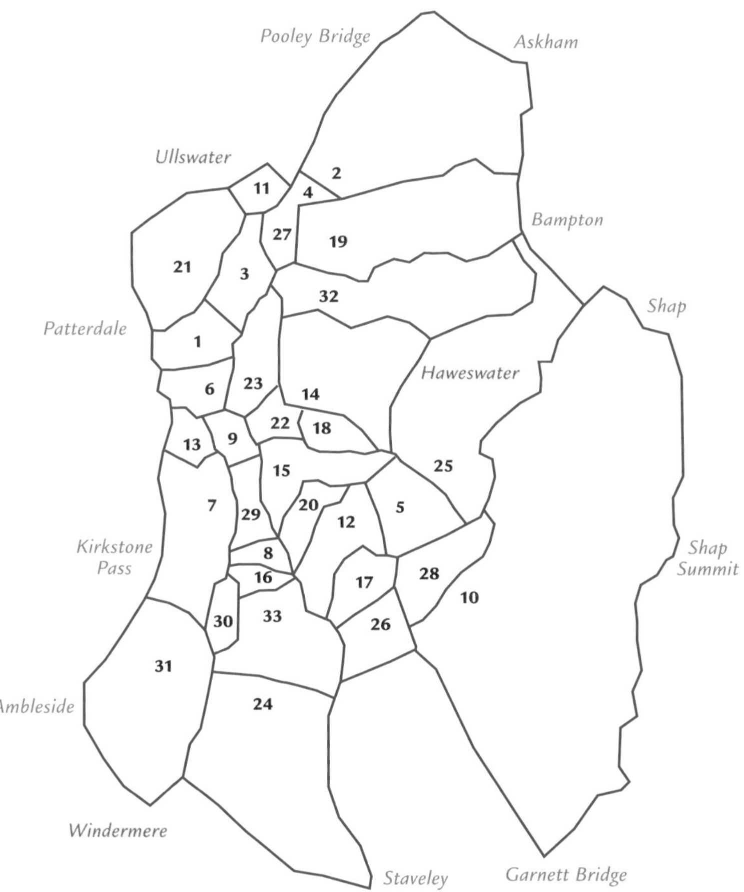

Fell chapters

STARTING POINTS

LOCATION	GRID REFERENCE	PARKING	BUS
1 Kirkstone Pass	401081	P	B
2 Caudale Bridge	403115	L	B
3 Hartsop	410131	P (voluntary fee)	B
4 Deepdale Bridge	399144	L	B
5 Patterdale	396159	P&D	B
6 Dalehead	434165	IN	
7 Martindale	434184	IN	
8 Sandwick	424196	IN	
9 The Hause	435193	P	
10 Fusedale	445194	IN	
11 Roehead	479236	L	
12 Askham	507235	IN	
13 Helton	498214	IN	
14 Helton Fell	488206	IN	
15 Cockle Hill	496195	IN	
16 Bampton	514183	L	
17 Moorahill	493182	IN	
18 Burnbanks	508162	P	
19 Mardale Banks	479119	L	
20 Mardale Head	469107	P	
21 Swindale	522143	IN	
22 Wet Sleddale	555114	P	
23 Shap Summit	554063	P	B
24 Hollowgate	548032	IN	
25 Bannisdale Bridge	543013	IN	
26 Plough Lane	530999	IN	
27 Sadgill	483056	IN	
28 Ullthwaite Bridge	456012	L	
29 Kentmere	456041	P&D	
30 Nunnery Beck	462043	L	
31 High Lane, Hallow Bank	464050	L	
32 Moor Howe	423006	IN	
33 Woundale	409067	L	B
34 Town Head	415040	L	B
35 Church Bridge	413027	L	B
36 Town End	405019	L	
37 Old Lakes Road	377038	P&D	B
38 Rydal Road	375047	P&D	B

P – formal car park
P&D – pay and display car park
L – lay-by parking
IN – informal parking

Bus services – **Kirkstone Rambler** seasonal service from Bowness to Glenridding. All year round the **108** Penrith to Patterdale and the **106/107** Penrith to Kendal (serves Shap).

Ill Bell from Nan Bield Pass | January 2013 MARK RICHARDS *linescape*

1 ANGLETARN PIKES *(567m/1860ft)*

Angletarn Pikes is a fell that merits all the time you can give it. Although it is most commonly climbed from either Patterdale or Hartsop in the Goldrill vale, ascents may spring from Martindale or Boredale as part of either a compact fell-round that can include Place Fell or Beda Fell or, on occasion, a greater round, including High Raise, Rampsgill Head and Rest Dodd.

Indulge yourself and wander to the shores of Angle Tarn, one of Lakeland's most enchanting mountain pools. Its situation, in a high basin south of the summit, is delightful. Find here two islets, and indeed a third knoll linked to the shore by an isthmus, which is a popular wild-camp pitch. Photographers will love the opportunities the tarn provides, especially as a foreground for a reflective vista of the Helvellyn range. Birds too find the lake alluring, and on occasion geese can be encountered honking rowdily. Walkers on the Coast to Coast Walk give it their fleeting admiration, while fellwalkers unshackled by such time constraints can linger long and appreciate other aspects of the fell. On the secret eastern flank find Heck Crag and Cove, wild places more than matched by the tarn's outflowing beck into the Goldrill vale, which itself provides a fascinating little-tried gorge ascent, although steep intermediate ground means that it is not suitable for every walker.

 ↑ Chiselled profile of the summit bastion from the north

ASCENT FROM PATTERDALE (5)

Via Boredale Hause 400m/1310ft 2.9km/1¾ miles

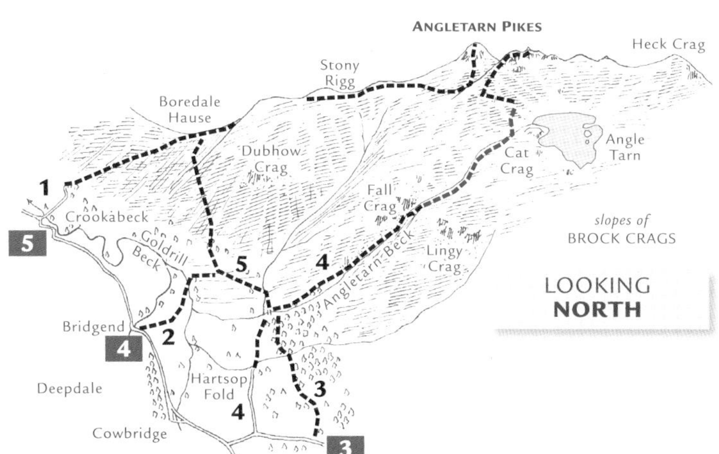

1 Head S through the narrow street between the village shop and White Lion Hotel to bear left with the no through road leading over Goldrill Beck. This leads by a cluster of properties and bears left to be confronted by gates. Guided by the slate sign 'Angle Tarn, Boredale Hause' go through the gate and after 50m swing up right. Climb the steep bracken slope, keeping to the lower of the two adjacent paths to reach Boredale Hause, with plenty of opportunities to stop and admire the rising crescendo of a view back over Patterdale. On meeting a path rising from the right, ford Stonebarrow Gill above the fold and keep with the path, which has some pitching as it leads through a gill notch. As you come upon a fine bird's-eye view down over the Goldrill Beck valley to Brothers Water, the path forks. Take the higher path, which runs under the summit bastion, which can be climbed either from the north or more simply from the south.

ASCENT FROM DEEPDALE BRIDGE (4)

Via Boredale Hause 400m/1310ft 3.2km/2 miles

2 From the road bridge follow the short lane E between cottages to a kissing-gate and embark on a meadow traverse by way of a stile, kissing-gate and finally a stile onto an open track. Keep on to cross the Goldrill Beck bridge and swing left to an acute track junction. Bear right signed 'Hartsop'. After 70m come to a further acute track junction and here break up left on a path engineered during the laying of the Hayeswater aqueduct pipeline. The ascent is minimal for a while, giving plenty of scope to enjoy the beautiful vale, and only latterly does it climb more earnestly to reach the pass,

Lower falls in Angletarn Beck

converging with a path from Patterdale. Come above a spoil bank and fold to bear right on a partly pitched path (part of the Coast to Coast Walk). This leads through a nick to come upon a lovely downward view to Brothers Water. When the path forks, take the upward way which leads under the summit ridge. Either veer left on a minor path and gain the ridge from the north, or more naturally continue to break up from the south.

ASCENT FROM HARTSOP (3)

Via Angletarn Beck 440m/1445ft 3km/2 miles

3 Begin at the wooden signpost a matter of 30m west from the car park, and rise upon a concrete roadway, via a gate, that provides access to the outside world for two elevated bungalows. The roadway enjoys lovely views before dipping to a three-way fork. Keep ahead, guided by a yellow waymark, and pass Grey Rigg along a

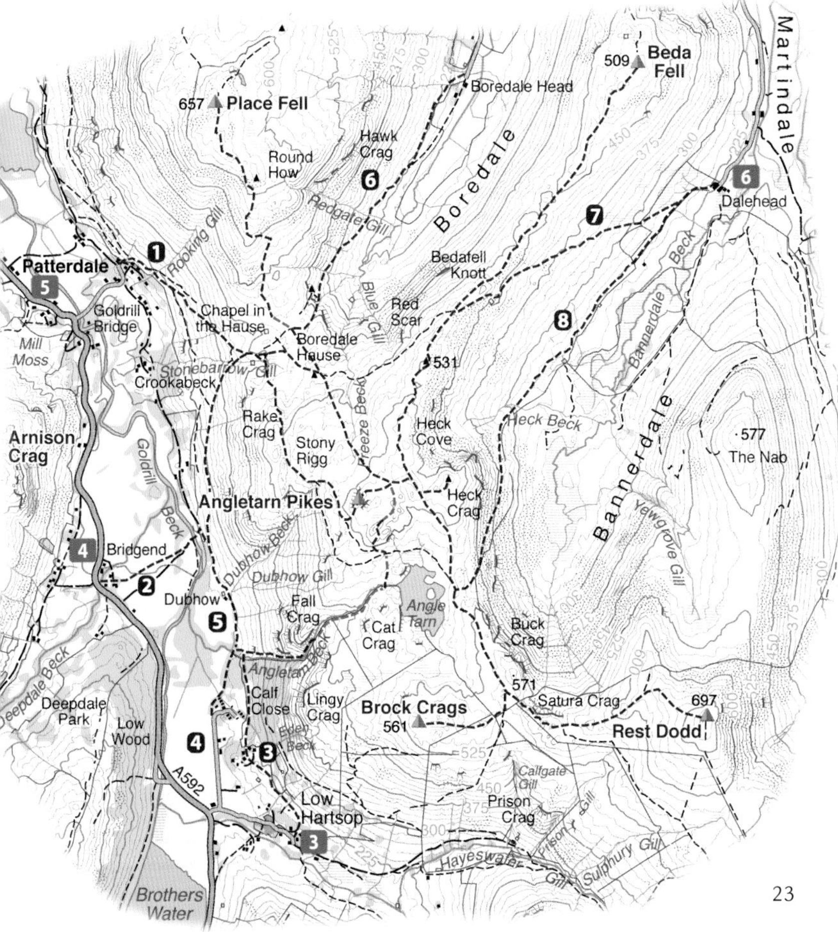

confined passage to a hand-gate. Thereafter the path declines via rocky ground and a small ford of the ambitiously named Eden Beck to go through a hand-gate and ford the target beck beneath an impressive set of leaping falls.

Via Hartsop Fold 420m/1380ft 2.9km/1¾ miles

4 Alternatively, you may opt for a more casual start, avoiding early ascent, by following the approach road back towards the main valley road and turning right 50m short at a white house, Langton Adventure Centre, along the byroad signed 'Hartsop Fold'. After the chalet park this becomes a confined path leading to a gate, ford and footbridge spanning Angletarn Beck.

Fall Crag and the upper falls of Angletarn Beck

Bear up right on the north bank to meet a fording lateral path. The ascent is obvious, although there are moments when a steady step is needed as you work up the rocky flank that accompanies a sequence of lovely cascades. Fall Crag eventually intervenes, and you are obliged to ford and progress with a wall close left. Views towards Brothers Water give rise to many a backward glance. At a wall junction turn right (SE) and follow this wall over damp fell, approaching the next wall junction. Drift half-left to avoid marshy ground and pass through a narrow wall-gap (former shepherding gate) and complete the ascent pathless up the grassy bank.

Via Boredale Hause **450m/1475ft 4.2km/2½ miles**

5 From the footbridge over Angletarn Beck follow on with the open track secreting the Hayeswater aqueduct pipeline. Dubhow Beck is briefly channelled before a ford brings the path beside a wall, the path duly arriving at the point where the aqueduct begins its climb to Boredale Hause. Follow this rising track (as with Routes 1 and 2).

ASCENT FROM SANDWICK (8 – off map N) OR THE HAUSE (9 – off map N)

Via Boredale Hause **450m/1475ft 6km/3¾ miles**

6 Boredale has no casual parking, so instead park at Sandwick or The Hause. By either start point advance with the minor country road into Boredale (the valley name means 'the valley with a store-house') to approach the furthest farmstead. A permissive path veers up right short of the gate entry into Boredale Head, thereby avoiding

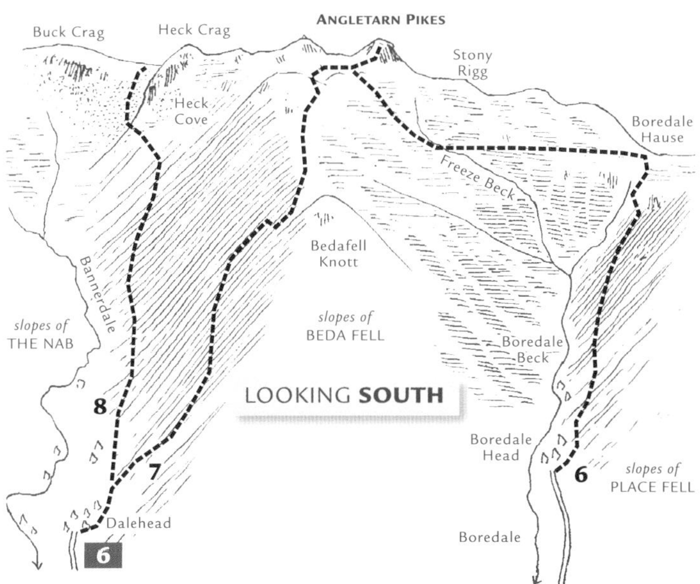

East peak from the summit

disturbance within the intimate environs of the farmstead. Climb to a ford and contour above the tree-sheltered dwellings to connect with the open bridle track (which otherwise runs through the farmyard). The seclusion of the dale head is manifest on the steady rise, which comes up beneath a lead mine retaining wall to where the old path hairpins right. Keep on through the stony gully, passing inspection covers on the Hayeswater aqueduct. The path comes up onto the undulating Boredale Hause. Veer left on a bridle path, being sure to break right at a cairn, where the route turns S to ford Freeze Beck high up as the shapely profile of the main summit ridge of Angletarn Pikes comes into view. The path draws left onto the saddle; here find a path that bears right to avoid a peaty hollow en route to the summit ridge.

ASCENT FROM MARTINDALE (7)

Via Bedafell Knott 355m/1165ft 3km/2 miles

7 Park 50m short of the farmyard at Dalehead. Refrain from passing through the farmyard. Instead, go right by the deer notice at the turning point, ford the gill and go through the hand-gate. Bear up left above the farmstead enclosure and go over a plank-bridge to rise with the green track and come beside the field-wall. Quickly spot a sign directing up on a lateral path, which is little more than a sheep trod at this point. After fording a tiny gill this becomes more significant as it rises to a gate/stile where a fence meets the wall of an insular enclosure. The bridle path mounts steadily on a long diagonal course. Ignore the quad track which takes a short-cut up the flank of the fell to the skyline ridge; it is better by far to keep with the age-old inter-dale route. High up, come upon the lower walls of a bothy (a room with a view alright) overlooking Heck Cove. The ridge arrives with a tiny cairn at the cross-paths. Turn left and follow the lovely ridgeway SSW, soon to be tantalised by the castle of Angletarn Pikes. Come above Heck Cove to follow a comparatively minor branch path right, which quickly beelines to the shapely summit ridge of the west peak.

Via Heck Crag 360m/1180ft 3.8km/2½ miles

8 A scenically surreptitious ascent, ill suited for descent. Begin as Route 7, but keep the intake wall close left on a level course. After a fence-gate the green way leads on into Bannerdale, looking down upon a sycamore-shaded field barn and then a ruin incorporated in the adjacent wall. The Nab is the big presence throughout this phase of the journey, and – given good fortune – a herd of red deer may be seen quietly grazing in the dale-bottom pasture. The path drifts slightly away from the wall as it approaches a gate (do not go through). Heck Cove is the focus of attention, with Heck Crag looming ahead, and as the path mounts it comes under its spell, with a strange glacial hollow at its base. The path now embarks on an altogether more flimsy course, traversing the steep slope with patches of scree on a very narrow trod – watch your footing. As next Buck Crag dominates the view ahead, the path climbs to come beside the higher section of the wall. Duly, and with much anticipation, the path comes over the brow. Spread out in the shallow hollow below is the sparkling jewel of Angle Tarn. Bear right with the regular path, forking right again to keep with the rising path going N as it heads back towards the top of Heck Crag (its own summit cairn may be visited). Depart from the ridge path left to reach the summit on a thin path over intervening marshy ground.

The Helvellyn range in view across Angle Tarn

THE SUMMIT

The fell has the most unusual summit arrangement. Two parallel spine ridges of hard volcanic rock 200m apart vie for supremacy, defended to the north by a peaty hollow. The eastern top has a cairn, but concedes a few metres to the western top, which has the better view, too, with the fells surrounding Deepdale especially impressive.

The southern aspect of the summit ridge

SAFE DESCENTS

The popular path skirting round to the south and east of the summit bastion offers the best line of escape in inclement weather; veer north to reach Boredale Hause for Patterdale.

RIDGE ROUTES

BEDA FELL ↓ 135m/445ft ↑ 80m/265ft 2.9km/1¾ miles

Head E off the summit ridge, crossing the marshy ground to join the ridge path. Now turn N, with a consistent path all the way. Watch your step in negotiating Bedafell Knott and in coping with some marshy ground on the approach to the summit.

BROCK CRAGS ↓ 105m/345ft ↑ 100m/330ft 2.2km/1½ miles

There are several variations possible, even the direct boggy beeline. However, keeping to a stricter sense of a ridge route head E to unite with the path from Beda Fell. This path declines SE and, joining the popular path from Boredale Hause, runs on above the eastern shores of Angle Tarn. Rising behind Buck Crag find a path forking right, short of an intervening wall; this leads down to a gateway, but don't go through. Bear right (W), with the wall first to the left and then right, before stepping over and through a pool-filled hollow to reach the summit cairn.

PLACE FELL ↓ 180m/590ft ↑ 270m/885ft 2.7km/1¾ miles

Depart E to connect with the minor path crossing W–NW into the headstream of Freeze Beck. Coming down, merge with the bridle path straddling the Beda Fell ridge

Angletarn Pikes backed by Place Fell from Brock Crags

from Bannerdale. Stride over the undulating saddle of Boredale Hause and link onto the newly enhanced path winding onto Place Fell.

REST DODD ↓ 90m/300ft ↑220m/720ft 3km/2 miles

Follow suit with the path to Brock Crags. However, keep to the regular path, crossing a wall and the awkward bedrock on top of Satura Crag, after which the path splits. Take the left-hand option, rising from E to NE onto the grassy ridge. Keep climbing where the path forks again, mounting over the brow to find the summit cairn lurking beyond a peaty step.

PANORAMA

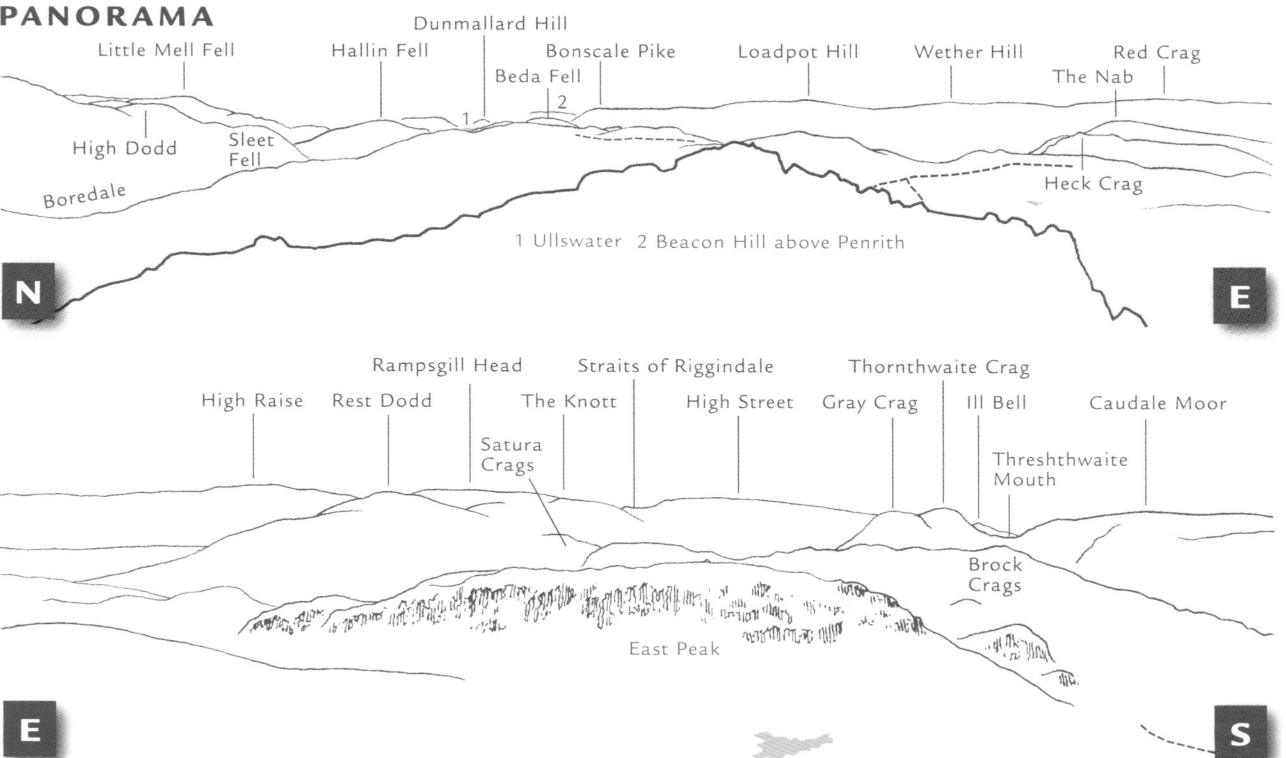
Dunmallard Hill
Little Mell Fell
Hallin Fell
Bonscale Pike
Loadpot Hill
Wether Hill
Red Crag
Beda Fell
The Nab
1
2
High Dodd
Sleet Fell
Heck Crag
Boredale
1 Ullswater 2 Beacon Hill above Penrith
N
E
Rampsgill Head
Straits of Riggindale
Thornthwaite Crag
High Raise
Rest Dodd
The Knott
High Street
Gray Crag
Ill Bell
Caudale Moor
Satura Crags
Threshthwaite Mouth
Brock Crags
East Peak
E
S

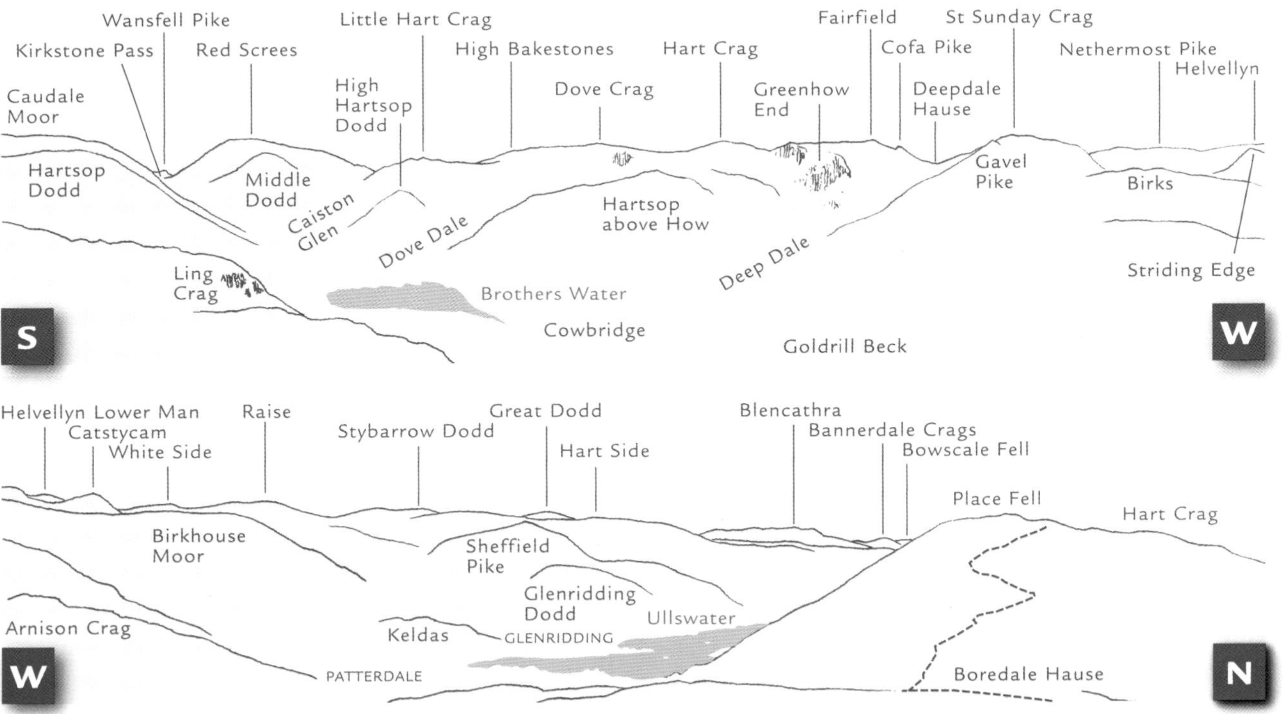
Wansfell Pike
Kirkstone Pass
Red Screes
Little Hart Crag
High Bakestones
Hart Crag
Fairfield
Cofa Pike
St Sunday Crag
Nethermost Pike
Helvellyn
Caudale Moor
High Hartsop Dodd
Dove Crag
Greenhow End
Deepdale Hause
Hartsop Dodd
Middle Dodd
Caiston Glen
Dove Dale
Hartsop above How
Gavel Pike
Birks
Deep Dale
Ling Crag
Brothers Water
Striding Edge
S
Cowbridge
Goldrill Beck
W
Helvellyn Lower Man
Catstycam
White Side
Raise
Stybarrow Dodd
Great Dodd
Hart Side
Blencathra
Bannerdale Crags
Bowscale Fell
Place Fell
Hart Crag
Birkhouse Moor
Sheffield Pike
Glenridding Dodd
Ullswater
Arnison Crag
Keldas
GLENRIDDING
W
PATTERDALE
Boredale Hause
N

2 ARTHUR'S PIKE *(533m/1749ft)*

Viewed from the foot of Ullswater Arthur's Pike has a strong identity, which is all but lost from other angles, as strictly it is no more than the leading shoulder of Loadpot Hill. Many's the walker who ventures to this grand little summit and turns tail, content with the view and rejecting the lure of Loadpot. Well, the view is so good, the effort sufficient and the maze of ways a delight. Not one trod attempts to climb the western shield of irregular crags, as they prohibit assault. The fell-top lies a suitable distance from a convenient road – perhaps this is one of its virtues – so walkers get a good leg stretch over open country from Roehead, Askham or Helton. Indeed, some may find the perfect harmony of lake and fell by taking the cruise from Pooley Bridge on the Ullswater steamer. Alight at the Howtown jetty and climb via Bonscale Pike to revel in two cairned viewpoints before wending easily down via The Cockpit to Roehead and continuing by the single-track road into the village.

Mountain limestone scarp at Heugh Scar

↑ Arthur's Pike escarpment from low on Hallin Fell

ASCENT FROM ROEHEAD (11)

Via The Cockpit 320m/1050ft 4.7km/3 miles

1 At the top of the single-track road from Pooley Bridge find a generous parking verge. Pass through the gate and follow the open track all the way up to the cairn, almost on the brow, and here bear off right on the firm dry path which leads to The Cockpit. Keep right with the main path and shortly after the ford find a small cairn that marks the point of departure from the popular bridleway. To all intents this is the Roman road, climbing at an easy gradient up Barton Fell. After 1.6km (1 mile) take the right-hand fork to cross the infant Aik Beck, steering towards the palpable summit, although paths seem to bypass it, and cut back N to reach the cairn.

Via Heughscar Hill 320m/1050ft 5.8km/3½ miles

2 An attractive extended variant – ideal if you have in mind to make Arthur's Pike the culmination of your fell day, as this brings a bonus limestone hill-scarp into the equation. A matter of 100m above the gate on the open track find a rough trod breaking half-left up the slope and climbing to where the wall-corners under a bower of mature trees. The grass path continues NE to duly unite with a more regularly used grass track beyond the prominent limestone outcrop of Heugh Scar. Bear up right easily onto the scarp-top and follow the brink, with evidence of surface clints, to where a path forks right, declining, as towards the distant Arthur's Pike scarp. This path comes to a lower scarp broken by old quarry hollows and a large cairn, and bears on down the short way to join the regular way from Winder Hall. Follow on left, coming down to cross Roehead bridleway at the marker cairn and join the firm path winding on a contouring course to The Cockpit.

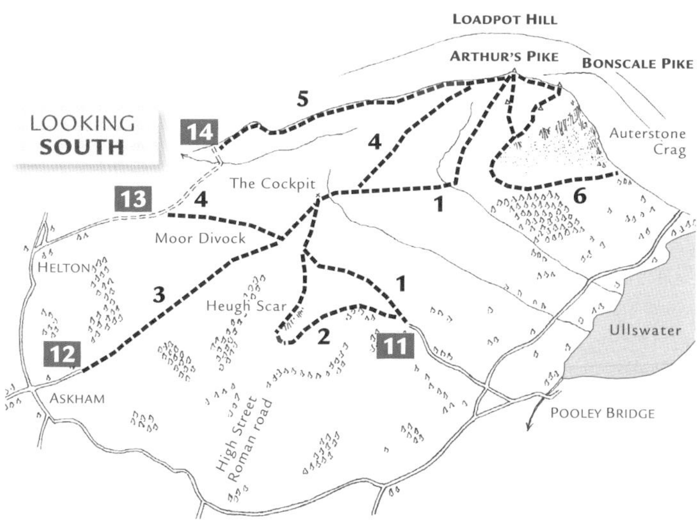

ASCENT FROM ASKHAM (12)

Via The Cockpit 330m/1085ft 6.2km/4 miles

3 Askham is one of Cumbria's prettiest villages, with well-tended cottages decorating an irregular green, two pubs, a village shop and a delectable tea-room – all quite sublime. At the top end of the street find a parking space opposite a bungalow and before a cattle grid. Follow on with the roadway, quickly bearing right with the track, with the wall close right. Rising by a hipped stone barn veer onto the greenway to a gate where the open common is entered. Follow on with the close-cropped grass trod aiming for the tip of the distant shelter belt. A matter of 50m short of this, bear half-left with the declining greenway which leads down to a crossing of the Roehead/Helton bridleway. Go straight on across the marshy moor, as with Route 4, direct to The Cockpit.

ASCENT FROM HELTON (13)

Via Moor Divock 235m/770ft 5km/3 miles

4 A lovely green-turfed trail leads off from the open road, passing the enigmatic Cop Stone ('cop' means 'viewpoint'). The trail avoids sink holes and marshy ground until at a cross-ways it departs left, crossing a very marshy tract of moor to reach The Cockpit stone circle, yet another reminder of the historic significance of this locality. Here the trail links up with Routes 1 and 2; but as a variant to those routes, keep faith with the regular way to ford the inset Aik Beck, and then bear up left (SW) on a regular path. After 1.6km (1 mile) the path inexplicably veers left as the summit hoves into view – keep your eye on the knoll and pace off the trail to the top. Be aware that the fell up to and around the summit is a maze of paths, the frequent of dog walkers, wavering wanderers and serious sheep.

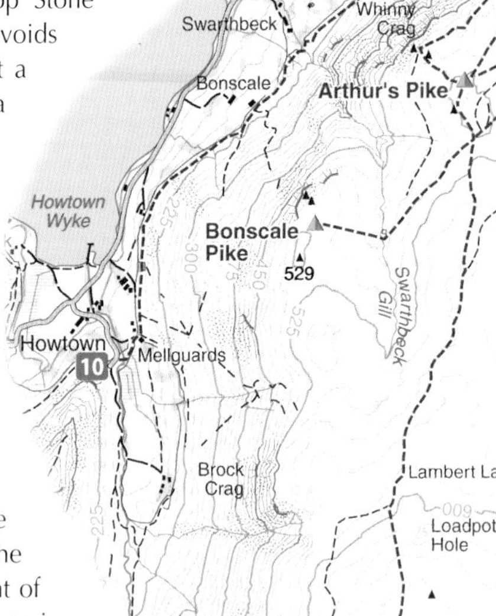

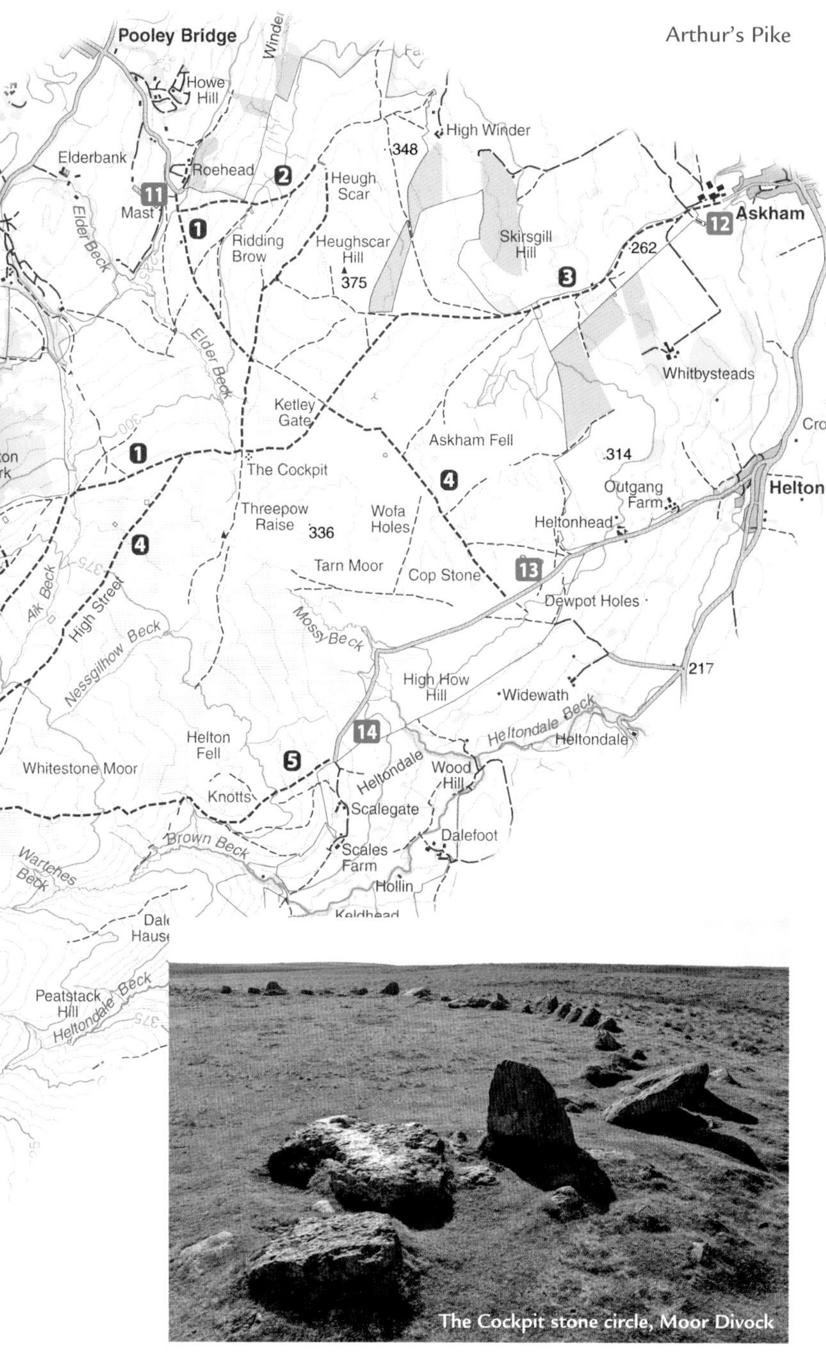

The Cockpit stone circle, Moor Divock

Auterstone Crag

ASCENT FROM HELTON FELL (14)

Via Knotts 230m/755ft 3.3km/2 miles

Drive S from Askham within the lovely Lowther valley to the equally enchanting hamlet of Helton. Turn up through the community onto the fell-road heading SW across the open common bounding Moor Divock. Car parking space is abundant, but for this Helton Fell approach continue until 200m short of the gate accessing the enclosures leading to Scalegate and Scales Farm ('no through road' daubed on stone and private letter box). **5** The walk begins (marshy underfoot) by following the wall up, and as this bears left continue SW, crossing over the low saddle of Knotts to run on right with a worn track to a ford bearing the lovely name of Jennie Brewster's Well. The regular passage of a shepherding quad bike ensures the old path is well marked as it heads up the grassy fell westward to unite with the High Street Roman road path (Route 1) on Whitestone Moor. Head straight across – a strong sheep path invites, but dwindles to nothing when an intermediate cairned top comes into view. Aim to this and bear right on a tangible path to the summit.

ASCENT FROM FUSEDALE (10)

Via White Knott 400m/1310ft 5.5km/3½ miles

6 A really good fell circuit can be undertaken from Howtown by sweeping over Arthur's and Bonscale Pikes. Follow the popular bridleway as it passes through the gate at Mellguards. During the early part of its course the path runs beside a wall and crosses Swarth Beck by a plank-bridge. **Warning** Do not attempt an ascent via the gorge of Swarth Beck – it well merits its name, as 'swarth' means 'dark and

Brink beacon overlooking Sharrow Bay

forbidding'. There is one notable rock-wall that elevates the ascent into the realm of graded scrambling, so please keep well clear. The continuing bridle path is a delight and gives scope to admire the craggy shield of Auterstone Crag, crowned by Arthur's Pike. Although the summit is set back, the forward cairn is frequently visible. After a fenced tank and as the intake wall at the top of Barton Park draws near, find an old path veering right through the bracken. This swings up to round the north side of White Knott and leads onto the regular scarp-edge path.

On the near horizon you will see two cairns, and separate paths lead to each. The right-hand cairn is on the line leading to the forward viewpoint cairn, from where you head back up the fell SE to reach the summit. The left-hand cairn is a sighter for the summit. Consult Bonscale Pike and the connecting route which skips through the upper 'tame' section of Swarth Beck to fashion the round trip.

THE SUMMIT

The summit, identified by a modest cairn, is an ideal place to ponder the peace of the fells, but for a really good view the forward viewpoint cairn should be visited. It is located to the north-west as the scarp of Whinny Crag begins to become profound. Pass a smaller cairn en route to the prime spot. The old beacon is suffering from being built too soon, as my father would say, exposed to the slings and arrows of a harsh climate and neglect. However, it is not neglected by appreciative visitors, for whom this is one of the most sensational spots above Ullswater.

The summit cairn

Arthur's Pike escarpment from Bennethead

SAFE DESCENTS

Any path in the tangle of heather and rough moor grass that leads you NE (for Moor Divock), or for that matter E (for the Helton fell-road), will see you safe. The western scarp from Swarth Beck to White Knott has not one breach for sure descent.

RIDGE ROUTE

BONSCALE PIKE ↓ 40m/130ft ↑ 35m/115ft 1.3km/¾ mile

A clear path leads S then SW, angling easily into the upper valley of Swarth Beck by the remains of a wash-fold. Stepping through the rushes, rise gently W to reach the cairn on the grassy summit.

LOADPOT HILL ↓ 20m/70ft ↑ 160m/525ft 2.7km/1¾ miles

Walk S to join a good path which duly unites with the Roman road on a gently swelling ridge. Some 100m after passing Lambert Lad (standing stone set in the old track groove) bear left, climbing on the regular ridge path to reach the OS column on the plateau top.

PANORAMA

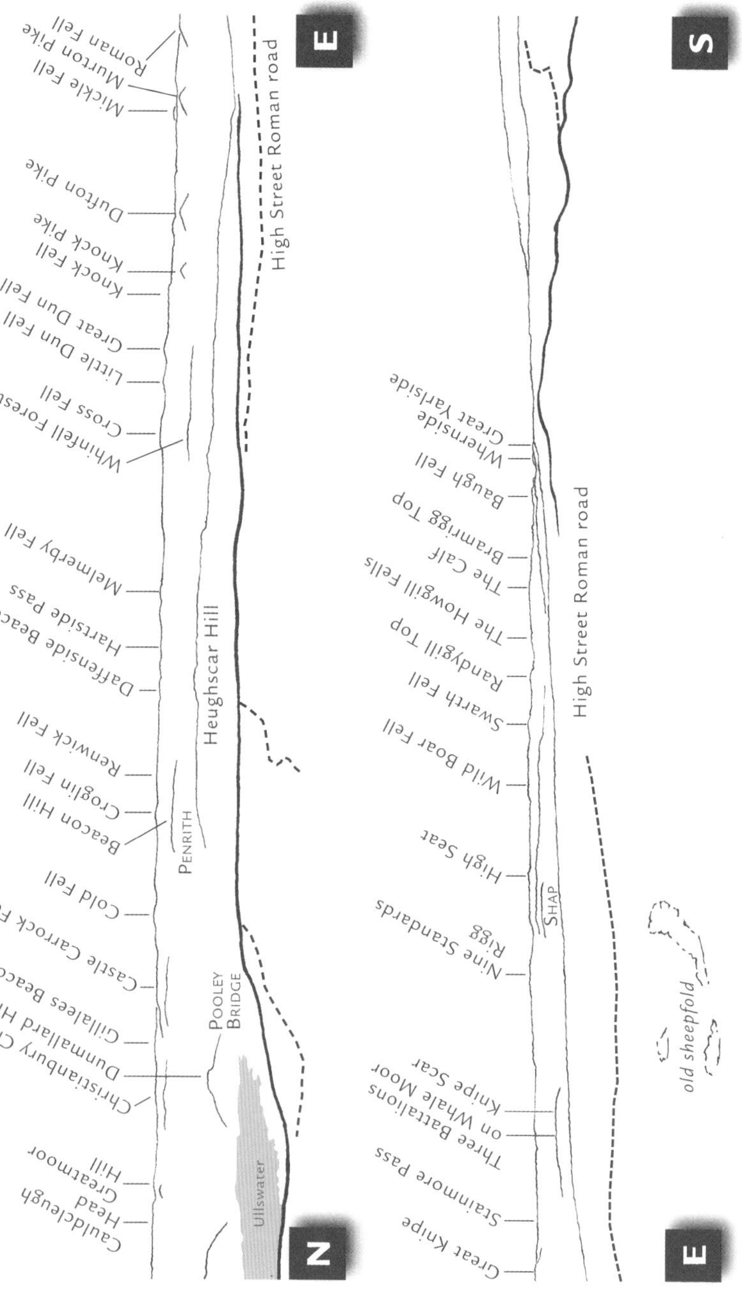

N

Cauldcleugh Head
Greatmoor Hill
Christianbury Crag
Dunmallard Hill
Gillalees Beacon
Castle Carrock Fell
Cold Fell
Beacon Hill
Croglin Fell
Renwick Fell
Daffenside Beacon
Hartside Pass
Melmerby Fell
Whinfell Forest
Cross Fell
Little Dun Fell
Great Dun Fell
Knock Fell
Knock Pike
Dufton Pike
Mickle Fell
Murton Pike
Roman Fell

Ullswater
Pooley Bridge
Penrith
Heughscar Hill
High Street Roman road

E

E

Great Knipe
Stainmore Pass
Three Battalions on Whale Moor
Knipe Scar
Nine Standards Rigg
Shap
High Seat
Wild Boar Fell
Swarth Fell
Randygill Top
The Howgill Fells
The Calf
Bramrigg Top
Baugh Fell
Whernside
Great Yarlside

High Street Roman road
old sheepfold

S

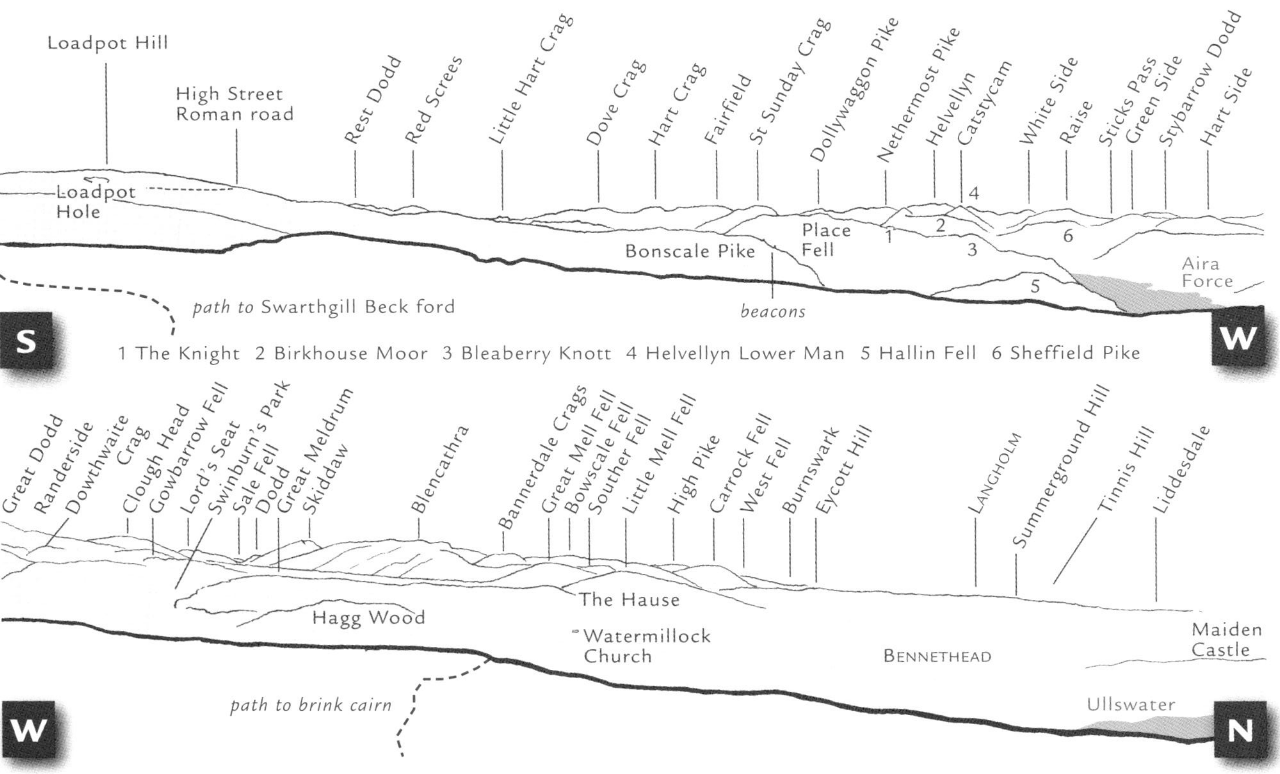
Loadpot Hill
High Street
Roman road
Loadpot
Hole
Rest Dodd
Red Screes
Little Hart Crag
Dove Crag
Hart Crag
Fairfield
St Sunday Crag
Dollywaggon Pike
Nethermost Pike
Helvellyn
Catstycam
White Side
Raise
Sticks Pass
Green Side
Stybarrow Dodd
Hart Side
4
Place
Fell
1
2
6
Bonscale Pike
3
Aira
Force
5
path to Swarthgill Beck ford
beacons
S
W
1 The Knight 2 Birkhouse Moor 3 Bleaberry Knott 4 Helvellyn Lower Man 5 Hallin Fell 6 Sheffield Pike
Great Dodd
Randerside
Dowthwaite
Crag
Clough Head
Gowbarrow Fell
Lord's Seat
Swinburn's Park
Sale Fell
Dodd
Great Meldrum
Skiddaw
Blencathra
Bannerdale Crags
Great Mell Fell
Bowscale Fell
Souther Fell
Little Mell Fell
High Pike
Carrock Fell
West Fell
Burnswark
Eycott Hill
Langholm
Summerground Hill
Tinnis Hill
Liddesdale
The Hause
Hagg Wood
Watermillock
Church
Bennethead
Maiden
Castle
path to brink cairn
Ullswater
W
N

3 BEDA FELL *(509m/1670ft)*

Rising between the Howegrain Beck valley and the secretive Boredale on a long spur ridge from Angletarn Pikes, Beda Fell lies in the heart of Martindale – and the impulse to climb it is hard to resist. This characterful peak is best comprehended from Brownthwaite Crag, from where its craggy eastern face is prominent, although Hallin Fell and Steel Knotts are equally good vantage points. Although the fell is a ridge climb pure and simple, it also offers several lateral connections for the explorer, with the tapered northern extension over Winter Crag a delight to tramp. Paths straddle this portion of the ridge in two places, while where the fell merges with the main massif a bridle path slants up from Dalehead on course for Boredale Hause. This latter path gives scope to make an entertaining round trip off the ridge by either Howe Grain or Boredale. The fell name, truncated in dialect speech, is of unknown root or meaning.

↑ Beda Fell from the slopes of Hallin Fell

ASCENT FROM THE HAUSE (9)

Via Winter Crag 330m/1085ft 2.7km/1¾ miles

1 While some walkers may be content with following the public road down the hill and forking right to cross Howegrain Beck bridge, the more relaxing route follows the footpath that is ushered immediately right before the road descends, signed 'Doe Green'. This leads by a wall-stile and traverses a pasture above Hause Farm to a high wall-stile, with all eyes intent on Beda Fell (left). After the next kissing-gate pitch downhill on the path to reach the road. Cross the bridge and on the rise come onto the left-hand bank following the wall up to the track. Go left signed 'Mauldslack'. As the walled lane opens on the right, climb up by the wall to reach the low ridge top. Turn left and ascend S onto Winter Crag, a real treat, although the bottom section of path can be hard to find when the bracken has grown high. A modest rock groove is the only caution. The views down on Martindale Old Church are worth studying. The ridge path faithfully adhered to duly arrives on the ultimate ground, with plenty of excuses en route to halt and look back in pleasure at the fabulous view.

St Martin's Church backed by Winter Crag

New Church/Old Church link path 16m/50ft 0.9km/½ mile

A handsome alternative start, connecting to the open common beside the old church. **2** Pass up by St Peter's Church, keeping the wall close right, rounding a bluff to a gate. Once the brief lane opens, keep left, coming by a seat to head over the access track to Cotehow (cottage). Pass on beside the wall to a gate and soon join the dale road advancing into the open meadow.

ASCENT FROM MARTINDALE OLD CHURCH (7)

Via Winter Crag 325m/1065ft 2.3km/1½ miles

Walkers may join the north ridge either side of Winter Crag more directly by starting from the open common beside the historic church. **3** Follow the road S to cross Christy Bridge and bear off the road in passing the farmstead. Ignore the slate sign 'bridle path to Sandwick', and keep up and angle right above the wall with crags close above. The clear path leads up onto the ridge precisely at the metal seat, turning left to accompany the ridge and follow Route 2 over the crest of Winter Crag.

Via Knicklethorns 320m/1050ft 1.8km/1 mile

4 A second option is to stay with the road, passing a roadside barn with the curious name Knicklethorns. As the wall is lost on the right, angle up the slope, with the path coming above a wall; here switch up right to the ridge, with only bracken a summer hindrance.

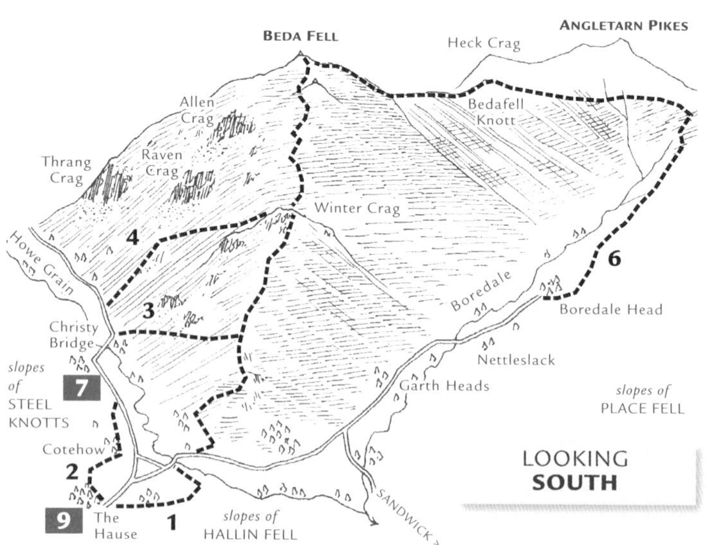

ASCENT FROM DALEHEAD (6)

Via Bedafell Knott 350m/1150ft 3.5km/2¼ miles

5 It might be noted that there is scope for the odd vehicle to sit on the verge at GR433178 or respectfully short of the turning point in front of the farmyard entrance gate at Dalehead – although NPA signage wisely discourages this. In any case, to walk the dale road is an unalloyed pleasure in its own right.

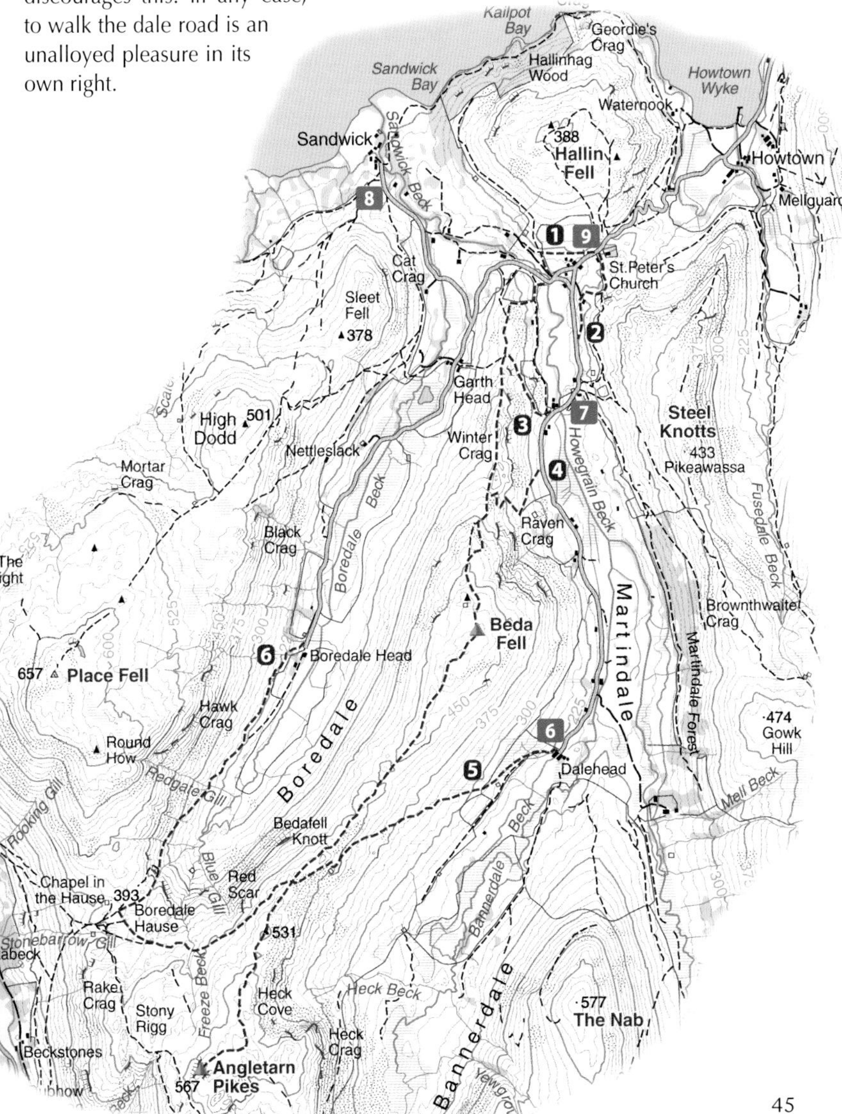

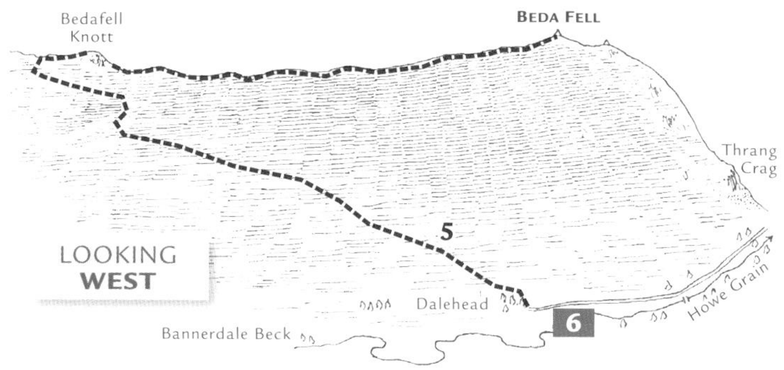

Martindale Deer Forest from Beda Fell

Cross Christy Bridge and follow the dale road by Henhow and Thrang Crag Farm to reach Dalehead. Here a deer conservation information panel draws attention to the paths to follow. The Nab and its bounding dales, Rampsgill Beck and Bannerdale Beck are correctly out of bounds to all casual visitors. The Martindale Deer Forest is the breeding ground of the oldest native red deer herd in England – we all should cherish this and keep disturbance to the absolute minimum.

Walk on through the farmyard via the gates following the rising track, with the intake wall close left. The green path moves up from the wall as the last tree is passed and reaches a gate/stile in a fence above a higher walled enclosure. The drove-path forges on SW up the flank of Beda Fell, revelling in its views of The Nab and Heck Crag. Higher up the path jockeys round a small ruin – a fine place for a walkers' bothy – in reaching the skyline. Turn right (NE) following the delightful spine of the ridge over Bedafell Knott to reach its high point at Beda Head.

ASCENT FROM SANDWICK (8)

Via Boredale Head 470m/1540ft 7.8km/5 miles

6 Follow the Boredale valley road, although it is possible to park short of Boredale Head Farm. Short of the farm gate veer up the bank right with a waymarked permissive path that fords a gill directly above the farm. It then contours above the intake wall to duly reconnect with the dale bridleway running on freely south-westward towards the dale

Summit of Beda Head

head. As the path steepens look for the retaining bank of an old mine up to the right. The track, now rough underfoot, avoids a 'retired' zig-zag path and climbs through a natural cutting with inspection covers to the Hayeswater aqueduct. Venturing onto the broad grassy saddle of Boredale Hause, swing left to join forces with the bridle path from Patterdale. This fords Freeze Beck and runs on NE high above a steep declivity to connect with the ridge path from Angletarn Pikes at a small cairn. Turn left – in effect maintaining your compass bearing – glancing over the left shoulder of Bedafell Knott and heading along the roller-coaster ridge to the summit.

THE SUMMIT

Known as Beda Head, the summit knoll is a popular spot to pause right in the midst of the Martindale valleys, although the views are perhaps not as brilliant as might be expected – this being a fell to admire, rather than to admire from. The panoramic outlook is fine enough for anyone who values peace and quiet in a comparatively high place. A ragged cairn occupies the highest point.

SAFE DESCENTS

Sizeable crags lie in wait down the north-eastern slopes, so stick unwaveringly to the ridge path in poor weather. Winter Crag adds interest to the northern descent, without threatening real hazard, although even it can be avoided via a path that dips off the ridge, right, at the foot of the primary descent.

RIDGE ROUTE

ANGLETARN PIKES ↓ 80m/265ft ↑ 135m/445ft 2.9km/1¾ miles

The ridge path leads confidently SSW, level for a time but including a couple of notable rises, especially Bedafell Knott, after which it crosses the ridge-straddling bridle path at a small cairn. Continue, watching for the chiselled profile of the western summit. Coming above Heck Cove follow a comparatively minor branch path right which beelines to the shapely summit ridge.

PANORAMA

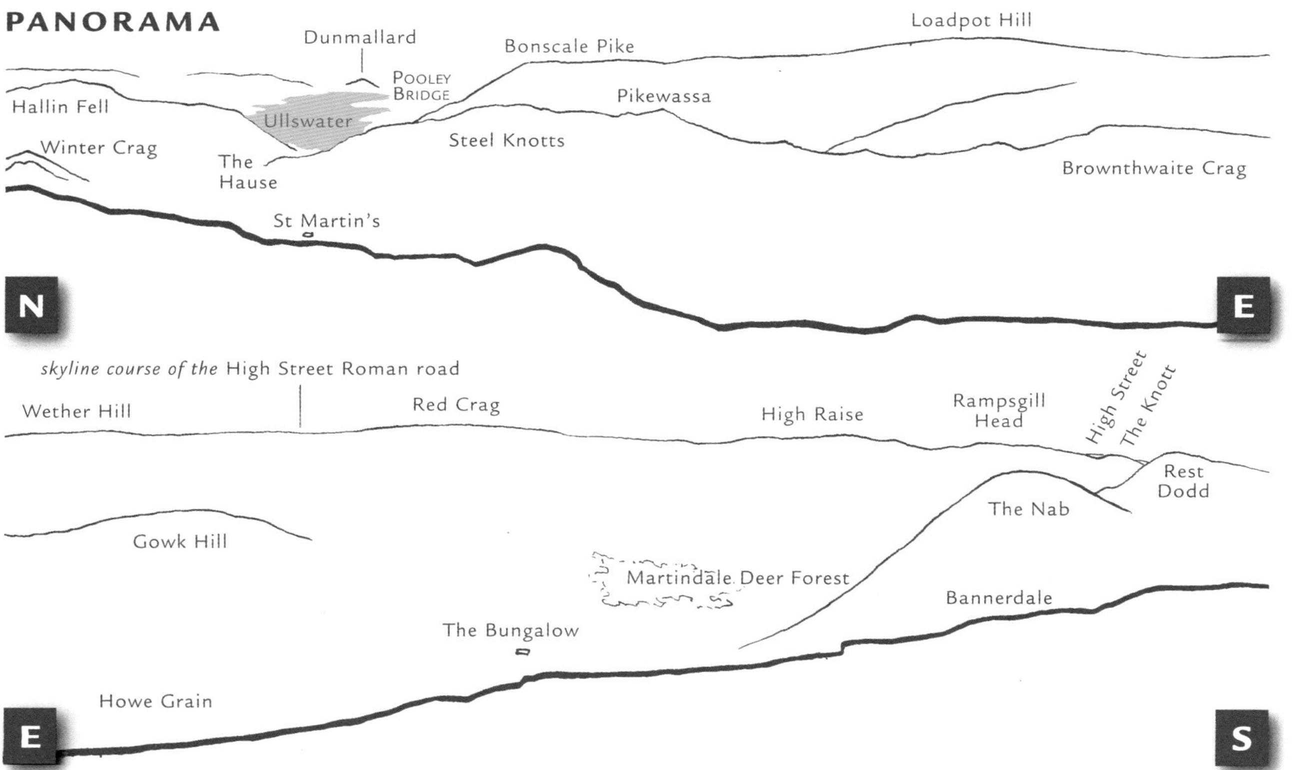
Dunmallard
Pooley Bridge
Bonscale Pike
Loadpot Hill
Hallin Fell
Ullswater
Pikewassa
Winter Crag
The Hause
Steel Knotts
Brownthwaite Crag
St Martin's
N
E
skyline course of the High Street Roman road
Wether Hill
Red Crag
High Raise
Rampsgill Head
High Street
The Knott
Rest Dodd
The Nab
Gowk Hill
Martindale Deer Forest
Bannerdale
The Bungalow
Howe Grain
E
S

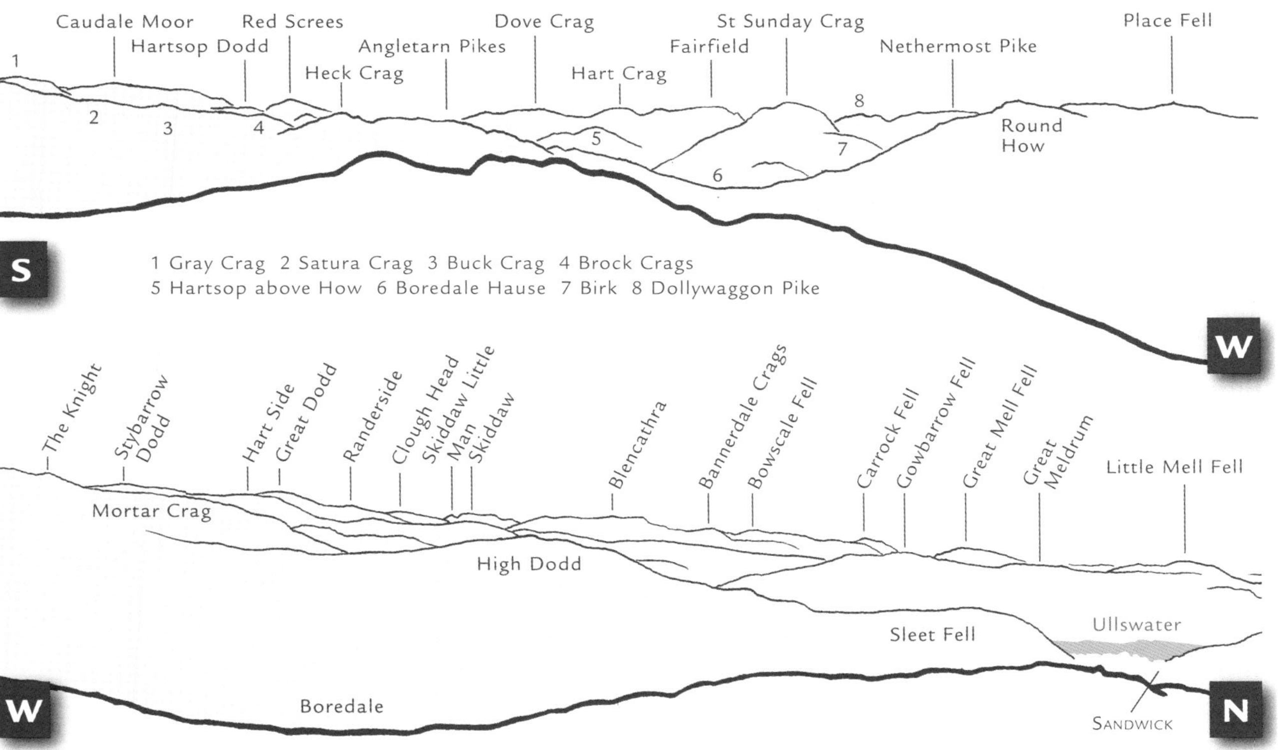
Caudale Moor
Hartsop Dodd
Red Screes
Heck Crag
Angletarn Pikes
Dove Crag
Hart Crag
Fairfield
St Sunday Crag
Nethermost Pike
Place Fell
Round How
1
2
3
4
5
6
7
8
S
W
1 Gray Crag 2 Satura Crag 3 Buck Crag 4 Brock Crags
5 Hartsop above How 6 Boredale Hause 7 Birk 8 Dollywaggon Pike
The Knight
Stybarrow Dodd
Hart Side
Great Dodd
Randerside
Clough Head
Skiddaw Little Man
Skiddaw
Blencathra
Bannerdale Crags
Bowscale Fell
Carrock Fell
Gowbarrow Fell
Great Mell Fell
Great Meldrum
Little Mell Fell
Mortar Crag
High Dodd
Sleet Fell
Ullswater
W
Boredale
Sandwick
N

4 BONSCALE PIKE *(529m/1736ft)*

Viewed from Ullswater, and best of all from Hallin Fell, there is no doubt that Bonscale Pike is handsome. But it is a front, a façade without back or sides. Strictly it is an extended shoulder of Loadpot Hill, and in another setting it would be deemed a sham. But not here – Bonscale Pike contributes massively to an appreciation of Ullswater and is a climb for the delectation of landscape connoisseurs. It is separated from escarpment compatriot Arthur's Pike by one of the district's most forbidding ravines, Swarthbeck Gill, a 'no go' place for all normal fellwalkers; it's as well to know that fact before you casually plot it into your travels. There are several lines of ascent, all of which stem from Howtown and are thus perfect as an accompaniment to a cruise on the Ullswater steamer (although being diesel powered, it is steamer in name only).

Lower beacon with Sharrow Bay Hotel

 ↑ Bonscale Pike from Waterfoot boat-house

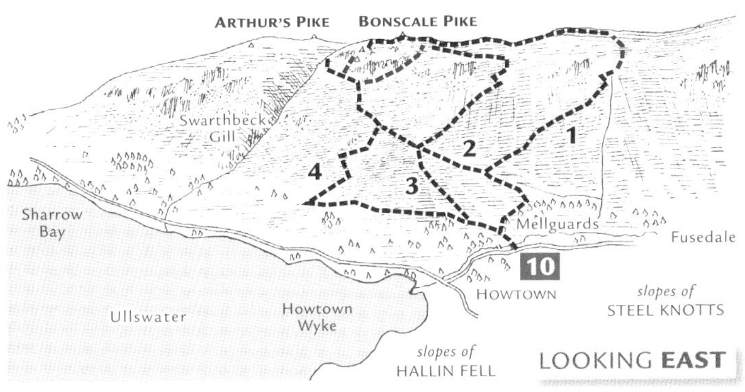

ASCENT FROM FUSEDALE (10)

Via Mellguards 360m/1180ft 1.9km/1¼ miles

1 Park beyond the cattle grid on the Cote Farm access road from Howtown Hotel as it enters Fusedale. From the four-way signpost leave the open road at once to cross the clapper-bridge spanning Fusedale Beck and rise within the walled lane to a gate entering the gravel drive to Mellguards, the prominent white house. Go through the gate by the house door and at once bear up right, following the intake wall to continue a short distance beyond where this angles right. Veer left in a rising groove leading onto a shoulder, and here find an old drove-path steering up right. This climbs above the gill and is lost as a path on the grassy rise to the plateau. On joining the ridge path, turn left due N to reach the summit.

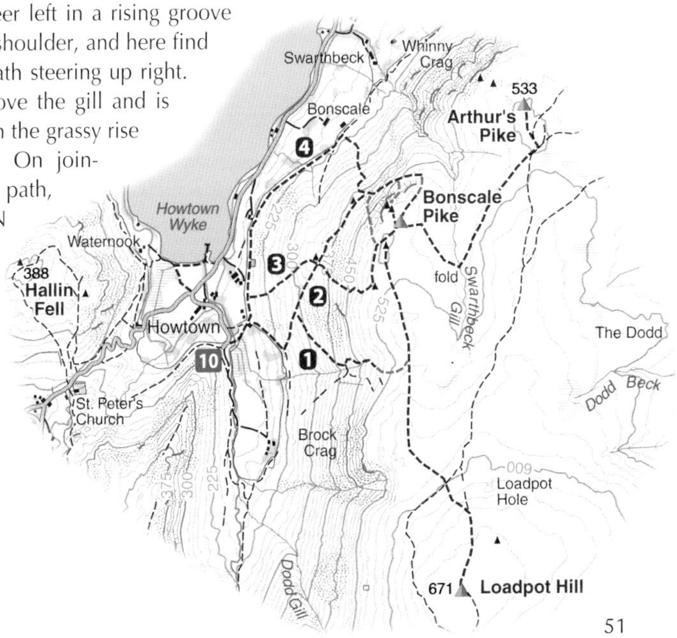

Via the under-scarp 350m/1150ft 1.7km/1 mile

2 A more interesting variant continues to where the fell shoulder broadens further, passing a cairn set on a boulder. Ignore the path rising right – this is Route 3. Instead, continue forward on a largely contouring line passing a second cairn among boulders to meet up with a rising groove, a seldom followed drove. Follow this by a small cairn. There are now three options. First, as a prominent headland become visible above veer right and, keeping the boulder field to the left, climb onto this headland, now with a natural groove onto the ridge. Turn left to reach the summit. The second option is to continue until both beacon pillars become visible, then veer right again, this time following a wide grassy passage up between two crags to reach the lower beacon. En route notice the small overhanging boulder with a wall set beneath – most odd. The third option continues to pass the end cliff and round the ridge-end to find easy ground before swinging back right to the summit.

Via shoulder route 360m/1180ft 1.6km/1 mile

3 Go through the gate beside Mellguards and follow the regular level bridleway beside the wall. Some 60m after passing the power-line pole step right, just before a green inspection cover. A popular path climbs directly (by error this is frequently followed in descent, but is not a good way down, being steep up this initial bracken-clad bank). Two steepish sections prove it inferior to Route 1, as pigeon-hole erosion steps are developing. Its one great virtue is the view back to the craggy Steel Knotts ridge and Hallin Fell above Howtown Wyke (the bay with the steamer jetty). Coming onto the grassy alp arrive at the boulder with a cairn perched on top. This time continue uphill with the scree slope to the left. The groove latterly zigzags to reach the skyline, curving left by a cairn in the rushes to contour along the scarp edge to the summit.

Via old drove 370m/1215ft 2.2km/1½ miles

4 A steep alternative, this route is invariably 'happened upon' in descent when the lateral path of Route 2 is missed. Follow the level bridleway from the Mellguards gate beside the intake wall, passing the base of a walled copse. Some 20m before a ruined barn over the adjacent intake wall, with the crags seen high above, climb the steep fellside, finding the beginnings of the zig-zag drove which duly is joined by Route 2 as the upper tier of crags comes close.

Bonscale Pike summit cairn

Swarthbeck Gill ravine

THE SUMMIT

Being far from a holistic fell, the summit is not a certain science. There are cairns on two knolls above the beacons, yet the ground continues to rise back from them. In this guide, the accompanying panorama is taken from the lower cairn, although most walkers will be more intent on surveying Ullswater from the beacon cairns – and why not… it is an uplifting sight, and copious time should be spent in unhurried admiration.

SAFE DESCENTS

It is advisable to avoid the immediate craggy ground beneath the summit. Follow the scarp-top path S to where it heads down, thereby keeping to consistently grassy terrain. For all the steepness, you are assured of comfortable footing all the way down to Howtown Hotel and the steamer jetty.

RIDGE ROUTES

ARTHUR'S PIKE ↓ 35m/115ft ↑ 40m/130ft 1.3km/¾ mile

A definite path leads E then SE to ford Swarthbeck Gill at an old wash-fold, then trends NNE to gain the summit cairn.

LOADPOT HILL ↓ 20m/65ft ↑ 165m/540ft 2km/1¼ miles

Follow the right path S. This dips and rises onto a damp shoulder above Brock Crag, then slants SE, climbing to cross the High Street Roman road and connect with the regular ridge path to the summit.

PANORAMA

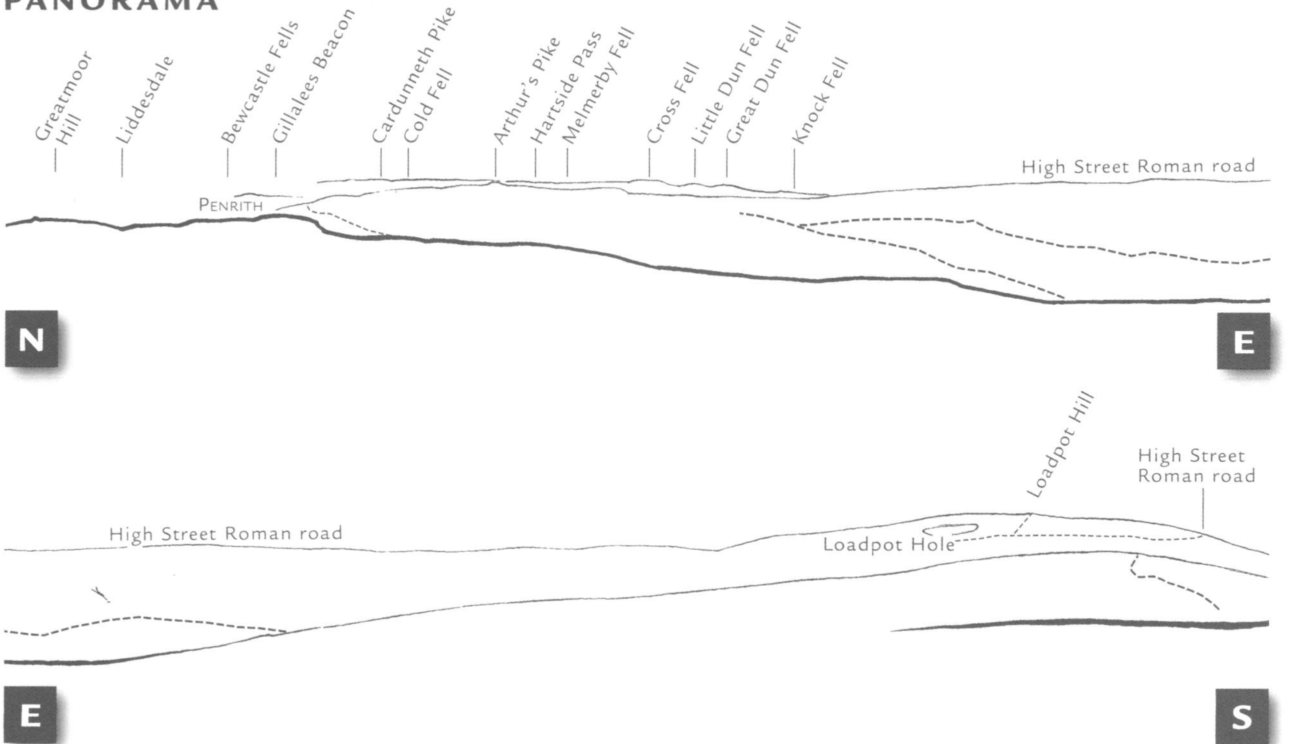
Greatmoor Hill
Liddesdale
Bewcastle Fells
Gillalees Beacon
Cardunneth Pike
Cold Fell
Arthur's Pike
Hartside Pass
Melmerby Fell
Cross Fell
Little Dun Fell
Great Dun Fell
Knock Fell
High Street Roman road
PENRITH
N
E
Loadpot Hill
High Street Roman road
High Street Roman road
Loadpot Hole
E
S

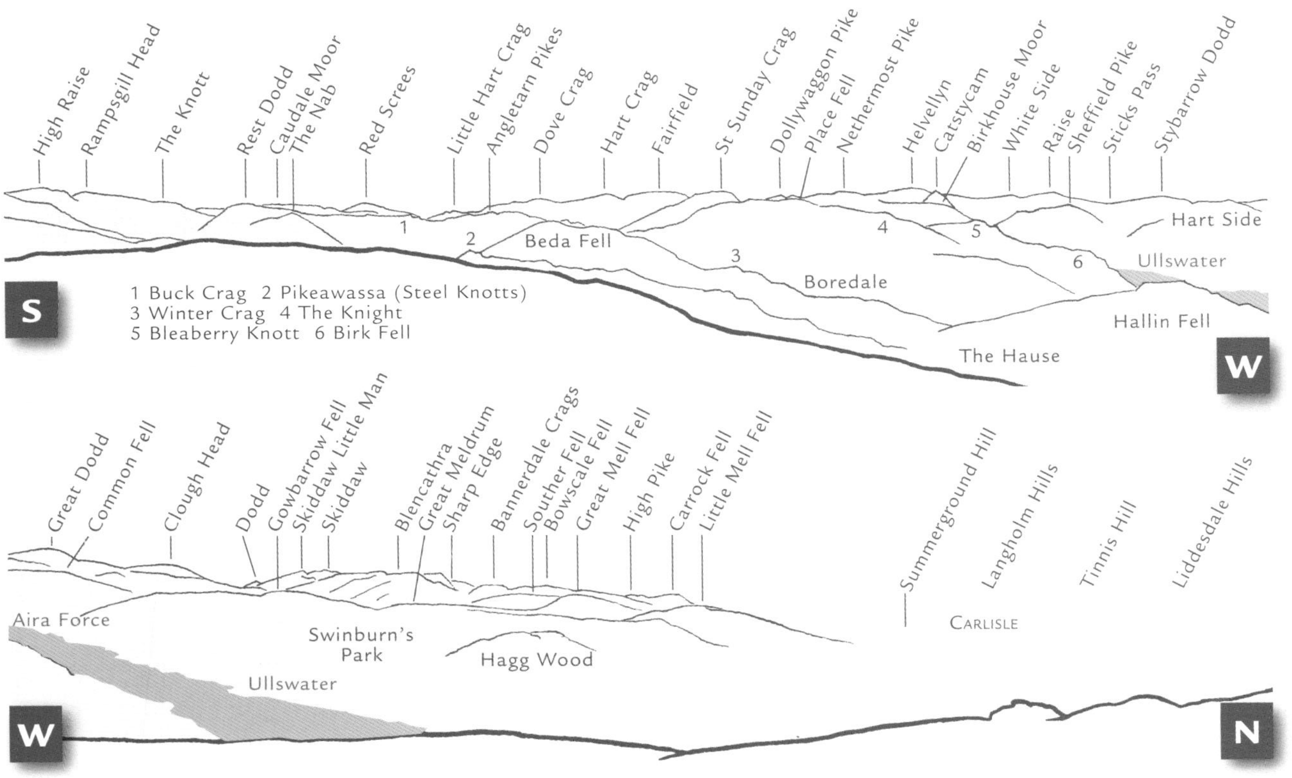
High Raise
Rampsgill Head
The Knott
Rest Dodd
Caudale Moor
The Nab
Red Screes
Little Hart Crag
Angletarn Pikes
Dove Crag
Hart Crag
Fairfield
St Sunday Crag
Dollywaggon Pike
Place Fell
Nethermost Pike
Helvellyn
Catstycam
Birkhouse Moor
White Side
Raise
Sheffield Pike
Sticks Pass
Stybarrow Dodd
Hart Side
1
2
Beda Fell
3
4
5
6
Ullswater
Boredale
Hallin Fell
The Hause
S
1 Buck Crag 2 Pikeawassa (Steel Knotts)
3 Winter Crag 4 The Knight
5 Bleaberry Knott 6 Birk Fell
W
Great Dodd
Common Fell
Clough Head
Dodd
Gowbarrow Fell
Skiddaw Little Man
Skiddaw
Blencathra
Great Meldrum
Sharp Edge
Bannerdale Crags
Souther Fell
Bowscale Fell
Great Mell Fell
High Pike
Carrock Fell
Little Mell Fell
Summerground Hill
Langholm Hills
Tinnis Hill
Liddesdale Hills
Aira Force
Swinburn's Park
Hagg Wood
Carlisle
Ullswater
W
N

5 BRANSTREE *(713m/2339ft)*

Lost in the mists of time, when fell names began to be coined in upper Mardale, farmers would have referred to the great hill to the west as High Street, its Roman roots lingering in folk memory, and the steep slope immediately to the east as Brant-stree, meaning 'steep hillside'. The notion of a 'road' inferred by the Roman name was not in their minds; it was a simple colloquialism. Branstree is certainly steep when viewed from Haweswater perspectives. From elsewhere it is less imposing and, together with High Howes, is of some girth. Invariably the fell ascent is combined with Selside Pike, whether begun from Mardale Head (most commonly), Swindale, Wet Sleddale or Longsleddale; the latter option frequently involves Grey and Tarn Crags, for all the intervening drop between.

The only dwelling associated with the fell, Mosedale Cottage, is a treasure for seekers after simple lodgings in a wild setting. Linked to the Mountain Bothies Association, this former quarry-manager's and shepherd's abode has been restored to use by local enthusiasts and should be appreciated and respected. Above it looms a massive slate quarry, long derelict, with no railway or easy line of transport; stone hauling must always have been a major undertaking from this remote dale head.

Mosedale Cottage

↑ Branstree from Adam Seat

ASCENT FROM MARDALE HEAD (20) OR MARDALE BANKS (19)

Via Hopegill Beck 485m/1590ft 3.8km/2½ miles

1 Use the shoreline path (or the road) from the Mardale Head car park. After crossing the little bridge spanning Hopegill Beck take the path climbing right to a kissing-gate and regain the road. Turn right, and immediately after crossing the Hopegill Beck road bridge go through the hand-gate to be confronted by a chaos of beck, boulders and trees. At once switch right to follow an obvious groove drove-path. This winds up, passing under the cheek of the Hollow Stone, a large tilted boulder, and progresses steadily, with the roar of the long mare's-tail cascades a constant accompaniment. When the bracken is up, getting close to the waterfalls is impossible, but at other times can be achieved, although the confines are ill suited to generous casual inspection. Higher up, as the slope eases, come by two ruins – the upper has the taller walls. See the tapered window slot, which must have given a draughty view upon Mardale. The path becomes far less certain from this point on. After passing a small fold keep to the right of a great swathe of damp tussocks, with a large wash-fold close to the beck confluence. There is no path, nor need of one, on the steady pull up the north ridge. All the excitement occurs over your shoulder, so periodic pauses are quite in order to glory in the craggy face of High Street and its supporting Rough Crag ridge and hanging valley combe cradling Blea Water. Two handsome cairns greet you on the Artlecrag Pike brow. The name 'Artlecrag' seems to harbour reference to a Viking family name, 'Arnketill'. The altogether less impressive summit lies further back (south-west), near the fence/wall junction.

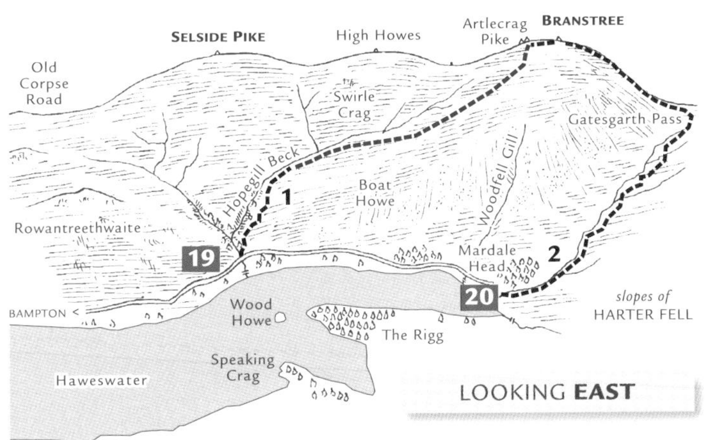

Via Gatescarth Pass 460m/1510ft 2.7km/1¾ miles

Unlike most routes in the area this track has the occasional visitation from 4x4 leisure vehicles, and has been engineered to as best as possible cope. **2** From the three-way signpost follow the left-hand arm signed 'Public Byway Gatescarth Pass'. The track rises via a gate in harmony with Gatescarth Beck and with two multiple hairpin sections climbing to the brow. At your comfort, after the new path veers right and before the gate in the saddle-straddling fence, break off left to wade through the marshy flats to join the rising fence that climbs uneventfully to the summit plateau.

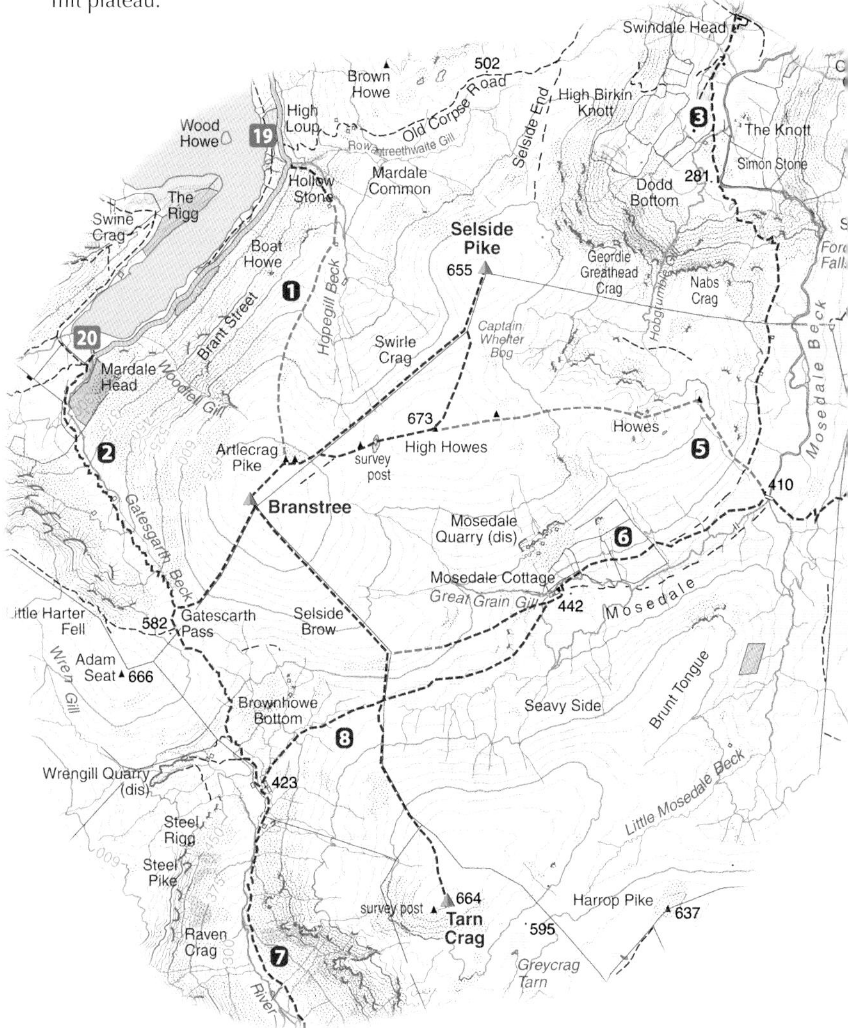

ASCENT FROM SWINDALE (21 – off map N)

Via Mosedale 560m/1840ft 8.2km/5 miles

3 Follow the road by Truss Gap (the only active farm in the valley) to the road-end at Swindale Head. Continue within the gated drove-way, passing the stone barns by an irregular walled lane. After a gate/wall-stile cross the outflowing beck from Dodd Bottom and follow the moraine track, soon coming along a narrow section between the great basin of Dodd Bottom, clearly once the location of a considerable tarn, and Swindale Beck. The path swings up the rising moraine, revealing the drama of this wild sanctuary, with the contrasting ravines of Forces Falls (left) and Hobgrumble spilling almost sheer into Dodd Bottom and drawing walkers' attention. The old bridleway takes several sharp hairpin turns in negotiating the rough dale-head slope.

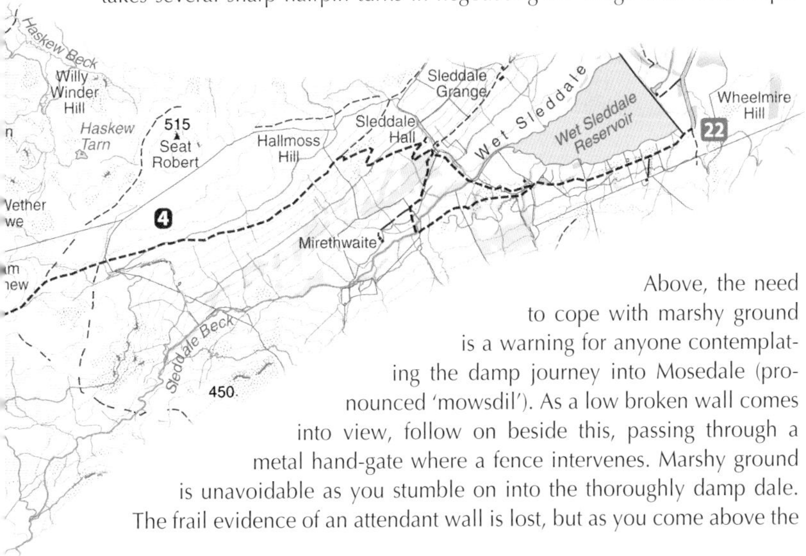

Above, the need to cope with marshy ground is a warning for anyone contemplating the damp journey into Mosedale (pronounced 'mowsdil'). As a low broken wall comes into view, follow on beside this, passing through a metal hand-gate where a fence intervenes. Marshy ground is unavoidable as you stumble on into the thoroughly damp dale. The frail evidence of an attendant wall is lost, but as you come above the

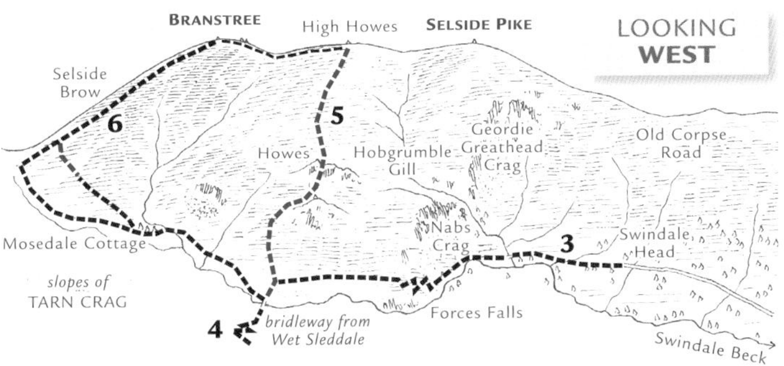

broad bridge in the dale bottom turn off the path and climb with a quad track beside a tiny gill to reach the ridge-end rocky top adorned by a small cairn of Howes. This point is the en route target for a grand long approach from Wet Sleddale (Route 4).

ASCENT FROM WET SLEDDALE (22)

Via Sleddale Hall to Mosedale footbridge 230m/755ft 5.6km/3½ miles

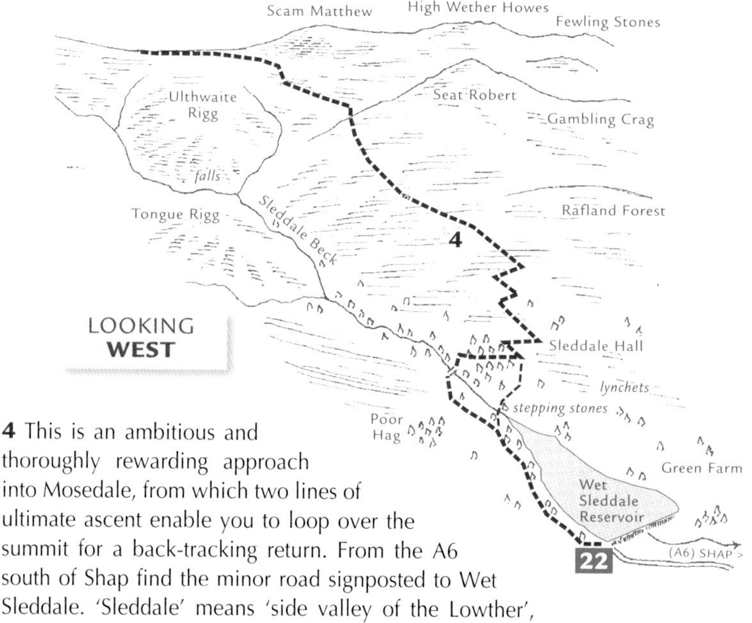

4 This is an ambitious and thoroughly rewarding approach into Mosedale, from which two lines of ultimate ascent enable you to loop over the summit for a back-tracking return. From the A6 south of Shap find the minor road signposted to Wet Sleddale. 'Sleddale' means 'side valley of the Lowther', with the 'damp' connotations to distinguish it from its near neighbour Longsleddale. Within 1.6km (1 mile) this road leads to a car park beside the dam.

Follow the open track directly via gates, and on coming to the head of the reservoir by a ruin there is a choice. The footpath heads on over the footbridge with matching handrails and veers right to cross a wall ladder-stile and a fence-stile to a crude set of stepping stones over Sleddale Beck. After any rain the second stone will be submersed and therefore challenging to negotiate, as the water is deep. In which case the better option is the concessionary path, which veers half-left at the ruin and crosses the single hand-railed plank-bridge some 40m upstream. Damp ground predominates, and white-topped stakes guide the route to a handsome stone bridge (be amazed by the underside, simply bristling with stalactites). Ascend the pasture to a fence-stile and bear right, with the track winding up through the deer-fenced woodland. Coming to a barn and sheep pens, bear left with the open track which winds up the Sleddale Hall, and keep on the track as it continues hairpinning up the pasture

Wet Sleddale Reservoir from above Sleddale Hall

to a gate. Now contouring on, notice directly below in the valley two high-walled enclosures; these were built to corral red deer. The track advances well above the dale beck and therefore is too distant from the great cascades at its head.

The next gate brings the track over the undulating shoulder of Scam Matthew, and after merging with a quad track it arrives at an askew gate overlooking Mosedale. Follow the zig-zag path down inevitably damp slopes to cross the broad plank-bridge spanning Mosedale Beck. Routes 5 and 6 spring from this point.

Via High Howes **570m/1870ft 9.6km/6 miles**

5 Head straight across the valley, climbing to the right of a minor gill with crags up to the right. This grass path leads to a rocky crest with a cairn (at 544m/1785ft). Ascend the Howes ridge SW, weaving through the easy outcropping to find a tarn and a delightful rock-pool, while also enjoying fine views right down into the upland hollow of Hobgrumble Beck and through to Swindale Head. The ridge above is less enchanting, with a steady plod leading past a tiny memorial stone, 'Edward Dodds 1911', to reach the minor cairn on High Howes (673m/2208ft) between Selside Pike and Branstree. At last a path appears – follow this ridge trod W, slipping between a pair of tarns to encounter the Haweswater aqueduct survey post, a robust stone-built structure which has long lost a purpose, other than as a landmark in mist. The path continues to cross the fence and clamber up to the two stately cairns on Artlecrag Pike, built on a bedrock of vertically split slate. The summit lies a further 200m due SW.

Edward Dodds memorial on High Howes

Looking down the Gatescarth Pass track

Via Mosedale Cottage 560m/1840ft 10km/6¼ miles

6 From the Mosedale Beck bridge bear left and duly engage in a sequence of damp and pool-challenged sections of track which lead via gates to Mosedale Cottage (Mountain Bothies Association). The ford of Great Grain Gill offers the biggest obstacle just short of the bothy. Above the bothy looms the spoil bank of a mighty slate quarry, worth perusing for the ghosts of an industry long past. Trees have been planted above, which may eventually soften the raw scar. The bothy (part shepherd's residence), a classic of its kind, provides the simplest of overnight lodgings, serving all who genuinely respect its wild mountain setting. Although it is difficult to ignore a thick scent of burnt coal after prolonged non-occupancy, open the windows to freshen things up as you arrive if you plan to stay.

Passing on beyond the dwelling and the sheltering conifers, note a fork in the ways. The bridleway keeps low, slanting left through the wild corridor at the head of the dale to reach a gate. Turn right and ascend beside the fence. As a variant, keep company with the rising quad track that comes onto a shoulder. The track is lost, with a sheep path your only guide – follow this on a contouring course to reach the point where the rising fence meets a wall. Cross the fence, join the ascending path and follow the wall to the fence-stile leading onto the summit.

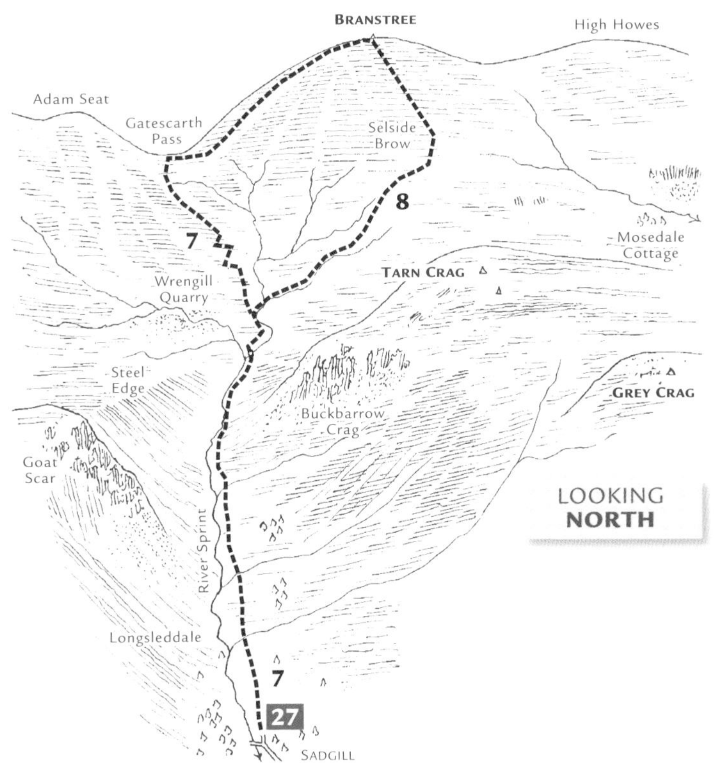

ASCENT FROM SADGILL (27 – off map S)

Via Gatescarth Pass 540m/1770ft 5km/3 miles

7 From Sadgill Bridge follow the drove-lane up the dramatic mountain corridor at the head of Longsleddale. Periodically exposed to wash-out damage, the lane passes close to the impressive Buckbarrow Crag before switching up cobbling close to a fine set of cascades, which are hard to see from within the walled lane. Keep to the track via two gates, zigzagging up the slope N to the Gatescarth Pass. Go through the gate in the saddle and, to avoid the worst of the marsh, stride on a further 50m before veering right and duly reconnecting with the fence to ascend NE to the summit.

Via Selside Brow 530m/1740ft 5.3km/3¼ miles

8 As a simple variant of Route 7, after the first gate advance to a signpost, short of the sheep-pens. Follow this to head right over a ford and up the periodically marshy Brownhowe Bottom to the gate in the broad saddle. Do not go through, but instead ascend left beside the fence at the angle; the fence becomes a wall rising up Selside End to the stile at the top.

THE SUMMIT

A circular concrete Ordnance Survey disc pinpoints the actual summit – this curious device matches those on several summits in the area, including Blencathra. A fence straddles the summit dome, running from Gatescarth Pass diagonally NE towards Selside Pike, while a wall leads towards the top from the SE. Find only a few stones for a cairn – all else is grass. The best views are to be had from the western edge of the summit plateau, from where Harter Fell, Mardale Ill Bell and High Street are seen to perfection.

SAFE DESCENTS

The ridge fence leads SW direct to Gatescarth Pass, a secure route for Mardale Head and Longsleddale. The wall from the fence/wall junction leads equally easily down to the marshy hollow at the head of Mosedale, from where it is simple enough to reach Longsleddale by curving SW through Brownhowe Bottom to join the Gatescarth track. Mosedale (E) is an altogether damper experience, en route to Swindale, although Mosedale Cottage is a valuable refuge only 1km away.

RIDGE ROUTES

SELSIDE PIKE ↓ 115m/375ft ↑ 55m/185ft 2km/1¼ miles

Head NE to the pair of sturdy cairns marking Artlecrag Pike, and from there drift right to accompany the ridge fence. You have two options. In mist stick resolutely beside the fence to the shelter cairn on Selside Pike. Alternatively, on a fine day, step over the plain wire fence, pass the stone survey frame and splice through the attractive pair of tarns onto the grassy ridge of High Howes. Pass on from the excuse

Summit Ordnance Survey triangulation disc with the tall cairn on Artlecrag Pike on the horizon

for a summit cairn, with the evident path continuing NE via the peaty depression of Captain Whelter Bog and climbing to the turn in the fence on the summit.

TARN CRAG ↓ 205m/670ft ↑ 155m/510ft 2.6km/1½ miles

Head SE, cross the fence-stile and follow the wall down Selside Brow, latterly in the company of a fence, to cross the broad saddle rising over peat groughs, keeping the fence close left. Higher up cross a stile on a consistent path S to the summit.

PANORAMA

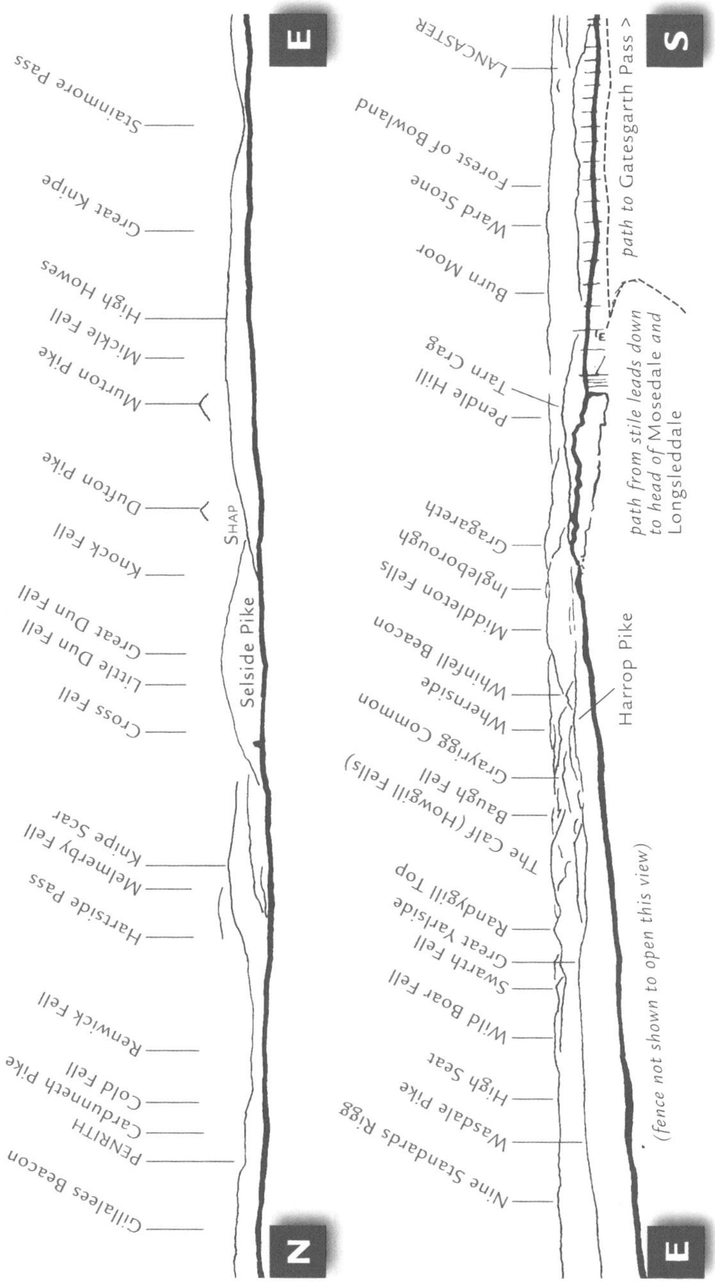

N

Gillalees Beacon
PENRITH
Cardunneth Pike
Cold Fell
Renwick Fell
Hartside Pass
Melmerby Fell
Knipe Scar
Cross Fell
Little Dun Fell
Great Dun Fell
Selside Pike
Knock Fell
SHAP
Dufton Pike
Murton Pike
Mickle Fell
High Howes
Great Knipe
Stainmore Pass

E

E

Nine Standards Rigg
Wasdale Pike
High Seat
Wild Boar Fell
Swarth Fell
Great Yarlside
Randygill Top
The Calf (Howgill Fells)
Baugh Fell
Grayrigg Common
Whernside
Whinfell Beacon
Middleton Fells
Ingleborough
Gragareth
Pendle Hill
Tarn Crag
Burn Moor
Ward Stone
Forest of Bowland
LANCASTER

(fence not shown to open this view)

Harrop Pike

path from stile leads down to head of Mosedale *and* Longsleddale

path to Gatesgarth Pass >

S

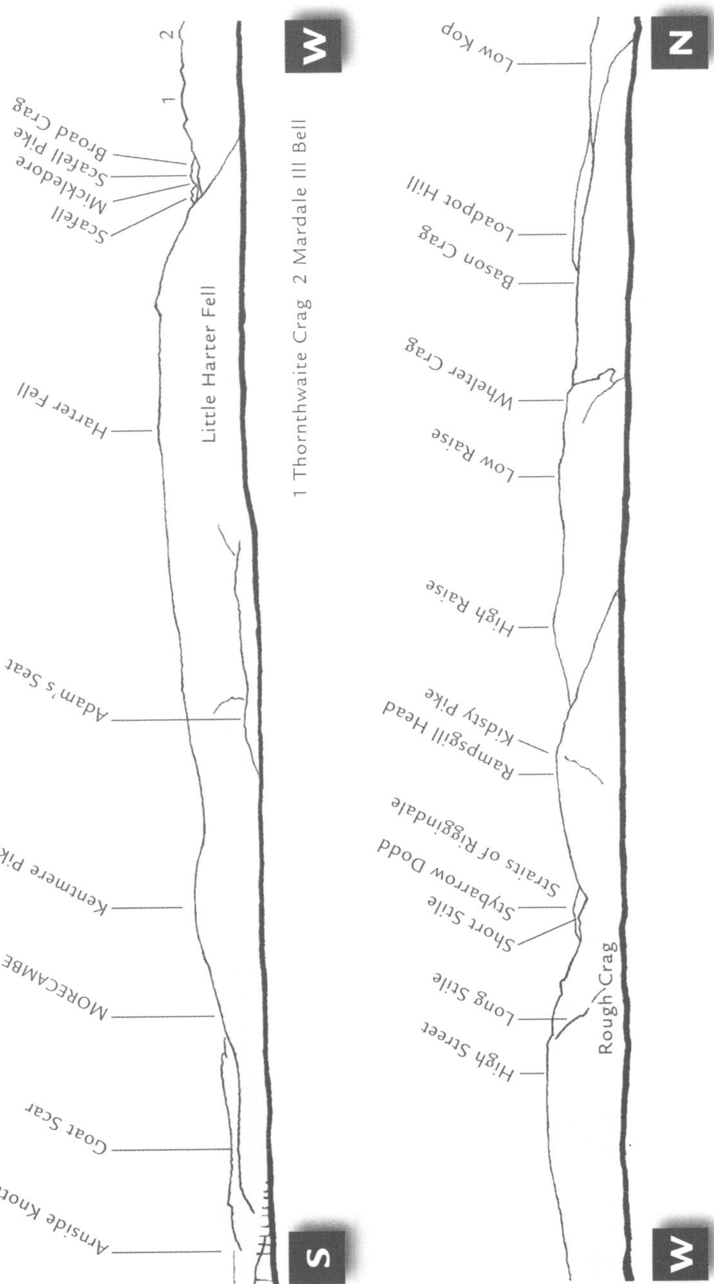
W
S
Arnside Knott
Goat Scar
MORECAMBE
Kentmere Pike
Adam's Seat
Harter Fell
Little Harter Fell
Scafell
Mickledore
Scafell Pike
Broad Crag
1
2
1 Thornthwaite Crag 2 Mardale Ill Bell
N
W
Low Kop
Loadpot Hill
Bason Crag
Wheler Crag
Low Raise
High Raise
Kidsty Pike
Rampsgill Head
Straits of Riggindale
Stybarrow Dodd
Short Stile
Rough Crag
Long Stile
High Street

6 BROCK CRAGS *(561m/1841ft)*

While some fells are gifted as fine subjects to look at, Brock Crags is far more a place to look from. For all its comparatively lowly height the summit situation, above Hartsop, overlooking the confluence of Hayeswater and Pasture Becks and the broad Goldrill Beck glen, is scenically superb. Most eyes will be drawn to Gray Crag, but the fells around Deepdale are equally as compelling. The fell name alludes to the 'rocks frequented by badgers', although you are more likely to encounter a small herd of red deer on the less frequented slopes. The southern slopes of the fell are dotted with thorn, while the western declivity, sheltered by Lingy Crag, is richly wooded. The hamlet of Low Hartsop is invariably shortened to Hartsop in conversation, the farming settlement of High Hartsop, upstream from Brothers Water, having long been wiped from maps. The fell shares custody of Angle Tarn with the Pikes of that name, and walkers will enjoy an exploration of this wild basin, adventurously visited by climbing by its outflow beck. Although most will content themselves with gaining the ridge by following the grassy groove up the southern flank of the fell, the odd few will love the testing gradient of the wall that beetles straight up.

Gray Crag from Brock Crags

↑ Brock Crags from the west slopes of Rest Dodd

ASCENT FROM HARTSOP (3)

Via Angletarn Beck 430m/1410ft 2.6km/1½ miles

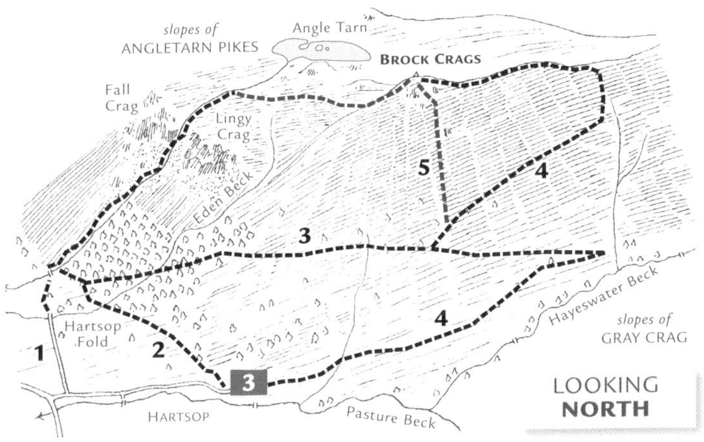

All primary ascents begin from Hartsop. **1** None is more exciting than the intimate climb by Angletarn Beck; note the use of the term 'exciting' – this is not a casual stroll. From the Hartsop car park it is possible to avoid the early ascent by following the approach road back towards the main valley road, then turn right 50m short at a white house, Langton Adventure Centre, along the byroad signed 'Hartsop Fold'. After the chalet park this becomes a confined path leading to a gate, ford and footbridge spanning Angletarn Beck. Bear up right on the north bank to meet a fording lateral path.

2 The lateral path begins at the wooden signpost a matter of 30m from the Hartsop car park, opposite Styan Bew, and rises upon a concrete roadway via a gate (the roadway provides access to the outside world for two elevated bungalows). The roadway enjoys lovely views before dipping to a three-way fork. Keep ahead, guided by a yellow waymark and passing Grey Rigg, along a confined passage to a hand-gate. Thereafter the path declines via rocky ground and a small ford of the ever-aspirational Eden Beck to go through a hand-gate and ford the target beck beneath an impressive set of leaping falls. The ascent is obvious, although there are moments when a steady step is required as you work up the rocky flank, accompanied by a sequence of lovely cascades. Fall Crag eventually intervenes, and walkers are obliged to ford and progress with the wall close left. Views towards Brothers Water give rise to many a backward glance. At a wall junction turn right (SE) and follow this wall over damp fell. Approaching the next wall junction, drift left to avoid marshy ground and pass through a narrow wall-gap (shepherding gate) and complete the ascent up the grassy bank.

Fall Crag and Angletarn Beck

Via the southern slope 430m/1410ft 3.2km/2 miles

The popular ascent, via the groove on the southern flank of the fell, can be reached by two lines of approach. This way has one further variant, the steep direct climb beside the wall direct to the summit, which is surprisingly entertaining – and good for the legs and lungs!

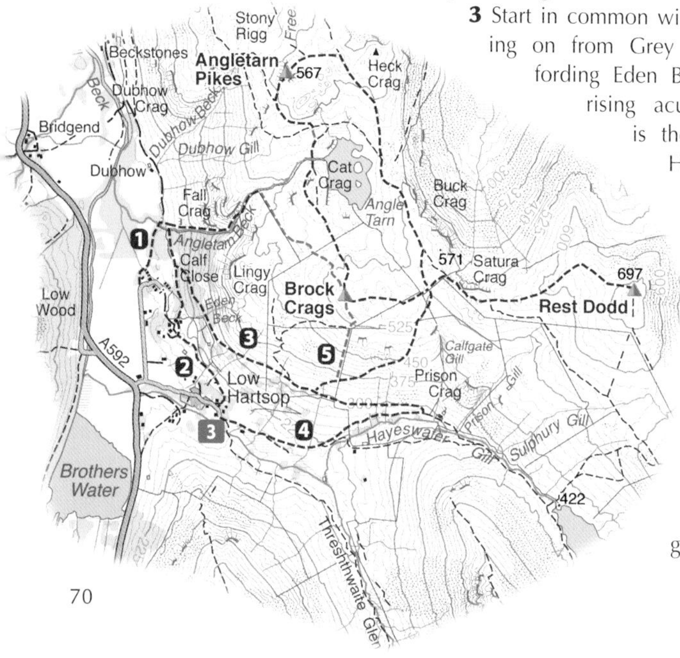

3 Start in common with Route 2, passing on from Grey Rigg, and after fording Eden Beck find a path rising acutely right. This is the course of the Hayeswater aqueduct, a loose gravel path rising through the rocky Calf Close wood. The path eases and comes along the open fellside as a green track via a kissing-gate, now with a fence right, to reach the point where an old drove-path veers up the fellside north-eastward. **4** This point can be attained from the opposite direction by following the dale track E from the car park, passing the sheep-pens by a gate. After the cattle grid, keep with the ribbon of tarmac as it rises with the wall left and passes through a gate en route to the waterworks building. However, just short of the building turn acutely left and follow a green-way (line of buried aqueduct pipe) that contours back along the fellside to come above the walled enclosures. It meets up with Route 3 at the point where the grooved path angles up the fell acutely right and thereby comes to and through the wall-gap. The drove-path mounts at a steady trajectory, revelling in fine views up the Pasture Beck valley and to the shapely ridge of Gray Crag. The path comes onto the ridge top, slipping through an old fence-line gate and over a broken wall to reach an old gateway in a further wall. Go through and, with paths in three directions, turn left. The ridge path steps over the next wall, now with a wall right, then veers right over a low broken wall and advances through a damp peaty hollow, with two distinct pools, to reach the summit cairn.

Via south slope direct 380m/1245ft 2.5km/1½ miles

5 The sterner direct option follows the wall directly up from the wall-gap (see Route 4). Keep the wall close right, climbing the grass slope; several sections of wall remarkably survive up this slope – fearsome for any wall-builder. A bold volcanic buttress marks the end of the steep ground and offers a good spot to pause and admire the view back. As the wall drifts right, bear up half-left to pass a rock pool and reach the summit.

Volcanic outcrop perched high above Hartsop

THE SUMMIT

A notable and most satisfying, if infrequently visited, viewpoint. A grassy seat beside a modest cairn is a place of peace and scenic pleasure, given a clement day. The fells rimming Dove and Deep Dales claim greatest attention, although the chiselled ridge of Gray Crag weighs in to the south, tantalising the camera.

SAFE DESCENTS

The best option in poor weather is to follow the ridge path E by the pool hollow. Cross a wall and a second wall to come to a shallow dip, where a path veers S, angling naturally down the slope SW. At the foot turn left with the green-way to join the waterworks' tarmac roadway, going sharp right with this down to Hartsop.

RIDGE ROUTES

ANGLETARN PIKES ↓ 100m/330ft ↑ 105m/345ft 2.2km/1½ miles

The are two options. The more direct heads N, passing through a wall-gap and skirting to the left of Cat Crag to come round to where the tarn outflow is forded at the broken wall-end. It rises to the regular path, slanting up left onto the rocky-ribbed summit – but this is not strictly the ridge route. The natural line is to go E, slipping

Summit looking to Gray Crag

Cat Crag from across Angle Tarn

through the pooled hollow and over and then alongside a broken wall. After stepping over a second lateral wall come down into a shallow hollow and bear left. This path leads onto the popular path trending NNW above the eastern shores of Angle Tarn. Take the right-hand fork level with the tarn's promontory, rising till level with Heck Crag's top, then swing left to reach the narrow rocky ridge of the summit over intervening marshy ground.

REST DODD	↓ 30m/100ft	↑ 20m/65ft	1.8km/1 mile

Head E with the ridge path through the pooled hollow and over a broken wall. Keep with the line of the wall through a depression and rise to join the main ridge path from Angle Tarn at a gateway. Cross the bedrock top of Satura Crag and, as this dips, keep with the left-hand path mounting onto the grassy subsidiary ridge. At the crest the path swings SE, climbing to the brow. A peat step later and you are by the summit cairn.

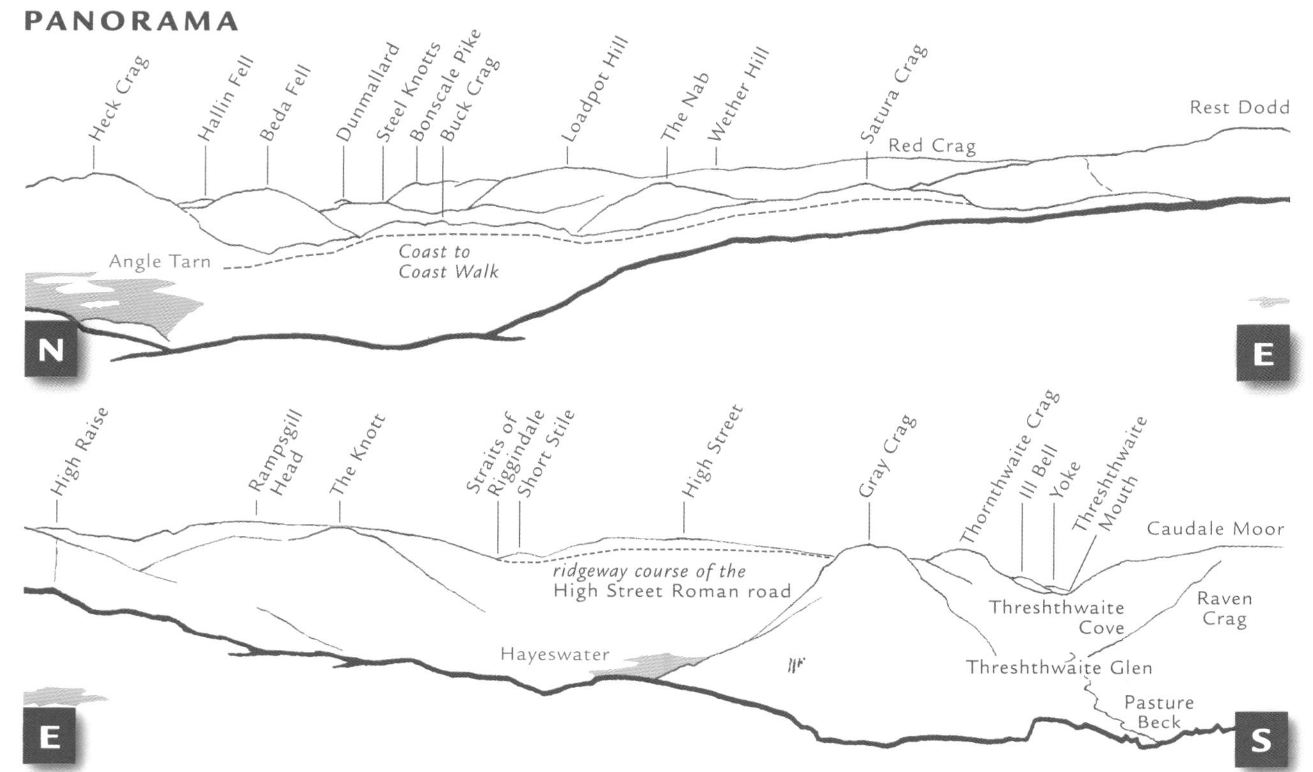
PANORAMA
Heck Crag
Hallin Fell
Beda Fell
Dunmallard
Steel Knotts
Bonscale Pike
Buck Crag
Loadpot Hill
The Nab
Wether Hill
Satura Crag
Red Crag
Rest Dodd
Angle Tarn
Coast to Coast Walk
N
E
High Raise
Rampsgill Head
The Knott
Straits of Riggindale
Short Stile
High Street
Gray Crag
Thornthwaite Crag
Ill Bell
Yoke
Threshthwaite Mouth
Caudale Moor
ridgeway course of the High Street Roman road
Threshthwaite Cove
Raven Crag
Hayeswater
Threshthwaite Glen
Pasture Beck
E
S

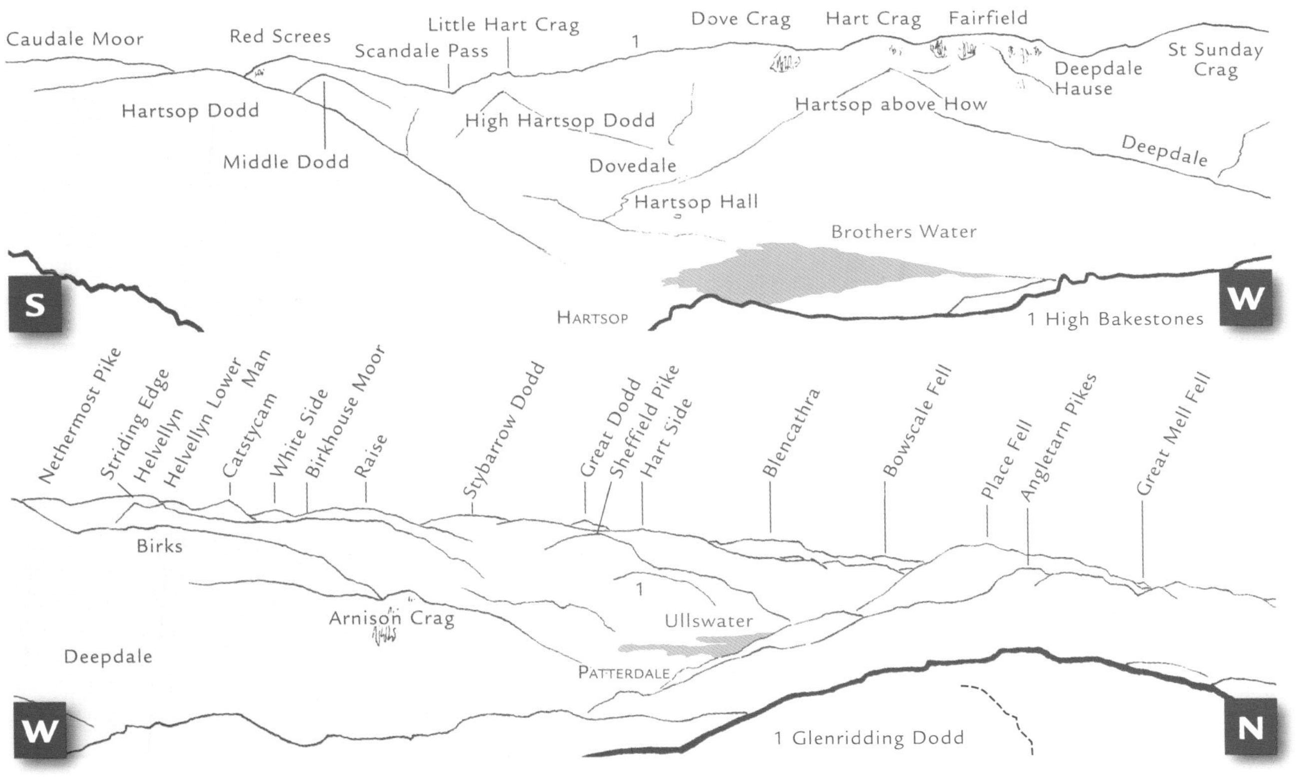

Caudale Moor
Red Screes
Scandale Pass
Little Hart Crag
1
Dove Crag
Hart Crag
Fairfield
Deepdale
Hause
St Sunday
Crag
Hartsop Dodd
Middle Dodd
High Hartsop Dodd
Dovedale
Hartsop above How
Deepdale
Hartsop Hall
Brothers Water
S
HARTSOP
1 High Bakestones
W
Nethermost Pike
Striding Edge
Helvellyn
Helvellyn Lower
Man
Catstycam
White Side
Birkhouse Moor
Raise
Stybarrow Dodd
Great Dodd
Sheffield Pike
Hart Side
Blencathra
Bowscale Fell
Place Fell
Angletarn Pikes
Great Mell Fell
Birks
1
Arnison Crag
Ullswater
Deepdale
PATTERDALE
W
1 Glenridding Dodd
N

7 CAUDALE MOOR *(764m/2507ft)*

Caudale Moor has great individuality. While the Kirkstone Pass gives it a high umbilical connection with the Near Eastern Fells and one attractive elevated start, around the compass there are enticing dale-floor ascents to mesh into a grand mountain day. Of Caudale Moor's four biggest ridges one is sufficiently abrupt to have been annexed as a separate fell, Hartsop Dodd. The two ridges embracing Woundale St Raven's Edge and Hart Crag make fine mid-point objectives, while a real favourite is the north ridge from Caudale Bridge, with the interest of a high-sited slate quarry explored en route. The wild Threshthwaite Glen fully merits its Scottish resonance, mounting to the 'Mouth', while the corresponding southern approach, up Trout Beck, is altogether more open, although decidedly damper too.

 ↑ Caudale Moor from Cowbridge

ASCENT FROM HARTSOP (3)

Via Threshthwaite Cove 590m/1935ft 4.4km/2¾ miles

1 Exit the car park and bear immediately right, crossing Walker Bridge. Follow the gated track leading into the Pasture Beck valley. Gray Crag has first claim of your attention on this approach, but on swinging into Threshthwaite Glen Raven Crag looms mightily up to the right as you weave up through the moraine and boulders on a firm path. As Threshthwaite Cove is entered pitching is evident, most noticeably on the steep headwall climb to Threshthwaite Mouth. Notice that the Tongue of the Mouth 'protrudes' a disconnected distance down the Trout Beck valley! Turn sharply up right, negotiating minor rocky steps to reach the plateau.

Via Hartsop Dodd 610m/2000ft 3.5km/2¼ miles

2 This abrupt route climbs over Hartsop Dodd and follows the continuing north ridge direct to the summit (see HARTSOP DODD Route 1).

ASCENT FROM CAUDALE BRIDGE (2)

Via Caudale Beck 580m/1905ft 3km/2 miles

3 Walk over the road bridge to find, up the bank above the gate, a wall-stile. Ascend upon a retained path beside the wall to embark on the engineered zig-zag grooves, created for the laborious hauling of slate from the remarkable high-situated Caudale Quarry. Take the path slanting right, but be watchful to veer left again. (The continuing path actually reaches an adit on the west side

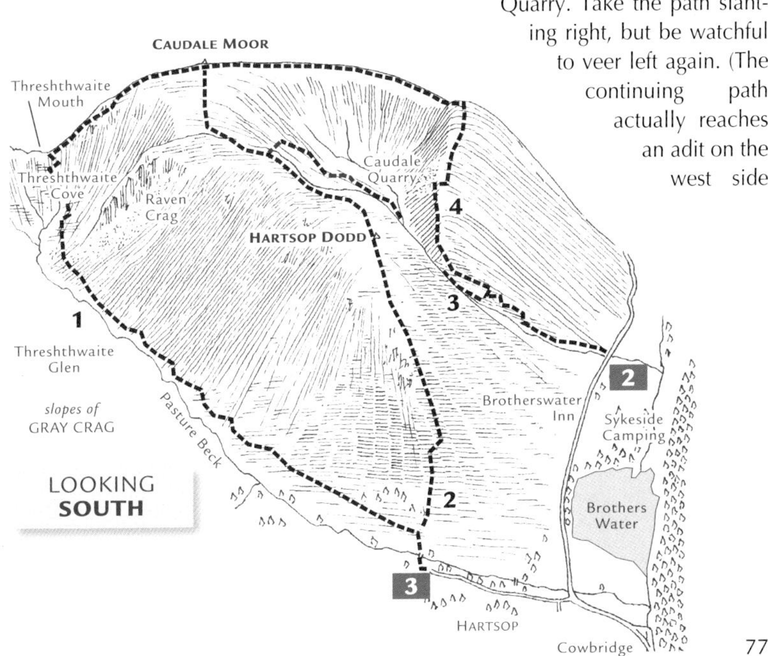

Caudale Quarry backed by Dove Crag

of the fell and is no place for sedate walkers to safely gain the ridge.) The grooved haul-path has periodic water run-out points that seem to have functioned very well in keeping the path secure from over deepening. The climb to Caudale Quarry represents the main labour of the ascent as a whole. Take a few minutes out to peruse the dilapidated remnants – ruined works sheds, a collapsed adit and much slate spoil tell their own story of times past. The opening of this quarry coincided with the wholesale transition from heather thatch to stone-tiled roofs on all levels of building and would have been initiated by the Dalemain Estate. The ridge is smartly joined only some 40m to the right and is followed on an ever lessening gradient up Rough Edge to the handsome cairn on John Bell's Banner. There is an expanse of summit area with a shallow trough in its midst, with several sheets of water to attract the camera in capturing the cloud reflections. Aim E to join the wall, and find the summit cairn 30m NE beyond the wall junction.

Via The Tongue 570m/1870ft 3.2km/2 miles

4 A canny little option, useful in poor conditions as an easy line on and off the fell. Start as Route 3, but retain company with Caudale Beck on a drove-path below the wall. Coming to a waters-meet step up right over the wall and hop over Caudale Beck to begin the old zig-zag groove path up The Tongue. Seldom followed by walkers, the way peters out, but simply keep on to reach a wall-corner with integral sheep-creep. Keeping the wall to the right, ascend to find a groove-drove slanting half-left leading to the ridge wall, and here turn right to complete the ascent.

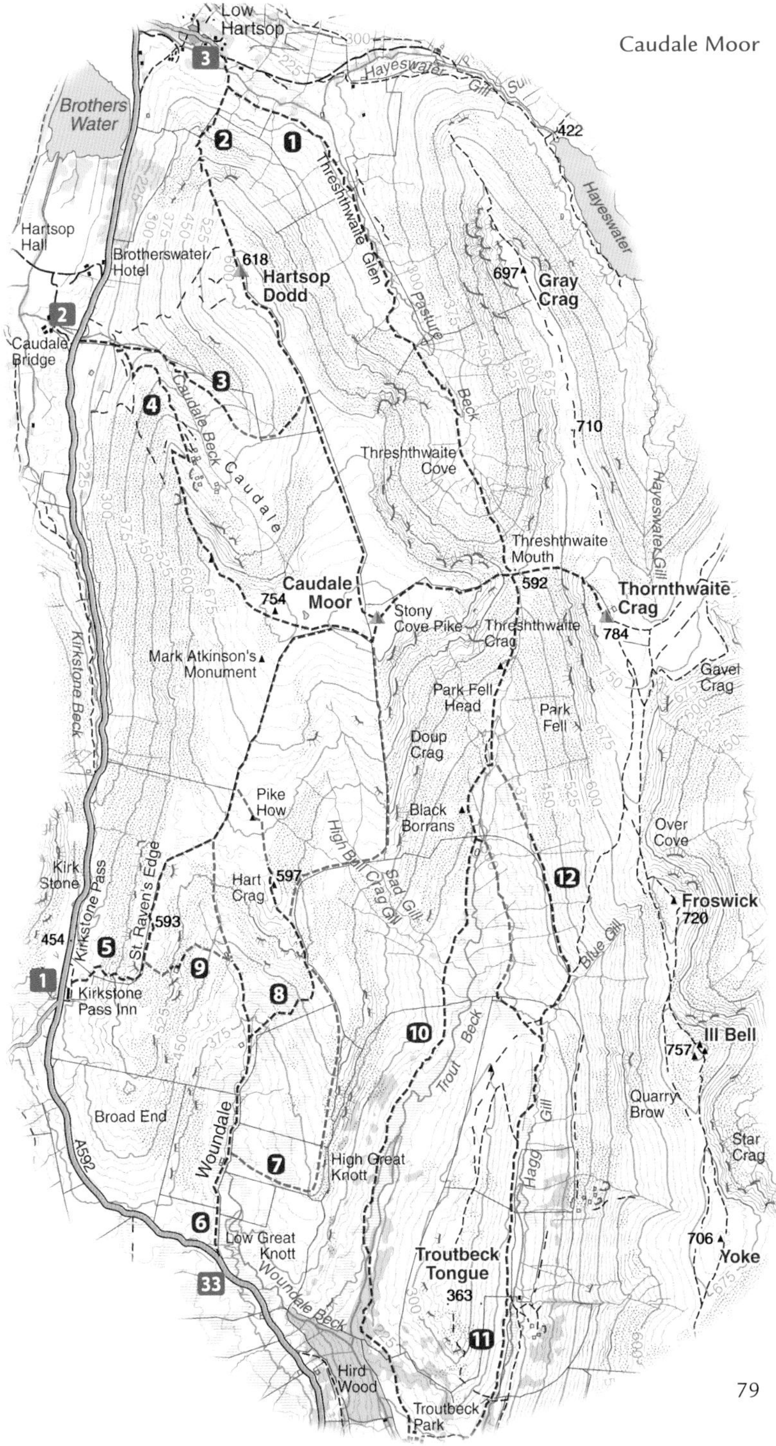
Low Hartsop
3
Hayeswater Gill
Brothers Water
2
1
422
Threshthwaite Glen
Hayeswater
Hartsop Hall
Brotherswater Hotel
618
Hartsop Dodd
697
Gray Crag
2
Caudale Bridge
Pasture
3
4
Caudale Beck
Beck
710
Threshthwaite Cove
Caudale
Hayeswater Gill
Threshthwaite Mouth
592
Caudale Moor
754
Thornthwaite Crag
Stony Cove Pike
Threshthwaite Crag
784
Mark Atkinson's Monument
Kirkstone Beck
Gavel Crag
Park Fell Head
Park Fell
Doup Crag
Pike How
Black Borrans
High Bell Crag Gill
Over Cove
Kirk Stone
Hart Crag
597
12
Kirkstone Pass
St. Raven's Edge
Sad Gill
Froswick
720
593
454
5
Blue Gill
1
9
Kirkstone Pass Inn
8
10
Ill Bell
757
Trout Beck
Broad End
Quarry Brow
Woundale
Hagg Gill
Star Crag
7
A592
High Great Knott
6
Low Great Knott
706
Yoke
33
Woundale Beck
Troutbeck Tongue
363
11
Hird Wood
Troutbeck Park

ASCENT FROM KIRKSTONE PASS (1)

Via St Raven's Edge 350m/1150ft 3.2km/2 miles

Mark Atkinson's cairn on John Bell's Banner

5 This is very much a there-and-back route to the top, as circuits are just not possible. Propelled by the energy of a high start, rather than from the trio of turbines bringing power to the Kirkstone Inn, the popular path from the large car park climbs via stiles to the ridge top and the large cairn on St Raven's Edge. Keeping close company with the ridge wall head N, slipping through a depression at the head of Woundale. Maintain allegiance to the wall, which is a sure guide to the summit. En route make a point of locating the cairn monument to Mark and William Atkinson on John Bell's Banner, towards the western edge prior to where the wall bears east. While there is no doubting the sentiment behind the desire to mark anyone's passing on a high and dearly loved hill, custodians of the fell environment are at pains to keep the fells wild and minimise the sense of them being a garden of rest.

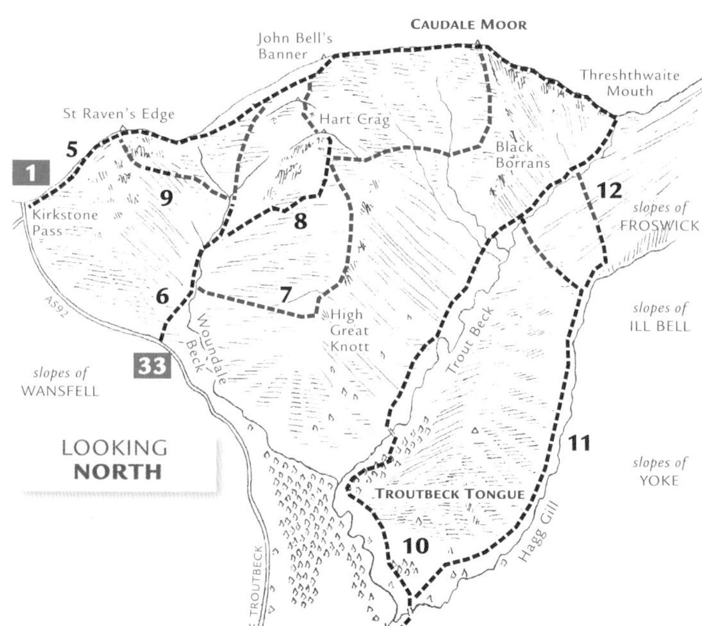

Flag bridge and wash-fold in Woundale

ASCENT FROM WOUNDALE (33)

The strange dale-name appears to mean 'the twisted valley', as in 'winding', although from the Kirkstone Road it's a straight march from bottom to top. Four routes stem from the dale-floor track in Woundale onto the south-west ridge of Caudale Moor.

Direct 460m/1510ft 4km/2½ miles

6 The gated track leads via a broad flagged bridge over Woundale Beck, with a classic sheep-wash fold. Heading up-dale by a glacial rigg, see a lone roofless stone barn on the far bank, then reach a second entire wash-fold, an unusually high situation for such a practical shepherding structure from yesteryear. Keep on, holding a slight bias right with the feeder gill, to reach the ridge wall and main path to John Bell's Banner.

Via Hart Crag 470m/1540ft 4.9km/3 miles

7 Stout stock fencing prevents lower access to the Hart Crag ridge. It is possible to go through a gate some 50m beyond the lower wash-fold where Woundale Beck is crossed and wander up the damp fellside, with the ridge-straddling wall close right,

Froswick and Ill Bell from east of Stony Cove Pike

to gain the ridge at High Great Knott. Keep to the spine of the ridge, enjoying the views into the upper Trout Beck valley to the distinctive twin peaks of Froswick and Ill Bell. A netting fence is crossed in the next cross-wall and then higher wooden rails at the next wall junction. Hereon accompany the ridge wall to join a quad track. **8** This quad-bike track stems from Woundale at the wall end and bears steadily up onto the ridge. Weave through the ridge-top outcropping by an old wall, which includes a bedrock peak, to reach a prominent cairn on the crest of Hart Crag itself. When the old wall falters in a marsh follow on with a dwindling path that climbs over Pike How to join the ridge to John Bell's Banner. As a variant to connecting with the regular ridge, veer right following the solid wall down to ford Bull Crag and Sad Gills and join company with the true south ridge. Follow the rising wall almost direct to the summit; there is no hint of a path, as there is no way up via Sad Gill from the Trout Beck valley. More importantly, there is no way of crossing the wall at Black Borrans – please heed, especially walkers influenced by the Wainwright guide!

Via St Raven's Edge 510m/1675ft 4.8km/3 miles

9 From the higher wash-fold (see Route 6) an old quarry-way once struck up the left-hand slope – now not visible until almost at the quarry, itself a fascinating remnant with a roofless bothy amid the slate tip. Above this a shallow pecked-out cavern and rake-cutting gives cause to pause and peruse this long forgotten scene of human endeavour. Climb directly up from here onto St Raven's Edge to join the regular path from Kirkstone Pass.

ASCENT FROM TROUTBECK, TOWN HEAD (34 – off map S)

Via Trout Beck 670m/2200ft 8.5km/5¼ miles

10 A journey in two parts. The early phase follows the tarmac Ing Lane through the meadows – this single-track road leads from Town Head to Park Farm and is a popular stroll. Beyond the farm the walk takes on an altogether rougher, wilder complexion. Pass by the Westmorland barn and round the back by the sheep-handling pens, guided by the footpath arrow onto a track rising by a gate. The path weaves on along an open woodland way to cross a broad slate bridge spanning Trout Beck. This fascinating rustic stone structure must be stout to have resisted the not infrequent hydraulic drummings of the beck at times of flood. The trail trends up a decidedly damp dale, grazed by suckler cattle, and comes to a fixed hurdle (where you would expect a hand-gate!). Climb over and continue with the path, negotiating the fringes of bracken and sedge marsh and passing an old sheep-pen complex to reach and go through a wooden gate in the upper-dale enclosure wall. Further damp ground leads by the first of several small cairns, and there is a moment where ascending walkers go straight on, but descending walkers have created a path right. This is recommended, as it leads to the top of the upper rowan gorge – in two sections with their lovely cascades. The upper section of the path is less about the intimate and more about the rousing craggy heights above, as Threshthwaite Crag looms above and the trail slants up the grassy fringe of scree to the col of Threshthwaite Mouth. Here turn up the rock steps, left, accompanying the ridge wall.

Via Hagg Gill 670m/2200ft 8.5km/5¼ miles

11 A variant, that is better underfoot for longer, joins the footpath signposted right off the road – immediately after Hagg Bridge and before Park Farm. Rise up the pasture, crossing a gill to reach and go through a kissing-gate. Bear right with the stony track, which enters the lovely glen of Hagg Gill via a sequence of gates and en route passes below two long abandoned slate quarries. The name reflects the fact that the valley was once a managed woodland – 'hagg' means 'to hack or chop timber'. This route also coincides with High Street Roman road, so there is a certain romance in the notion of treading an ancient thoroughfare. On the rise of the Roman road towards the third gate bear off left with a track to go through a sheep-handling pen, via two gates, to enter the Trout Beck valley pasture. Contour, keeping above the worst of the marsh to cross a ford just beyond a sheepfold complex and before the final enclosure wall. Go through the near gate to link with Route 9.

Via upper dale 710m/2330ft 8.5km/5¼ miles

12 As a further variation to Route 10, keep with the Roman road through the next gate, and as the adjacent field-wall drifts left follow suit on a narrow trod that contours into the dale-head pasture. Evidence of a path is quickly lost when the company of the wall is forsaken. Contour to reach the dale beck immediately above the rowan-filled gorge, ford and join the main path to the col (Route 10).

THE SUMMIT

A large cairn occupies the top, set away from the straddling ridge wall. As befits a fell with a 'moor' name, the summit has a certain plateau-like quality. Although the immediate vicinity of the cairn is less expansive, the presence of ridge-top walls conveys

Caudale Moor summit cairn

the sense of shepherding, rather than a mountaineering environment. Further west a shallow hollow holds a tarn, missed by most walkers. However, the cairns above the north ridge and Mark Atkinson's cairn on John Bell's Banner are popular situations from which to enjoy fine views to north and west. Most walkers content themselves by sitting on the southern periphery, gazing towards the distant Windermere.

SAFE DESCENTS

The walls come into their own when safety is an issue. Go W for Kirkstone Pass and N for Hartsop, and opt to decline into the Caudale Beck valley rather than traversing Hartsop Dodd for easiest going. But avoid the wall heading due S, as this does not give an escape, and the wall to Threshthwaite Mouth (E) has rock steps just above the col that call for caution.

RIDGE ROUTES

HARTSOP DODD ↓ 30m/100ft ↑ 175m/575ft 2.2km/1½ miles

Follow the ridge wall N, keeping to the west side; this is a sure guide to the apparently lowly summit. But note that when you descend further to Hartsop or Caudale Bridge, consistently steep ground is encountered.

THORNTHWAITE CRAG ↓ 190m/625ft ↑ 170m/560ft 1.5km/1 mile

Walk E, soon joining company with the ridge wall that eventually plummets to Threshthwaite Mouth, with several rather awkward rock-steps to handle – never as easy in descent. As it crosses the undulating col the wall climbs steep ground, accompanied by an appallingly loose trail. Walkers are encouraged to consider alleviating the pressure both on their knees and the trail itself by veering left as the rocky ground is reached. Cross the ridge wall and head NE, and once you have crossed the north-running wall, bear back right (pathless) onto the ridge, thereby keeping entirely to grass. Later, the broken ridge wall is rejoined to reach the most handsome of beacon cairns.

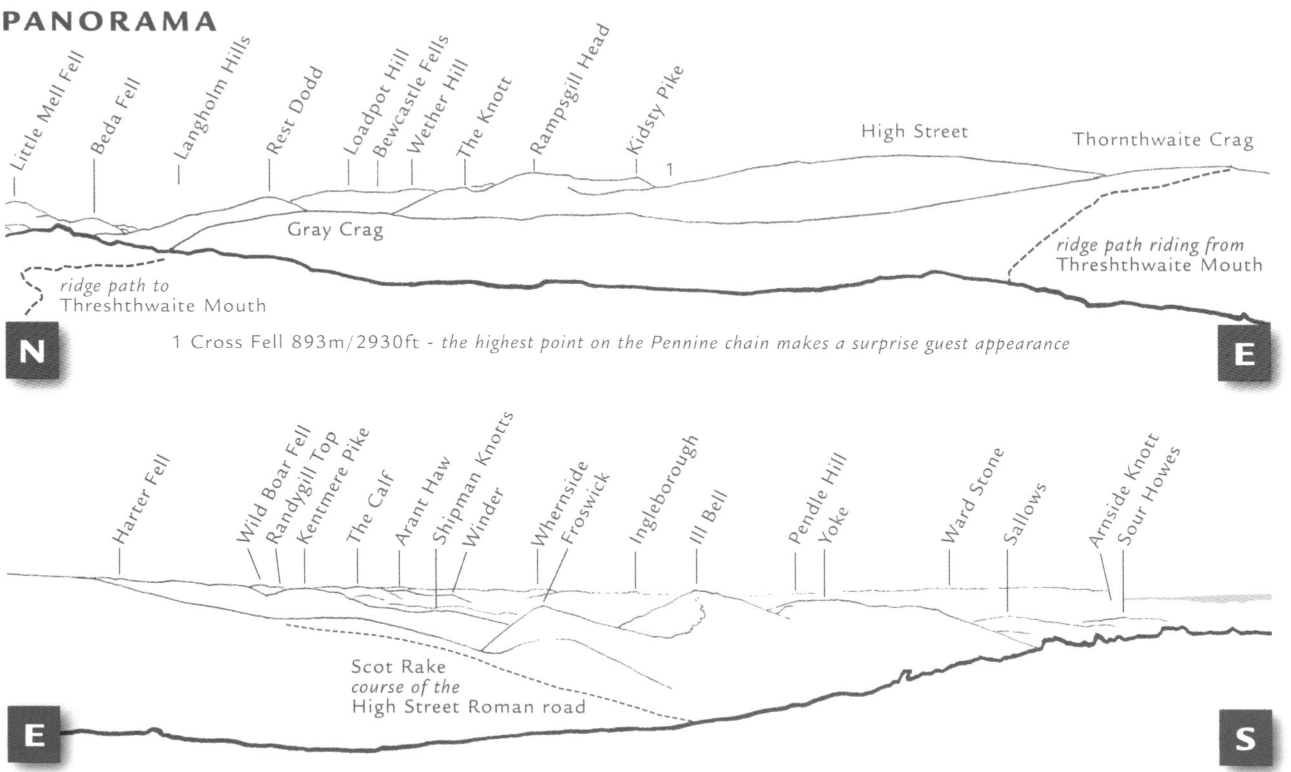
PANORAMA
Little Mell Fell
Beda Fell
Langholm Hills
Rest Dodd
Loadpot Hill
Bewcastle Fells
Wether Hill
The Knott
Rampsgill Head
Kidsty Pike
1
High Street
Thornthwaite Crag
Gray Crag
ridge path to Threshthwaite Mouth
ridge path riding from Threshthwaite Mouth
N
1 Cross Fell 893m/2930ft - the highest point on the Pennine chain makes a surprise guest appearance
E
Harter Fell
Wild Boar Fell
Randygill Top
Kentmere Pike
The Calf
Arant Haw
Shipman Knotts
Winder
Whernside
Froswick
Ingleborough
Ill Bell
Pendle Hill
Yoke
Ward Stone
Sallows
Arnside Knott
Sour Howes
Scot Rake
course of the High Street Roman road
E
S

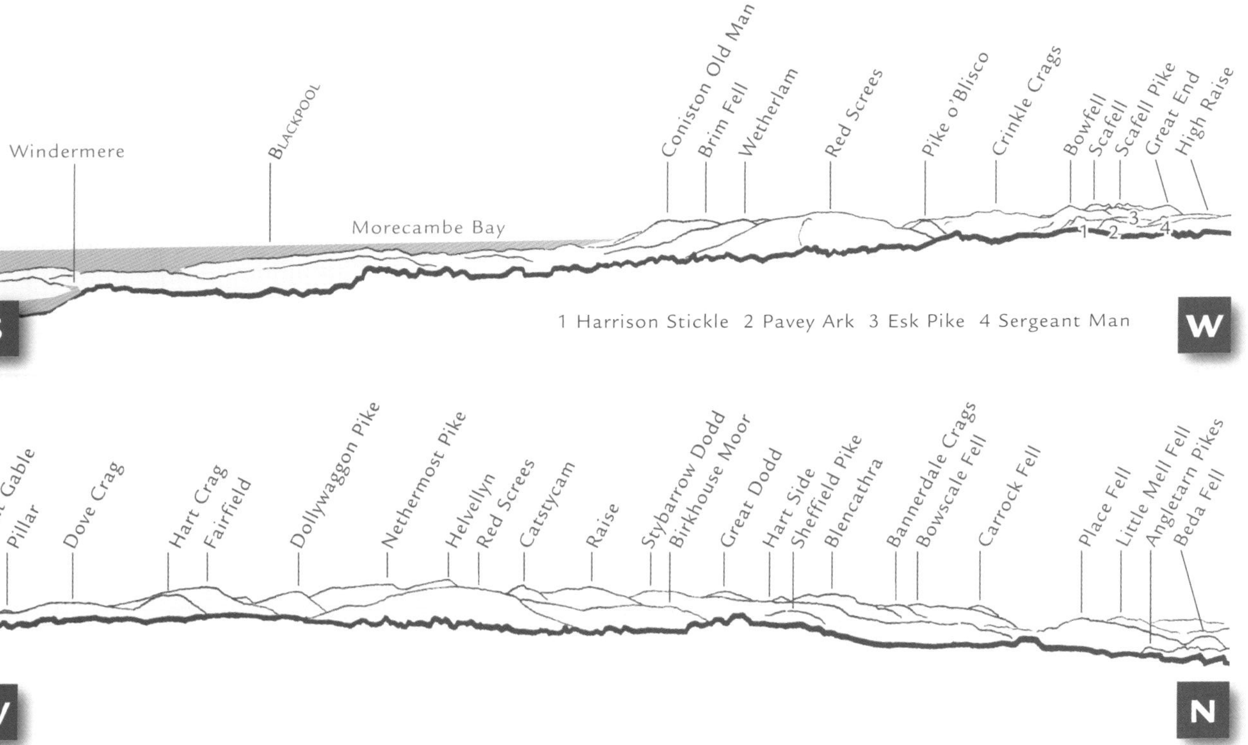
Windermere
Blackpool
Morecambe Bay
Coniston Old Man
Brim Fell
Wetherlam
Red Screes
Pike o'Blisco
Crinkle Crags
Bowfell
Scafell
Scafell Pike
Great End
High Raise
S
W
1 Harrison Stickle 2 Pavey Ark 3 Esk Pike 4 Sergeant Man
Great Gable
Pillar
Dove Crag
Hart Crag
Fairfield
Dollywaggon Pike
Nethermost Pike
Helvellyn
Red Screes
Catstycam
Raise
Stybarrow Dodd
Birkhouse Moor
Great Dodd
Hart Side
Sheffield Pike
Blencathra
Bannerdale Crags
Bowscale Fell
Carrock Fell
Place Fell
Little Mell Fell
Angletarn Pikes
Beda Fell
W
N

8 FROSWICK *(720m/2362ft)*

In height Froswick is the junior partner to Ill Bell – the two forming almost (but not quite) a matching pair – and these conical fells have great visual appeal. The origin of the fell name (pronounced 'frozik') is rather obscure, suggesting a lingering association with a lost farmstead in a chilly situation close below. Unlike its higher twin, the fell has no eastern line of ascent, although the Roman road up Scot Rake does offer a simple approach from the west. What the Roman militia thought of the climb from Hagg Gill can only be surmised, but it is less of an issue in descent, of course, and entirely on grass. The fell is generally climbed as walkers head along the ridge path connecting Ill Bell with Thornthwaite Crag.

The Roman road embarks on Scot Rake

 ↑ Ridge path from Thornthwaite Crag

ASCENT FROM TROUTBECK, TOWN HEAD (34)

Via Scot Rake

600m/1970ft 6.7km/4¼ miles

1 Follow Ing Lane from Town Head. Immediately after crossing Hagg Bridge bear right via the stile (currently superfluous, as the fence is missing) and follow the footpath up the pasture via a minor gill to go through the kissing-gate and join the farm track. Go right, following the track via gates through the Hagg Gill valley. At the top, exit by the gate and step up on the grassy way with a wall close left and Blue Gill right. Where the wall contours off left, turn your mind more purposefully to the ascent. The grassy trod may be as old as the hills (or Romans!), but it is a modest presence and has one small rock-step, which would not have been there 2000 years ago!

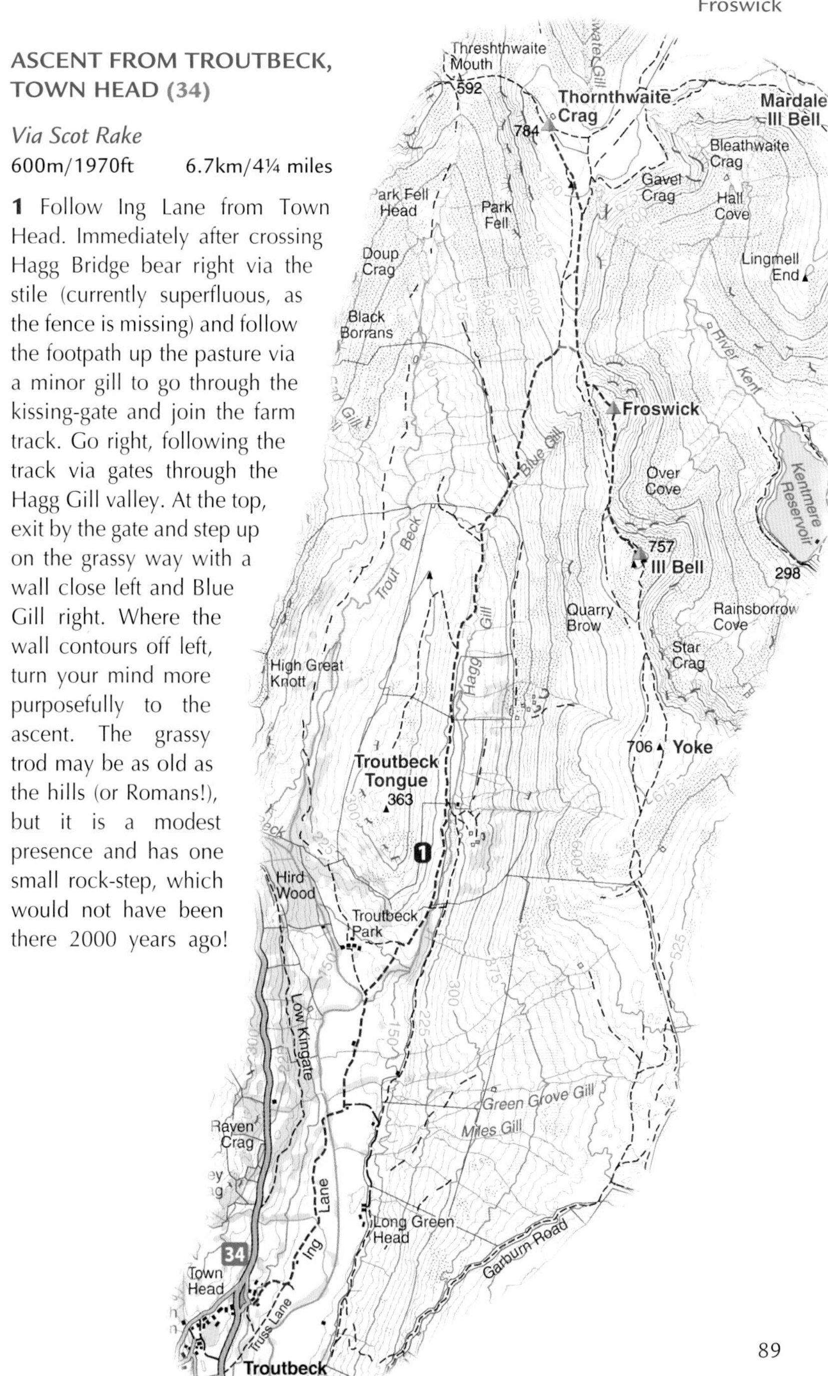

Froswick from Ill Bell's north-east ridge

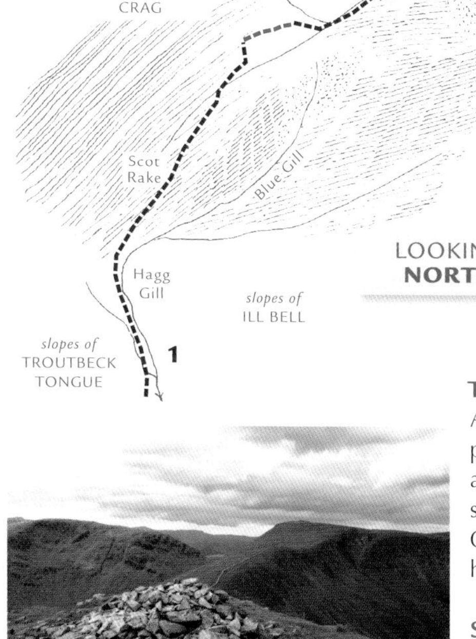

Froswick summit cairn

After curving through a shallow re-entrant, the path comes by loose stones, wash-out from a tiny gill. Directly above this leave the ancient 'road' and ascend the grassy slope to the col, joining forces with the well-tended ridge path climbing excitedly to the summit.

THE SUMMIT

A small dome centred upon a cairn provides the perfect place to stop and study big brother Ill Bell to the south across the crucible of Over Cove and, to the north-east, the headwall of the Kentmere valley.

SAFE DESCENTS

The quickest route to valley level is by Scot Rake, reversing the one prime ascent route for Troutbeck. Otherwise, head S as to Ill Bell and use the fell-runners' route from the saddle that contours along the upper western slopes onto Yoke and so down to the Garburn Pass for Troutbeck or Kentmere.

RIDGE ROUTES

ILL BELL ↓70m/230ft ↑ 105m/345ft 0.8km/½ mile

Head due S to the col, from where the one honest trail angles SE, with two optional paths above the prominent buttress. The path closest above the buttress gives the more handsome views into Over Cove.

THORNTHWAITE CRAG ↓ 95m/310ft ↑ 160m/525ft 1.7km/1 mile

Keep tight to the ridge path leading NW down to the col, from where modern path-work has secured a good firm trail, and climb N to a skyline cairn among a few rocks. From here easier ground is reached, trending NW to the beacon cairn.

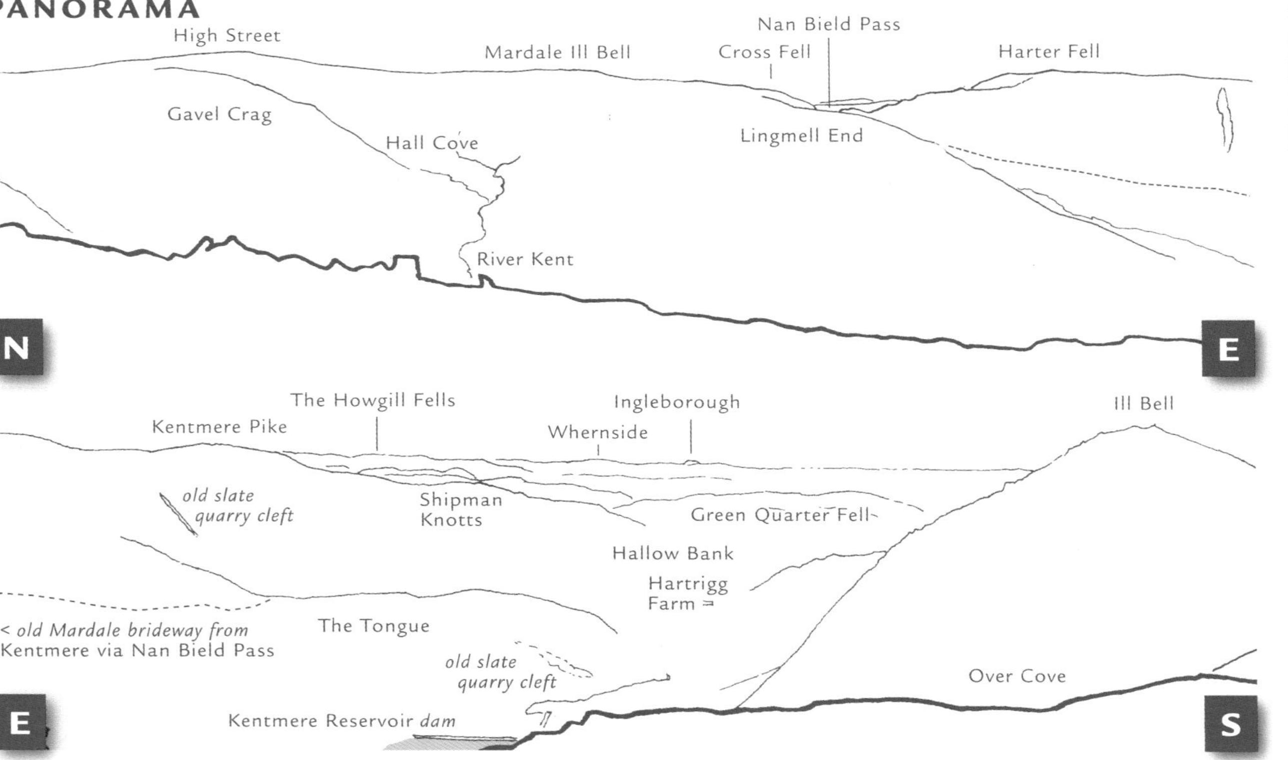
PANORAMA
High Street
Mardale Ill Bell
Cross Fell
Nan Bield Pass
Harter Fell
Gavel Crag
Hall Cove
Lingmell End
River Kent
N
E
The Howgill Fells
Ingleborough
Ill Bell
Kentmere Pike
Whernside
old slate quarry cleft
Shipman Knotts
Green Quarter Fell
Hallow Bank
Hartrigg Farm
The Tongue
< old Mardale brideway from Kentmere via Nan Bield Pass
old slate quarry cleft
Over Cove
Kentmere Reservoir dam
E
S

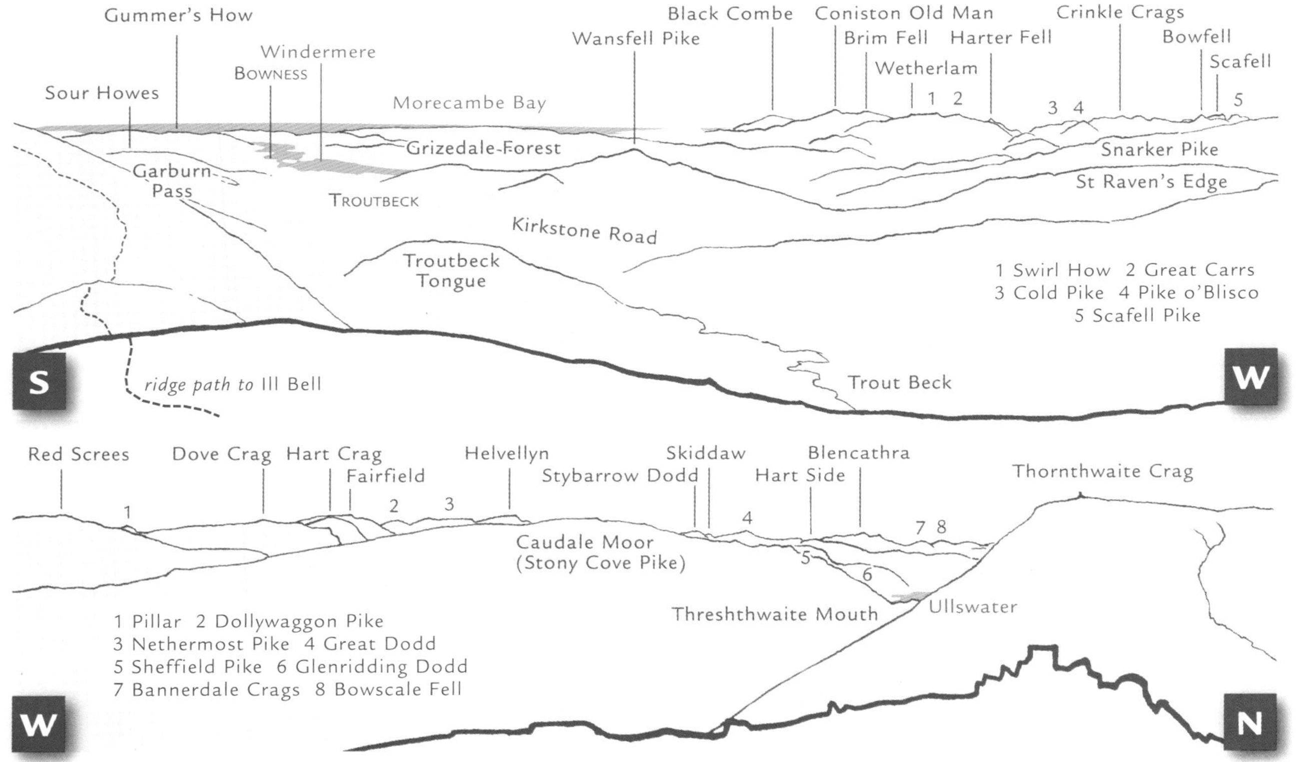
Gummer's How
Windermere
Bowness
Sour Howes
Morecambe Bay
Wansfell Pike
Black Combe
Coniston Old Man
Brim Fell
Harter Fell
Wetherlam
1 2
Crinkle Crags
Bowfell
Scafell
3 4
5
Grizedale-Forest
Garburn Pass
Troutbeck
Snarker Pike
St Raven's Edge
Kirkstone Road
Troutbeck Tongue
1 Swirl How 2 Great Carrs
3 Cold Pike 4 Pike o'Blisco
5 Scafell Pike
S
W
ridge path to Ill Bell
Trout Beck
Red Screes
Dove Crag
Hart Crag
Fairfield
Helvellyn
Stybarrow Dodd
Skiddaw
Hart Side
Blencathra
Thornthwaite Crag
1
2
3
4
7 8
Caudale Moor
(Stony Cove Pike)
5
6
Threshthwaite Mouth
Ullswater
1 Pillar 2 Dollywaggon Pike
3 Nethermost Pike 4 Great Dodd
5 Sheffield Pike 6 Glenridding Dodd
7 Bannerdale Crags 8 Bowscale Fell
W
N

9 GRAY CRAG *(697m/2287ft)*

Travellers heading south from Patterdale towards Brothers Water catch a fleeting glimpse of this ridge-end fell and sense a bulkiness belying its actual slender proportions. Rising between the Threshthwaite Glen and Hayeswater, Gray Crag forms a grand start to a fell-round via Thornthwaite Crag to either Caudale Moor or High Street. Walkers may reach the ridge from Threshthwaite Mouth, but the common line stems from Wath Bridge, an abrupt climb rewarded with great views.

Hayeswater Gill

↑ Gray Crag from the A592

ASCENT FROM HARTSOP (3)

Via north ridge 510m/1675ft 2.5km/1½ miles

1 An inevitably stiff start, but what a fine ridge to follow! Set off from the Hartsop car park (free parking, donations for the village school appreciated in the collection box). Advance along the bridleway signed 'Hayeswater', passing the large sheep corral. The tarmac strip is forsaken after a gate, and the open track followed down to cross the Hayeswater Gill bridge – note the stone ruins associated with the 19th-century Myers' Head Lead Mine down to the right. The rough track rises by a gate, passing a rustic stone barn, and after a kissing-gate climbs easily onto where there is evidence of a walkers' path stepping off onto the near fellside right. This path climbs the steep grass slope, angling left to avoid the skyline outcropping, with a spot of wash-out damage evident. The path rounds the crags to gain the north ridge proper. This narrow ridge, a fellwalkers' delight, leads assuredly and handsomely onto the summit plateau.

2 As a variant to Route 1, follow the metalled roadway from the cattle grid as it rises above Wath Bridge to come by the waterworks' building onto a path. This leads to a wall-stile directly over the inflow of Calfgate Gill into Hayeswater Gill, an

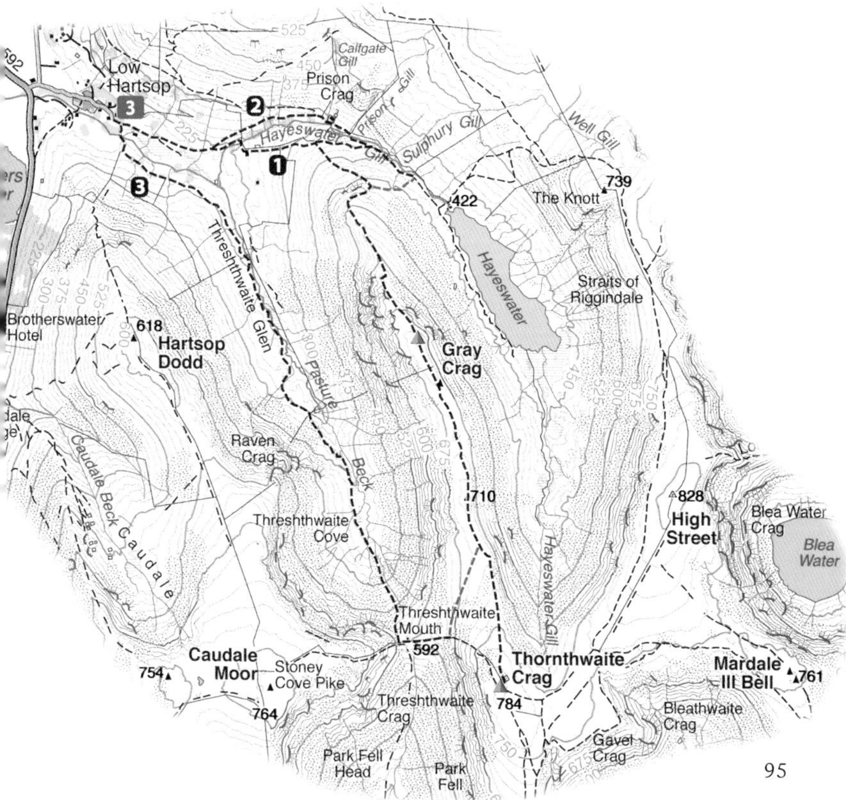

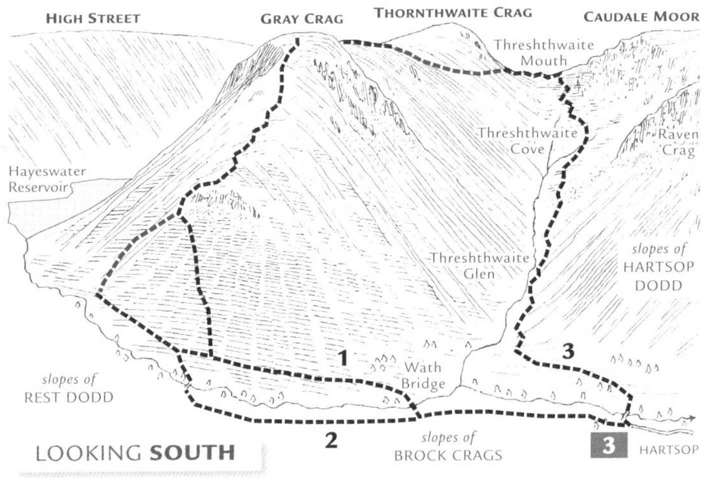

interesting moment. Cross the footbridge, taking time to enjoy the excited tumbling waters. The path slants up to join the reservoir track (although you might be tempted to hold off joining it until you've had a look at the great waterfall down to the left). Follow the track towards Hayeswater dam, taking to the steep grassy slope at random some time after the point where a wall is seen descending to Hayeswater Gill from the north-east, after the amazing cascades of Sulphury Gill. Climb pathless grassy slopes almost due W onto the ridge, where the direct route comes above the ridge-end outcropping.

Via Threshthwaite Glen **570m/1870ft 5.5km/3½ miles**

3 Such a grand valley name suggests an impressive arena, and Threshthwaite certainly lives up to expectations. Depart the car park, turning sharp right, signed 'Pasture Beck', by the gate and crossing Walker Bridge. Keep company with the gated track, which leads into Threshthwaite Glen. High to the right, partitioning Hartsop Dodd from Caudale Moor, the serrated edge of Raven Crag catches the eye, with the somewhat less imposing craggy face of Gray Crag to the left. The valley, strewn with glacial rock debris and moraine, takes its name from 'the clearing with a thatch dwelling', where the thatch would have been of heather divots. The valley path winds up through a wall-gap and larger boulders at the quite distant base of Raven Crag, entering the enigmatic Threshthwaite Cove, where the walker is embraced in a wild mountain corrie. The path has received recent stone pitching attention, all the more necessary on the steep climb to the so-called Threshthwaite Mouth. The unique name for the hause was clearly coined by observers in the Trout Beck valley, where sits the proverbial Tongue. Follow the broken wall left towards Thornthwaite Crag,

Gray Crag from Hartsop Dodd

but as the slope steepens veer left, traversing the fellside to cross over a lateral wall and join the ridge path. This heads over the intermediate top and through the cross-ridge wall to reach the summit with some ease.

THE SUMMIT

Punctuating the ridge walk, the summit cairn rests upon a grassy patch. The best views are cautiously from the nearby edges on either side of the ridge. Hayeswater is quite a subject from the eastern edge – notice the simply massive accumulation of debris on the far shore. It would seem to have collapsed from on high some hundreds of years ago, creating a gully chiselling out The Knott from the main mass of Rampsgill Head.

SAFE DESCENTS

When heading N upon the one ridge path be mindful of the cliff at the ridge-end and take evasive action with the path – taking either side. If in doubt head for Hayeswater dam, joining the access track down to Hartsop.

RIDGE ROUTE

THORNTHWAITE CRAG ↓ 50m/165ft ↑ 140m/460ft 2km/1¼ miles

The ridge path leads SSE, crossing two walls, the second wall coming quickly after a knoll some 14m/45ft higher than Gray Crag, from where the ridge eases up by the wall to the beacon cairn.

PANORAMA

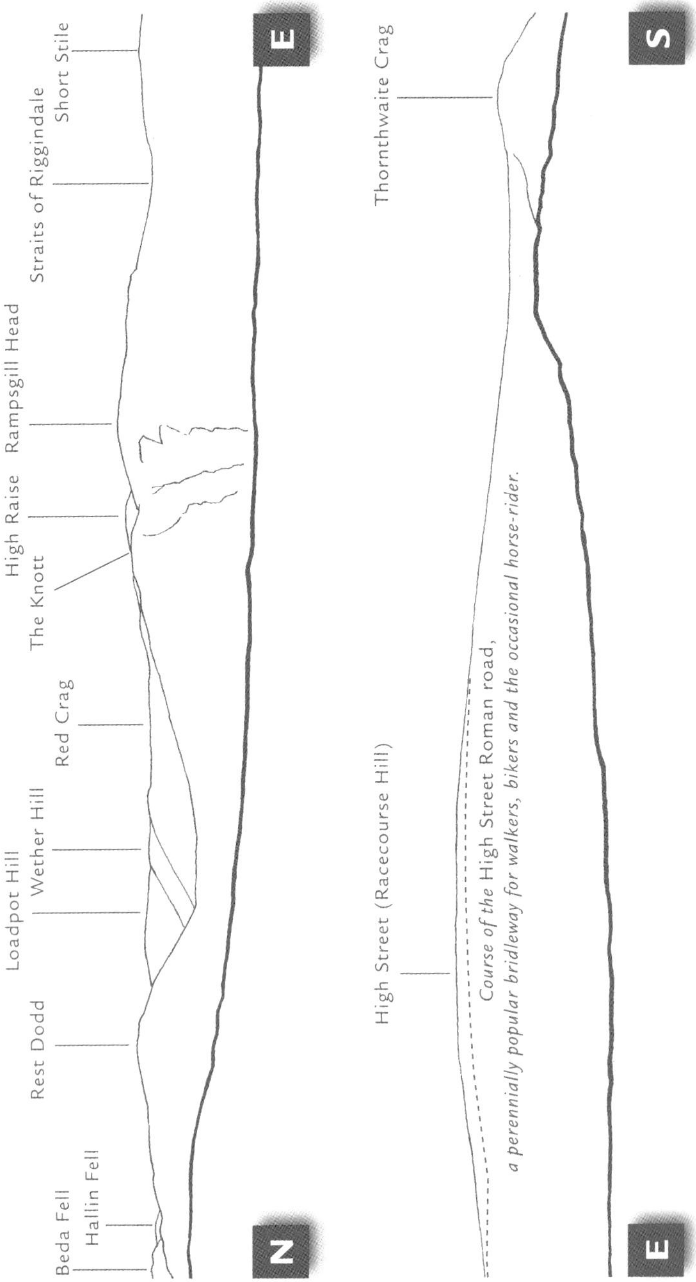

N – E

Beda Fell
Hallin Fell
Rest Dodd
Loadpot Hill
Wether Hill
Red Crag
The Knott
High Raise
Rampsgill Head
Straits of Riggindale
Short Stile

E – S

High Street (Racecourse Hill)
Thornthwaite Crag

Course of the High Street Roman road*,*
a perennially popular bridleway for walkers, bikers and the occasional horse-rider.

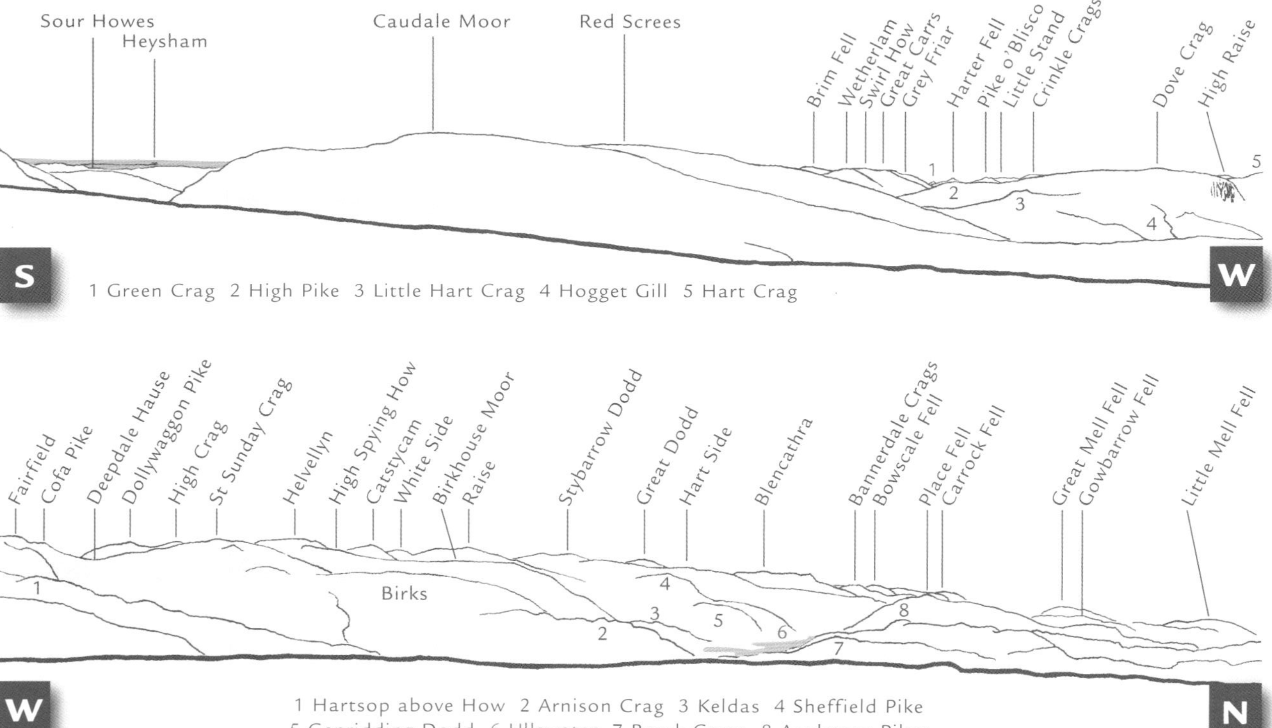
Sour Howes
Heysham
Caudale Moor
Red Screes
Brim Fell
Wetherlam
Swirl How
Great Carrs
Grey Friar
Harter Fell
Pike o'Blisco
Little Stand
Crinkle Crags
Dove Crag
High Raise
S
W
1 Green Crag 2 High Pike 3 Little Hart Crag 4 Hogget Gill 5 Hart Crag
Fairfield
Cofa Pike
Deepdale Hause
Dollywaggon Pike
High Crag
St Sunday Crag
Helvellyn
High Spying How
Catstycam
White Side
Birkhouse Moor
Raise
Stybarrow Dodd
Great Dodd
Hart Side
Blencathra
Bannerdale Crags
Bowscale Fell
Place Fell
Carrock Fell
Great Mell Fell
Gowbarrow Fell
Little Mell Fell
Birks
W
N
1 Hartsop above How 2 Arnison Crag 3 Keldas 4 Sheffield Pike
5 Genridding Dodd 6 Ullswater 7 Brock Crags 8 Angletarn Pikes

10 GREY CRAG *(638m/2093ft)*

This is where it all can be said to begin – Lakeland that is. While rooted in the majesty of upper Longsleddale, Grey Crag also sends out four lonely ridges south and east towards the A6. This is territory of a different character to that known and revered as Lakeland. These ridges give scope for long days far from the crowds. Here it is possible to experience a kind of soothing solitude, engaging with the wild, where walkers are much more likely to encounter red deer, red grouse and birds of prey than on the popular fells.

Not unsurprisingly most walkers claim their fell-top from Sadgill, in the thrilling arena at the head of Longsleddale, and invariably include Tarn Crag in a compact rambling day. Some, indeed, venture on to claim Branstree and Selside Pike before backtracking down the historic Gatescarth Pass track and quarryman's lane – a fine expedition, sure enough. Yet the more haunting pleasure is experienced only by those who journey the less trodden ridgeways.

 ↑ Cairn on Long Crag, looking to a distant Grey Crag

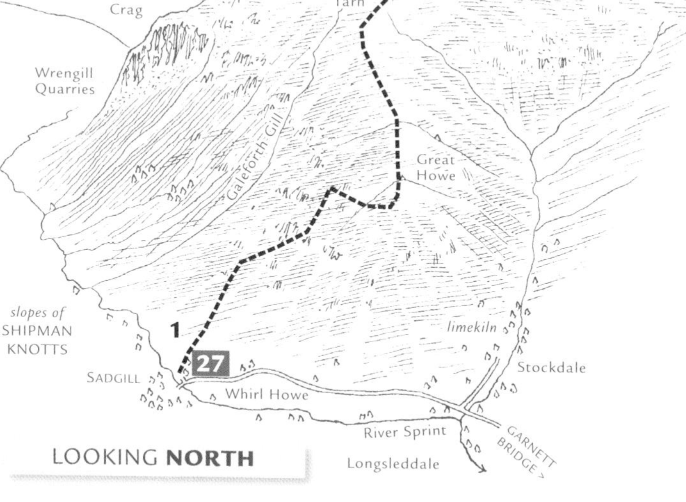

ASCENT FROM SADGILL (27)

Via Great Howe 450m/1475ft 2.4km/1½ miles

By far the shortest and most popular line of travel. **1** Direct from the lane-end parking space close to Sadgill Bridge find a field-gate, from which access land is accessed. Target the fence-gap at the top, ascend the pasture bank (interspersed with outcropping), then crossing a gill to reach what turns out to be a stile. The path heads on up a stony gully onto a shelf – a marvellous point to admire the craggy wilds of upper Longsleddale

and down on the delightful setting of Sadgill, which looks anything but sad! Where a wall is encountered find also a waymark post that guides the path right to where the wall switches to a fence. At this point cross the stile, with dog-gate, and continue up the ridge above onto Great Howe. The path sweeps past a cairned knoll without a second glance, but you shouldn't miss the opportunity to gaze back down on the lower reaches of Longsleddale. The path now runs on along a level, inevitably damp moorland on a northern bias before swinging to the right as it rises to a stile at a fence-corner. The path now angles eastward, avoiding outcropping, to reach the summit cairn.

Grey Crag summit cairn

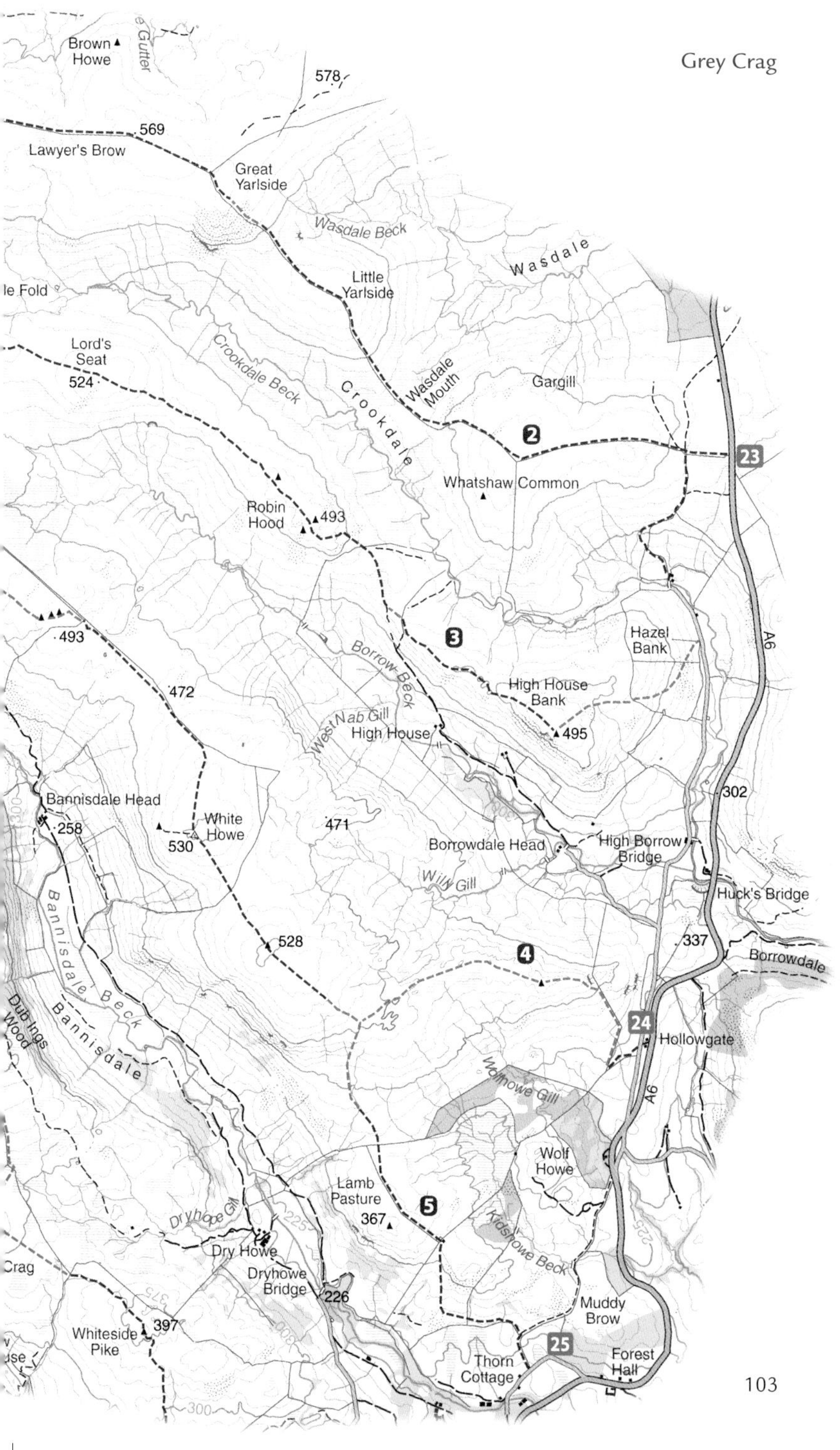
Brown Howe
578
569
Lawyer's Brow
Great Yarlside
Wasdale Beck
Wasdale
le Fold
Little Yarlside
Lord's Seat
524
Crookdale Beck
Crookdale
Wasdale Mouth
Gargill
2
23
Whatshaw Common
Robin Hood
493
493
3
Hazel Bank
A6
Borrow Beck
472
High House Bank
West Nab Gill
High House
495
302
Bannisdale Head
258
White Howe
530
471
Borrowdale Head
High Borrow Bridge
Willy Gill
Huck's Bridge
Bannisdale Beck
528
337
4
Borrowdale
Dub Ings Wood
Bannisdale
24
Hollowgate
Wolfhowe Gill
A6
Wolf Howe
Lamb Pasture
Dryhope Gill
367
5
Kidshowe Beck
Dry Howe
Crag
Dryhowe Bridge
226
Muddy Brow
Whiteside Pike
397
25
Forest Hall
Thorn Cottage

ASCENT FROM A6 SHAP SUMMIT (23)

Via Great Yarlside 340m/1115ft 6.9km/4¼ miles

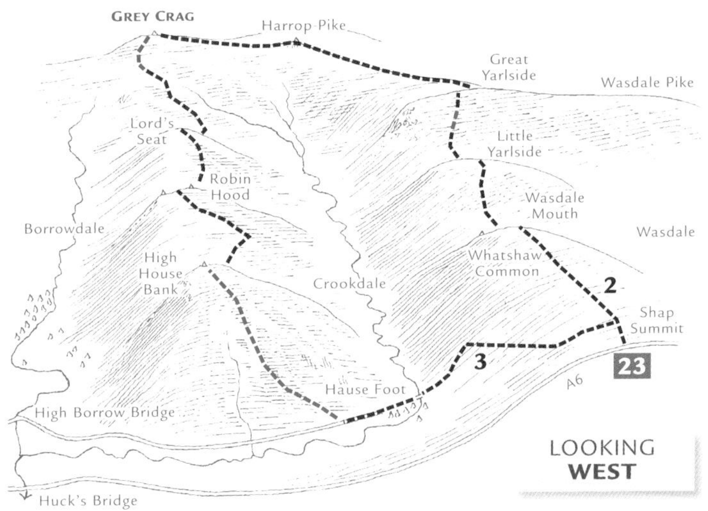

2 The long lay-by on Shap summit provides a grand high-level springboard for the eastern approach to the adjacent summits of Grey and Tarn Crags. Carefully cross the padlocked gate and follow the track to the crossing with the old Shap Road – presently exposed following the laying of a gas pipeline. Head on in the company of the ridge wall onto Whatshaw Common, with scant evidence of a path. The name 'Whatshaw' might have derived from 'the common connected with Walter's wood'. The wall and, briefly, fence provide a sure guide over typical upland herbage with the odd damp hollow, notably in the depression of Wasdale Mouth. Ahead is a steady climb into Little Yarlside, now upon a quad track. See the considerable outcropping of Yarlside Crag over the wall to the left. Next take on the final real climb of this approach, onto Great Yarlside. Ignore the deliberately evasive course of the quad track and stick close to the wall. Great Yarlside means 'the Lord's high pasture', a tract of country which evidently extended from Wasdale through into upper Crookdale, to judge by the post-Viking reference to Lord's Seat on the lower parallel ridge. Pass through a gate and keep company with the fence as a quad track merges on the right from Wasdale Pike. After a further loose-fitting gate advance to the outcropped headland of Harrop Pike, with its old wall and striking cairn, suggesting an ancient boundary point. Descend and, after a fence merges from the left, cross the adjacent fence and follow the clear path to and beyond the fence-corner, drifting S to the summit of Grey Crag.

Via High House Bank 480m/1575ft 8km/5 miles

A comparatively low undulating ridge runs between the twin headwaters of Borrowdale, providing an absorbing 'lost in the fells' approach to the fell-top and the basis of a return route for a circular expedition when combined with Route 4. **3** With this in mind, start from Shap summit – for all that this requires a modest descent at the start. Upon reaching the cross-ways, go through the hand-gate left and follow the old road, which soon becomes a broad green-way curving down to a gate. Beyond, the old highway curves left to a further gate leading into improved pasture. Follow the wall down to a gate into a short lane by Hause Foot (an attractively landscaped abode). Cross Crookdale Bridge and advance beyond the line of Leylandii, bearing off right short of the road-gate. The ascent proper begins by slanting up Hazel Bank. First pass under the power line and close by the pylon, then slip through the broken wall to continue up the steep rough pasture slope to find a quite obscure through-stone stile almost at the top, where the wall swings over the brow (with a netting top). The summit cairn on High House Bank (495m/1624ft) is in view, but the slope ahead is tough tussock grass, so slow progress will be made to this fine little crest – a worthwhile spot to pause and admire Borrowdale beyond the A6 towards the distant Howgills.

Follow the ridge, periodically peering down on the farmstead of Borrowdale Head and High House, administering the shepherding of the joint headwater valleys. Come to a gate in the ridge-straddling fence and advance W to join the regular quad track. This is your faithful guide almost all the way to Grey Crag. From the next gate the path swings up left to gain the crest of the enigmatically named Robin Hood, the beacon cairn a fine spot to rest a moment. The quad track follows the spine of the ridge into friendly outlaw territory it would seem! The next rise is Lord's Seat, although there is no cairn. The east top makes a fine spot from which to admire Yarlside Crag

High House Bank from Robin Hood

Summit of Whiteside Pike looking to White Howe

– might there be a few rock-climbs there for the intrepid? Continuing W the track avoids the outcropping above Crookdale in rising to the intermediate skyline, where a fence running N–S is encountered. While the fence is easiest to cross at a fixed gate near a fence-junction, there is little difficulty in crossing at the point where the track comes alongside the fence. Eroding peat drainage is the only obstacle on the early rise NE that leads through small outcropping to the summit.

ASCENT FROM HOLLOWGATE (24)

Via White Howe 550m/1805ft 8.2km/5 miles

4 While the round trip from Shap summit may catch your attention, perhaps the most natural circuit begins from Hollowgate Farm. It traverses the ridge above onto Fawcett Forest and climbs over White Howe before heading for Mere Crag and Grey Crag, then returning via the Robin Hood ridge (Route 3).

Park on the verge beside the hen-hut above Hollowgate Farm on the old road, which forks from the A6 immediately north of the Kendal Caravans depot – the pre-M6 site of the famous Jungle Café (lorry stop). Opposite the west entrance to the farm, go through the field-gate (currently padlocked, but not to inhibit walkers, so you are obliged to climb carefully over). A green track leads to a further gate, and beyond this bear sharp right and follow the rising fence (on the line of a buried gas pipeline). As the ridge-top gap is neared, veer left up the bank and follow the switchback ridge to a small cairn above a pool. This is a grand spot to view High House Bank across Borrowdale and the course of the A6, as well as back east towards the shapely fells flanking the dale. There is no hint of a path on the undulating ridge, which has a few

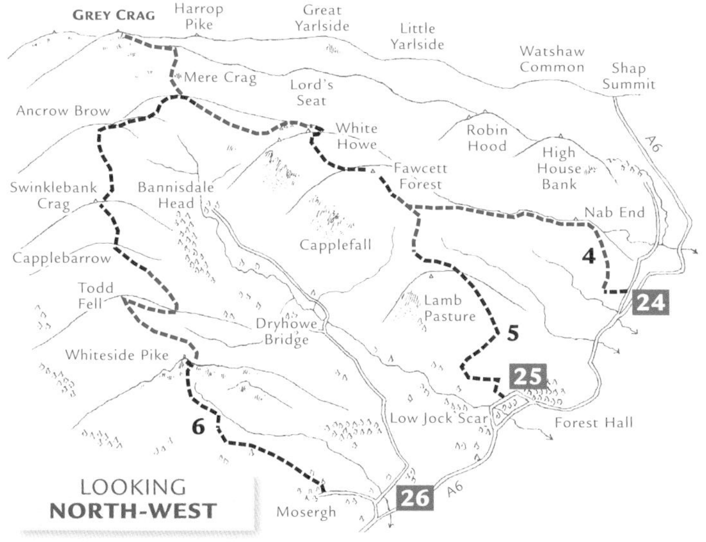

minor incident outcrops that are easily avoided on the rise to the spine of Fawcett Forest. Here a path is found, coming up from Lamb Pasture (Route 5).

ASCENT FROM BANNISDALE HIGH BRIDGE (25)

Via Lamb Pasture 630m/2065ft 8.6km/5¼ miles

5 Another start can be made off the old Shap highway – long gone to seed. Find a quiet looping back-road by Low Jock Scar and a bridleway signed off this above Thorn Cottage. The old Shap road, now a green track, rises to a gate. From here leave the old way and follow the farm track left, passing through a further gate in a fence. As this fades bear up right, thereby avoiding the otherwise dense cover of bracken, onto the ridge. Here a curious shed stands beside a gate. Go through and, keeping the ridge fence close left, traverse the dip slope of Lamb Pasture, coming down to a gate. Ahead the continuing path falters after crossing a gill. Climb naturally onto the fell, where the path re-establishes a presence en route to the cairn on this nameless top of Fawcett Forest. The path declines, crosses a wall-stile and clambers onto the more substantial cairned top of White Howe. Note a spur path that leads to a cairn commanding a superb bird's-eye view down on the seldom comprehended upper quarter of Bannisdale Head – even to Lakeland aficionados, this is a lost valley. The main thread of the ridge path veers N and accompanies the wall, and after an awkward step up clambers over a ladder-stile, whereupon the continuing path is lost. A lateral rock rib with three casual cairns gives a line to follow left before the route traverses the marshy ground NW, eventually assisted by a quad track, onto the dry turf at the very head of Bannisdale. Coming to a fence/broken wall on the brow, cross and descend on the remains of the wall, slipping through a damp hollow at the head of Brow Gill. Go through a metal gate close under Mere Crag.

Mere Crag

Mere Crag is not 'mere', in fact most visitors will consider it quite impressive. A huge clean face of volcanic rock invites competent climbers, although even they need a rope, as the presence of two metal belay loop stakes above the crag attest. The crag might be considered to mark the top of Borrowdale. The ridge fence slips easily up past the crag, and as the ground levels go over the fixed gate and traverse the peaty origins of Stockdale Beck, weaving up through the minor outcropping to the summit cairn. This achieved, most walkers will retrace their steps before opting to make a skyline horseshoe of Bannisdale their rewarding mission by reversing Route 6.

ASCENT FROM PLOUGH LANE, SELSIDE (26 – off map S)

Via Whiteside Pike 615m/2020ft 9.5km/6 miles

6 Come off the A6 and follow the byroad that is the sole means of access to secretive Bannisdale. Parking is poorly served, although verge space exists where Light Water is culverted under the road. Follow the branch-road as to Mosergh Farm, and short of the buildings an unsurfaced lane is signed right (N). Follow this, rising to a handling pen with galvanised gates, the main gate oddly padlocked. Therefore gain entry into access land via the side hand-gate. The green track is quickly forsaken on angling half-right into the Light Water valley, your sights firmly fixed on reaching the summit of Whiteside Pike. There is little hint of a consistent path, even when close to. A small plaque reflects the importance the peak has within the local parishes, and the cairn certainly does it justice. A path is now apparent wending NW down the heather moor and through a shallow valley to find a new wall-stile close to the wall junction. On entering pasture the path is again lost, although the appealing option of venturing to the top of Todd Fell should not be lightly dismissed, as it provides a remarkable view into Longsleddale. (The author disturbed a snoozing red deer in a patch of bracken on his climb to this grand little viewpoint – which actually translates as 'the frequent of foxes'.)

Angle down NE to a ladder-stile into a marsh and keep left, now following the fence up to join a track, and go through a gate in a lateral fence. Walkers may find it interesting to locate the line of stone stoops that clearly formed an old fence-line above Dub Ings Wood, situated on the irregular east slope before the gate. The ridge path sweeps on, not hidebound to the fence in crossing Capplebarrow ('the horse pasture hill'). Further N, after coming close by the fence, a water obstacle is met. The ground close to the fence is very marshy, and to the right of this water lingers as a permanent tarn, so keep right and skirt it as well you can. In coming back to the fence, walkers may find a quaking bog that makes an interesting trampoline! Swinklebank Crag has a cairn over the broken fence and a fine view to boot. Step back and continue with the fence left over Ancrow Brow and then a broken wall to gain the brow at the very head of Bannisdale, uniting with Route 5 to venture on to Grey Crag.

THE SUMMIT

A small plateau of the most minor outcropping centres upon a cairn, while more significant rock exists to the south and west.

SAFE DESCENTS

The path heading WSW is your faithful guide to a dale harbour, Sadgill in upper Longsleddale. After crossing a fence-stile, this path curves S along the damp ridge to Great Howe, never failing as a path.

RIDGE ROUTE

TARN CRAG	↓ 40m/130ft	↑ 65m/215ft	1.4km/1 mile

Head N to come to the projecting corner of a fence. Keep the fence close right on peaty ground, even though this makes the path less obvious for a short distance. Your attention will be more gripped by the possibility of damp feet as the basin to the north of Greycrag Tarn is crossed, although it is less daunting (soft) than first impressions may suggest. Coming up the bank, the path duly veers away from the fence to reach the cairn and, close by, the Haweswater survey pillar.

Ill Bell range over Longsleddale from Todd Fell

PANORAMA

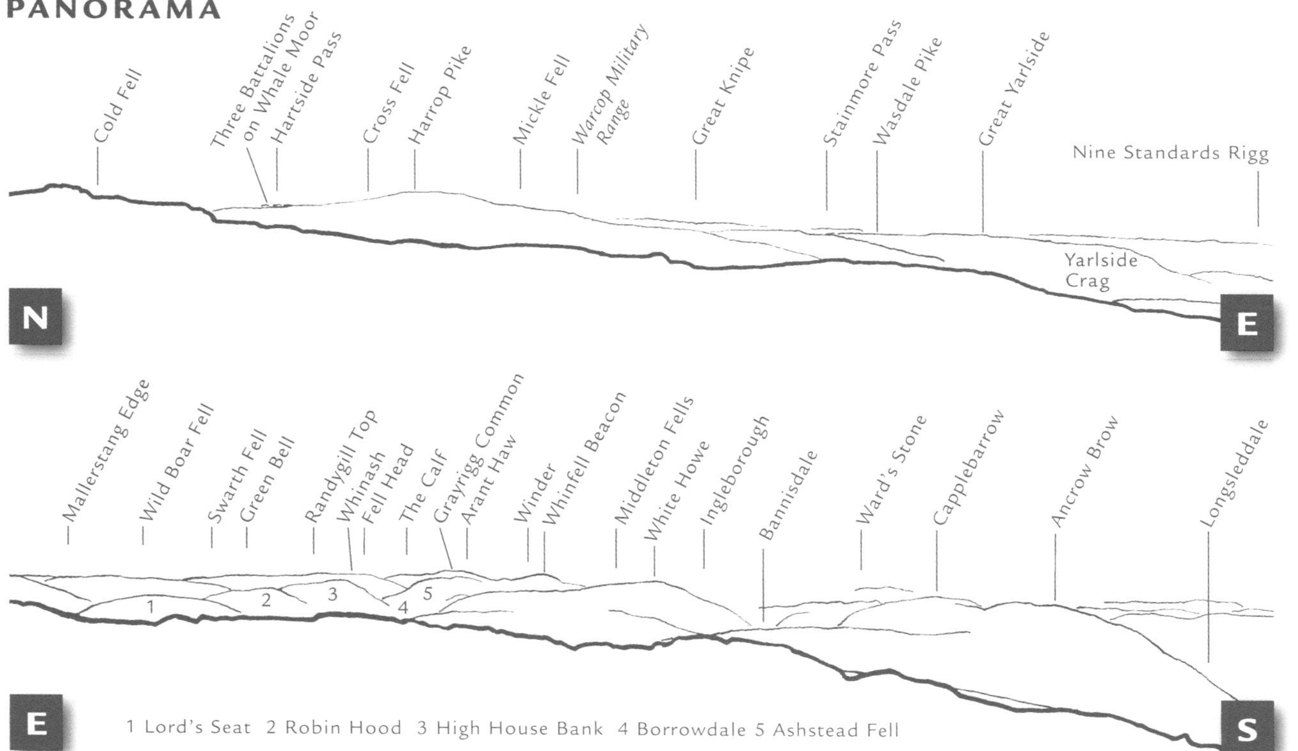
Cold Fell
Three Battalions on Whale Moor
Hartside Pass
Cross Fell
Harrop Pike
Mickle Fell
Warcop Military Range
Great Knipe
Stainmore Pass
Wasdale Pike
Great Yarlside
Nine Standards Rigg
Yarlside Crag
N
E
Mallerstang Edge
Wild Boar Fell
Swarth Fell
Green Bell
Randygill Top
Whinash
Fell Head
The Calf
Grayrigg Common
Arant Haw
Winder
Whinfell Beacon
Middleton Fells
White Howe
Ingleborough
Bannisdale
Ward's Stone
Capplebarrow
Ancrow Brow
Longsleddale
1
2
3
4
5
E
S
1 Lord's Seat 2 Robin Hood 3 High House Bank 4 Borrowdale 5 Ashstead Fell

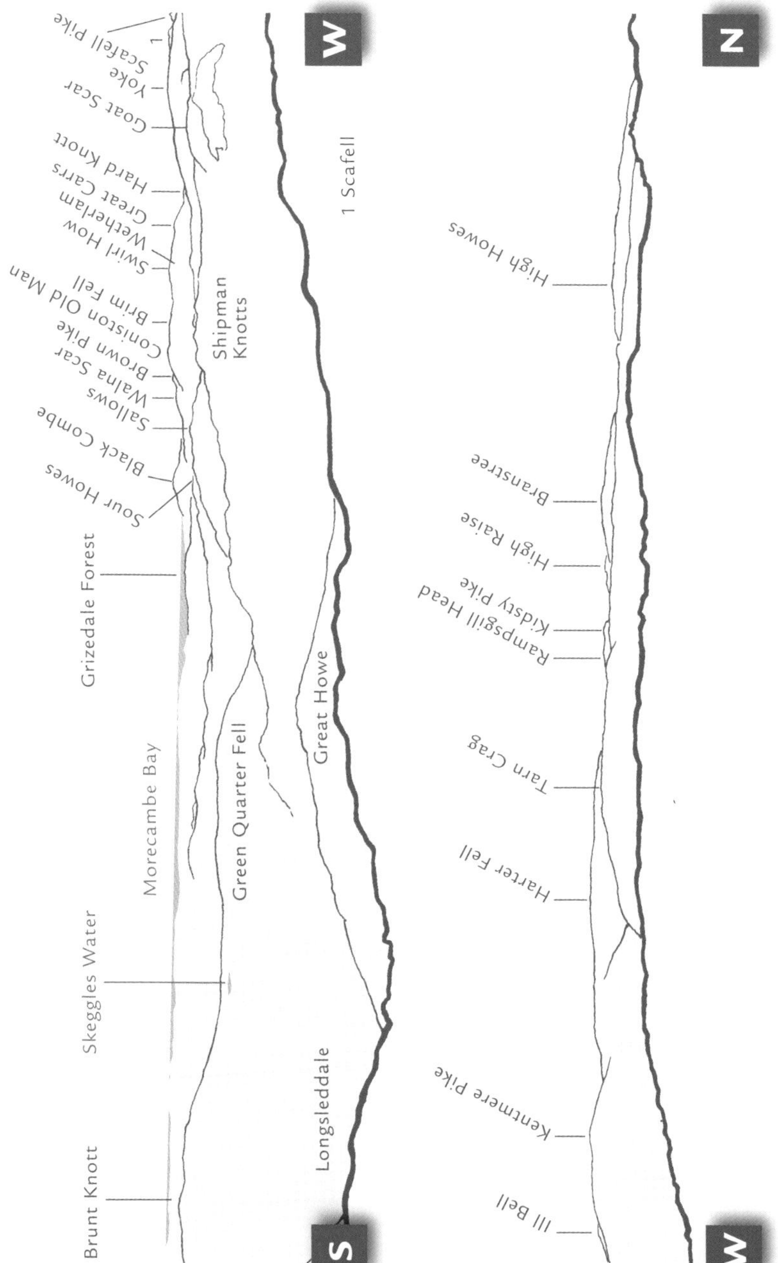
W
N
1 Scafell
Scafell Pike
Yoke
Goat Scar
Hard Knott
Great Carrs
Wetherlam
Swirl How
Brim Fell
Coniston Old Man
Brown Pike
Walna Scar
Sallows
Black Combe
Sour Howes
Shipman Knotts
Grizedale Forest
Morecambe Bay
Green Quarter Fell
Great Howe
Skeggles Water
Longsleddale
Brunt Knott
S
High Howes
Branstree
High Raise
Kidsty Pike
Rampsgill Head
Tarn Crag
Harter Fell
Kentmere Pike
Ill Bell
W

11 HALLIN FELL *(388m/1273ft)*

A fell for all seasons and all-comers – but watch your footwear, the steep grass can be slippery! Hallin Fell is a brilliant introduction to the scenic pleasures of Ullswater and, perhaps more importantly, the perfect initiation into the delights of fellwalking itself. Parents should bring their children – and grandparents for that matter. If you've never stood on a Lakeland fell-top before, then Hallin lets you know how wonderful an experience it can be. The setting is sumptuous, steep and rugged, with a sylvan petticoat fringing the shore, and there is the option of visiting the summit as a wonderful accompaniment to a journey on the lake steamer. It turns a tourist excursion into a modest but memorable mountain day. Among the range of options, walkers can girdle the fell at low level or part way up on the south side, follow the throng from The Hause, or wend more peaceably up the north and west slopes. Everything about this fell is pleasurable – it's a real little gem. Cherish it.

Hallin Fell summit cairn

 ↑ Hallin Fell from the slopes of Bonscale Pike

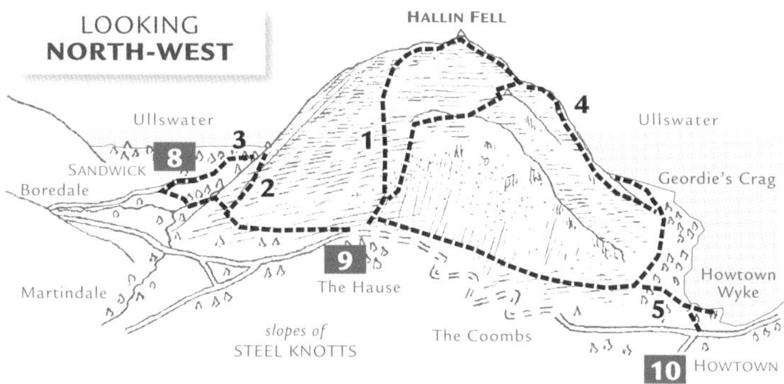

ASCENT FROM THE HAUSE (9)

Direct 150m/490ft 0.7km/½ mile

1 Step across the open road from The Hause, parking beside St Peter's Church. Ascend unhindered NNW to the summit. The normal and natural practice is to continue in a natural exaggerated loop, descending N from the landmark cairn and curving right to visit a lower cairn overlooking the Howtown Wyke landing stage before tilting back down to The Hause. Several casual variant paths exist within this area, beating back the bracken.

Via the west ridge 190m/625ft 1.6km/1 mile

2 A scenically blessed quiet way. Follow the footpath heading W off the roadside verge. This leads by three wall-stiles above the refurbished Hause Farm, commanding marvellous views of Beda Fell and the Martindale valleys. Coming onto a bank, veer uphill with the path to join a lateral path drifting left above the intake wall. As this path moves downhill watch for a path angling gently up right. This comes above a badger sett

and curves right more steeply, then turns left under rocks with a bield. Coming onto a rock rib, bear right to reach the plainer slope and gain the summit rocks.

ASCENT FROM SANDWICK (8)

Via the west ridge 240m/785ft 1.6km/1 mile

3 The hugely popular shoreline path leads E from the hamlet of Sandwick via gates. Come by Sandwick Bay – 'the sandy shore' is the sure origin of the name; the 'bay' is tautologically superfluous, as 'wick' was Viking for 'a bay'. After going through the kissing-gate in the wood break up right and follow the wall steeply to a hand-gate out of the woodland. Continue in harmony with the rising wall to join the path described in Route 2.

Via the north-east ridge 235m/770ft 2.5km/1½ miles

4 Keep to the rough woodland way through Hallinhag Wood, where the term 'hag' meant to 'coppice or chop trees', clearly suggesting that this woodland has long been a source of timber. Coming above Kailpot Bay and the great ice-smoothed headland adorned with Scots pines come through a kissing-gate and along the shore rounding Geordie's Crag. Here perhaps watching the flow of the Ullswater steamer or canoeists from the Outward Bound Centre directly across the water. As the path comes above a tree-bowered wall watch for a path turning sharply up the fell. Turn to task and follow this direct to the summit.

Townhead, Sandwick

Kailpot Crag and Hallin Fell from across Ullswater

ASCENT FROM FUSEDALE (10)

Girdle route 190m/625ft 4km/2½ miles

5 This is a great little walk for travellers on the steamer, who are not inclined to climb to the summit, or guests at Howtown Hotel, relishing a parade to absorb the beauty of the locality. Embark on the orbiting path around the fell, with paths converging close to Waternook and rising to steps and a kissing-gate. Go left, keeping to the higher path and traversing the rough east slope of the fell up to The Hause, where walkers join Route 2. Continue down by the wall into Hallinhag Wood to join the woodland way right. There is plenty of cause to pause from time to time, and many a potential trip on the roots and rocks!

THE SUMMIT

The magnificent square-built beacon illustrated in Wainwright's guide has suffered over the intervening 60 years, but, not withstanding the disruption to its upper tier, it still stands as a mighty landmark. It makes a worthy objective, perched proud as punch upon a bare rock plinth. The view down the lower reach of Ullswater will hold your attention, watching 'the toings and froings' of the steamers.

SAFE DESCENTS

Follow the regular grassy trail SE to The Hause for the surest ground.

PANORAMA

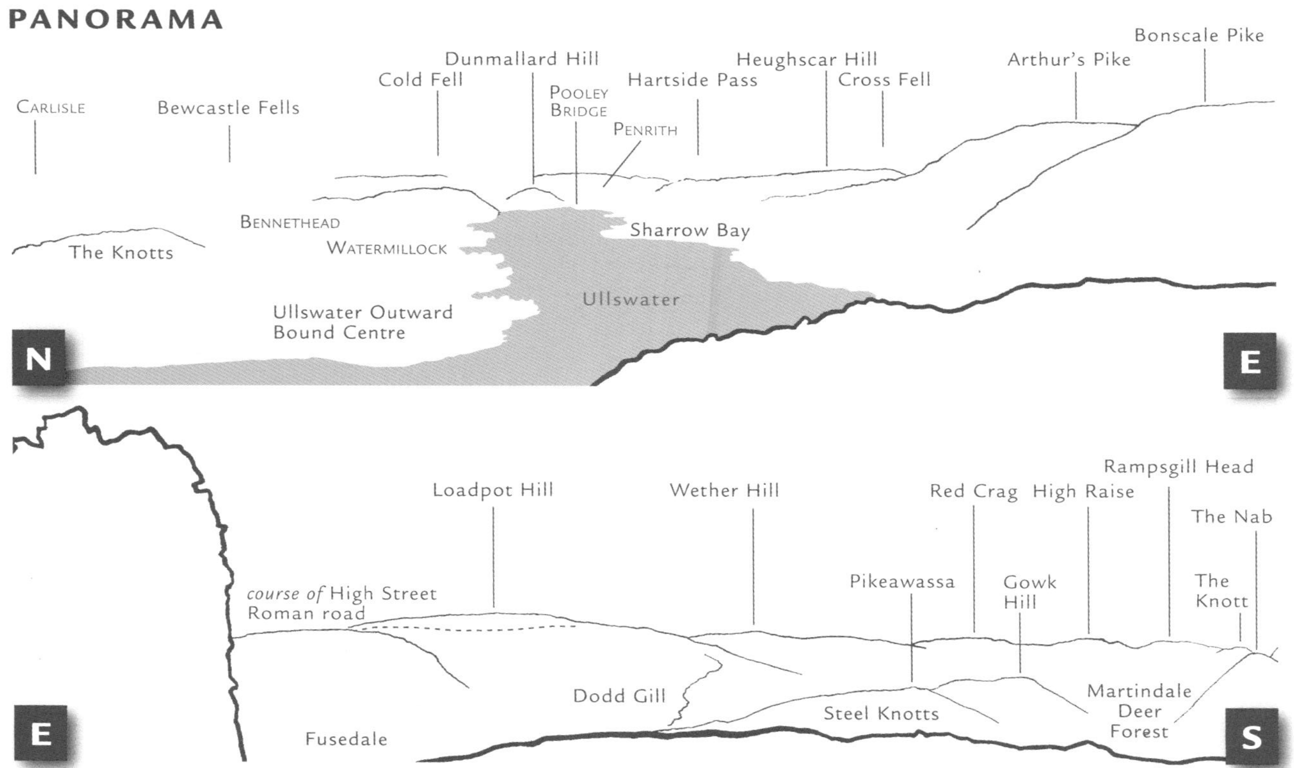
Carlisle
Bewcastle Fells
Cold Fell
Dunmallard Hill
Pooley Bridge
Penrith
Hartside Pass
Heughscar Hill
Cross Fell
Arthur's Pike
Bonscale Pike
The Knotts
Bennethead
Watermillock
Sharrow Bay
Ullswater
Ullswater Outward Bound Centre
N
E
Loadpot Hill
Wether Hill
Red Crag
High Raise
Rampsgill Head
The Nab
course of High Street Roman road
Pikeawassa
Gowk Hill
The Knott
Dodd Gill
Steel Knotts
Martindale Deer Forest
Fusedale
E
S

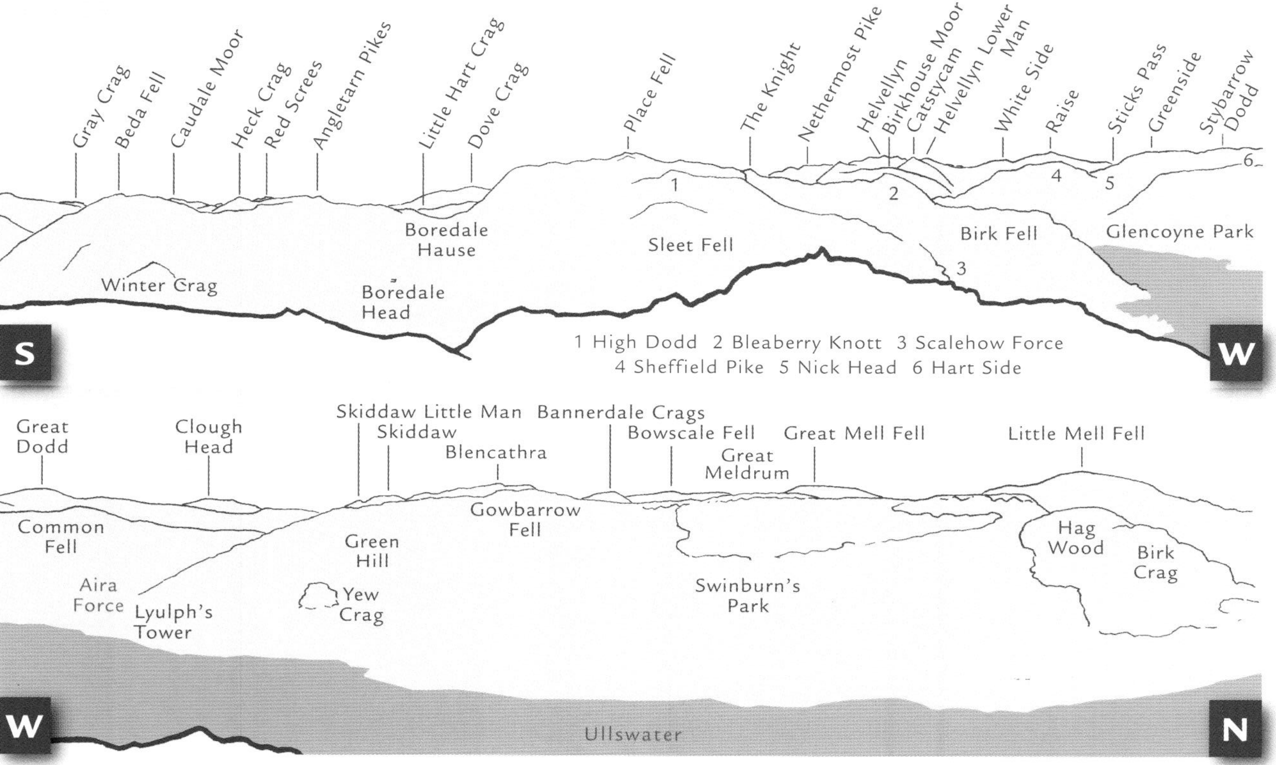

Gray Crag
Beda Fell
Caudale Moor
Heck Crag
Red Screes
Angletarn Pikes
Little Hart Crag
Dove Crag
Place Fell
The Knight
Nethermost Pike
Helvellyn
Birkhouse Moor
Catstycam
Helvellyn Lower Man
White Side
Raise
Sticks Pass
Greenside
Stybarrow Dodd
Boredale Hause
Sleet Fell
Birk Fell
Glencoyne Park
Winter Crag
Boredale Head
S
W
1 High Dodd 2 Bleaberry Knott 3 Scalehow Force
4 Sheffield Pike 5 Nick Head 6 Hart Side
Skiddaw Little Man
Bannerdale Crags
Great Dodd
Clough Head
Skiddaw
Blencathra
Bowscale Fell
Great Meldrum
Great Mell Fell
Little Mell Fell
Common Fell
Gowbarrow Fell
Green Hill
Hag Wood
Birk Crag
Aira Force
Lyulph's Tower
Yew Crag
Swinburn's Park
W
Ullswater
N

12 HARTER FELL *(778m/2553ft)*

Mardale comes to an abrupt and impressive halt on Harter. While much attention is taken looking west to Riggindale and its adjacent ridges, there is no doubting what is the head of this drowned dale. Either side of its great craggy presence are two popular passes. Gatescarth, the eastern saddle, carries a track into Longsleddale that at times is made available for 4x4 drivers to test the off-road capacity of their rough, tough vehicles. The high western col, Nan Bield Pass, is an exclusively pedestrian adventure with a long history of use, and rustic stone pod shelters beside Small Water are proof of the discomforts of travellers to and from Kentmere in the past.

Strictly, the summit lies at the termination of a long northward-rising ridge, dividing Longsleddale from Kentmere. Ascents from both valleys tend to be either along this spinal ridge or from the lateral passes, although some walkers may make grassy plods from the Ull Stone on the Kentmere side and via Wren Gill on the east. The fell name suggests it has long been associated with red deer and particularly as the rutting ground of mature stags.

 ↑ Harter Fell from the road to Mardale Head

ASCENT FROM MARDALE HEAD (20)

Via Nan Bield Pass 525m/1720ft 3.2km/2 miles

A really good fell climb – constantly ascending, constantly attractive to the eye. **1** From the car park where the Haweswater road terminates go through the kissing-gate and rise to the wall-corner where three paths diverge. Take the middle route signed 'Public bridleway Nan Bield Pass Kentmere'. The heavily trod path leads via successive gates up through the moraine to come close to the fine cascades issuing from Small Water. Cross at the outflow and swing round the west side of the tarn, coming by a trio of stone shelters. These are symptomatic of the time, before the flooding of Mardale, when this route was an important four-season social and trade link between Mardale and Kentmere. The path has received essential pitching repair all the way to the pass, where the alcove 'seat' forms a partial block to southerly draughts. 'Nan Bield' means 'Anne's shelter', and many a passing walker still appreciates the brief shelter it affords ahead of the final pull to the top. Turn up left (E) and weave your way to the plateau. Views on both sides of this, the west ridge, are excellent, so take your time. Arrive on the plateau, from where a line of cairns guides to the summit cairn, short of the ridge fence.

The upper frenzy of hairpins rising from Kentmere to Nan Bield Pass

Via Gatescarth Pass 535m/1755ft 3.5km/2¼ miles

Not exactly a mirror of the Nan Bield route, but a natural return for a simple round trip. Early on Harter Crag dominates, and the going is solid throughout. **2** From the three-way signpost follow the left-hand arm signed 'Public Byway Gatescarth Pass'. The

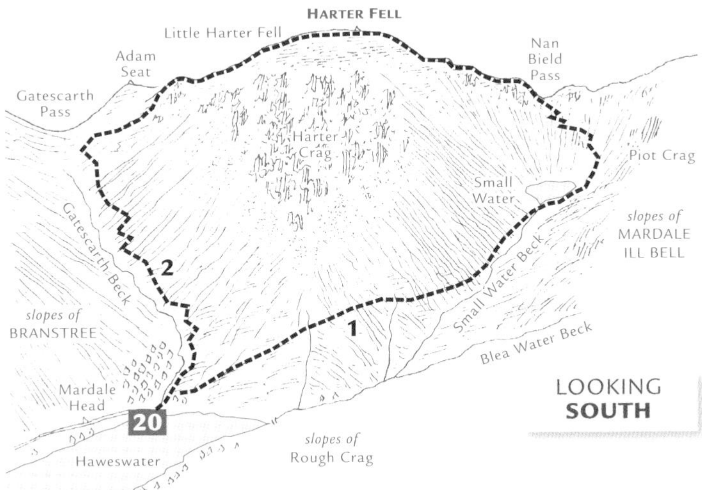

track rises via a gate in harmony with Gatescarth Beck, and with two multiple hairpin sections climbs to the brow, where a new trail swings right from the byway, 120m short of the gate in the saddle-straddling fence. The gravelly trail is actually inverted subsoil excavated to secure a durable surface and guides all walkers the one way. Hence the cairn on Adam Seat, with its H/L-inscribed estate boundary stone of 1924, is a seldom visited side show (appreciated by fell connoisseurs). Coming onto the brow enjoy the fine views back of Branstree and, higher, Haweswater, notably from the prominent cairn on Little Harter Fell above a rock etched with a large Ordnance Survey bench-mark. Continuing beside the fence pass a further pair of cairns, this time entangled

Little Harter Fell in winter raiment

Benchmark above Harter Crag

with old metal stakes, to duly reach the summit. This has its own collection of unsightly stakes, although these do not detract from the point itself, which is hugely uplifting.

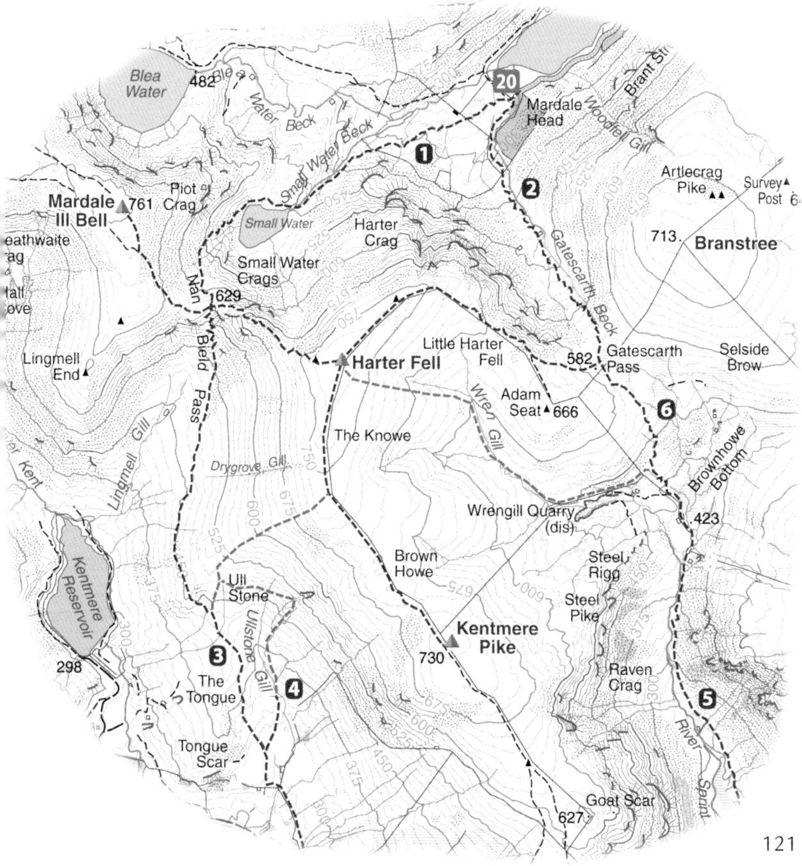

ASCENT FROM NUNNERY BECK (30 – off map S) OR HALLOW BANK (31 – off map S)

Via Nan Bield Pass 645m/2115ft 7km/4½ miles

3 There are two starting points. The first option is from the shallow parking bay where Nunnery Beck slips by the road immediately north of Green Quarter on the single-track road to Hallow Bank. Walk up the road to find the old bridleway signed 'Nan Bield'. This is Low Lane and gives a lovely lower dale approach to Overend by a series of gates. The second option is to start from the larger lay-by in High Lane, after the road-gate and before the Stile End bridle track. In this instance follow either the road or bridleway through the hamlet of Hallow Bank, coming down the gated roadway to Overend. Beside the white-washed farmhouse diverge right, guided by the old slate sign 'To Mardale'. The bridleway leads by gates to a footbridge spanning Ullstone Gill and after the final gate curves up the bank onto the ridge of the Tongue, beating back the dense bracken. Notice the old slate-quarry workings high up to the right. Further workings trace the consistent seam on the west slope of The Tongue and palpably on Rainsborrow Crag. The normal line stays with the bridleway – peel your eyes for an engraved bedrock underfoot – before the path steps up on Smallthwaite Knott and contours well above Kentmere Reservoir, in its final stages tackling acute hairpins to reach the col of Nan Bield. From the bield wind-break bear up right, working a steady course on a secure path to the plateau.

The wind-shelter and bench in Nan Bield Pass

Via the Ull Stone 590m/1935ft 5.3km/3¼ miles

4 A more direct route to the summit lies above the Ull Stone. Intrepid explorers will relish finding a second slate waymarker stone (after the one at Overend) off to the right, part-way up the rising path from the gate above the Ullstone Gill footbridge – it is obscured by the bracken unless you make a strenuous effort to locate it. This is both the original line of the age-old bridleway (shortcut by descending walkers) and the haul-route of slate from the old quarry, which can be seen high on the west slope of Kentmere Pike. The roving fellwalker will relish getting up close and personal with this amazing gash. It is a stiff clamber by a broken wall and much spoil. Standing in the lower portion you can look up to see a waterfall at the very top – and a wall above that to prevent sheep (and descending walkers) from inadvertently tumbling in!

The lateral connection to the Ull Stone is awkward going, but without hazard, yet most walkers will be content to stick with the Nan Bield bridleway until the Ull Stone is more obviously accessible above. At that point, forsake the regular path for sheep trods en route to this unusually large, tilted, glacially plucked rock. Climb on above, keeping first left, then right, to avoid all hint of outcropping. The reward for the toil is the ridge fence on The Knowe and a grassy trail left (N) to the summit.

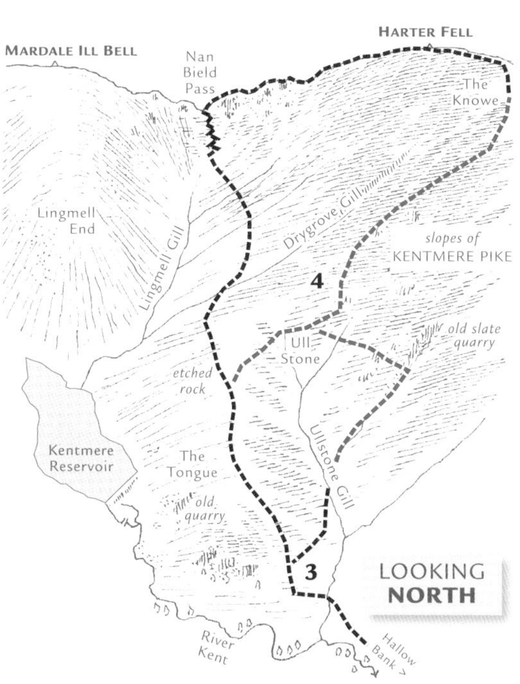

ASCENT FROM SADGILL (27 – off map S)

Via Wrengill Quarry 600m/1970ft 5.4km/3½ miles

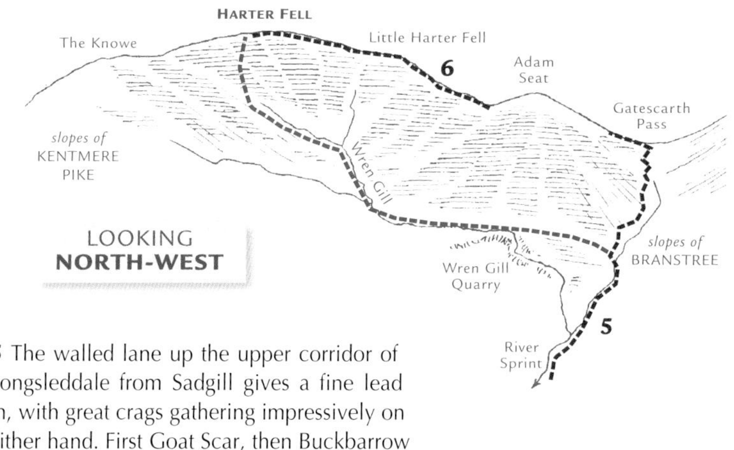

5 The walled lane up the upper corridor of Longsleddale from Sadgill gives a fine lead in, with great crags gathering impressively on either hand. First Goat Scar, then Buckbarrow Crag, captivates attention. After the pitched incline go through a gate and cross the stone bridge, the path following on as an open track. After a kissing-gate (where the broad gate is padlocked) it begins the ascent beyond the fold. At the third hairpin bear off left on a short track to a padlocked galvanised gate. Head W above the wall which bars off the stony confusion of Wrengill Quarry. The old water pipe is encountered, and then its connected breached race that once tapped a flow out of Wren Gill to power a quarry pump. Ford Wren Gill and follow the dwindling gill to its high-pastured and rough source to ultimately attain the skyline and a stile in the ridge fence close to the summit cairn.

Via Gatescarth Pass 615m/2020ft 6km/3¾ miles

6 Hold course with the zig-zagging track climbing from Brownhowe Bottom to the fence in the broad saddle. Go through the gate and after 150m veer left upon the regular made-path which leads up the scarp edge, via Little Harter Fell, assuredly to the summit.

THE SUMMIT

While stone walls may tumble, metal fences, when past their best, should be removed completely. But all too often much remains, as is the case on Harter, where stakes left lying about have been gathered by the tidying instincts of passing walkers and amassed on the summit cairn. But, of course, they don't make a tidy heap even then. However, there is a tidy view from this wonderful high plateau – packed with drama in the foreground and excitement in the long-range. The replacement fence does little to detract from the extensive views east towards the Pennines and Howgills. Most

Summit cairn, a chaotic ensemble of rock and discarded fence posts

attention will be focused east over the neighbouring Ill Bell and High Street range, with eyes peeled to see many a favourite fell – Coniston Old Man, Crinkle Crags, Scafell Pike, Great Gable, Pillar and Helvellyn, with even Blencathra making an appearance over the Straits of Riggindale.

SAFE DESCENTS

For Mardale and Longsleddale follow the ridge fence and continuing trail E to Gatescarth Pass. This avoids rocky ground entirely. Heading S with the fence along the spine of the ridge takes you over Kentmere Pike and Shipman Knotts, where an easy line avoiding rock can be followed for Hallow Bank, which has been adopted by the local shepherd on his quad.

RIDGE ROUTES

KENTMERE PIKE	↓ 80m/265ft	↑ 35m/115ft	1.8km/1 mile

The ridge fence is a sure guide S. After a gentle dip in the ridge a wall is encountered, leading quickly to the summit, with the OS column sited over a stile in the wall.

MARDALE ILL BELL	↓ 145m/475ft	↑ 130m/425ft	1.7km/1 mile

Head W with a couple of cairns aligned to the lip of the plateau, from where a consistent path weaves down the stepped ridge to Nan Bield Pass. The continuing path veers up left from the stone alcove, enjoying fine views of Ill Bell before slanting NW, with some recent stone pitching, onto domed top.

PANORAMA

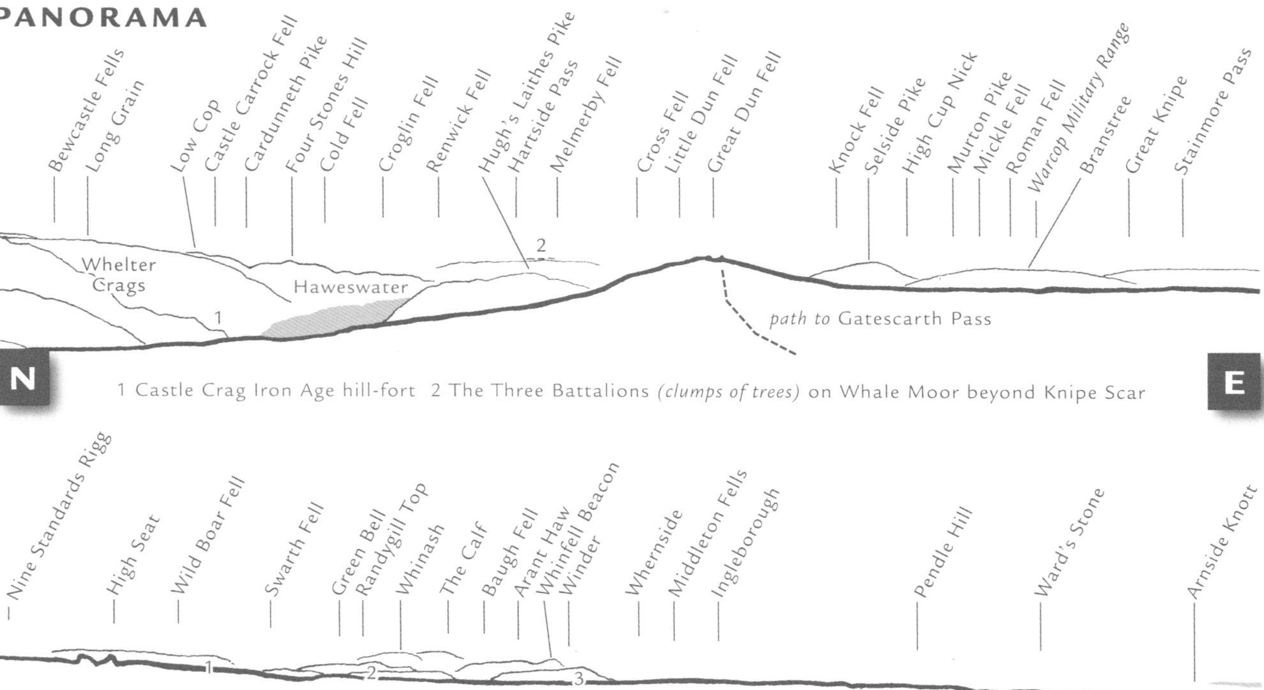
Bewcastle Fells
Long Grain
Low Cop
Castle Carrock Fell
Cardunneth Pike
Four Stones Hill
Cold Fell
Croglin Fell
Renwick Fell
Hugh's Laithes Pike
Hartside Pass
Melmerby Fell
Cross Fell
Little Dun Fell
Great Dun Fell
Knock Fell
Selside Pike
High Cup Nick
Murton Pike
Mickle Fell
Roman Fell
Warcop Military Range
Branstree
Great Knipe
Stainmore Pass
Whelter Crags
Haweswater
1
2
path to Gatescarth Pass
N
E
1 Castle Crag Iron Age hill-fort 2 The Three Battalions (clumps of trees) on Whale Moor beyond Knipe Scar
Nine Standards Rigg
High Seat
Wild Boar Fell
Swarth Fell
Green Bell
Randygill Top
Whinash
The Calf
Baugh Fell
Arant Haw
Whinfell Beacon
Winder
Whernside
Middleton Fells
Ingleborough
Pendle Hill
Ward's Stone
Arnside Knott
1
2
3
E
S
1 Great Yarlside 2 High House Bank 3 White Howe

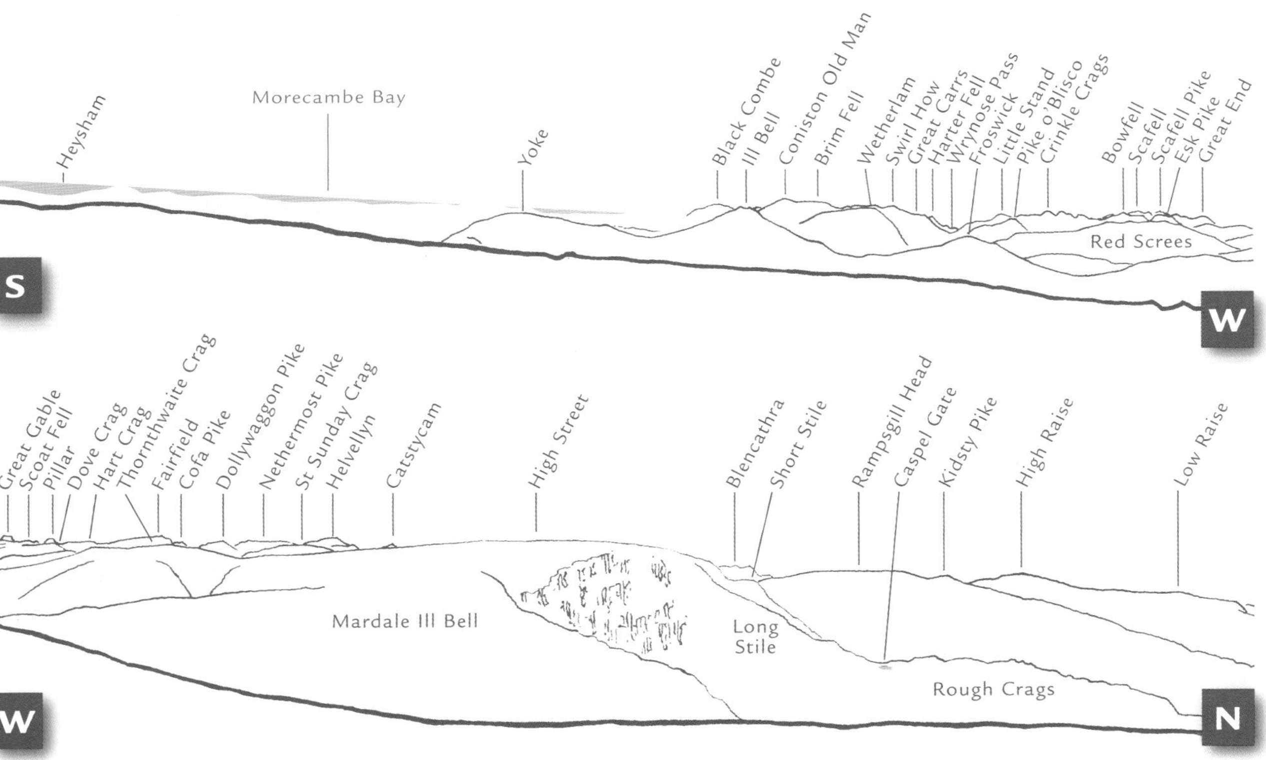
Heysham
Morecambe Bay
Yoke
Black Combe
Ill Bell
Coniston Old Man
Brim Fell
Wetherlam
Swirl How
Great Carrs
Harter Fell
Wrynose Pass
Froswick
Little Stand
Pike o'Blisco
Crinkle Crags
Bowfell
Scafell
Scafell Pike
Esk Pike
Great End
Red Screes
S
W
Great Gable
Scoat Fell
Pillar
Dove Crag
Hart Crag
Thornthwaite Crag
Fairfield
Cofa Pike
Dollywaggon Pike
Nethermost Pike
St Sunday Crag
Helvellyn
Catstycam
High Street
Blencathra
Short Stile
Rampsgill Head
Caspel Gate
Kidsty Pike
High Raise
Low Raise
Mardale Ill Bell
Long Stile
Rough Crags
W
N

13 HARTSOP DODD *(618m/2028ft)*

Hartsop vale, 'the valley of the deer stag', is home to Brothers Water. At one time there were two nucleated farmsteads here – that situated higher up the side of the dale was High Hartsop, hence High Hartsop Dodd (which is lower than Hartsop Dodd by 99m/325ft), and the present community was Low Hartsop, normally now simply referred to as Hartsop. The more sheltered setting ensured the lower hamlet's growth. Strictly, Hartsop Dodd is the blunt end of Caudale Moor's long north ridge. It provides a striking presence above Brothers Water and a marvellous viewpoint well meriting the stiff climb from either Hartsop or Caudale Bridge. Keen eyes will spot a long-forsaken shepherds' path on the east flank of the fell – forsaken for good reason, being mightily steep.

Reflections in Brothers Water

 ↑ Hartsop Dodd from Low Hartsop

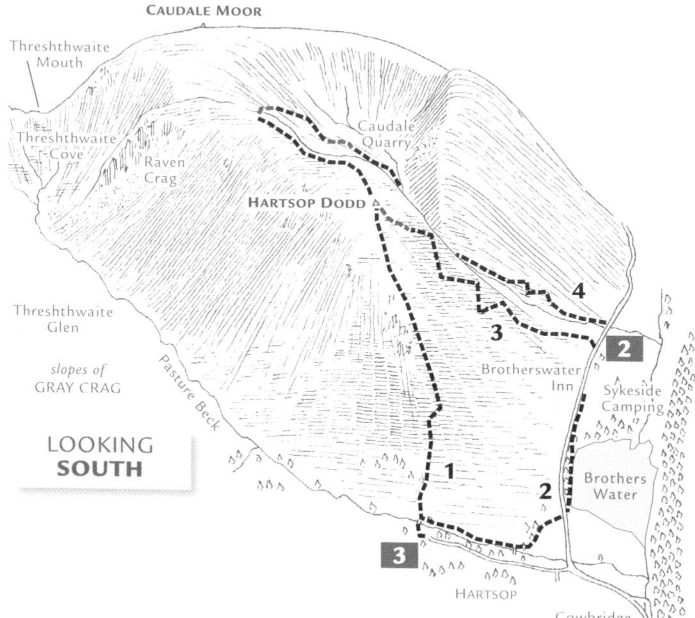

ASCENT FROM HARTSOP (3)

Via north ridge 435m/1425ft 1.6km/1 mile

1 Leave the car park and bear right crossing Walker Bridge. After the next gate/ladder-stile, where the track swings left step off onto the pasture and rise with the wall close right to a stile at the wall junction. Continue with some worn and some pitched hairpins to the top of the wall. The path persists up the steep blunt ridge, the climb providing many an excuse to pause and admire Brothers Water below and a fine backdrop of fells. Duly the butt end of the ridge wall is encountered, leading to the summit.

Valley connection via Brothers Water 40m/130ft 2km/1¼ miles

2 An appealing connection with Caudale Bridge, should a round trip devoted to this one fell be considered. After crossing Walker Bridge bear sharp right, following the beck downstream by gates and passing by the cottage row and farmsteading into a walled lane that constricts to a gate. Drop to the road and cross over, passing through the gap (sometime hand-gate) to wend beside the serene waters of Brothers Water. The woodland fringe adds charm to the intimate outlook across the lake. The path rises and runs on field-side of the ensuing bounding road to the road entrance to Sykeside/Hartsop Hall. Follow this by the grid and bear up through the car park of the Brotherswater Hotel, now beside the road towards Caudale Bridge.

ASCENT FROM CAUDALE BRIDGE (2)

Direct 420m/1380ft 1.2km/¾ mile

3 From the lay-by walk N to a footpath sign and hand-gate and enter the fell pasture, rising towards the beck and a ruin. But short of the ruin, coming near a broken wall, ascend directly with a predominately sheep-worn path. Pass up to the right of a thorn bush and duly come onto a more consistent path, which progresses steadily in determined zig-zags up the steep grassy west slope of the fell. The path is never more than a shallow groove, sometimes best identified by rushes, and is little affected by the pressure of recreational users, so there is a real sense of following in shepherds' footsteps. Coming onto the grassy brow of the fell, the path dissolves on the final stroll to the cairn.

Via Caudale Beck 430m/1410ft 2.5km/1½ miles

4 This is the ideal line of descent in misty conditions. Cross the wall-stile up to the right of Caudale Bridge. Follow the embanked path beside the wall, but keep with the beck as the popular path (a former quarrymen's haul) to Caudale Moor's north-west ridge is encountered. The adjacent wall is lost for a time as the beck constricts. At a beck confluence step up over the wall and skip over the beck, now rising with a definite zig-zag groove up The Tongue. Rising SE, higher up the groove is less evident on the approach to a wall-corner (with sheep-creep). Go over, keeping the wall right until a distinct grooved path slants left gaining ground to the ridge. Here join company with the regular ridgeway beside the wall easing N to the summit.

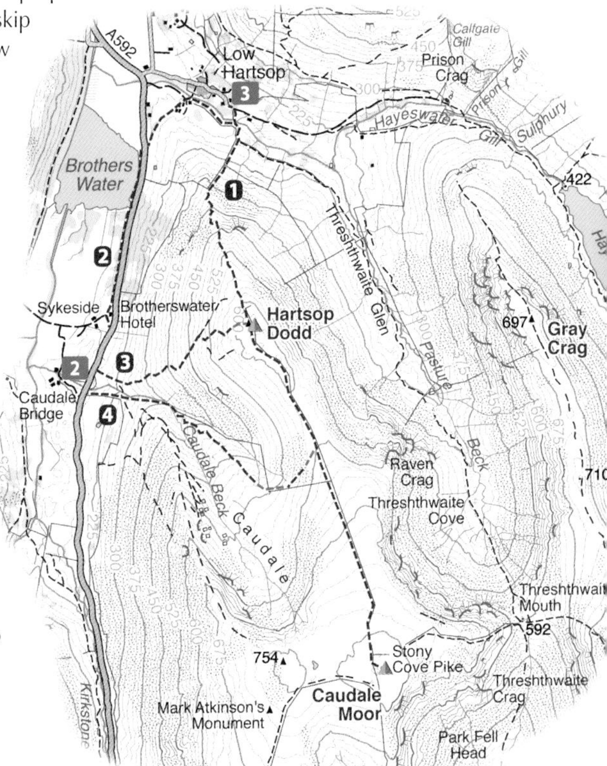

Summit wall and cairn on Hartsop Dodd

THE SUMMIT

The precise summit is marked by a weathered hardwood stake set into the broken ridge wall. Most visitors pay it little heed as they find all the satisfaction of the climb beside the large cairn 'borrowed' from the ridge wall and set on the grassy platform a few paces to the west. The best of the view is indeed to the west, with the grand craggy backdrop of Dovedale centre stage.

SAFE DESCENTS

The path N to Hartsop is short and steep, but unfailing in its destiny. If gentler ground is sought, walk SSE beside the ridge wall and bear off with the old drove that angles SW down by a broken wall at its corner. At the trace of a hog-hole step over and rediscover the drove descending The Tongue to the confluence with Caudale Beck. Soon after, find dale sanctuary on the Kirkstone road just above the Brotherswater Hotel.

RIDGE ROUTE

CAUDALE MOOR ↓ 30m/100ft ↑ 175m/575ft 2.2km/1½ miles

About as uncomplicated as can be conceived. Follow the ridge wall S.

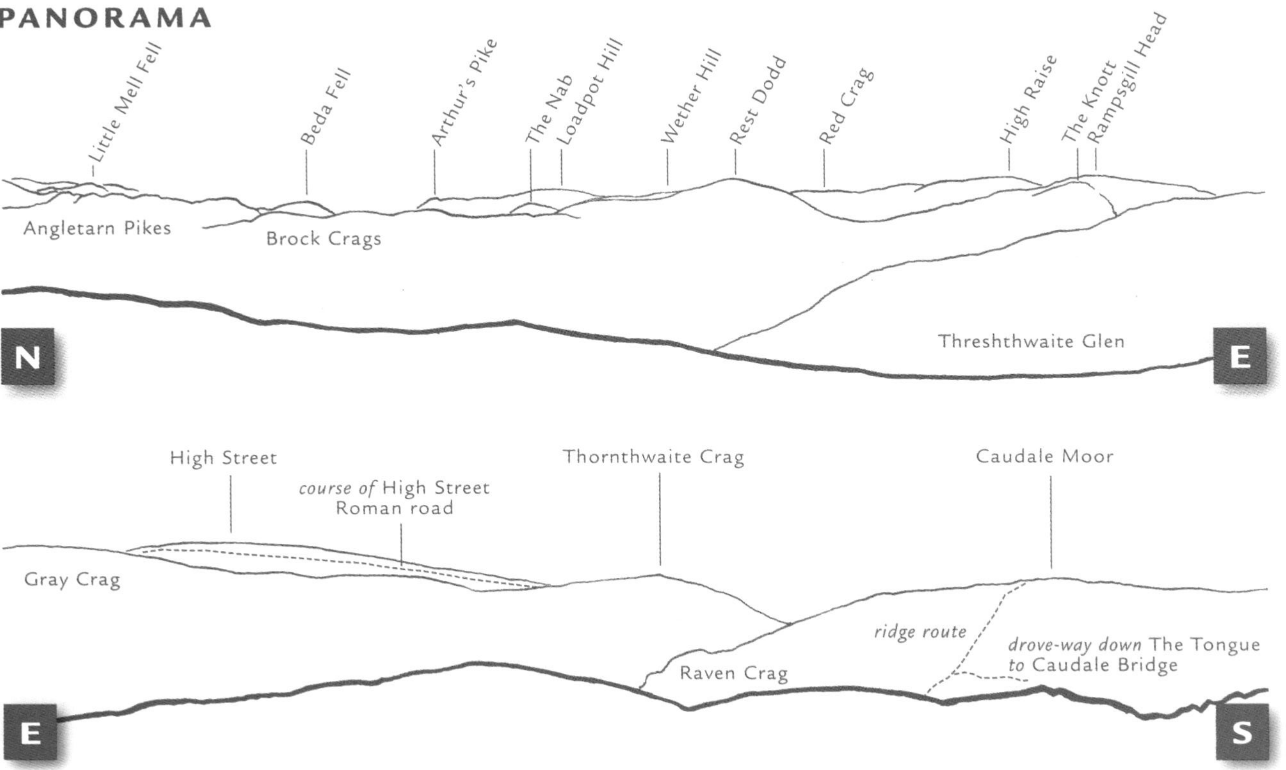
PANORAMA
Little Mell Fell
Beda Fell
Arthur's Pike
The Nab
Loadpot Hill
Wether Hill
Rest Dodd
Red Crag
High Raise
The Knott
Rampsgill Head
Angletarn Pikes
Brock Crags
Threshthwaite Glen
N
E
High Street
course of High Street
Roman road
Thornthwaite Crag
Caudale Moor
Gray Crag
ridge route
drove-way down The Tongue
to Caudale Bridge
Raven Crag
E
S

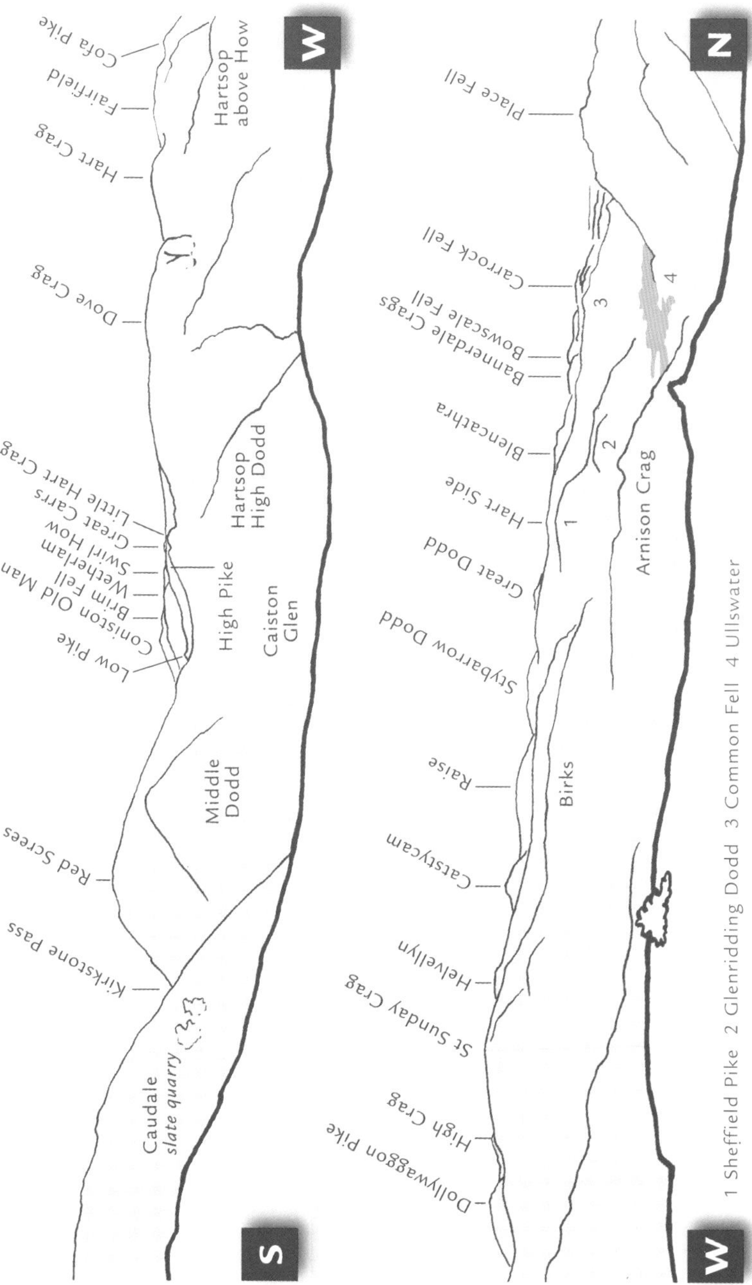

1 Sheffield Pike 2 Glenridding Dodd 3 Common Fell 4 Ullswater

14 HIGH RAISE *(802m/2631ft)*

Winter aspect of High Raise up the Longgrain Gill valley

Simply to stand on the summit of High Raise is a modest walking achievement in itself, as the peak is far set and aloof. The fell name suggests a place of revere, as the term 'raise' frequently alluded to 'an ancient burial place', although the likely reference was to Low Raise, where there are the remains of a tumulus. The second highest summit in the High Street range, High Raise is an obvious addition to any thorough exploration of the Far Eastern Fells, and invariably its scalp is taken on the fine skyline trek from Martindale. But there are a few other lines to consider from either end of Haweswater, penetrating the wilds of Measand Beck, climbing over the Long Grain ridge via Low Raise, or venturing by the great amphitheatre of Whelter Crags, with its crag-topping Iron Age fort.

 ↑ Whelter Crags, High Raise

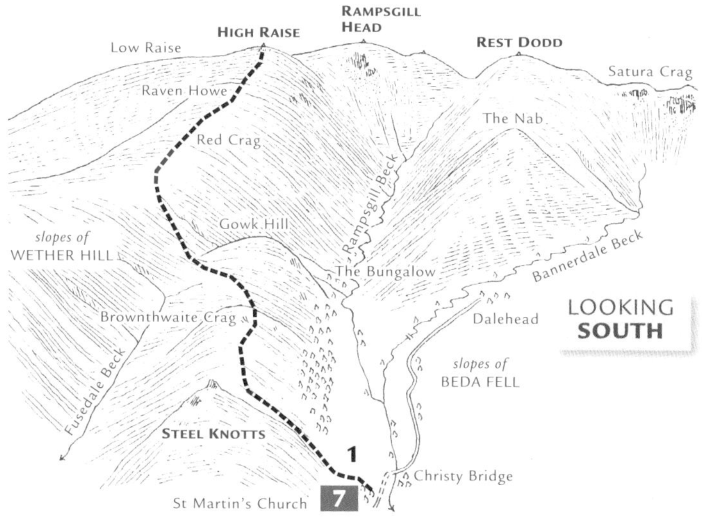

ASCENT FROM MARTINDALE OLD CHURCH (7 – off map N)

Via Keasgill Head 640m/2100ft 6km/3¾ miles

1 A common route to the top, integral with Martindale's southern skyline clockwise horseshoe walk, and upliftingly scenic throughout. From the verge follow the footpath rising directly behind the Old Church – regular use keeps the bracken at bay. Pass through a wall-gap (hand-gate missing) onto the ridge, coming over the rocky shoulder of Brownthwaite Crag, an exceptional viewpoint for the Howe Grain valley, across to Beda Fell and up the dale to The Nab. The path negotiates some pretty damp ground as it curves into the head of the Fusedale Beck valley, fording a gill beside two ruined shepherds' bothies. Curving right beyond Gowk Hill (derived from the local dialect term for 'cuckoo'), the path embarks on a steady pull across the western slopes of Wether Hill. Some part is in a groove, coming up by Mere Beck and offering a bird's-eye view down on The Bungalow in Rampsgill Beck valley – the red roof makes it hard to miss! There are two options high up. First, slip across the dry upper section of the gill to go through the gateway in the rising wall and follow on with the fence, with minimal evidence of a path. Second, stick with common practice and come up to the Roman road at Keasgill Head, swinging right with the wall, with peat groughs evident close left. Shortly the broken wall is crossed on a peaty trail that moves over to unite with the fence (and the short-cut route). Pass on by the undistinguished top of Red Crag and its peaty pool, Redcrag Tarn, to go through a hand-gate where the fence moves across to unite with a consistent ridge wall. Head on over Raven Howe, arriving at a stile where a fence breaks right from the wall-end. The stony summit is shortly gained off to the left from the Roman road.

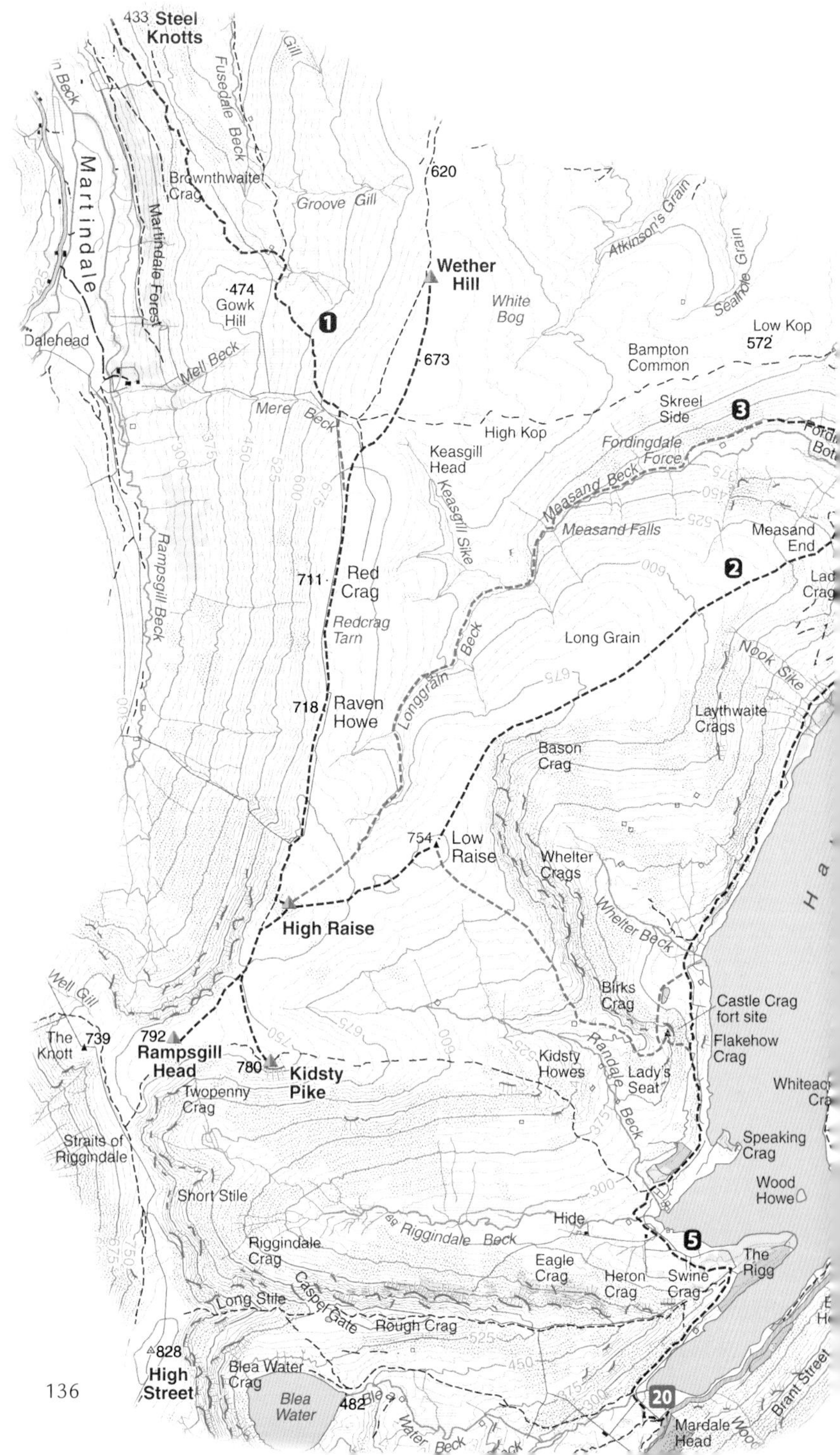

433 Steel Knotts
Fusedale Beck
Gill
Martindale
Brownthwaite Crag
Martindale Forest
Groove Gill
620
Wether Hill
White Bog
Atkinson's Grain
Sealhole Grain
474 Gowk Hill
Dalehead
Mell Beck
673
Low Kop 572
Bampton Common
Skreel Side
Mere Beck
High Kop
Keasgill Head
Keasgill Sike
Fordingdale Force
Measand Beck
Measand Falls
Measand End
Rampsgill Beck
711
Red Crag
Redcrag Tarn
Long Grain
Nook Sike
Longgrain Beck
718
Raven Howe
Laythwaite Crags
Bason Crag
754
Low Raise
Whelter Crags
Whelter Beck
High Raise
Well Gill
Birks Crag
Castle Crag fort site
The Knott 739
792 Rampsgill Head
780 Kidsty Pike
Kidsty Howes
Randale Beck
Lady's Seat
Flakehow Crag
Twopenny Crag
Straits of Riggindale
Speaking Crag
Wood Howe
Short Stile
Hide
Riggindale Beck
Riggindale Crag
Eagle Crag
Heron Crag
Swine Crag
The Rigg
Long Stile
Caspel Gate
Rough Crag
828 High Street
Blea Water Crag
Blea Water
482
Mardale Head
Brant Street

ASCENT FROM BURNBANKS (18 – off map E)

Via Measand End 620m/2035ft 7.3km/4½ miles

2 Follow the waymarked reservoir track from the hamlet of Burnbanks, which is also part of the Coast to Coast Walk. From the car park walk up the roadway by the chalet bungalows, switching right by two hand-gates out of the woodland belt. Turn W, accompanying a good track with progressively better views across the great 'lake'. A large deer-exclusion gate/fence brings the trail into an area of sapling sheathes within a newly planted enclosure surrounding the lower reaches of Measand Beck. There are two ways up to the footbridge on the threshold of Fordingdale Bottom. The quickest bears up right by the wall soon after the deer-exclusion fence/gate, with a track rising right. As the wall turns right, follow suit, coming onto damper ground to draw alongside the deer-exclusion fence and duly reach and go through a gate out onto the bracken-clad fellside. Keep beside the fence, passing by another gate, to duly reach the footbridge over Measand Beck. Alternatively, the more exciting option continues to the gated footbridge at the foot of The Forces. Step off right from the regular path and ascend in harmony with this rousing ravine of Measand Beck. This is a fascinating section – take whatever safe options you can find to admire the various falls and cascades within the tangle of rocks and native trees. However, the best of the falls are denied to walkers. At the top the path goes

Remnant peat hag on Long Grain (2012)

through a gate in the deer-exclusion fence and marches on to the footbridge. This is a point of decision, as two routes break from this spot.

Standing on the west side of the Measand Beck footbridge the primary option heads SW, but be sure to hold to the slightly right-hand option as bracken intervenes. The regular way, used by quad bikes, is more direct than the old drove shown on maps. This weaves up Measand End via a rock and then grassy groove onto the broad pasture above Lad Crags. The slope eases amid terrain interspersed with eroded groughs. As the higher plateau is reached, pass a slender peat hag, which will be gone within a decade. The quad path marches along the expansive Long Grain ridge towards Low Raise.

Take the opportunity to visit the edge, eventually to view the great combe beneath Whelter Crags, with Bason Crag in the foreground. The two names of the latter are tautological – 'bason' means 'basin', and Whelter is the rare Scandinavian 'hwilftar', meaning 'an amphitheatre'. The ancient stones comprising Low Raise have been reworked into a substantial cairn, and the remnant stone heap into a wind-shelter. The term 'raise' means 'a tumulus' and must have held ancestral significance upwards of three millennia ago. The ridge path turns SW to reach the summit.

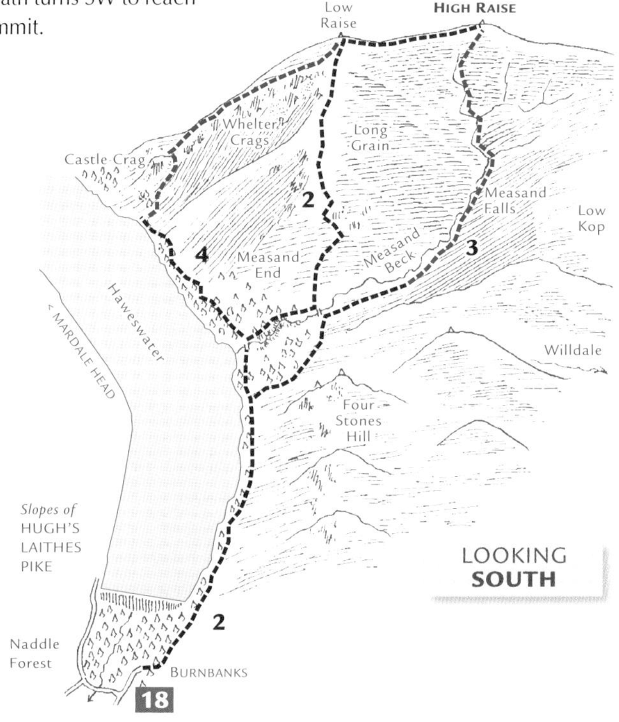

Via Measand Falls 645m/2115ft 8km/5 miles

Measand Falls in Longgrain Gill

3 The watery, unfrequented option begins from the east side of the top footbridge and follows the path running level along the base of the fell at the edge of the great basin of Fordingdale Bottom, clearly once a shallow tarn. As a sheep trod it becomes less evident as it comes above the large sheepfold complex, the layout suggestive of a sheep-wash, a Bampton Common gathering point. Come above Fordingdale Force, now upon rocky ground, to become more intimate with the gorge. The fellsides on either side of the beck are steep, but pose no problem to the well-adjusted mountain-goat fellwalker. Skreel Side, above, is a popular haven for small red deer herds – keep your eyes open and move quietly. Some way up the gorge a substantial waterfall comes into view. Keep up to overcome the awkward approach, then move down to inspect the 8m high Measand Falls. The valley has a few more rough moments above this point, but nothing to hamper the determined gill-wanderer. Keep to the left-hand watercourse at the fork, holding to Longgrain Beck, and follow this basically SW. Ultimately rise on tough moor, but easier angled fell, targetting the stony summit of High Raise.

Via Whelter Crags 720m/2360ft 8.5km/5¼ miles

4 A route familiar to all Coast to Coasters, who will invariably be met as you wander on SW from the foot of The Forces. The path has much to commend it scenically, though is probably best adopted as a return route following an ascent by Measand End. There is one scree-fringe section en route to a small footbridge spanning Whelter Beck, with its holly-laced ravine beneath. Step up right some 50m after the footbridge and skirt to the right of the small walled conifer copse to climb the broad gully between crags, the more prominent left-hand cliff being Castle Crag. There is some trace of the zig-zag path higher up, although it is apparent only when the bracken is suppressed by winter. Make a move left at the top to visit the Iron Age hill-fort site. A natural rampart fronted by a wall is surmounted by a shattered wall more than 2000 years old, with space for hut dwellings being immensely limited. The tiny native kinship would have resorted to this waterless place only at times of extreme peril and for very short periods of time. As a viewpoint it is an exciting station from which to train your eyes upon Haweswater's peat-darkened waters.

Haweswater from Castle Crag

Backtrack to weave your way up onto Lady's Seat, the ridge above Birk Crag, and find a path that ventures to a ruined bothy and fold. Turn then to task, ascending the minor outcropping of the broad ridge bounding Whelter Crags. Expect no path upon this seldom climbed ridge. The name 'whelter' is Viking for 'an amphitheatre', also reflected in the name Bason Crag, meaning 'cliff of the basin'. The top of Low Raise is achieved with no little relief – it's a tough old climb – and the reward is a stout cairn and the lowest of wind-shelters built from the loose tumulus relic. A clear path, emphasised by quad-bike use, leads on SW to the main summit.

ASCENT FROM MARDALE HEAD (20)

Via Castle Crag **625m/2050ft 5.8km/3½ miles**

5 Leave the car park via the kissing-gate. As the wall turns right under the bower of an oak, follow suit, following the sign 'Fellside path to Bampton'. The path duly runs on via a hand-gate and three footbridges, the last a broad walk over Mardale Beck. Go right, duly slipping over the ridge-end, sheltered to the right by the conifers of The Rigg, and trend easily down left into the valley of Riggindale. There is access to the RSPB eagle viewpoint, left, from before the copse and the curious stone-row-lined path after. The path leads over successive footbridges – Bowderthwaite, spanning Riggindale Beck, and then Randale Beck bridge. Hold faith with the trail, passing below a conifer plantation, and with a wall right much of the way until the trail rises by thorn bushes onto the shoulder of Flakehow Crag, a handsome elevated viewpoint. Here there are two options to get to the top of the first headland. Either turn

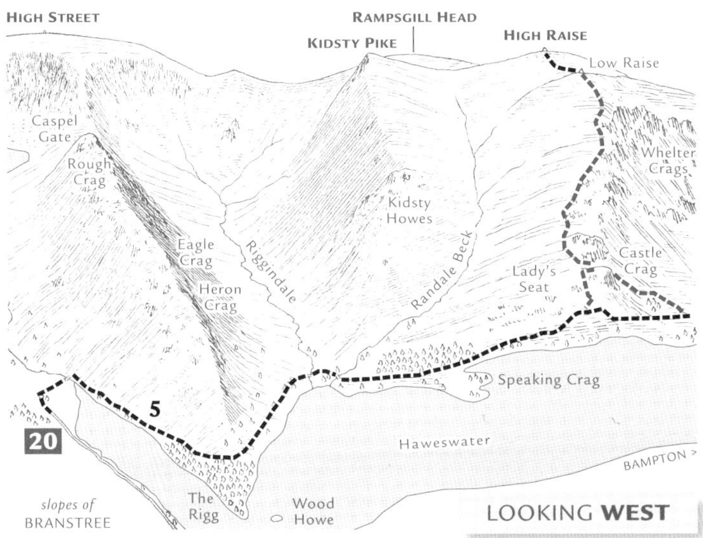

Looking upon the crown of Castle Crag hill-fort

directly left, climbing to the top of the hill-fort via the steep slope left of Castle Crag. A scree-top path leads onto a grass and heather bank – although steep, it is within normal tolerances and very direct. Alternatively, descend with the continuing path until some 50m short of Whelter Beck footbridge, then turn up left, joining forces with Route 4.

High Raise summit cairn

THE SUMMIT

The stony summit is unique in the High Street range and lends the place a special quality, as well as providing foreground interest when composing a photograph. The views are generous in all directions, as might be expected from such an elevated spot. The Pennines form a consistent skyline on the eastern arc, while the Helvellyn range dominates the western view, with several major fells, including High Street, Coniston Old Man, Crinkle Crags, Bowfell, both Scafells, Great Gable, Skiddaw and Blencathra, well in evidence. Coy additions include Eskdale's Harter Fell and Eel Crags, and much else elsewhere to absorb the student of fine fell scenery.

SAFE DESCENTS

Walkers are inevitably a long way from habitation – the nearest road is Mardale Head. To reach that point, follow the ridge route S to Kidsty Pike, joining the well-made path heading E down by Kidsty Howes – there are some tricky moments as you emerge on steep ground leading into Riggindale. Hartsop is the nearest settlement, reached by following the skyline route S then W over Rampsgill Head to join the regular path glancing down by The Knott into the Hayeswater Gill valley. Strictly, if you follow a ridge path you will find safe haven, eventually.

RIDGE ROUTES

KIDSTY PIKE ↓ 50m/165ft ↑ 25m/80ft 0.9km/½ mile

Join the Roman road which slips over the west side of the summit, descend SSW, and from the depression take the left fork, curving round the head of Randale direct to the summit.

RAMPSGILL HEAD ↓ 50m/165ft ↑ 40m/130ft 1km/½ mile

From the depression SSW of the summit take the right-hand path, coming naturally onto the brow to find the summit cairn beyond the impressive craggy edge.

WETHER HILL ↓ 160m/525ft ↑ 34m/110ft 3.5km/2¼ miles

This route was surveyed by the Romans, so you can expect directness, as indeed transpires. Follow the ridge path N, crossing a stile where a fence meets a wall. Keep with the wall, and where this ends go through a hand-gate then accompany the fence as it passes Redcrag Tarn and veers half-right to cross the broken wall and run on through the shallow depression at Keasgill Head. Here two paths are evident, both leading on to the cairn at the far end of the broad damp ridge of Wether Hill.

The Roman road leads north to Loadpot Hill

PANORAMA

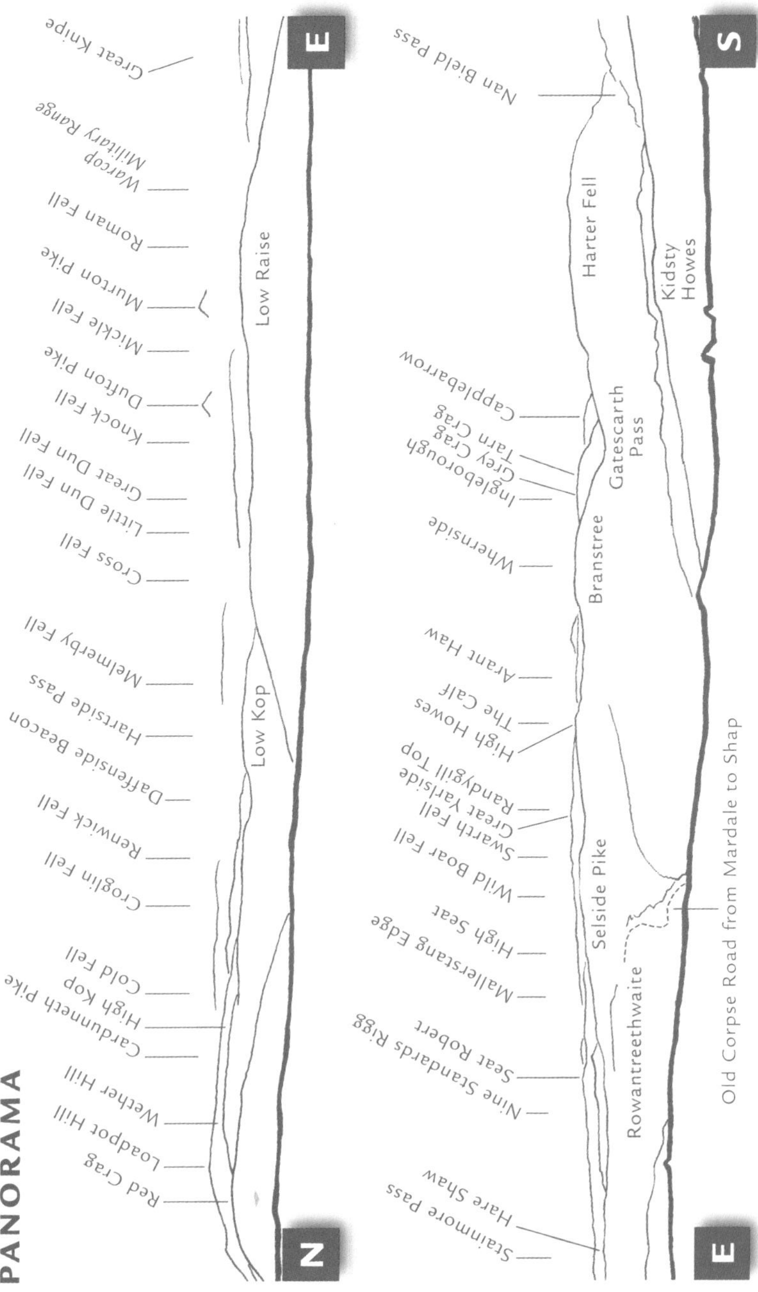
N
E
S
E
Red Crag
Loadpot Hill
Wether Hill
Cardunneth Pike
High Kop
Cold Fell
Croglin Fell
Renwick Fell
Daffenside Beacon
Hartside Pass
Melmerby Fell
Low Kop
Cross Fell
Little Dun Fell
Great Dun Fell
Knock Fell
Dufton Pike
Mickle Fell
Murton Pike
Low Raise
Roman Fell
Warcop Military Range
Great Knipe
Stainmore Pass
Hare Shaw
Nine Standards Rigg
Seat Robert
Mallerstang Edge
High Seat
Wild Boar Fell
Swarth Fell
Great Yarlside
Randygill Top
High Howes
The Calf
Arant Haw
Selside Pike
Rowantreethwaite
Old Corpse Road from Mardale to Shap
Wherside
Ingleborough
Grey Crag
Tarn Crag
Capplebarrow
Branstree
Gatescarth Pass
Harter Fell
Kidsty Howes
Nan Bield Pass

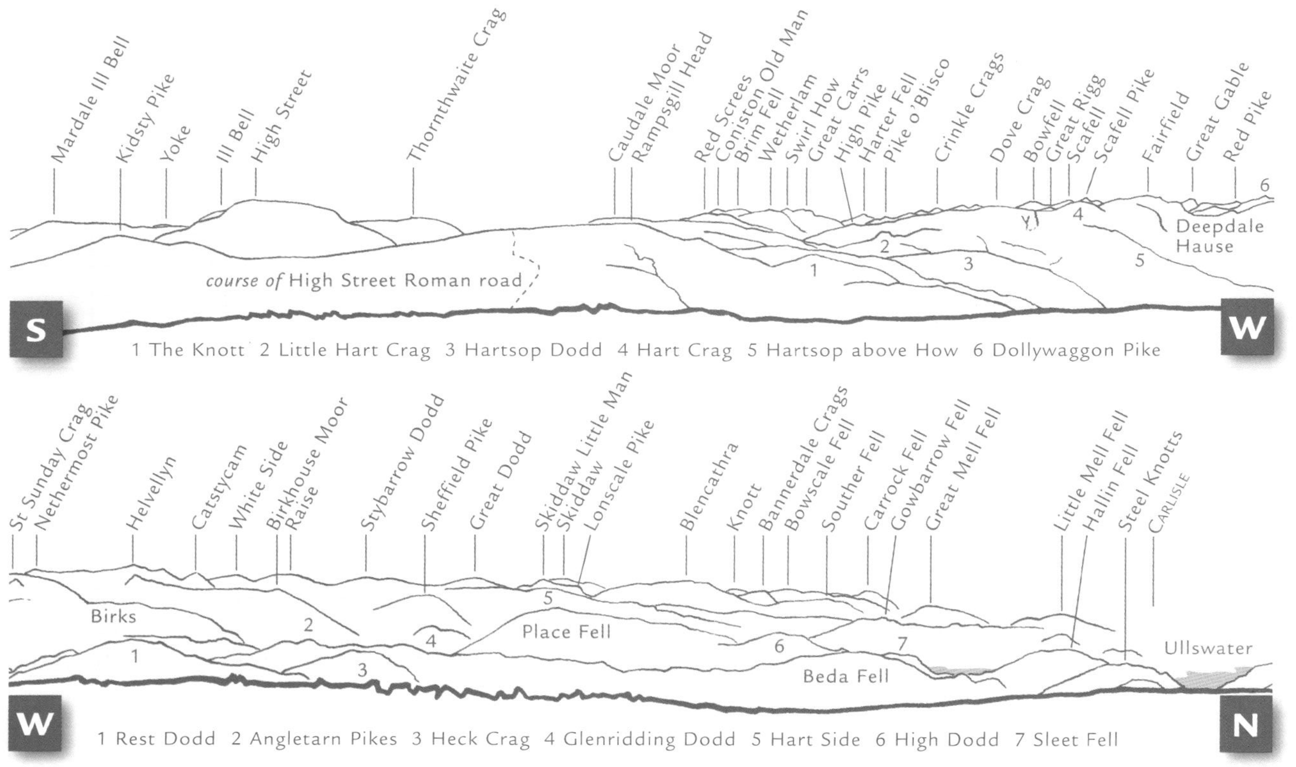

Mardale Ill Bell
Kidsty Pike
Yoke
Ill Bell
High Street
Thornthwaite Crag
Caudale Moor
Rampsgill Head
Red Screes
Coniston Old Man
Brim Fell
Wetherlam
Swirl How
Great Carrs
High Pike
Harter Fell
Pike o'Blisco
Crinkle Crags
Dove Crag
Bowfell
Great Rigg
Scafell
Scafell Pike
Fairfield
Great Gable
Red Pike
Deepdale Hause
course of High Street Roman road
S
W
1 The Knott 2 Little Hart Crag 3 Hartsop Dodd 4 Hart Crag 5 Hartsop above How 6 Dollywaggon Pike
St Sunday Crag
Nethermost Pike
Helvellyn
Catstycam
White Side
Birkhouse Moor
Raise
Stybarrow Dodd
Sheffield Pike
Great Dodd
Skiddaw Little Man
Skiddaw
Lonscale Pike
Blencathra
Knott
Bannerdale Crags
Bowscale Fell
Souther Fell
Carrock Fell
Gowbarrow Fell
Great Mell Fell
Little Mell Fell
Hallin Fell
Steel Knotts
CARLISLE
Birks
Place Fell
Beda Fell
Ullswater
W
N
1 Rest Dodd 2 Angletarn Pikes 3 Heck Crag 4 Glenridding Dodd 5 Hart Side 6 High Dodd 7 Sleet Fell

15 HIGH STREET *(828m/2717ft)*

The fell forms the high focus of the range – and, indeed, the summit of High Street has been a gathering place down the ages. The first significant roads in Britain were built by the Romans, promptly after they claimed authority over Britannia. Undaunted by physical obstacles, they swept a high road – hence the fell name – over the fells to connect their forts at Galava (Ambleside) and Brocavum (Brougham, near Penrith), first garrisoned by Syrian cavalry. Visible and used to this day, their high street ran up abruptly from the Trout Beck valley, via Scot Rake towards what is now a beacon on Thornthwaite Crag, then along the western brink of this central fell, exiting north via the Straits of Riggindale over Rampsgill Head. The road can hardly ever have lain dormant, as travellers will have always found it far too useful. In more recent centuries shepherds from neighbouring valleys met on the plateau to reclaim wayward sheep and enjoy sporting rivalry, including fell-pony races, with wagers and much merriment – hence the fell's alternative name, Racecourse Hill. The classic ascent is via Rough Crag from Mardale Head, with a fine circuit including either Kidsty Pike or Mardale Ill Bell. In addition, longer dedicated climbs can be considered from Hartsop, Troutbeck and Kentmere.

 ↑ High Street from Twopenny Crag

ASCENT FROM HARTSOP (3)

Via The Knott 700m/2300ft 5.4km/3½ miles

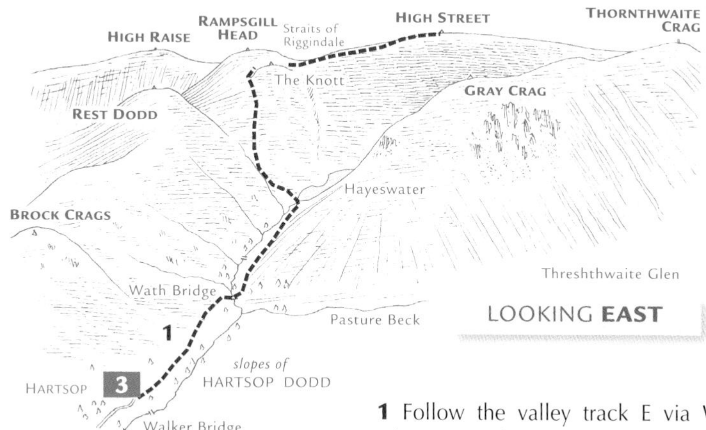

1 Follow the valley track E via Wath Bridge, ascending to Hayeswater dam. Bear left with three possible lines up the flank of The Knott – the more natural heads N to come up by the wall to join the popular path from Angle Tarn, part of the Coast to Coast route, hence the added wear. A peaty rise has some pitching, and higher a loose gravel trail leads through a wall-gap and round the northern side of The Knott, although some may wish to follow the broken wall up to the large cairn on top for its grand view back down on Hayeswater. The main path swings S on the level beside the wall and comes down through the narrow section of the ridge known as the Straits of Riggindale.

Straits of Riggindale

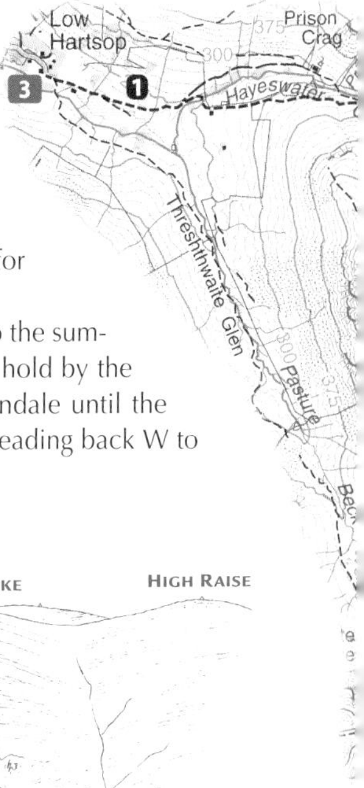

Notice this place-name contains two nautical terms – 'straits', normally associated with a constricted current of water, and 'riggin', the rope-work on a tall ship; both are of Viking origin. The latter alludes to the angle of the facing slopes running down into Riggindale. Keep the wall close right, ignoring the passage through that was the course of the Roman road. Come onto the minor cairned top of Short Stile for a special view into Riggindale.

Continue through the pooled depression and rise to the summit. Alternatively some may find it more attractive to hold by the pathless eastern edge to prolong the interest in Riggindale until the cairn is met at the top of the Long Stile ridge, before heading back W to the wall and the summit.

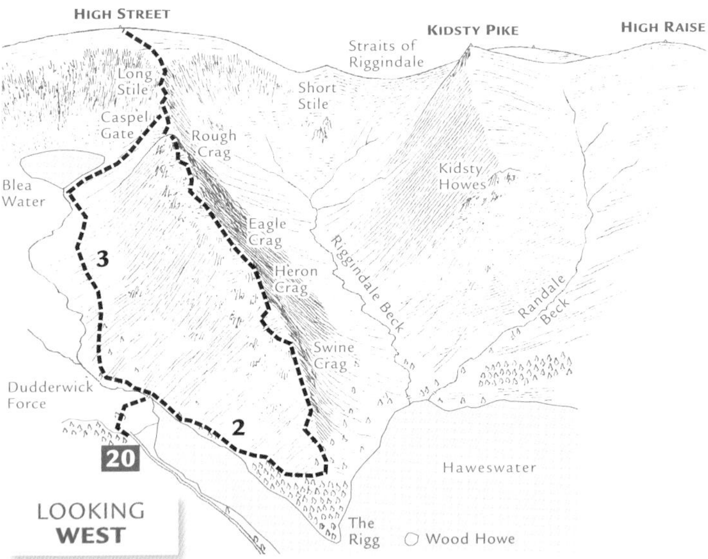

ASCENT FROM MARDALE HEAD (20)

Via Rough Crag ridge 620m/2035ft 4.7km/3 miles

There is more than a hint of similarity with Helvellyn and Striding Edge in the geography of the blunt buttress ridge of Long Stile, with the Rough Crag crest running down to the shores of Haweswater. There is even the magic of an adjacent great corrie lake in Blea Water.

2 Go through the kissing-gate, and where three paths diverge under the bower of an oak follow the 'Fellside path to Bampton', ushered right. This path is commonly followed by ornithologists venturing to the Riggindale viewing hide to strain their eyes for the famous, if sadly solitary Golden Eagle. Eagles have

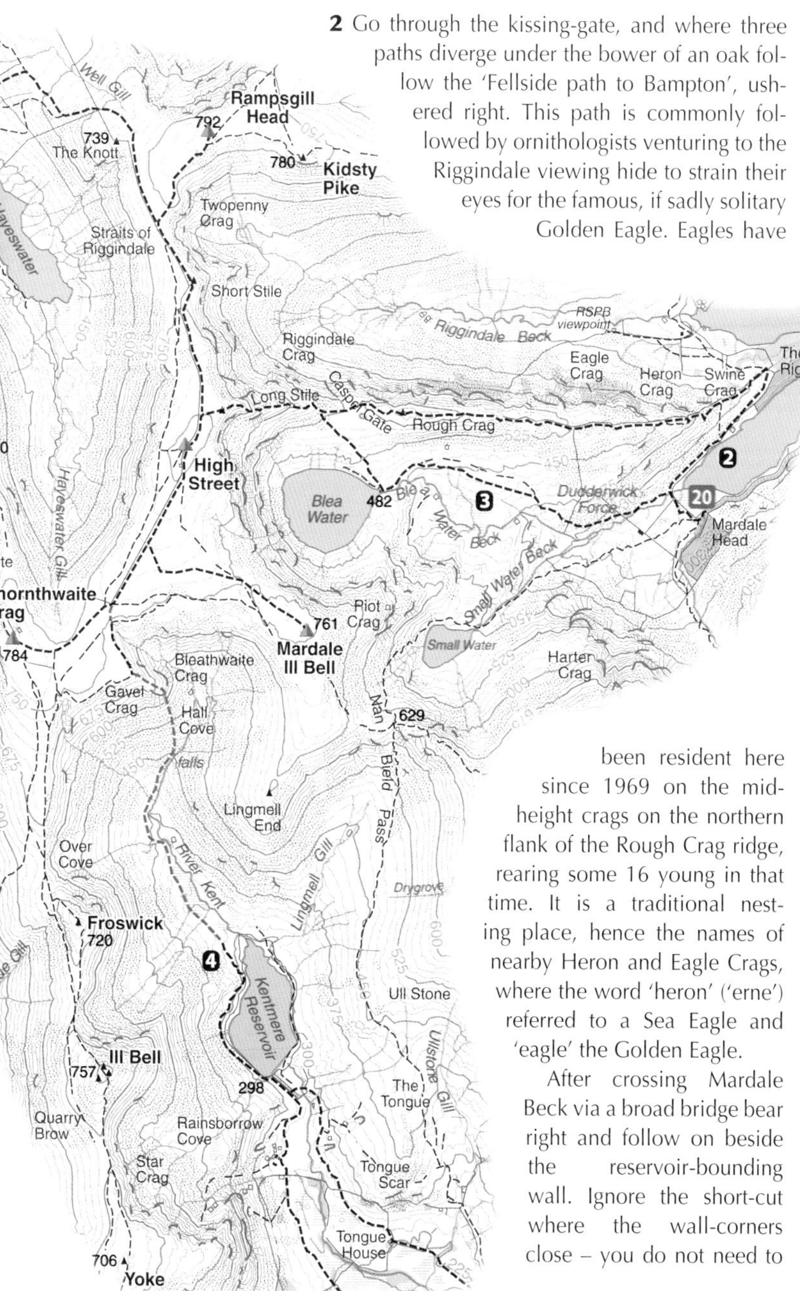

been resident here since 1969 on the mid-height crags on the northern flank of the Rough Crag ridge, rearing some 16 young in that time. It is a traditional nesting place, hence the names of nearby Heron and Eagle Crags, where the word 'heron' ('erne') referred to a Sea Eagle and 'eagle' the Golden Eagle.

After crossing Mardale Beck via a broad bridge bear right and follow on beside the reservoir-bounding wall. Ignore the short-cut where the wall-corners close – you do not need to

The Rigg projecting into Haweswater

Bracken kiln in Riggindale

contribute to further unsightly erosion. Continue to the shelter of the conifers on The Rigg, go through the gateway and veer left, joining the rising ridge adorned lightly with birch. Eagle Crag lies high ahead on the broken flank of the ridge, while on the right the great scoop of Riggindale, culminating in the peak of Kidsty Pike, draws the eye, as they both do throughout this ascent. The path slips through a gap by a sheep-creep, meets up with the short-cut and, passing a large cairn, begins the first proper climb, ignoring the wall's defiant line.

The path comes back in company with the wall shortly, then drifts left. But watch where the path seems to pass along the flank here, and veer right on the rock-ramp to regain the wall's handsome line. From this point the wall is your companion until the last step of the ridge, where it is lost. The brief rocky steps accomplished, the fine ridge top of Rough Crag forms a triumphant culmination. Pass the crest-topping cairn and decline in order to pass to the right of the pool in the enigmatically named Caspel Gate. Critically this is **not** a cross-over point on the ridge, as crags lurk on the east side. The Long Stile spur ridge looms ahead, and the path copes confidently with its numerous stepped stages to reach the brink cairn. From here bear half-left to reach the summit.

Via Blea Water 590m/1935ft 3.6km/2¼ miles

3 Begin as per Route 2, but at the instant you cross the broad bridge spanning Mardale Beck bear left and follow the old way. After the first gate see Dudderwick Force (waterfall) down to the left, a suitable subject for an artist's consideration. The path rises through a second gate, after which eyes will be drawn towards a fine fall in Bleawater Beck, with a sturdy juniper clinging to its upper lip. Beyond, the path

Tarn in Caspel Gate

traverses marshy ground, although the line of an aqueduct pipe provides a drier alternative to the dam outflow of Blea Water. 'Blea' means 'blue, although invariably the tarn appears pitch black! Directly from the concrete dam a path climbs the moraine, angling up the slope to connect with the ridge path west of the Caspel Gate tarn as the rockier ground at the foot of Long Stile is met.

ASCENT FROM KENTMERE (29 – off map S) OR HALLOW BANK (31 – off map S)

Via Hall Cove 680m/2230ft 8km/5 miles

4 This route, more than any, emphasises the remote nature of the fell by tracing the upper course of the River Kent towards its source in Hall Cove. It offers an opportunity to experience a little-visited rocky spur. There are two early valley approaches. From the vicinity of St Cuthbert's parish church in Kentmere village (limited parking), by either the road or green lanes, venture onto the private road to Hartrigg and continue on with the track to Kentmere Reservoir dam. The same spot can be reached from Hallow Bank by the gated dale-floor footpath via Overend and Tongue House (barn). From the barn advance to a ladder-stile to reach an area of slate spoil where once a quarrymen's bridge spanned the dale beck. Beyond, contour the banks to a point just beyond the man-made reservoir's outflow ravine. There cross a plank-bridge and stepping stones to then cross the cobbled and stepped outflow channel itself by a gated bridge to reach the reservoir track. Keep to the path running along the western side of the reservoir, halfway drifting down to avoid rocky ground. As the

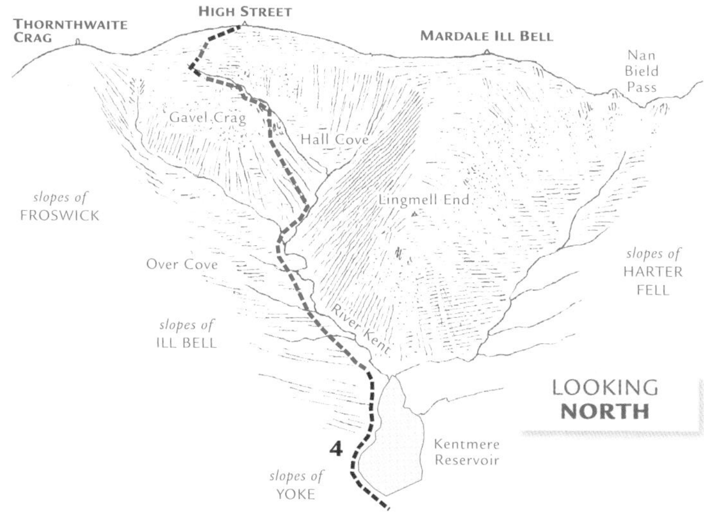

reservoir is passed so is clear evidence of a path through the damp dale-floor herbage well left of the Kent, which for all its beck dimensions retains the name of 'river'. Coming near a wash-fold bear up left with the moraine ridge and trace along the top of this feature, sustaining company with the Kent.

Walkers can continue upstream right up through Hall Cove with minimal discomfort, but the better adventure is to take on the Gavel Crag ridge. Reaching a notable

Rough Crag and High Street from Selside Pike

waterfall is the cue to take leave of the beck and ascend the steep fellside. Some may drift half-left and avoid most of the rocky ground, but the seasoned campaigner will have no problem unlocking the ridge above. After the initial boulders the ridge becomes a succession of small irregular outcrops, calling for canny manoeuvres as you work your way, bit by bit, up the prow. Grass is found as the rocky shield is beaten and walkers climb onto the spine of the ridge to find the contouring path skirting the edge. Go right with this and, as the scree-streaked re-entrant that is the headstream of the Kent is reached, bear up N on the grassy moor to join the wall leading direct to the summit column.

THE SUMMIT

While Roman road engineers took the pragmatic course along the western brink of the fell, the estate-defining wall traced the highest ground, and while this has greatly tumbled in the modern era, it is sufficient to ensure a welcome wind-break for rest and recuperation, a little distance either side of the Ordnance Survey column. To the south, a small holding pen is a curious old shepherding feature. The summit is otherwise a bleak place. Perhaps the fell-pony races kept to the Roman road, although the turf on the west side of the summit wall looks a far better race-track today. The view is mighty and generous, as might be hoped and expected of this elevated spot, with all the real potential held in the western arc. The Coniston and Langdale fell groups are well in evidence, the latter backed by the Scafells, as too is the angular form of Great Gable and, in a gap in the Helvellyn range, High Stile peeps through between Fairfield and Dollywaggon Pike. A special and little appreciated viewpoint is that over Blea Water from the path to Mardale Ill Bell. Walk SE – there is no path – until the slope begins to threaten crags, and then find several vantage points to enjoy the real drama of High Street.

SAFE DESCENTS

Clearly the greatest dangers lie to the east, but a well-developed path system comes to walkers' aid in hostile conditions. For Mardale Head use the Mardale Ill Bell ridge path S then SE to Nan Bield Pass, thereby avoiding the steep ground of Long Stile. Although, if you can handle the rocks of Long Stile, the branch right from Caspel Gate to the outflow of Blea Water makes a comparatively sheltered way down. For points W the solution is far easier to contemplate, with the way down to Hartsop attained by following the ridge wall N via the Straits of Riggindale and keeping by the wall and subsequent trail W down into the Hayeswater valley or Angle Tarn for Patterdale.

RIDGE ROUTES

MARDALE ILL BELL ↓ 80m/260ft ↑ 15m/50ft 1.7km/1 mile

Walk S on the east side of the ridge wall to where a new path is found (created by inverting the substrate). This trail leads S then SE on a gentle gradient down, and as the new trail ends keep to the low ridge to reach the summit cairn.

Eagle Crag from the Rough Crag ridge path

RAMPSGILL HEAD ↓ 130m/425ft ↑ 95m/310ft 2km/1¼ miles

Those who relish following the Roman road should head W to encounter it short of the steep brink of the Hayeswater valley. There is no doubting the Roman track. Go N to slip through the ridge wall on the gentle rise in the Straits of Riggindale. Alternatively, you may enjoy keeping to the east side of the ridge wall from the OS column and visiting the cairn on top of Short Stile before rejoining the wall to the gap. As the path climbs from the gap bear off right at the fork coming over the top of Twopenny Crag. Keep to the edge, now travelling E, to find a path-fork which guides direct to the summit cairn.

THORNTHWAITE CRAG ↓ 75m/245ft ↑ 30m/100ft 1.6km/1 mile

Follow the ridge wall on the west side declining to where the broken wall breaks right. Follow this right (20m) to join the Roman road and follow this, curving W to the beacon cairn.

PANORAMA

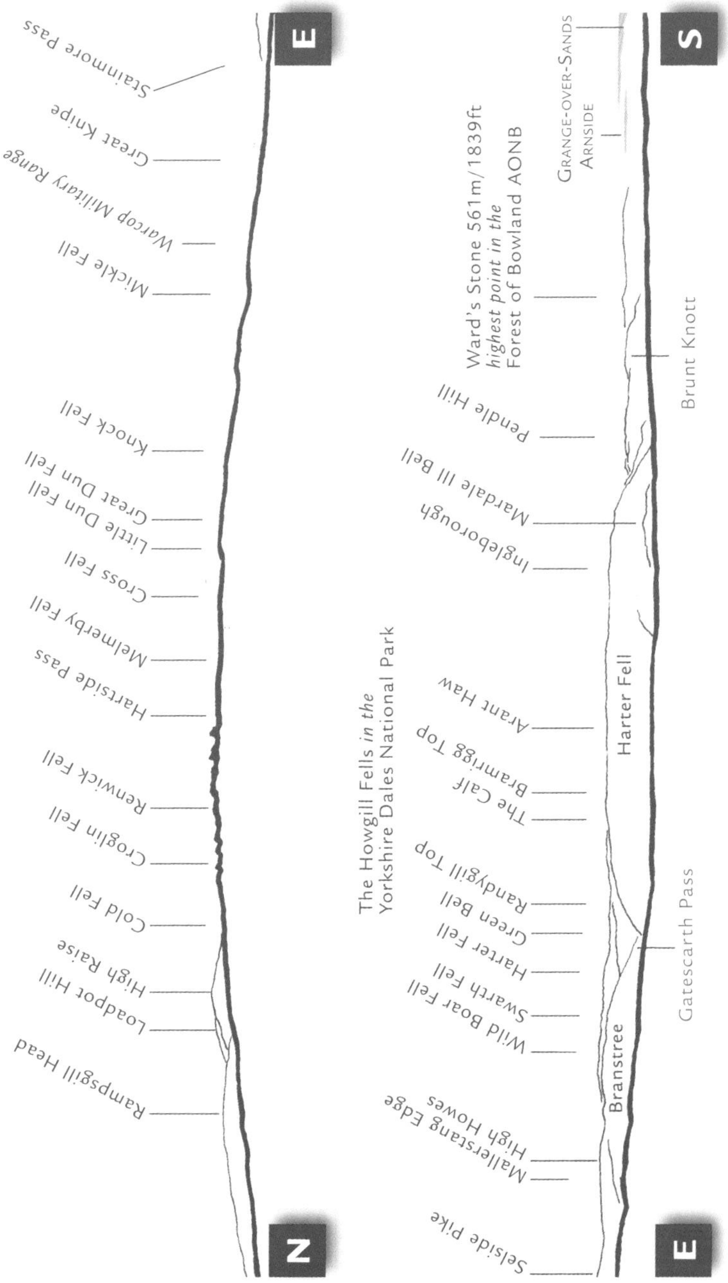

N

Rampsgill Head
Loadpot Hill
High Raise
Cold Fell
Croglin Fell
Renwick Fell
Hartside Pass
Melmerby Fell
Cross Fell
Little Dun Fell
Great Dun Fell
Knock Fell
Mickle Fell
Warcop Military Range
Great Knipe
Stainmore Pass

E

E

Selside Pike
Mallerstang Edge
High Howes
Branstree
Wild Boar Fell
Swarth Fell
Harter Fell
Green Bell
Randygill Top
Gatescarth Pass
The Howgill Fells *in the* Yorkshire Dales National Park
The Calf
Bramrigg Top
Arant Haw
Harter Fell
Ingleborough
Mardale Ill Bell
Pendle Hill
Brunt Knott
Ward's Stone 561m/1839ft *highest point in the* Forest of Bowland AONB
Arnside
Grange-over-Sands

S

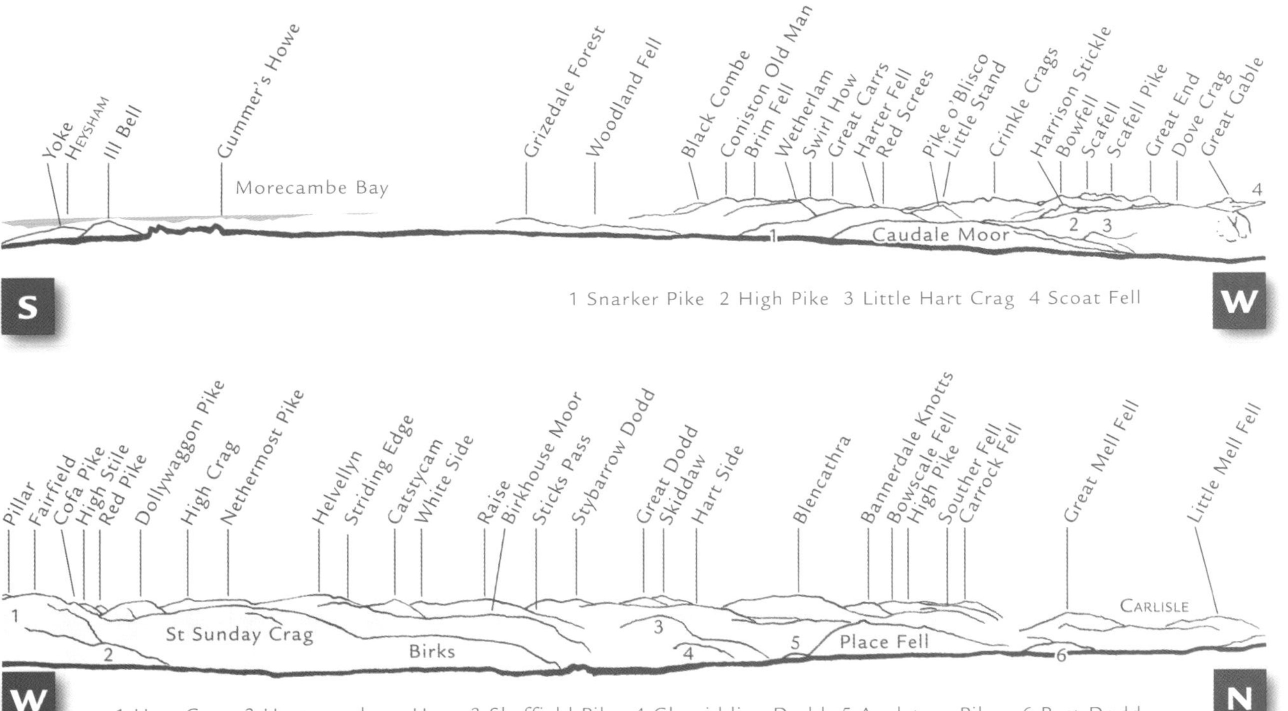
Yoke
Heysham
Ill Bell
Gummer's Howe
Morecambe Bay
Grizedale Forest
Woodland Fell
Black Combe
Coniston Old Man
Brim Fell
Wetherlam
Swirl How
Great Carrs
Harter Fell
Red Screes
Pike o'Blisco
Little Stand
Crinkle Crags
Harrison Stickle
Bowfell
Scafell
Scafell Pike
Great End
Dove Crag
Great Gable
Caudale Moor
S
W
1 Snarker Pike 2 High Pike 3 Little Hart Crag 4 Scoat Fell
Pillar
Fairfield
Cofa Pike
High Stile
Red Pike
Dollywaggon Pike
High Crag
Nethermost Pike
Helvellyn
Striding Edge
Catstycam
White Side
Raise
Birkhouse Moor
Sticks Pass
Stybarrow Dodd
Great Dodd
Skiddaw
Hart Side
Blencathra
Bannerdale Knotts
Bowscale Fell
High Pike
Souther Fell
Carrock Fell
Great Mell Fell
Little Mell Fell
Carlisle
St Sunday Crag
Birks
Place Fell
W
N
1 Hart Crag 2 Hartsop above How 3 Sheffield Pike 4 Glenridding Dodd 5 Angletarn Pikes 6 Rest Dodd

16 ILL BELL *(757m/2484ft)*

One of the star attractions of the Far Eastern group, Ill Bell is the central member, with Yoke and Froswick, of a trio of very distinctive and characterful hills lying between the Troutbeck and Kentmere valleys. It is a simple mountain to admire and enjoy in any season. Almost everyone climbs the fell by the perennially popular ridge path, yet the route described here is a fabulous off-beat, mildly scrambling ascent – that by the steep NE ridge from out of the wild upper realms of the Kentmere valley. The fell name appears to mean 'the treacherous bell-shaped hill', where 'ill' means 'bad', as in 'ill tempered'. However, your mood is likely to remain upbeat and cheery, especially your sense of elation on visiting the summit.

Ill Bell from Nan Bield Pass

↑ Ill Bell from Hallow Bank

ASCENT FROM KENTMERE (29 – off map S) OR HALLOW BANK (31 – off map S)

Via north-east ridge 660m/2165ft 6.4km/4 miles

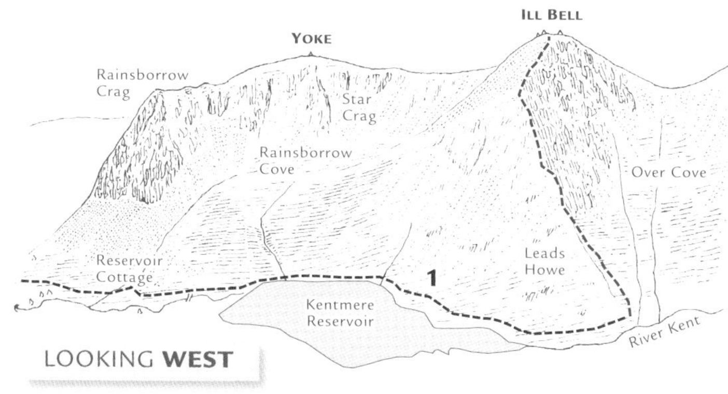

The perfect climb, deserving a warm summer's day – avoid in adverse weather. **1** Approach either by the road to Hartrigg Farm and subsequent gated track to Kentmere Reservoir or the dale-floor footpath from Hallow Bank. This latter comes to a ladder-stile after Tongue House (barn) and advances by slate spoil banks, contouring to veer down to a plank-bridge after the man-made reservoir outflow mini-gorge

Climbing the north-east ridge

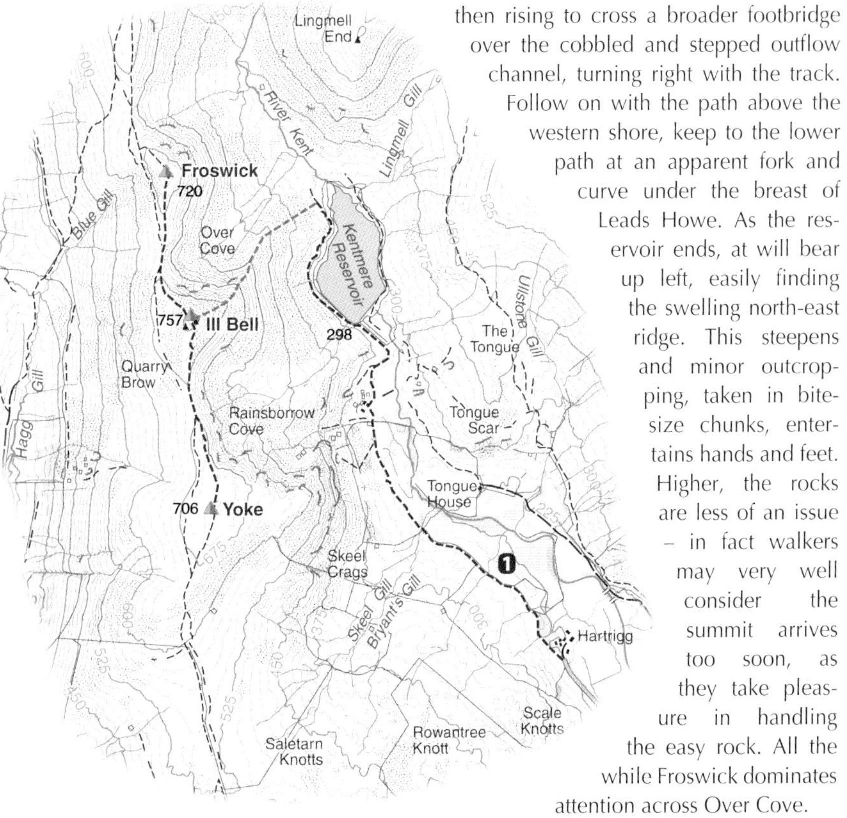

then rising to cross a broader footbridge over the cobbled and stepped outflow channel, turning right with the track. Follow on with the path above the western shore, keep to the lower path at an apparent fork and curve under the breast of Leads Howe. As the reservoir ends, at will bear up left, easily finding the swelling north-east ridge. This steepens and minor outcropping, taken in bite-size chunks, entertains hands and feet. Higher, the rocks are less of an issue – in fact walkers may very well consider the summit arrives too soon, as they take pleasure in handling the easy rock. All the while Froswick dominates attention across Over Cove.

THE SUMMIT

Nature and man have combined to achieve a place of great architectural merit. The vertically split slate bedrock underfoot is attractive in itself, but the greater harmony comes from the strategically sited cairns. Walkers may question which of the two main cairns stands on the higher ground. Less taxing is your deliberation on the view, which is magnificent – particularly south to Windermere and, in the west, held between Wansfell and Red Screes, the fells from Black Combe to Pillar centred upon the Scafells. To the north-west see the Helvellyn range overtopping Caudale Moor, while nearer, over Froswick, is the beacon cairn on Thornthwaite Crag, and to the north High Street above Hall Cove.

SAFE DESCENT

The ridge path S gives all the security you need via Yoke for the Garburn Pass for Troutbeck and Kentmere.

Trio of cairns on the summit

RIDGE ROUTES

FROSWICK ↓ 105m/345ft ↑ 70m/230ft 0.8km/½ mile

Stick religiously to the tried, tested and well-repaired path leading NW from either side of the north cairn outcrop.

YOKE ↓ 100m/330ft ↑ 50m/165ft 1km/½ mile

Due S the ridge path runs along the brink of Rainsborrow Cove, with a minor rise to reach the cairn on the summit rock dais.

PANORAMA

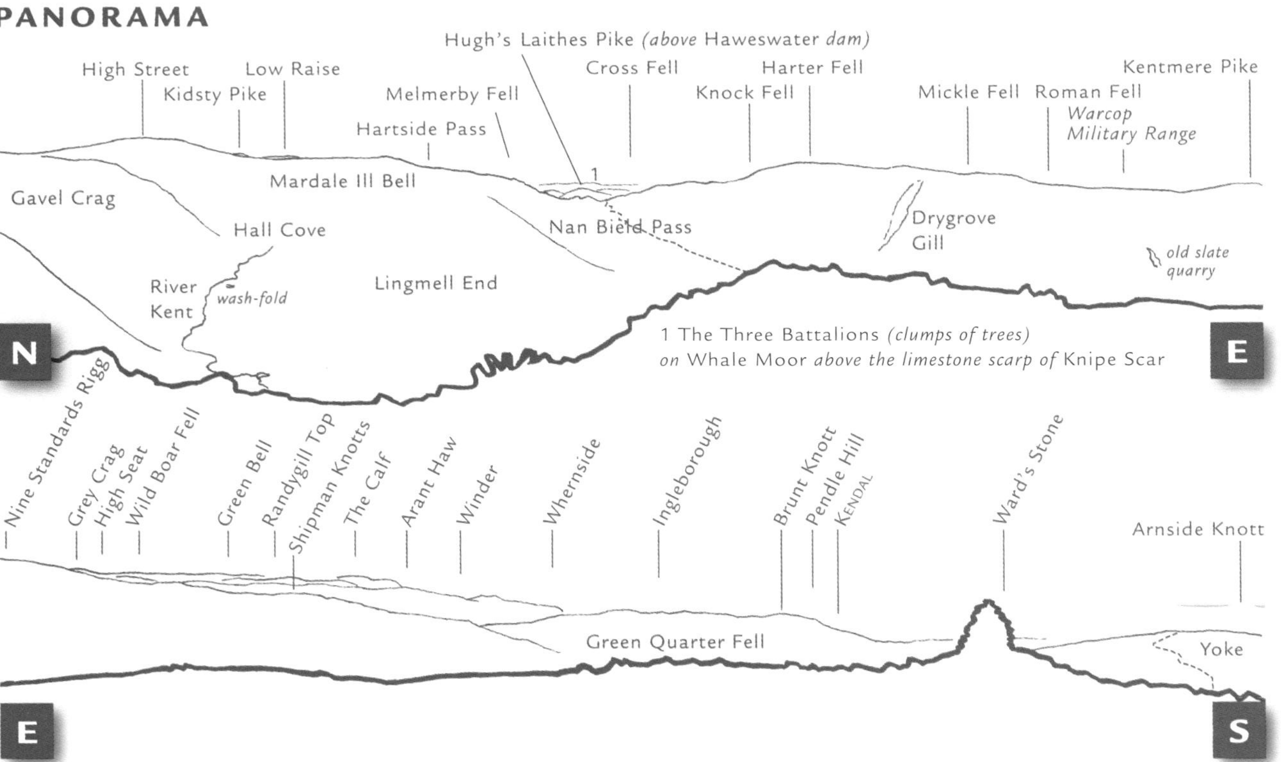
Hugh's Laithes Pike (above Haweswater dam)
High Street
Low Raise
Cross Fell
Harter Fell
Kentmere Pike
Kidsty Pike
Melmerby Fell
Knock Fell
Mickle Fell
Roman Fell
Warcop Military Range
Hartside Pass
1
Mardale Ill Bell
Gavel Crag
Hall Cove
Nan Bield Pass
Drygrove Gill
old slate quarry
River Kent
wash-fold
Lingmell End
N
1 The Three Battalions (clumps of trees) on Whale Moor above the limestone scarp of Knipe Scar
E
Nine Standards Rigg
Grey Crag
High Seat
Wild Boar Fell
Green Bell
Randygill Top
Shipman Knotts
The Calf
Arant Haw
Winder
Whernside
Ingleborough
Brunt Knott
Pendle Hill
KENDAL
Ward's Stone
Arnside Knott
Green Quarter Fell
Yoke
E
S

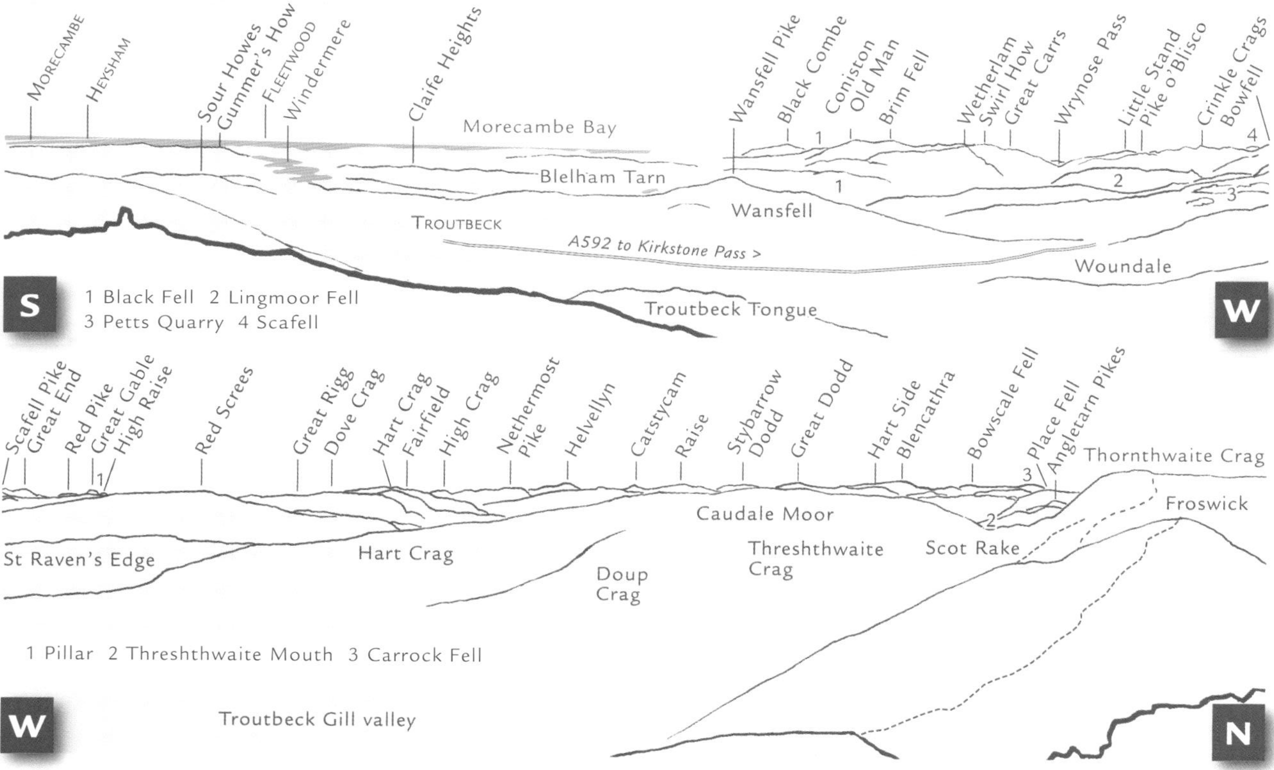
Morecambe
Heysham
Sour Howes
Gummer's How
Fleetwood
Windermere
Claife Heights
Morecambe Bay
Wansfell Pike
Black Combe
Coniston Old Man
Brim Fell
Wetherlam
Swirl How
Great Carrs
Wrynose Pass
Little Stand
Pike o'Blisco
Crinkle Crags
Bowfell
Blelham Tarn
Wansfell
Troutbeck
A592 to Kirkstone Pass >
Woundale
S
1 Black Fell 2 Lingmoor Fell
3 Petts Quarry 4 Scafell
Troutbeck Tongue
W
Scafell Pike
Great End
Red Pike
Great Gable
High Raise
Red Screes
Great Rigg
Dove Crag
Hart Crag
Fairfield
High Crag
Nethermost Pike
Helvellyn
Catstycam
Raise
Stybarrow Dodd
Great Dodd
Hart Side
Blencathra
Bowscale Fell
Place Fell
Angletarn Pikes
Thornthwaite Crag
Froswick
Caudale Moor
St Raven's Edge
Hart Crag
Doup Crag
Threshthwaite Crag
Scot Rake
1 Pillar 2 Threshthwaite Mouth 3 Carrock Fell
W
Troutbeck Gill valley
N

17 KENTMERE PIKE *(730m/2395ft)*

Goat Scar from Sadgill

The great ridge that forms the high divide between upper Kentmere and Longsleddale has two notable summits, Harter Fell and Kentmere Pike, and the latter in turn has two dependant summits, Goat Scar and Shipman Knotts. So while regular walkers climb the fell by the latter, or on occasion Withered Howe, the more inventive will look to Longsleddale to unfurl their fell. Goat Scar has a considerable presence above the hamlet of Sadgill, shielding the main mass of the fell from that valley base. However, this stubby spur is unassailable from the east. Instead, intrepid explorers admire it as they stride up the valley lane, and may choose to venture onto Steel Pike via Wrengill Quarry. This itself is a fascinating relic – a reminder of quarrying endeavour from recent centuries, demanding care and caution. So while the fell name owes shepherding allegiance to Kentmere, in fellwalking terms its finest qualities belong utterly to Longsleddale.

 ↑ Goat Scar and Kentmere Pike from Galeforth Brow

ASCENT FROM HALLOW BANK (31)

Via Withered Howe 470m/1540ft 4.8km/3 miles

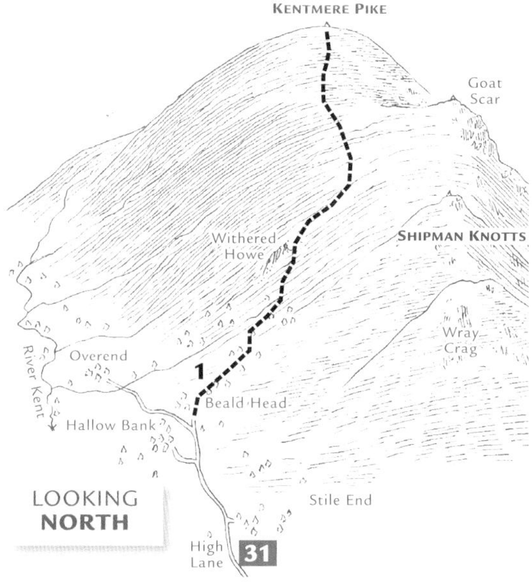

1 Follow the road into the hamlet of Hallow Bank. Keep right and below Brockstones to take the green track up from the garage by Beald Head to a gate onto a fell path. A consistent path, sometimes in a stony groove, by trees and bushes ensures a steady plod up to and through a gateless wall-gap, from where the top of the bastion outcrop of Withered Howe is niftily gained for a brilliant view of the upper Kentmere valley. From here, rushes cause the path to keep reasonably close order with the rising wall, but it does veer away N and NE before the wall falters, slanting over a gill-head to reach a ladder-stile. From here a direct line is taken on a regular path to the ridge wall and, thereby, to the summit.

ASCENT FROM SADGILL (27)

In effect there are three ways to the top from Sadgill, and all have a common opening stage from which to enjoy the theatre and drama of the wild dale head of Longsleddale. The walk leads N from Sadgill Bridge within the green stony-surfaced and walled lane, well removed from the meadows and dancing waters of the River Sprint. The lane runs comparatively close under Buckbarrow Crag and then switches sharply right and left with cobbling – a stony surface that is challenged by the occasional 4x4 vehicle that has licence to travel this way. At this point the Sprint thunders down a series of fine water shoots at Cleft Ghyll, from which walkers are denied easy access, although you may choose to hop over the metal railings to view them and then backtrack to continue. From the gate at the top and immediate bridge at the foot of Brownhowe Bottom walkers come upon their three choices.

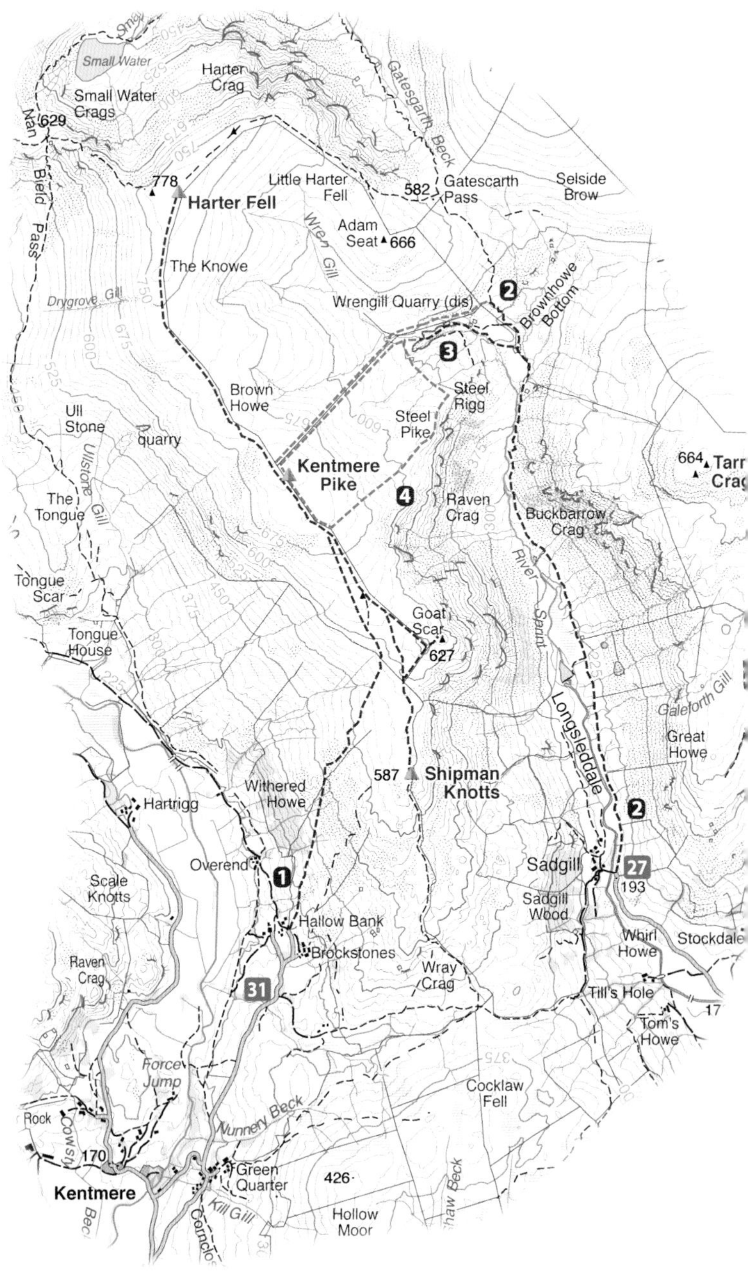
Small Water
Small Water Crags
Harter Crag
629
Nan Bield Pass
778
Harter Fell
Little Harter Fell
Gatesgarth Beck
582
Gatescarth Pass
Selside Brow
Adam Seat
666
Wren Gill
The Knowe
Drygrove Gill
Wrengill Quarry (dis)
2
Brownhowe Bottom
3
Brown Howe
Ull Stone
quarry
Steel Rigg
Steel Pike
Kentmere Pike
664
Tarn Crag
Ullstone Gill
The Tongue
4
Raven Crag
Buckbarrow Crag
Tongue Scar
River Sprint
Goat Scar
627
Tongue House
Longsleddale
Galeforth Gill
Great Howe
587
Shipman Knotts
Withered Howe
Hartrigg
2
Overend
1
Sadgill
27
193
Scale Knotts
Sadgill Wood
Hallow Bank
Whirl Howe
Stockdale
Brockstones
Raven Crag
Wray Crag
31
Till's Hole
17
Tom's Howe
Force Jump
Cocklaw Fell
Nunnery Beck
Rock
170
Green Quarter
426
Kentmere
Kill Gill
Hollow Moor

Wren Gill tumbling into Wrengill Quarry

Via Wren Gill 550m/1805ft 5km/3 miles

2 The simplest, safest and least exciting retains company with the bridle track via a kissing-gate gate (where the broad gate is padlocked) and begins the ascent beyond the fold. At the third hairpin bear off left on a short track to a padlocked galvanised gate. Head W above the wall which bars off the stony confusion of Wrengill Quarry. Walkers will encounter the old water pipe and then its connected breached race that once tapped a flow out of Wren Gill to power a quarry pump. Ford Wren Gill and continue SW, ascending beside the wall with little to consider except what might be the ultimate view. Anticipation becomes a reality as you cross the fence, where a gate once stood, at the junction with the wall and step onto the open ridge path. Go left, quickly completing the climb.

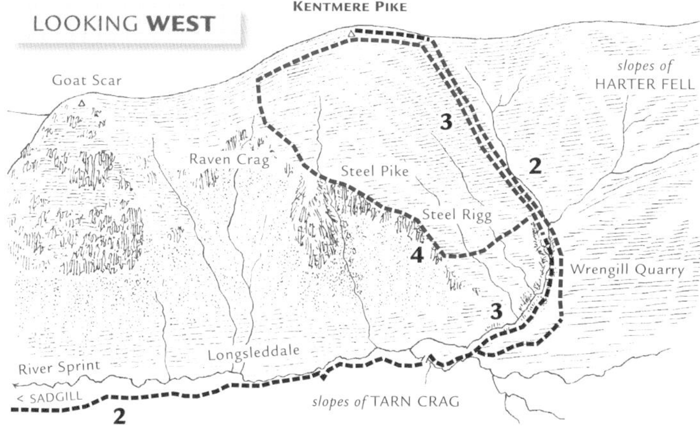

Slate quarry on the western flank

Via Wrengill Quarry 550m/1805ft 4.8km/3 miles

The next two routes have a common early quest. **3** After passing the three-way signpost the track enters a walled pen; at once depart left through a wooden gate. Advance to the slaty banks of the Sprint, where it undergoes an amazing transition. A scene of discordance and dereliction greets the eyes – thunderous waters have caused major wash-outs, with slate spoil banks adding to the visual clamour. Keep up right on a thin path as the ravine becomes more constricted, coming over a tunnel arch. Pass a level area with the vestige of an old workshop and rusting scoop to ascend an incline. See the massive gorge to the left and equally impressive retaining wall on the right on the rise to the next grassy platform, where further ruined workshops stand. The simply massive quarried ravine to the left will transfix your attention for a while. Notice the remnant mine rails protruding from just below the cave.

Keep to the right side, advancing to visit the remarkable waterfall beyond the two pillars that once carried an overhead track – footing is awkward, and the cavern beneath your feet forbidding. View the impressive arrival of Wren Gill as it tumbles into a hole akin to a limestone sink, disappearing through a chaos of boulders and seemingly blocking bedrock wall to emerge into the adjacent quarried canyon. Step back and complete your industrial journey beside Wren Gill. With excitement over, simply keep company with the wall/fence rising SW, a long unremitting climb, and at the top keep left to stand precisely beside the Ordnance Survey column.

Via Steel Pike 580m/1905ft 5.6km/3½ miles

4 From the top of the quarry skirt left, keeping above the topmost canyon and traversing the slope by two minor gills to clamber onto the edge of Steel Rigg. Hold the edge, coming beside a broken wall that has climbed out of the main valley. As the wall ends find a metal fence post. Formerly a fence ran up from here all the way to the ridge, and in effect the line of remnant posts are your guide to the point where the ridge wall and fence meet. Then complete the ascent beside the wall, again to stand beside the column. But before that take pleasure in the preceding cliff scenery. The main attraction is a significant gill which plunges down a gully and separates off as a spur cliff; this headland is called Steel Pike. The view down Longsleddale is fabulous and fully rewards the effort of adopting this unorthodox route.

THE SUMMIT

The ridge path sweeps past a stone cairn, but the actual Ordnance Survey summit is marked by a retired triangulation column. The pillar stands on the east side of the wall; fortunately a wall-stile has been provided, although only a proportion of visitors take the trouble to visit the edifice, content to sample the view from the west side, as this is less inhibited. Canny walkers stand on the top of the wall-stile and get the best of both worlds! Ill Bell and Froswick inevitably draw the eyes across upper Kentmere. Beyond crowd familiar heights to the west, although not Scafell Pike, which contrives to nestle precisely behind Ill Bell's summit.

SAFE DESCENTS

For Kentmere or Sadgill keep tight to the ridge over Shipman Knotts and use the quad-bike track to get down the final slopes and avoid rocky hindrance. The quickest route to a valley is on the north side of the wall/fence, descending NE to ford Wren Gill and subsequently join the Gatescarth Pass track into upper Longsleddale.

RIDGE ROUTES

HARTER FELL ↓ 35m/115ft ↑ 80m/265ft 1.8km/1 mile

The path accompanies a fence, with intermittent sections of wall, holding to the spine of the ridge N over The Knowe to the summit cairn.

SHIPMAN KNOTTS ↓ 170m/560ft ↑ 25m/80ft 2km/1¼ miles

There is a strict route and a scenic route. The former follows the wall and then fence and angles SSE down to a ladder-stile, where a fence converges acutely from the left. The scenic route makes for this point, but takes the time and trouble to visit the top of Goat Scar en route by keeping beside the fence, with some damp ground approaching the right-angled fence-corner. Here find a stile and access to the crown of the headland. A cairn marks the spot for a long contemplation, both up the dale to Buckbarrow Crag and downdale, the length of Longsleddale – quite spellbinding. Hopping back over the stile, continue with the fence close left to the aforementioned ladder-stile. Once over it, the path negotiates further damp ground and slips by a knoll – contender for the summit – to visit the cairn, which is strictly only a practical summit, not the actual summit, which lies out of bounds on the east side of the uncrossable ridge wall.

PANORAMA

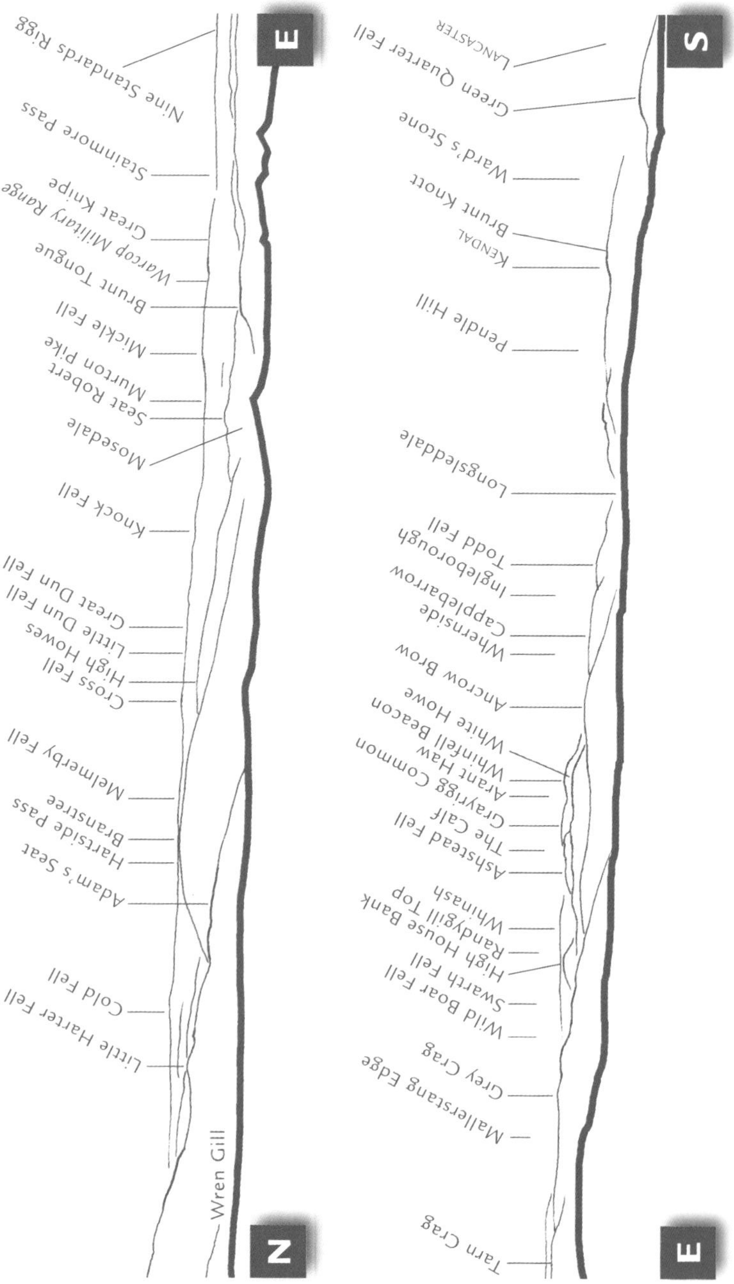

N

Wren Gill
Little Harter Fell
Cold Fell
Adam's Seat
Hartside Pass
Branstree
Melmerby Fell
Cross Fell
High Howes
Little Dun Fell
Great Dun Fell
Knock Fell
Mosedale
Seat Robert
Murton Pike
Mickle Fell
Brunt Tongue
Warcop Military Range
Great Knipe
Stainmore Pass
Nine Standards Rigg

E

E

Tarn Crag
Mallerstang Edge
Grey Crag
Wild Boar Fell
Swarth Fell
High House Bank
Randygill Top
Whinash
Ashstead Fell
The Calf
Grayrigg Common
Arant Haw
Whinfell Beacon
White Howe
Ancrow Brow
Whernside
Capplebarrow
Ingleborough
Todd Fell
Longsleddale
Pendle Hill
KENDAL
Brunt Knott
Ward's Stone
Green Quarter Fell
LANCASTER

S

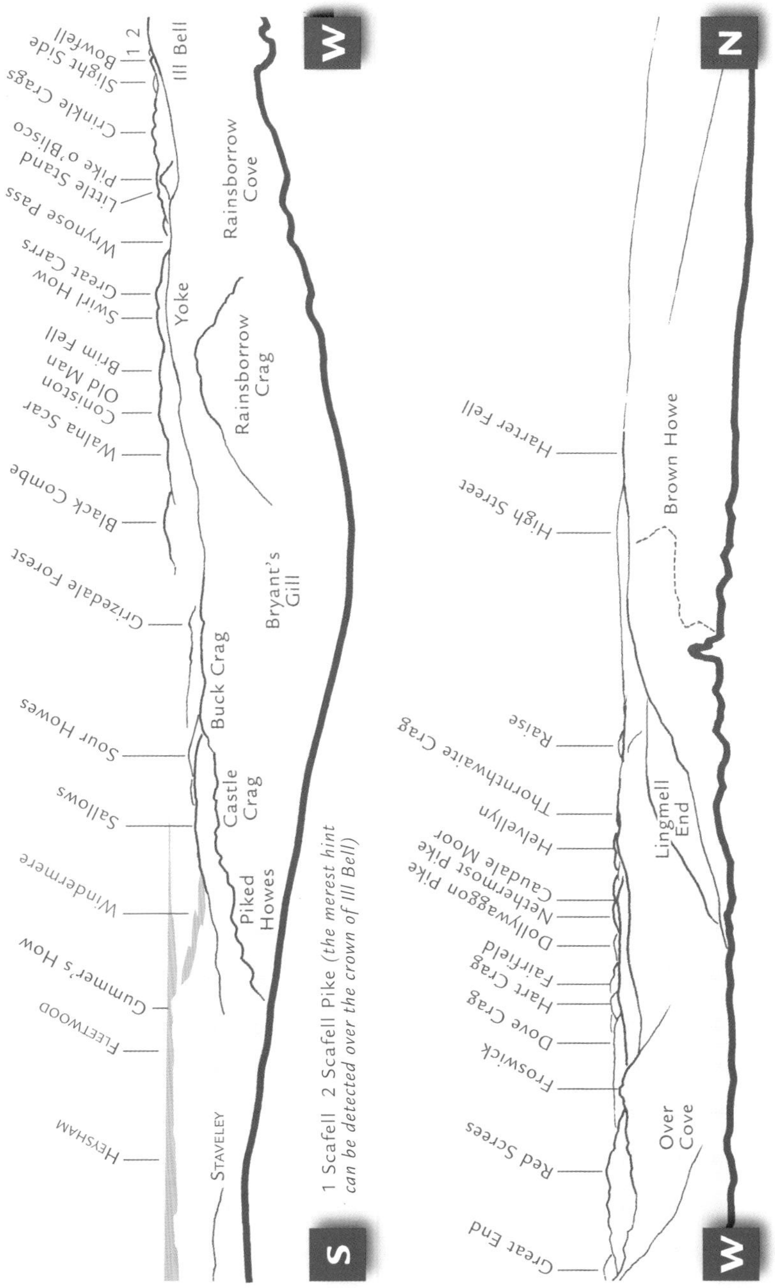
W
S
Ill Bell
1 2
Bowfell
Slight Side
Crinkle Crags
Pike o'Blisco
Little Stand
Wrynose Pass
Great Carrs
Swirl How
Brim Fell
Coniston Old Man
Walna Scar
Black Combe
Grizedale Forest
Sour Howes
Sallows
Windermere
Gummer's How
FLEETWOOD
HEYSHAM
Yoke
Rainsborrow Cove
Rainsborrow Crag
Bryant's Gill
Buck Crag
Castle Crag
Piked Howes
STAVELEY
1 Scafell 2 Scafell Pike (the merest hint can be detected over the crown of Ill Bell)
N
W
Harter Fell
High Street
Brown Howe
Raise
Thornthwaite Crag
Helvellyn
Nethermost Pike
Caudale Moor
Dollywaggon Pike
Fairfield
Hart Crag
Dove Crag
Froswick
Red Screes
Great End
Lingmell End
Over Cove

18 KIDSTY PIKE *(780m/2559ft)*

Easily visible from points east and identified from afar, travellers both on the A6 and even the M6 motorway know the distant peak of Kidsty Pike and seldom miss the opportunity to pick it out and judge the weather by how well it can be seen. The fell name means 'the peak of the steep playground of young goats'. The modern goats are the procession of Coast to Coast walkers who take in the peak. The southern slopes are uniformly steep. Indeed, the way up from Riggindale is a slow haul, especially for burdened trail-walkers engaged in a long westbound trek.

In truth the fell is nothing more than the extended eastern spur ridge of Rampsgill Head. In the sage fellwalker's day, Kidsty Howes was seldom crossed – the path that slices through the crest now has come into being as a direct result of the short-cutting habit of Coast to Coast walkers. Wash-out has caused further damage. The path between the summit and Kidsty Howes has been radically modified in recent years to accommodate the popularity of the route, with the substrate inverted to create an elegant walking trail.

 ↑ Kidsty Pike from the Straits of Riggindale

ASCENT FROM MARDALE HEAD (20)

Via Kidsty Howes 575m/1885ft 4.5km/2¾ miles

1 Go through the kissing-gate and where three paths diverge under the bower of an oak follow the 'Fellside path to Bampton' path, ushered right. This duly crosses Mardale Beck via a footbridge and naturally turns right, running on under the rough

A benchmark – chiselled arrow in stone made by a surveyor – in Randale Beck looking to Branstree

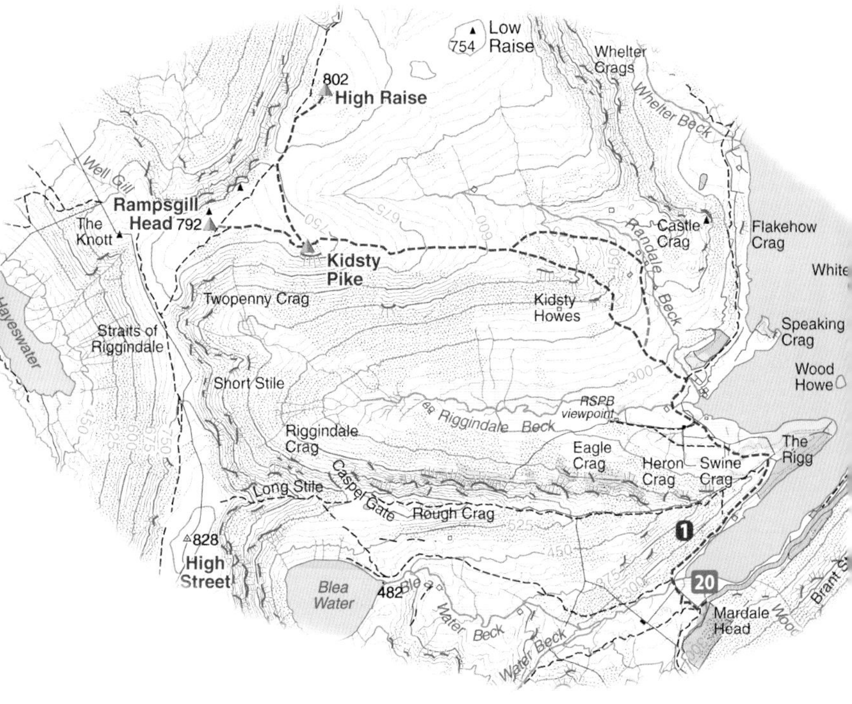

slopes of the Rough Crag ridge to slip over the spur of The Rigg, with its stand of conifers, to angle down into Riggindale. Slipping through a copse the path crosses Bowderthwaite Bridge, and short of the Randale Beck footbridge it takes a turn up the damp slope to embark on the steady climb bound for Kidsty Howes. Bracken has stolen all trace of the old shepherding path that in its day gave an easier line up the Randale Beck valley onto the northern slope of the ridge-end crest. Modern hasty hikers have made a mockery of such subtly appropriate route alignment. The path tackles the ridge; in ascent this is less uncomfortable than in descent. Once on the grassy fell above, join the snaking trail to the top.

THE SUMMIT

There is no doubting the summit – a cairn perched perilously on a small outcrop, from where the profound fall of the fell into Riggindale may take your the breath away, if the climb has not already claimed it! High Street is the centre of attention, but scan the skyline either side of Rampsgill Head to spot the Scafells, Pillar, Helvellyn and Blencathra.

Summit outcrop on Kidsty Pike

SAFE DESCENTS

In winter, when the bracken is down, walkers may sensibly opt to avoid Kidsty Howes where the modern trail ends. Instead drift far more easily into the Randale Beck valley, picking out the trace of the old path, which comes closer to the beck – but keep up in its latter stages, as there is a ravine.

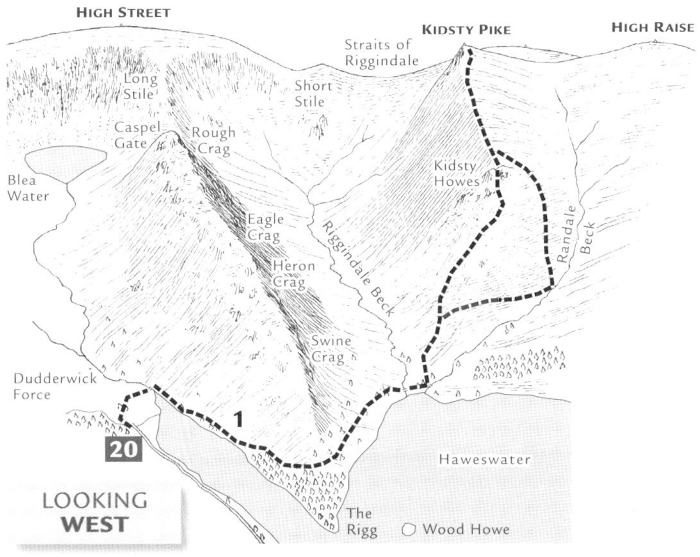

High Street from the summit gully

Kidsty Pike from the Old Corpse Road

RIDGE ROUTES

HIGH RAISE ↓ 25m/80ft ↑ 50m/165ft 0.9km/½ mile

An obvious path curves N across the headwaters of Randale. From the damp depression, where the Roman road is met, continue, rising to veer half-right onto the rocky top.

RAMPSGILL HEAD ↓ 10m/35ft ↑ 25m/80ft 0.5km/¼ mile

Follow the edge path W, and at the highest point break off right to reach the summit cairn within a mere few paces.

PANORAMA

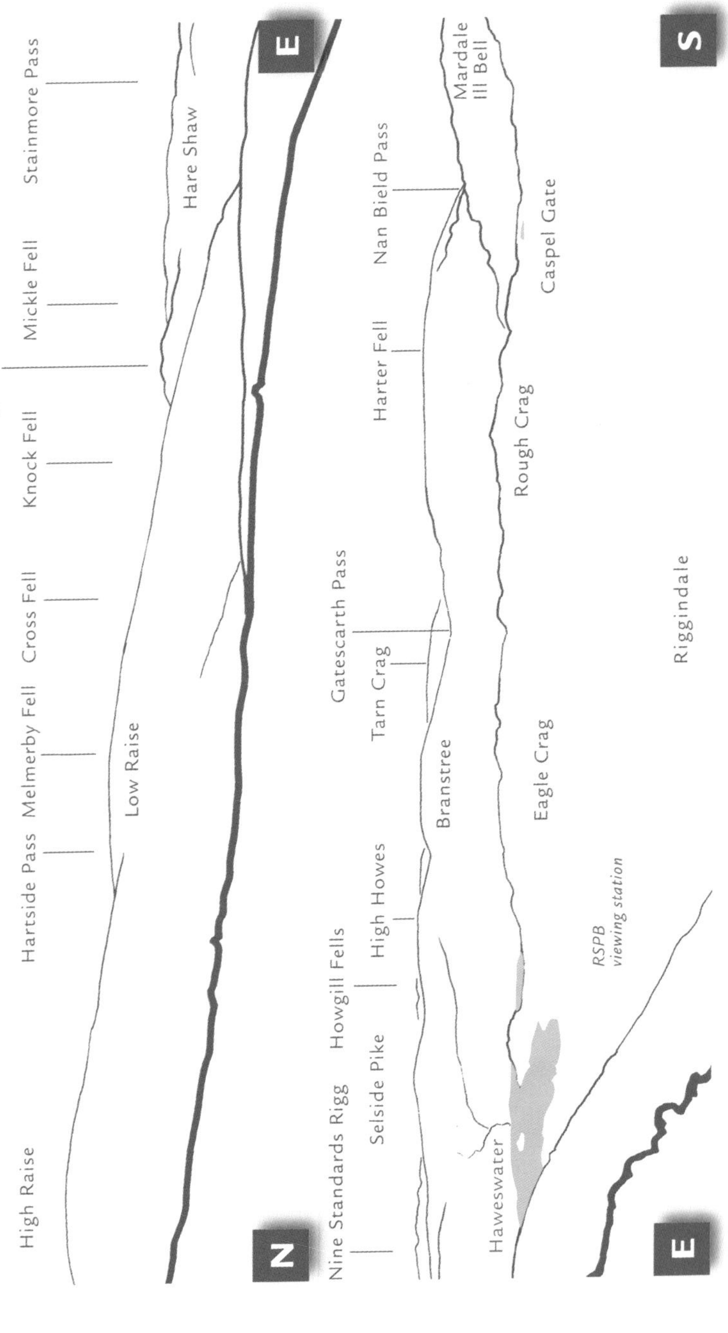

N
E
High Raise
Hartside Pass
Melmerby Fell
Cross Fell
Knock Fell
Hugh's Laithes Pike
Mickle Fell
Stainmore Pass
Low Raise
Hare Shaw
E
S
Nine Standards Rigg
Selside Pike
Howgill Fells
High Howes
Gatescarth Pass
Tarn Crag
Harter Fell
Nan Bield Pass
Mardale Ill Bell
Haweswater
Branstree
Eagle Crag
Rough Crag
Caspel Gate
RSPB viewing station
Riggindale

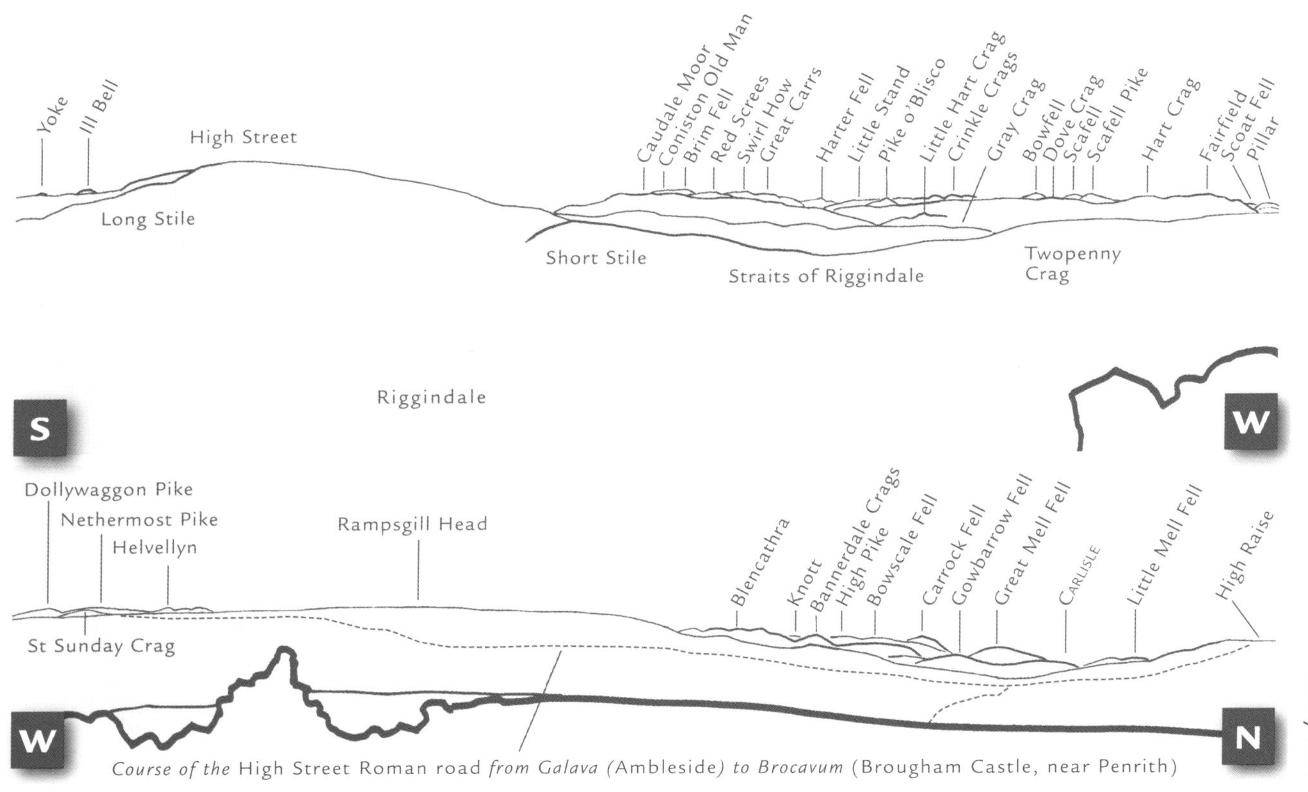
Yoke
Ill Bell
High Street
Long Stile
Caudale Moor
Coniston Old Man
Brim Fell
Red Screes
Swirl How
Great Carrs
Harter Fell
Little Stand
Pike o'Blisco
Little Hart Crag
Crinkle Crags
Gray Crag
Bowfell
Dove Crag
Scafell
Scafell Pike
Hart Crag
Fairfield
Scoat Fell
Pillar
Short Stile
Straits of Riggindale
Twopenny Crag
Riggindale
S
W
Dollywaggon Pike
Nethermost Pike
Helvellyn
Rampsgill Head
St Sunday Crag
Blencathra
Knott
Bannerdale Crags
High Pike
Bowscale Fell
Carrock Fell
Gowbarrow Fell
Great Mell Fell
Carlisle
Little Mell Fell
High Raise
W
N
Course of the High Street Roman road from Galava (Ambleside) to Brocavum (Brougham Castle, near Penrith)

19 LOADPOT HILL *(671m/2201ft)*

Forming the most northerly component of the High Street range, Loadpot has substantial proportions, even if it is a trifle unexciting. While the western slopes fall sharply into Fusedale, to the east and north the fell declines moorland fashion. The name 'Lode pot', first recorded in 1823, described the deep hollow from which it was thought that iron ore had been dug. Situated on the north side of the hill, it is actually identified tautologically as Loadpot Hole. It is now considered to have Roman origins and to have been a source of road-stone for their genuinely 'High Street', which ran close by at this point, avoiding the summit plateau over the scenic western shoulder of the fell. Where the Roman road realigns with the ridge on the south side of the summit plateau once stood Lowther House. The days when this was a shooting cabin are long departed, and only the bare outline remains. The poor herbage of the fell does not suggest it yielded many brace – although the bracing air will always have been abundant!

Looking west from the Roman road

↑ Loadpot Hill from Brock Crag

ASCENT FROM ROEHEAD (11)

Via The Cockpit 475m/1560ft 8.3km/5¼ miles

Lambert Lad

1 At the top of the single-track road from Pooley Bridge find a generous parking verge. Pass through the gate and follow the open track all the way up to the cairn almost on the brow. Bear off right on the firm dry path which leads to The Cockpit stone circle. Keep right with the main path, and shortly after the ford find a small cairn which marks the point of departure from the popular bridleway. Embark on the Roman road, climbing at an easy gradient up Barton Fell. The little top of Arthur's Pike may legitimately tempt you off right from the main path. But otherwise your destiny stretches out ahead, seemingly ever more distant!

Notice the old way comes into a groove, which switches right immediately after the standing stone known as Lambert Lad. The modern variant path avoids the groove, and promptly veers off the Roman way to climb the final slopes of the fell ahead due south. As an intriguing variant you may also drift half-left at this point to inspect Loadpot Hole, with its Roman associations, before completing the ascent over the near brow.

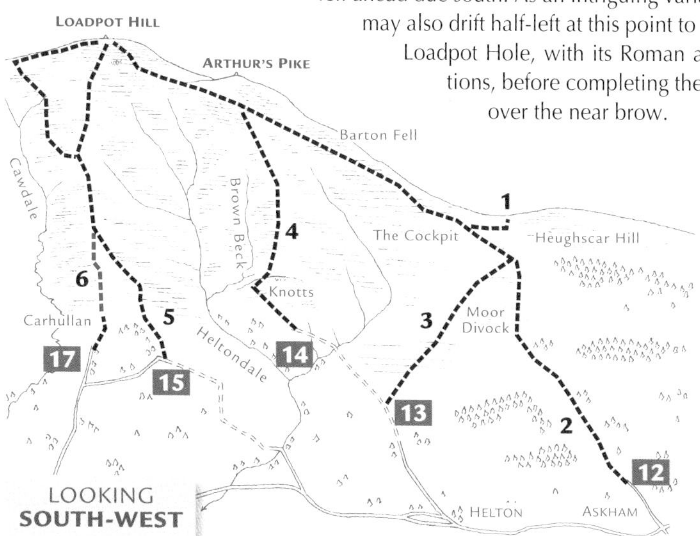

ASCENT FROM ASKHAM (12)

Via The Cockpit 475m/1560ft 8.3km/5¼ miles

2 From the Queen's Head and village store follow the road leading W rising towards a cattle grid. Just here find a car parking space and begin your walk. The tarmac road is forsaken for the bare bedrock limestone track rising by a hipped barn, and then a grassy trail up to a gate. Beyond, gaining access to the open common, keep to the clear turf trail heading W towards the end of the plantation. Just short, divert down half-left with the grass track. Cross the NW–SE trending track at Ketley Gate, a stone being all that is left of the 'gate'. The facing path leads across a tract of decidedly damp moorland to reach the dry oasis of The Cockpit, where this route joins Route 1.

ASCENT FROM HELTON (13)

Via Moor Divock
375m/1230ft 7.2km/4½ miles

Drive S from Askham within the lovely Lowther valley to the equally homogeneous little community of Helton. Turn up through the hamlet onto the fell-road heading SW across the open common bounding Moor Divock. **3** A lovely green turfed trail leads off, passing the enigmatic Cop Stone ('cop' means 'viewpoint'). The trail avoids sink holes and marshy ground until at a cross-ways it departs left, crossing the marshy tract of moor to reach The Cockpit stone circle, yet another reminder of the historic significance of this locality. Here the route links up with Route 1.

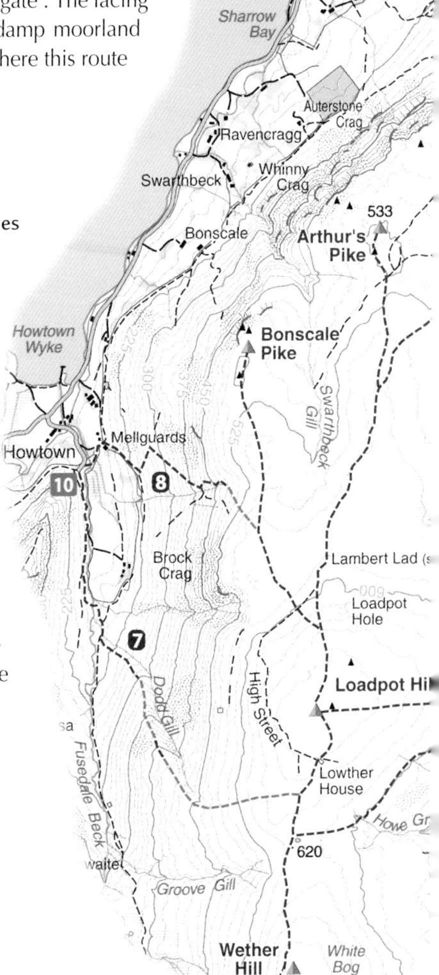

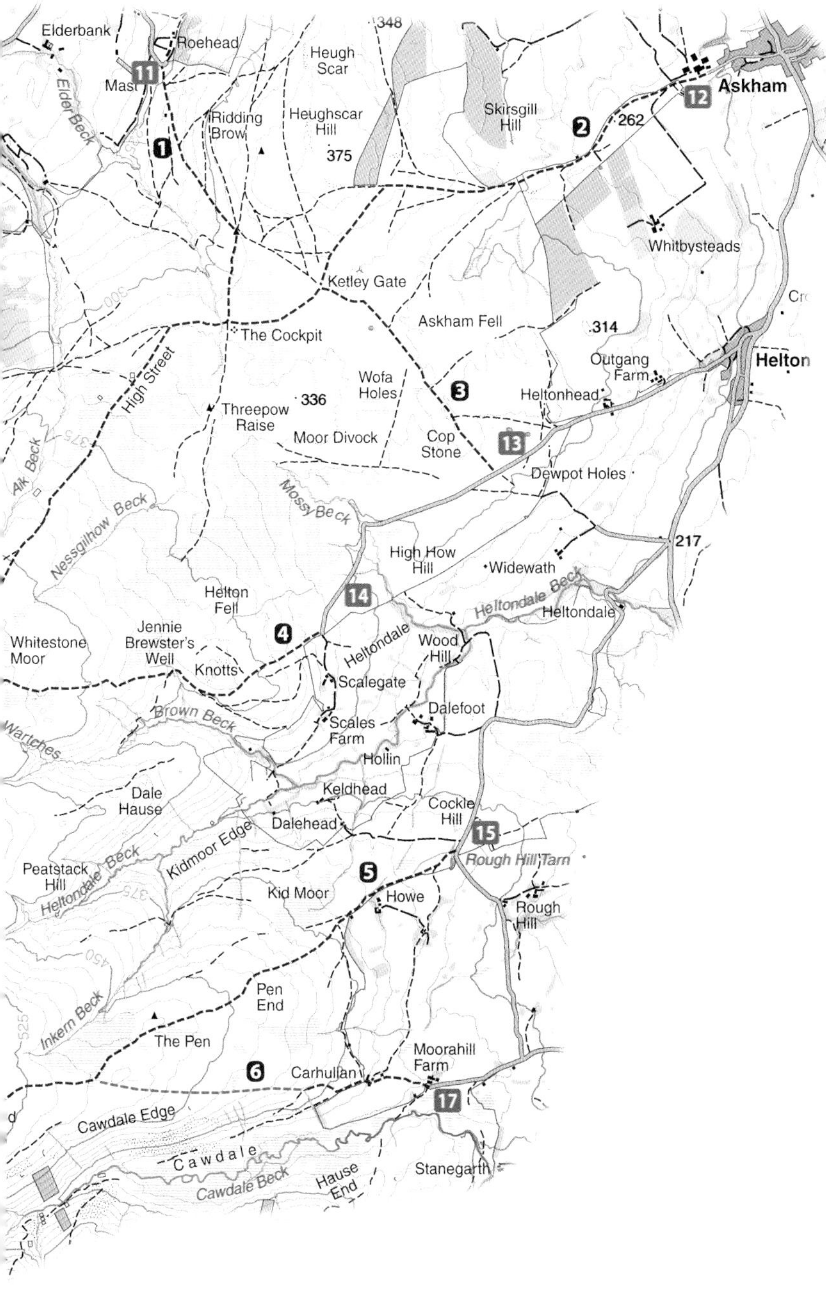
Elderbank
Roehead
348
Heugh Scar
Mast
11
Elder Beck
Ridding Brow
Heughscar Hill
375
Skirsgill Hill
2
262
12
Askham
1
Whitbysteads
Ketley Gate
300
Askham Fell
314
The Cockpit
Outgang Farm
Helton
High Street
Wofa Holes
3
Heltonhead
336
Threepow Raise
Moor Divock
Cop Stone
13
375
Alk Beck
Dewpot Holes
Mossy Beck
Nessgillhow Beck
217
High How Hill
Widewath
14
Heltondale Beck
Helton Fell
Heltondale
Jennie Brewster's Well
4
Whitestone Moor
Heltondale
Wood Hill
Knotts
Scalegate
Brown Beck
Dalefoot
Scales Farm
Wartches
Hollin
Keldhead
Dale Hause
Cockle Hill
Kidmoor Edge
Dalehead
15
Rough Hill Tarn
Peatstack Hill
Heltondale Beck
5
Kid Moor
Howe
Rough Hill
Pen End
Inkern Beck
The Pen
Moorahill Farm
6
Carhullan
17
Cawdale Edge
Cawdale
Cawdale Beck
Hause End
Stanegarth

ASCENT FROM HELTON FELL (14)

Via Knotts 370m/1215ft 5km/3 miles

Car parking space is abundant, but for this approach continue until 200m short of the gate accessing the enclosures leading to Scalegate and Scales Farm ('no through road' daubed on stone and private letter box). **4** The walk begins marshy underfoot by following the wall up, and as this bears left continue SW, crossing over the low saddle of Knotts to run on right with a worn track to a ford – bearing the lovely name of Jennie Brewster's Well. The regular passage of a shepherding quad bike ensures the old path is well marked as it heads up the grassy fell westward to unite with the High Street Roman road path (Route 1) on Whitestone Moor.

ASCENT FROM COCKLE HILL (15)

Via The Pen 355m/1165ft 4.3km/2¾ miles

5 From the verge parking follow the left-hand track as to Howe, passing on from the pool of Rough Hill Tarn. As the track turns in left keep up by the wall, and after a stone barn and tree shelter embark on the quad-track path up through the rushes, climbing steadily SW onto The Pen. The solitary cairn lies off the line of the regular path. The regular path copes with the odd damp patch in reaching the bield wall. The more regular way now bears up the fell W to reach the summit.

All that remains of the Lowther House shooting cabin

ASCENT FROM MOORAHILL (17)

Via Carhullan 360m/1180ft 5km/3 miles

'Carhullan' intrigues etymologists, who find it hard to unravel the origins of the farm name; equally tough is the storyline of Sarah Hall's fictional treatise *The Carhullan Army*. **6** Follow the walled lane from the gate and pass to the left of Carhullan farmhouse along a confined lane between barn walls. The track at bedrock steps up to reach a gate. Follow on with the wall left, but break up right onto the fellside, avoiding the bracken as best you can. The hint of an old path is quickly lost as a westward course is kept on an easy gradient. Follow this course duly to unite with the strong path from The Pen, which rises to pass beneath a bield wall. As a variant to the common walkers' way, bear off half-left after some 20m with the line of rushes defining an old drove-path on a SW line. This route ventures to the head of Cawdale and the pool in the saddle between Wether and Loadpot Hills. At this point switch N with the regular ridge path, passing up by the frugal remnants of Lowther House.

ASCENT FROM FUSEDALE (10)

Via Dodd Gill 500m/1640ft 3.2km/2 miles

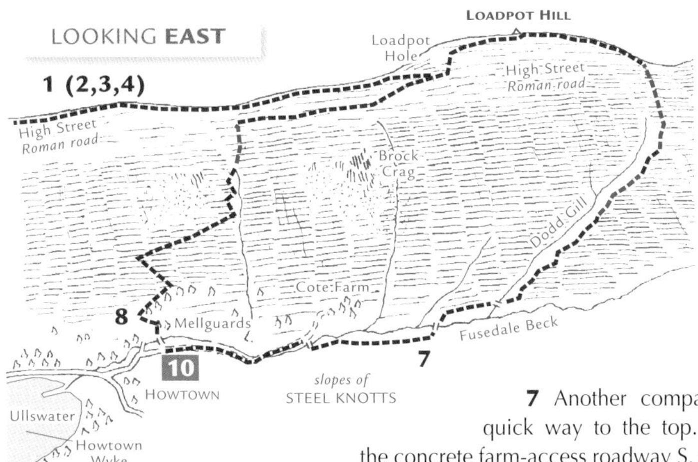

7 Another comparatively quick way to the top. Follow the concrete farm-access roadway S. Coming to a cattle grid bear right with the footpath over the stone-flag bridge and run on above the beck, coming down to recross Fusedale Beck by a wooden footbridge. Bear right and cross the plank-bridge spanning Dodd Gill. Now embark on the climb left; there is an intermittent path higher up coping with some stony ground. Coming above the gill, cross the lateral line of a strong sheep path and continue pathless to the join the ridge path in the intervening ground between the saddle and Lowther House. Turn left and pass up by the

Loadpot Hole, a source of Roman road-stone

ruin, being sure to keep to the northward ridge path to gain the summit plateau. The Roman way veers left at Lowther House – a fine promenade, but for all the quality of the view west over the Martindale fells, this is an unnecessary distraction for anyone intent on the summit. However, should you be prepared to vary your ultimate approach you will find this a lovely addition to the journey; cut back onto the plateau as the Roman way begins to decline off the shelf.

Via Mellguards 500m/1640ft 2.6km/1½ miles

The fell may appear distant from all valley stations, but this is a quick way to the top without question. Mind you, the steepness of the primary slope does mean it may be a 'slow' quick! Park beyond the cattle grid on the Cote Farm access road from Howtown Hotel entering Fusedale. **8** From the four-way signpost leave the open road at once to cross the clapper-bridge spanning Fusedale Beck and rise within the walled lane to a gate entering the gravel drive to Mellguards, the prominent white house. Go through the gate by the house door and at once bear up right following the intake wall; continue a short distance beyond where this angles right. Veer left in a rising groove leading onto a shoulder, and here find an old drove-path steering up right. This climbs above the gill and is lost as a path on the grassy rise to the plateau. Join the ridge-top path heading SSE and cross the Roman road to join the main path onto the summit plateau.

THE SUMMIT

The pasture plateau is focused upon an Ordnance Survey triangulation column. A small cairn lies 30m off the line of the regular flow of ridge walkers, to the east, composed of a handful of stones – some pure quartz – clustered around a Lowther/Dalemain estate boundary stone, possibly carried there following trophy finds in Loadpot Hole. The summit is not the best place to consider a view, there being no depth in any direction. The Helvellyn range has primacy, permitting just one glimpse beyond south-west to Coniston Old Man. To the north-west Skiddaw, Blencathra and company are unimpeded. The eastern horizon is every bit as full of detail towards the high Pennine chain, but too distant to fascinate for long.

SAFE DESCENTS

Distance is more the issue than craggy hazard. Join the Roman road N heading down to Moor Divock for Pooley Bridge, Askham or Helton. Head E for Bampton via Carhullan. However, the quickest route to a valley road at Howtown is W, but be mindful that the slopes running into Fusedale are very steep.

RIDGE ROUTES

ARTHUR'S PIKE ↓ 160m/525ft ↑ 15m/50ft 2.7km/1¾ miles

Head N with the regular ridge path, descending to join the Roman road. After a little over 1.6km (1 mile) bear off, in effect keeping N direct to the summit.

BONSCALE PIKE ↓ 165m/540ft ↑ 20m/65ft 2km/1¼ miles

Start N, but at the first fork veer NW on a path that crosses the Roman road and follows on down onto the broad undulating ridge. Make a point of visiting the pair of beacon cairns known as Bonscale Tower, close under the summit cairn, to revel in a fine view of Ullswater.

WETHER HILL ↓ 55m/180ft ↑ 53m/175ft 1.4km/¾ mile

Keep S with the evident ridge path. This passes down by the site of Lowther House to a depression with its glistening pool, then mounts the easy-angled peaty slope to the summit cairn.

PANORAMA

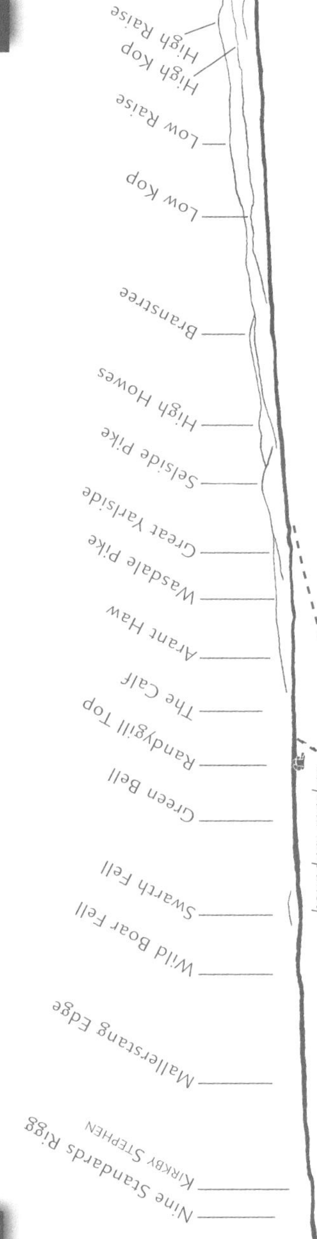
N
Christianbury Crags
Gillalees Beacon
Cardunneth Pike
Cold Fell
Croglin Fell
Renwick Fell
Hartside Pass
Melmerby Fell
Cross Fell
Little Dun Fell
Great Dun Fell
Knock Fell
Knock Pike
Dufton Pike
High Cup Nick
Murton Pike
Roman Fell
Mickle Fell
Warcop Military Range
Stainmore Pass
E
E
Nine Standards Rigg
Kirkby Stephen
Mallerstang Edge
Wild Boar Fell
Swarth Fell
boundary marker
Green Bell
Randygill Top
The Calf
ridge path to Wether Hill
Arant Haw
Wasdale Pike
Great Yarlside
Selside Pike
High Howes
Branstree
Low Kop
Low Raise
High Kop
High Raise
S

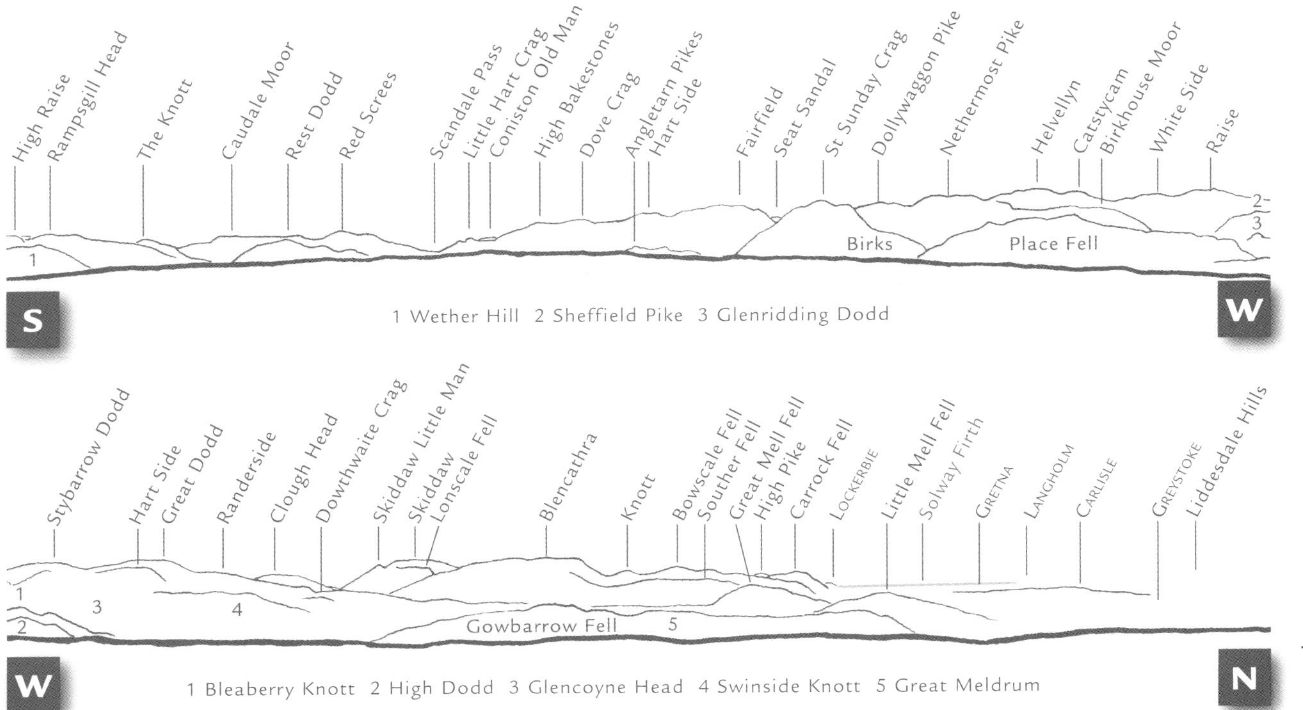

1 Wether Hill 2 Sheffield Pike 3 Glenridding Dodd

1 Bleaberry Knott 2 High Dodd 3 Glencoyne Head 4 Swinside Knott 5 Great Meldrum

20 MARDALE ILL BELL *(761m/2497ft)*

Lingmell End from Kentmere Reservoir dam

Mardale Ill Bell extends south-east from the mass of High Street, its northern slope defended by dark crags that hold snow and ice in winter. It has a stubby north-eastern ridge, also defended by crags partitioning the impressive corrie basins that contain two jewel tarns, known as the Mardale Waters – Blea and Small Water. To the south Lingmell End, a steep, less craggy arm, with no trace of the heather implied in the name, projects into the upper Kentmere valley. Off to the east of this ridge further crags flank the high connection with Harter Fell, over which an ancient pedestrian passage threads north to south, the Nan Bield Pass. The northern ascents are the best, but the long march from the south via Nan Bield provides a useful means of halving the Kentmere horseshoe, while the stiff climb from Kentmere Reservoir up Lingmell End will appeal to an intrepid minority. Little about the fell's profile can be considered bell shaped, but 'ill' suggests that it was considered Mardale's treacherous height, for whatever reason. Perhaps as the dales folk of Mardale adapted the name Branstree from High Street, so they borrowed again from Kentmere's eye-catching fell.

 ↑ Mardale Ill Bell from Selside Pike

ASCENT FROM MARDALE HEAD (20)

Via Nan Bield Pass 510m/1675ft 3.4km/2 miles

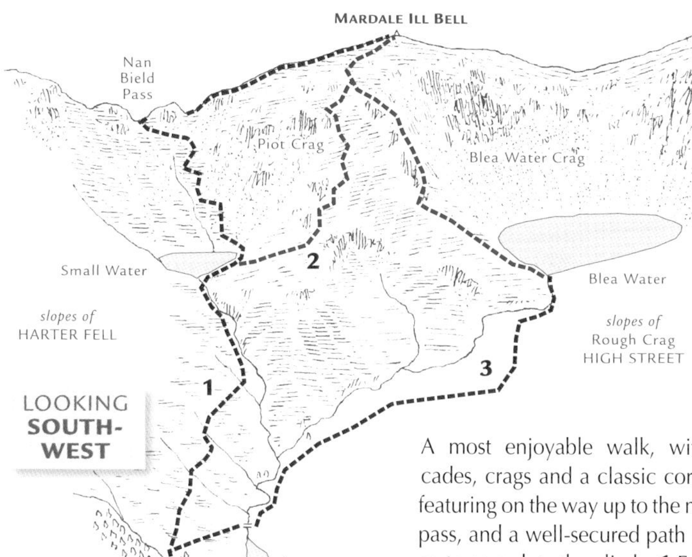

A most enjoyable walk, with cascades, crags and a classic corrie tarn featuring on the way up to the notched pass, and a well-secured path leading on to complete the climb. **1** From the car park where the Haweswater road terminates go through the kissing-gate and rise to the wall-corner where three paths diverge. Take the middle route, signed 'Public bridleway Nan Bield Pass Kentmere'. The heavily trod path leads up through the moraine, via successive gates, to come close to a sequence of beautiful cascades in the gill issuing from Small Water.

Cross at the outflow and swing round the west side of the tarn, coming by a trio of stone shelters. These pre-date the era of recreational walking and show how serious the inter-dale traverse could be in former centuries. The path has received essential pitching repair all the way to Nan Bield Pass, where the walled alcove forms a partial block to southerly draughts in this tight notch in the ridge. Bear right, rounding a splintered headland and stepping upon further big boulder pitching on the final easy clamber that leads onto easier ground and to the summit.

Small Water stone shelters

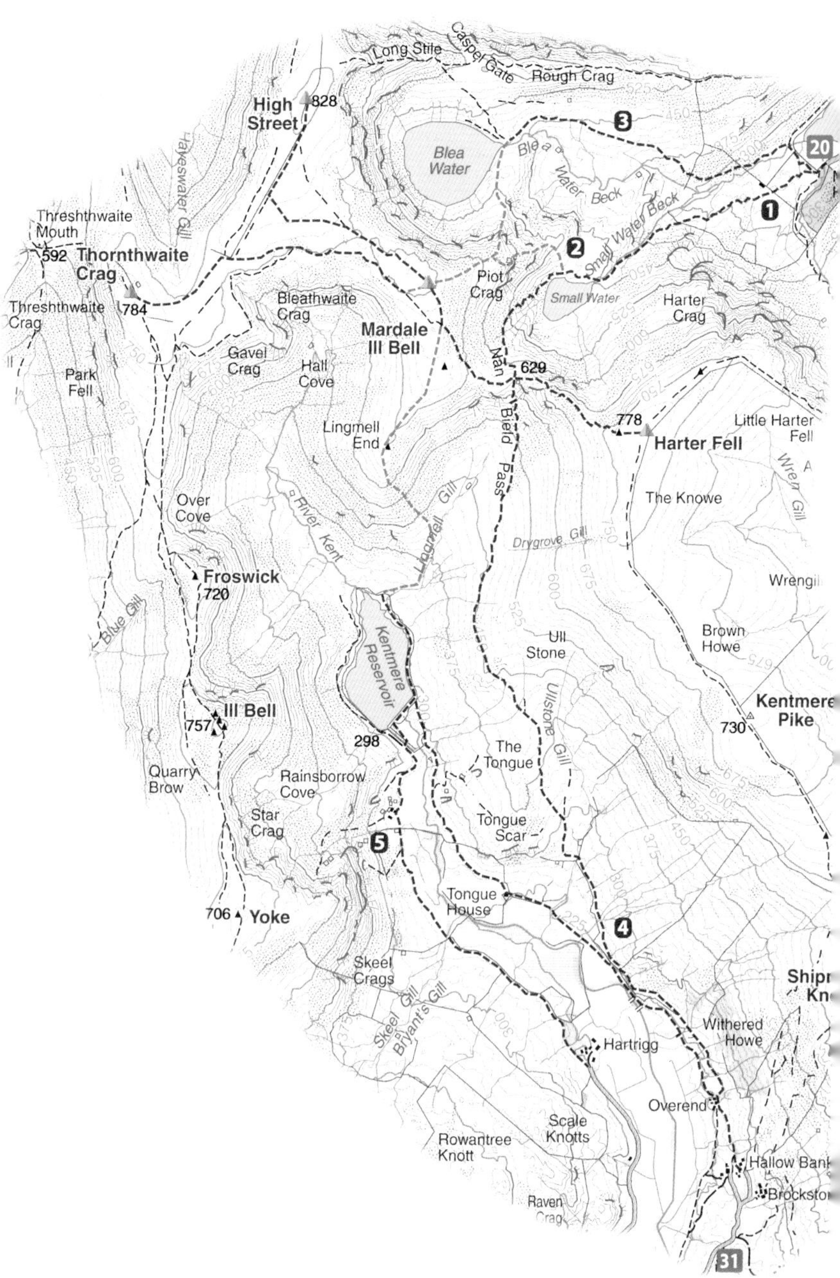
Long Stile
Caspel Gate
Rough Crag
High Street
828
Blea Water
Blea Water Beck
Small Water Beck
Threshthwaite Mouth
592
Thornthwaite Crag
784
Threshthwaite Crag
Bleathwaite Crag
Mardale Ill Bell
Piot Crag
Small Water
Harter Crag
Gavel Crag
Hall Cove
Park Fell
629
Nan Bield Pass
778
Harter Fell
Little Harter Fell
Lingmell End
The Knowe
Wren Gill
Over Cove
River Kent
Lingmell Gill
Drygrove Gill
Froswick
720
Wrengill
Blue Gill
Kentmere Reservoir
Ull Stone
Brown Howe
Ill Bell
757
Kentmere Pike
730
298
Ullstone Gill
The Tongue
Quarry Brow
Rainsborrow Cove
Star Crag
Tongue Scar
Tongue House
706
Yoke
Skeel Crags
Skeel Gill
Bryant's Gill
Hartrigg
Withered Howe
Overend
Scale Knotts
Rowantree Knott
Hallow Bank
Brockstone
Raven Crag
20
31

High Street from above Bleawater Crag

Via east ridge 500m/1640ft 2.6km/1½ miles

2 Break from Route 1 just short of the Small Water shelters, climbing the increasingly steep grass slope to the right of Piot Crag ('magpie cliff'). Above this, discover a tiny slate quarry, with the remnants of hut walls. It's an amazing situation, and hauling the prized stone down must have been a Herculean task. The grassy ridge above eases onto the summit.

Via the north ridge 520m/1705ft 3.2km/2 miles

Dudderwick Force

3 The east and north ridges converge well below the summit. To sample the individual pleasure of the latter requires an altogether different start. From the three-way sign (see Route 1) bear right and cross the Mardale Beck footbridge. Then turn left and follow the path that leads up by a gate, passing above the impressive tree-shaded Dudderwick Force to a further gate. Traipse up the sometimes damp moor well above Blea Water Beck, your destination the outflow of Blea Water. Blea Water entirely fills the basin below the imposing walls of Mardale Ill Bell and High Street. Ford the boulders beside the concrete dam and follow the grassy moraine ridge up to the rock arête. A minor rock-step gains your foothold onto the ridge – surprisingly, what appeared daunting from below on close acquaintance proves moderate; you can make it a rock scramble or hold to grassy steps. Higher up the view over Blea Water to the craggy face of High Street, flanked to the left by the shielding buttress of Bleawater Crag, directly below the summit of Mardale Ill Bell, is tremendous.

ASCENT FROM HALLOW BANK (31)

Via Nan Bield Pass 605m/1985ft 6.3km/4 miles

4 There are two starting points. The first is the shallow parking bay where Nunnery Beck slips by the road immediately north of Green Quarter on the single-track road to Hallow Bank. Walk up the road to find the old bridleway signed 'Nan Bield'. This is Low Lane and gives a lovely lower-dale approach to Overend by a series of gates. Alternatively, many walkers opt to start from the larger lay-by in High Lane, after the road-gate and before the Stile End bridle track. In this instance follow either the road or bridleway through the hamlet of Hallow Bank, coming down the gated roadway to

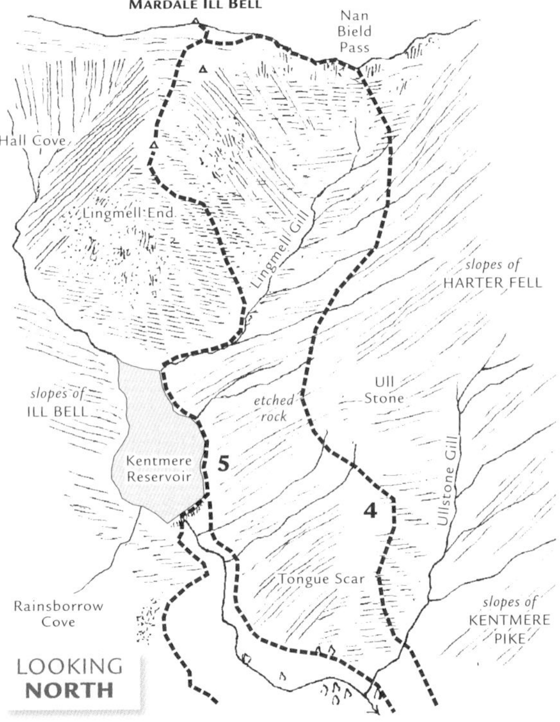

Old Mardale waymarker at Overend

Overend. Beside the white-washed farmhouse diverge right, guided by the old slate sign 'To Mardale'.

The bridleway leads by gates to a footbridge spanning Ullstone Gill and, after the gate, curves up the bank onto the ridge of the Tongue, easily beating back the dense bracken. Keen eyes will spot an engraved bedrock underfoot before the path steps up on Smallthwaite Knott and contours well above Kentmere Reservoir, eventually tackling the acute hairpins to reach the notch of Nan Bield. From the wind-break bear up left, curving round a rocky headland then upon large-boulder pitching onto the crown of the fell.

ASCENT FROM KENTMERE (29 – off map S) OR HALLOW BANK (31)

Via Lingmell End 610m/2000ft 7.3km/4½ miles

5 There are two early valley approaches. From the vicinity of St Cuthbert's parish church in Kentmere village (limited parking), by either the road or via green lanes, venture onto the private road to Hartrigg and follow on with the gated track towards Kentmere Reservoir, coming under Rainsborrow Crag and the slate quarries. Short of the dam cross the footbridge right over the overflow channel and veer left to come onto the dam, trending right. The same spot can be reached from Hallow Bank by the gated dale-floor footpath, via Overend and Tongue House (barn). From the barn advance to a ladder-stile to reach an area of slate spoil where once a quarrymen's bridge spanned the deeply etched dale beck. Beyond, contour the banks to the dam, joining up with the previous start to the route. Follow on with the ditch bank on the

Summit cairn on top of the outcrop

east side of the reservoir. Where Lingmell Gill enters, step over the wall and ford the gill. Ascend with the gill until a clear line can be detected up the steep fellside of Lingmell End. Much of this huge spur ridge is rotten scree and broken outcropping, excepting its south-eastern corner slope, which offers a grassy line. The climb calls for a grim resolution, ultimately coming to a cairn and taking a well-earned breather, with a fabulous view of Ill Bell the rich reward. The ridge north is open pasture, encouraging free-flowing strides to the summit. Walkers are likely to wonder how long ago the heather (ling) was lost from the now plain grass herbage.

THE SUMMIT

A tumbled cairn rests upon the lava shards of a mini Giant's Causeway outcrop. The view is not exactly something to write home about, but the best views are to be found from the edges, notably the northern brink upon Blea Water. It is enjoyable to spot the tantalising tops of Bowfell, Scafell and Scafell Pike just breaking the skyline immediately south of Thornthwaite Crag's beacon.

SAFE DESCENTS

The straightforward recourse is SE then E to Nan Bield Pass, from where Mardale Head (N) and Kentmere (S) are reached upon an actively used footpath.

RIDGE ROUTES

HARTER FELL ↓ 145m/475ft ↑ 130m/425ft 1.7km/1 mile

Follow the ridge path S then E – this has been given boulder pitching in places. Come down to the tight pass with its walled bield (wind break and seat). Continue E by several stepped stages onto the plateau. A brink cairn directs to the primary summit cairn short of the ridge fence.

HIGH STREET ↓ 80m/260ft ↑ 15m/50ft 1.7km/1 mile

Travel easily W, and from the shallow dip pick up a new trail created by inverting the substrate. This snakes up and across the grassy prairie, off the line of desire, and in so doing delays the turn up to the ridge wall leading to the summit.

THORNTHWAITE CRAG ↓ 60m/195ft ↑ 40m/130ft 1.8km/1 mile

Leave the summit SW to join the strong path that runs along the edge high above Hall Cove. Where this forks, keep W to pass the wall-end and join the Roman road heading SW to the beacon cairn.

Nan Bield Pass

PANORAMA

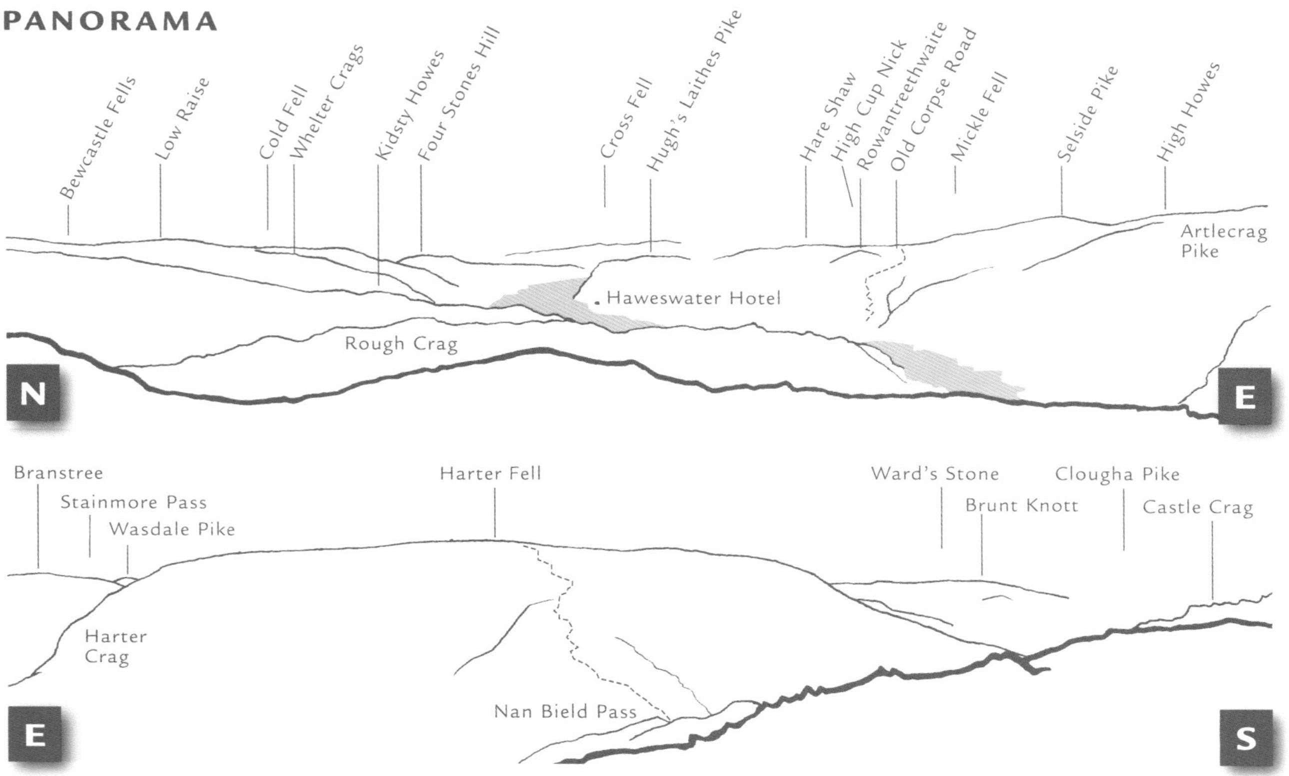
Bewcastle Fells
Low Raise
Cold Fell
Whelter Crags
Kidsty Howes
Four Stones Hill
Cross Fell
Hugh's Laithes Pike
Hare Shaw
High Cup Nick
Rowantreethwaite
Old Corpse Road
Mickle Fell
Selside Pike
High Howes
Artlecrag Pike
Haweswater Hotel
Rough Crag
N
E
Branstree
Stainmore Pass
Wasdale Pike
Harter Fell
Ward's Stone
Brunt Knott
Clougha Pike
Castle Crag
Harter Crag
Nan Bield Pass
E
S

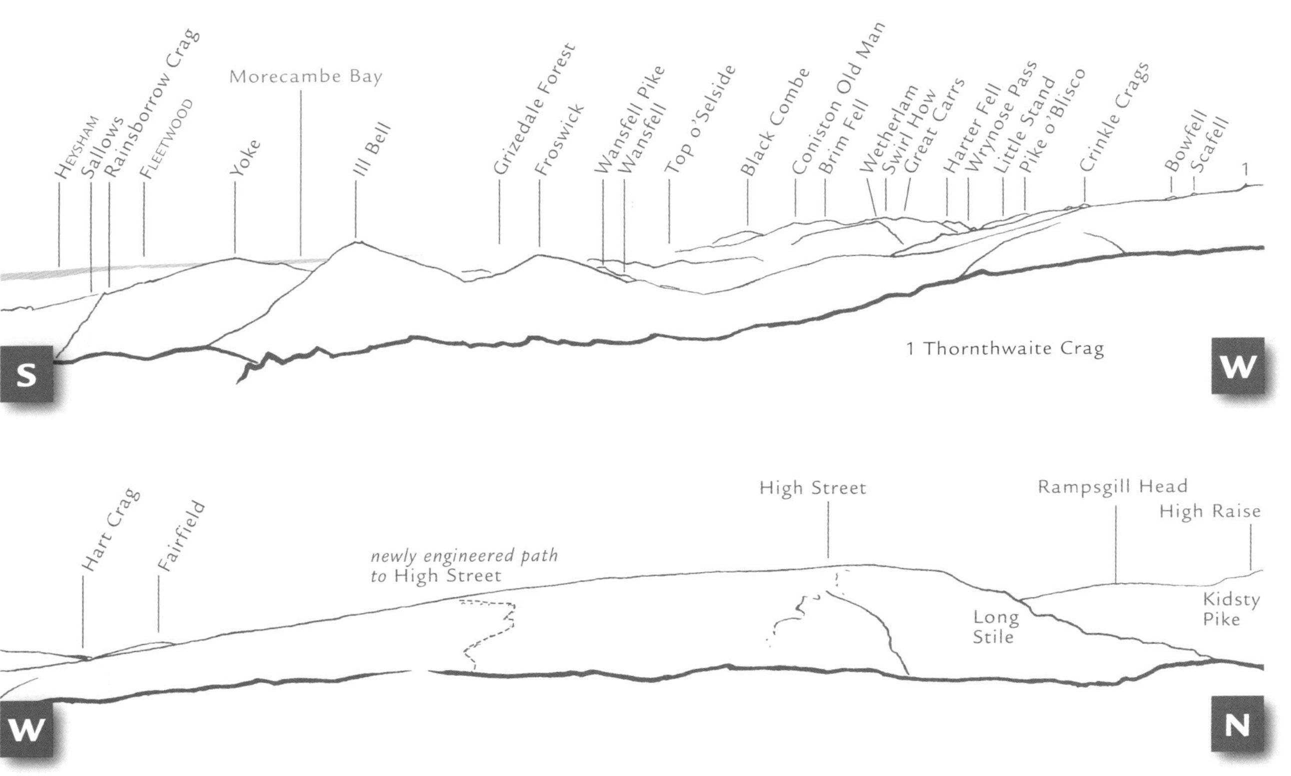
HEYSHAM
Sallows
Rainsborrow Crag
FLEETWOOD
Yoke
Morecambe Bay
Ill Bell
Grizedale Forest
Froswick
Wansfell Pike
Wansfell
Top o'Selside
Black Combe
Coniston Old Man
Brim Fell
Wetherlam
Swirl How
Great Carrs
Harter Fell
Wrynose Pass
Little Stand
Pike o'Blisco
Crinkle Crags
Bowfell
Scafell
1
S
1 Thornthwaite Crag
W
Hart Crag
Fairfield
newly engineered path to High Street
High Street
Rampsgill Head
High Raise
Long Stile
Kidsty Pike
W
N

21 PLACE FELL *(657m/2155ft)*

OS column on Place Fell summit

Mountains are comprehended as much by the eyes as by their measured scale, and Place Fell has all the individuality and proportionate qualities that make it a magnet to fellwalkers. Casual travellers view it with admiration from across Ullswater – its broad, shaggy, craggy, variegated slopes beautifully reflected in the lake. There is a convincing sense of spaciousness abroad ('spacious' being the probable original meaning of the fell name, first recorded as 'Plessefeld' in 1256). The main mass of the fell, defined by secretive Boredale, forms a bulwark to a fabulous summit crest, its crowning glory. Yet the more casual visitor may give pride of place to its shoreline path undulating through the trees from Sandwick to Patterdale by Silver Bay – invariably enjoyed in happy combination with a steamer cruise from/to the jetty at Howtown Wyke. Most walkers tackle the fell in isolation from the rest of the fell group in a short-day anti-clockwise circuit from Patterdale, climbing via Boredale Hause and descending via Low Moss into the Scalehow Beck valley. Yet, as you may guess, there are several great little adventures elsewhere, for instance by Sleet Fell, by Kilbert How and by Hare Shaw or Mortar Crag and The Knight.

 ↑ Place Fell from the Brotherswater Inn

ASCENT FROM PATTERDALE (5)

Via Boredale Hause 500m/1640ft 3km/2 miles

1 Pass through the narrows between the village shop and the White Lion upon the footway and turn left with the cul-de-sac road via Goldrill Bridge. Coming by cottages the road swings up left and comes to a gate, with a slate sign directing right through an adjacent gate for 'Boredale Hause'. The path duly turns right up the fellside

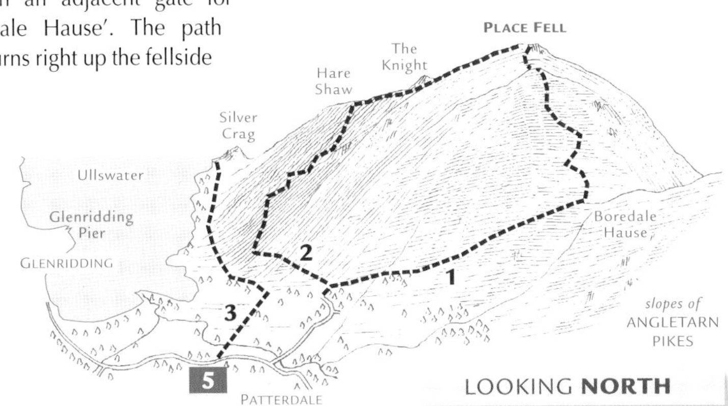

– indeed there are two groove paths rising one above the other with a similar goal, although the upper path is the one to take. The outlook is such that walkers will have many a cause to pause and admire the Patterdale vale. Come up to the small ruin, marked on maps 'Chapel in the Hause' – perhaps once a bad weather sanctuary. The popular path bears left from the broad saddle of Boredale Hause, now furnished with a modern trail winding up the southern slope onto the knoll of Round How, from where the slope eases, drawing walkers excitedly on to climb the final rock ridge.

The Knight backed by Helvellyn

Ice-smoothed bedrock on the shore path

Via Hare Shaw 525m/1720ft 3.5km/2¼ miles

2 Often followed in descent after climbing the fell from Boredale Hause, this route also provides a splendid little expedition working up through the juniper to gain The Knight. There are two lines of start, either via the track to Side Farm, from where the route turns left then quickly right to join the lateral bridle path; or join this earlier by crossing Goldrill Bridge in common with Route 1, but turn left to trace the green trail N. The lateral bridle-droveway is a lovely stroll. Where this comes onto a roche moutonnée rib veer up half-right, and the early green trail becomes more a stony trod, climbing through the

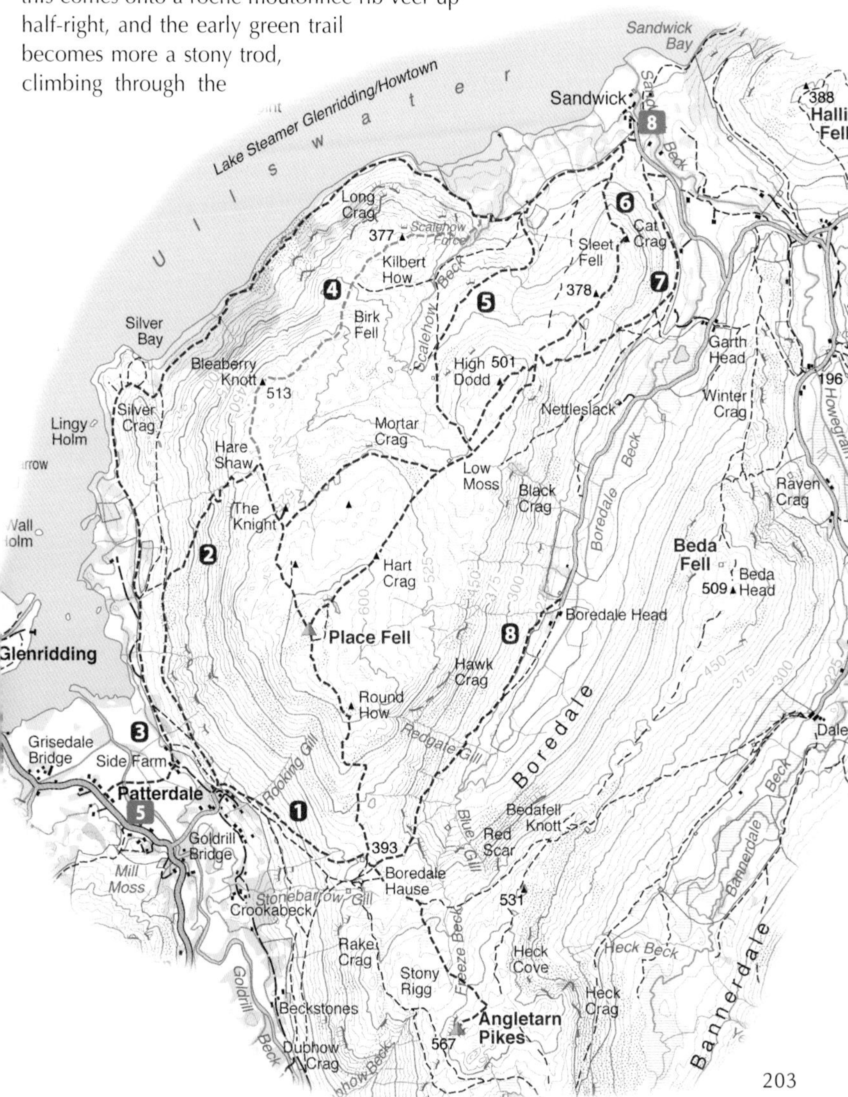

juniper thicket. Mounting ambition is matched by the growing scenic splendour, giving every excuse to stop from time to time to enjoy the 'over the shoulder' view. Gaining the brow at Hare Shaw the path switches right (SE) rising up the groove beside The Knight, its boiler-plated slopes a shining armour. This subsidiary peak demands a visit – walkers may clamber up the northern arête or stroll easily from the south off the regular path to the cairn, a minor triumph to enjoy. The route persists, passing a second laterally sited cairn en route to the summit.

Ullswater path – Patterdale to Sandwick 290m/950ft 6.5km/4 miles

3 Not an ascent per se, but the popular return to – or springboard from – Patterdale. It is normally enjoyed for its own sake as a sylvan stroll, with walkers giving total attention to the relationship of mountain and lake. Navigation is of the falling 'off the log' kind, and does not need spelling out. However, it is far more strenuous than might be expected, and there are sections where slippery rock and tree roots can greatly hamper your confident stride. There are lower and higher path options to Silver Bay. The more elevated inevitably has the better views well above the trees, and includes a mini 'pass' beside the Silver Crag headland, where a pool is passed and steps lead down by dense juniper to connect with the lower path.

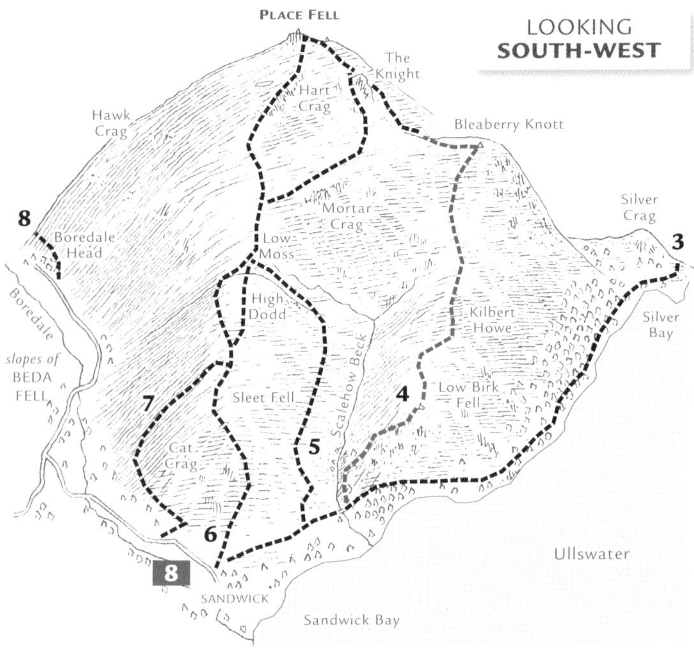

ASCENT FROM SANDWICK (8)

Via Birk Fell 525m/1720ft 4.3km/2¾ miles

The mantle of bracken leading onto Birk Fell should be no deterrent to accessing an exquisite fell-top – an unfrequented wild ridge-top domain, from which walkers may revel in a magnificent westward outlook towards the Helvellyn range.

4 From the ford keep with the regular path, which descends to cross a wooden footbridge over Scalehow Beck. Stay with the regular path as it zigs right and continues up beside the wall. However, before it reaches the top, break away left into the bracken and accompany a sheep trod that rises in harmony with the ravine, gaining splendid views of Scalehow Force, although summer verdance restricts the full glory. That summer growth, when reflected in the bracken, makes this a less than pleasant tussle. In mid-Victorian times the owner of the house, presently the home of Ullswater Outward Bound, sought to create a picturesque view across the lake, duly 'enhancing' the cascades with a few sticks of dynamite! On coming level with the great slab bear up right, weaving through the outcropping. Matters improve as the ridge proper is joined, leading to the prominent cairn on Low Birk Fell. The landmark wall-cairn appears untouched by time since it was first set up, which says a lot about the frequency of walking visitors.

A ridge-top path of sheep-path proportions leads SW over the bracken hollows and knobbles of Kilbert How. The ridge makes a big step up via the headland of

Rock headland below Kilbert How

Smeathwaite ('small clearing'), the path, created more by the odd descending walker, heading up the southern slope to come onto the ridge proper. The cairn indicated on OS maps no longer exists. A second prominent rise in the ridge off-set right, Bleaberry Knott, has a cairn and a wonderful view to boot. A small rock-step leads down to the marshy plateau of Bottom Heads – a great name! Pass a small slate working to join forces with Route 2 at Hare Shaw.

Via Scalehow Beck 490m/1610ft 3.8km/2½ miles

5 Leave the open road above the hamlet of Sandwick, signposted 'Patterdale'. Accompany the wall-side path, with its steady flow of happy family walkers, the majority intent on the enchantingly beautiful lakeside path between Howtown and Patterdale, invariably combined with a cruise on the steamer. Passing a bank-barn, ford the gill, and at once bear up half-left onto a turf drove-way. This has two options – that closer to the beck takes the greater foot-traffic, while the more pleasant underfoot keeps up to the top of the adjacent enclosure and climbs over High Knott, gliding up the valley until the two paths unite short of the old slate quarry. The route then continues to Low Moss and the large sheepfold, and joins the regular ridge route climbing SW over Hart Crag.

Via High Dodd and The Knight 520m/1705ft 4km/2½ miles

6 Leave the road above Townhead with the Patterdale path. At the top of the very first rise bear off half-left, climbing to pass a metal seat, and continue to keep company with the path climbing the ridge. Passing a scenically sited ridge-end cairn, cross over the old wall and hold to the spine of the ridge, passing a further cairned top to meet up with the path climbing the Boredale slope (Route 7). While some may keep with the prominent lateral path avoiding High Dodd, those with energy aplenty might prefer to take on the intermediate height by veering off and climbing the north-east slope on a thin path to reach the summit cairn (with evidence of minor slate extraction). The grassy path eases SW down to Low Moss to pass the sheepfold. Beyond, again, you may stick with the common way via Hart Crag, but a more exploratory option bears off right beyond the fold within a grassy groove that mounts W above Mortar Crag, with a further minor slate working above the path to the left. The path threads up a shallow passage, with the headland of The Knight up to the right. The splendid situation of the cairn set on this spur will tempt most to pay it an aside visit. The path quickly joins the route from Hare Shaw trending S, en route passing below a second, slightly less prominent headland cairn to reach the summit.

Via Low Moss 540m/1770ft 4km/2½ miles

7 From the open verge near the access to Bridge End follow the green sward path drifting W to a path confluence. Turn acutely left – this path basically contours to come above the intake wall. Drifting down beneath Cat Crag, the path then moves away from the wall on a steady climb along the eastern flank of Sleet Fell, quickly coming into union with a path climbing out of Boredale from Garth Heads. Reaching

The summit outcrop from the west top

the brow, the path hairpins as it is joined, on the level, by the direct Route 6 from Sandwick. The regular path keeps to the eastern side of High Dodd to arrive in the broad saddle of Low Moss. It lives up to its name, with a shallow pool in its midst and a ruined sheepfold – ideal for relief and a snack on a windy day. Sustaining a SW course ascend onto the rocky headland of Hart Crag, the bedrock making lovely foreground detail for creative photography. Beyond a further pool the fell's summit draws admiration and your boots irresistibly.

Via Boredale Head 550m/1805ft 6.4km/4 miles

8 Follow the Boredale valley road. Coming close to Boredale Head Farm, veer up the bank right with a permissive path. This fords a gill directly above the farmstead and contours above the intake wall to duly reconnect with the dale bridleway running on freely SW towards the dale head. Redgate Gill has recently taken a hit with wash-out, covering the green-way with stones. As the path steepens see the retaining bank of an old mine up to the right. The track, now rough underfoot, avoids a 'retired' zig-zag path (dashed green on OS maps) and climbs through a natural cutting with inspection covers to the Hayeswater aqueduct. Venturing on into the broad grassy saddle of Boredale Hause, unite with the popular path from Patterdale, now a made-way switching up to the right.

THE SUMMIT

This is one of the most satisfying summits in Lakeland, both in its immediate visual appeal and in its outlooks. The OS column perches proud as punch on the rocky peak, although the softer stone in its construction has fallen prey to etched graffiti. If this was the nature of the summit of Helvellyn, just think what plaudits it would garner. Few

Place Fell across the head of Boredale

St Sunday Crag and Dollywaggon Pike at the head of Grisedale

walkers skip over this top – the situation is spellbinding, enough to subdue eager energies for several magical moments, weather permitting. A conventional cairn rests on the western crest on ground that gives the finest view over Patterdale and into the wild recesses of Grisedale. St Sunday Crag and the craggy eastern faces of Dollywaggon and Nethermost Pikes, and the ridges and faces of Helvellyn and the high rolling skyline of summits running north towards Blencathra, all captivate. All around there is a no end to this bountiful fellscape. Down to the south see the almost square sheet of Brothers Water, perhaps catching the sun's rays in the Hartsop vale below Kirkstone Pass.

SAFE DESCENTS

Much of the fell is steep sided, so it is always wise to stick to the tried and tested paths. Most walkers tackle the fell in isolation to the rest of the fell group in a short-day anticlockwise circuit from Patterdale, climbing via Boredale Hause and descending via Low Moss. While this is fine as a way down, in adverse conditions walkers are best advised to backtrack to Boredale Hause for the swiftest, securest path to the valley.

RIDGE ROUTE

ANGLETARN PIKES ↓ 270m/885ft ↑ 180m/590ft 2.7km/1¾ miles

Step down S following the regular path over Round How and winding quite steeply down the new trail to Boredale Hause. Straddle the saddle SE to briefly join a bridleway, watching for a small cairn indicating departure half-right on a path that slips through the upper course of Freeze Beck. Coming onto a brow veer right SW, avoiding the marsh, to step onto the rock ridge and ponder the lack of a cairn!

PANORAMA

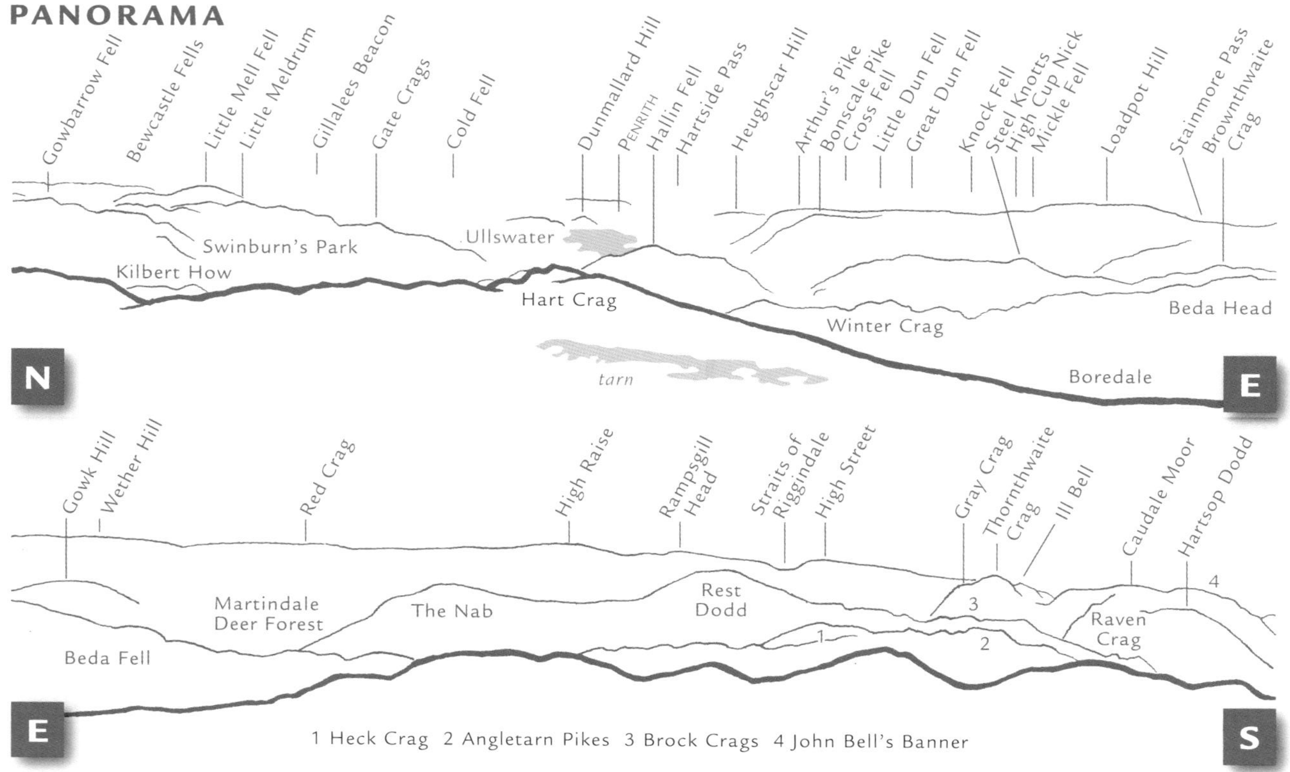
Gowbarrow Fell
Bewcastle Fells
Little Mell Fell
Little Meldrum
Gillalees Beacon
Gate Crags
Cold Fell
Dunmallard Hill
PENRITH
Hallin Fell
Hartside Pass
Heughscar Hill
Arthur's Pike
Bonscale Pike
Cross Fell
Little Dun Fell
Great Dun Fell
Knock Fell
Steel Knotts
High Cup Nick
Mickle Fell
Loadpot Hill
Stainmore Pass
Brownthwaite Crag
Swinburn's Park
Ullswater
Kilbert How
Hart Crag
Winter Crag
Beda Head
N
tarn
Boredale
E
Gowk Hill
Wether Hill
Red Crag
High Raise
Rampsgill Head
Straits of Riggindale
High Street
Gray Crag
Thornthwaite Crag
Ill Bell
Caudale Moor
Hartsop Dodd
4
Martindale Deer Forest
The Nab
Rest Dodd
3
Raven Crag
1
2
Beda Fell
E
S
1 Heck Crag 2 Angletarn Pikes 3 Brock Crags 4 John Bell's Banner

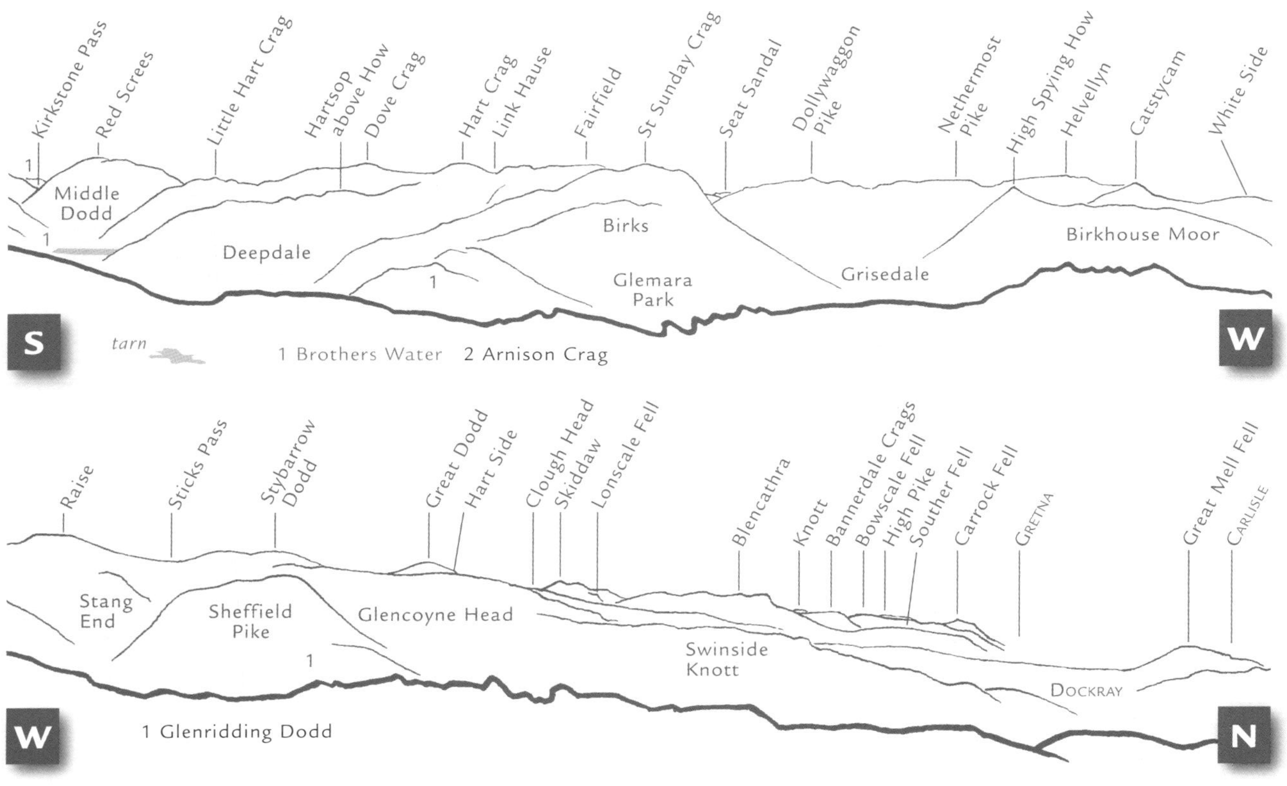
Kirkstone Pass
Red Screes
Little Hart Crag
Hartsop above How
Dove Crag
Hart Crag
Link Hause
Fairfield
St Sunday Crag
Seat Sandal
Dollywaggon Pike
Nethermost Pike
High Spying How
Helvellyn
Catstycam
White Side
1
Middle Dodd
1
Deepdale
1
Birks
Glemara Park
Grisedale
Birkhouse Moor
S
tarn
1 Brothers Water 2 Arnison Crag
W
Raise
Sticks Pass
Stybarrow Dodd
Great Dodd
Hart Side
Clough Head
Skiddaw
Lonscale Fell
Blencathra
Knott
Bannerdale Crags
Bowscale Fell
High Pike
Souther Fell
Carrock Fell
GRETNA
Great Mell Fell
CARLISLE
Stang End
Sheffield Pike
1
Glencoyne Head
Swinside Knott
DOCKRAY
W
1 Glenridding Dodd
N

22 RAMPSGILL HEAD *(792m/2598ft)*

The summit of Rampsgill Head has a three-way lynchpin significance – as the craggy head of the wild Rampsgill Beck valley and the cross-over point of two trade routes, the centuries-old Roman High Street and the perennially popular modern-age Coast to Coast Walk. There are higher summits to north and south, but none that have quite such importance.

Buttress below the northern edge looking into the Rampsgill valley

The waters of Rampsgill Beck, flowing due north into Howe Grain and Martindale, have created a deep trough beneath the fell. This 'lost valley' has no casual access and, like adjacent Bannerdale, deserves respect as a quiet sanctuary for the indigenous red deer. A native herd has lived hereabouts for centuries, even before the Romans made their presence felt. Lower down the dale a small woodland can be espied from the dale head – this may still harbour the understorey of wild garlic (ransoms) implied by the beck name. Beyond this, spot The Bungalow, a startling red-roofed dwelling, a holiday property owned by the Dalemain Estate. It was built as a game lodge in 1910 by the fifth Earl of Lonsdale in advance of a deer-shooting visit by the Kaiser of Germany, the bombastic Emperor Wilhelm II.

 ↑ Rampsgill Head from Rest Dodd

ASCENT FROM PATTERDALE (5)

Via Angle Tarn 725m/2380ft 7km/4½ miles

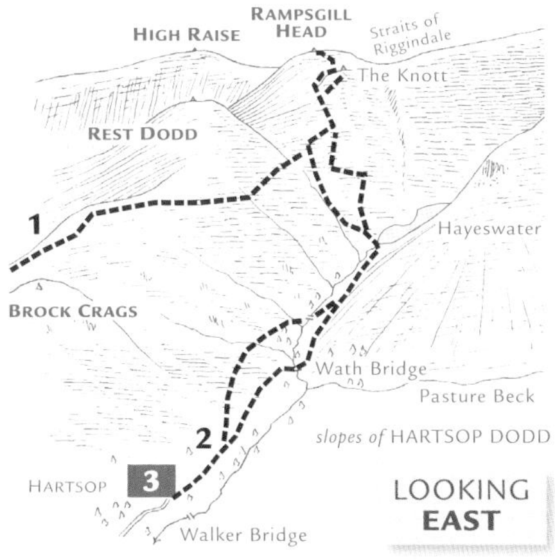

1 Take common cause with walkers intent on their Coast to Coast endeavour. Cross Goldrill Bridge and climb to Boredale Hause by the lower path coming up to Stonebarrow Gill, from where a part-pitched way leads through a gully and above the scarp, with a higher and a lower option as it passes under the main bastion of Angletarn Pikes. This leads round by the northern shore of Angle Tarn and on over the intermediary ridge above Buck Crag at the head of Bannerdale. Then, after slipping through a gateway over the rocky top of Satura Crag, take the right-hand fork to, in effect, contour across the southern slopes of Rest Dodd via a gateway at the head of Prison Gill. After fording Sulphury Gill (high above its fine cascades) join up with Route 2 on the rise by The Knott.

Western aspect seen over Hayeswater from Gray Crag

ASCENT FROM HARTSOP (3)

Via The Knott 610m/2000ft 4km/2½ miles

2 The situation provides two optional lines of ascent, tracking up the Hayeswater Gill valley to the dam, from where two further optional lines lead into harmony with the Coast to Coast route by peaty patch and gravelly trail, swinging round the shoulder of The Knott. Walkers may equally follow the wall onto this subsidiary outpost, where a large cairn suggests a moment's pause, before heading back down onto the regular way, turning right for a matter of 50m and bearing up left onto the dome of the fell.

THE SUMMIT

Rampsgill Head summit cairn

The summit cairn is but one of several that adorn this fell-top, two having sprung up near the northern brink, where walkers find greater satisfaction from a wonderful view. Most notably this point allows the closer inspection of a projecting buttress which seldom features in climbing annals, but on occasion will have drawn intrepid rock stars to carry up a rope. The greater view is heaped with detail inevitably concentrated to the west, with the high horizon of Fairfield and Helvellyn breached only by Scoat Fell, Ullscarf and Pillar. Left of Hart Crag see the Scafells, with Bowfell above, Dove Crag left again, the Crinkles, Eskdale Harter Fell and then the Coniston group, with the Old Man glimpsed above Red Screes.

SAFE DESCENTS

The regular thoroughfare W, descending promptly to the Hayeswater dam, gives a sure and safe line to a valley base, Hartsop.

RIDGE ROUTES

HIGH RAISE ↓ 40m/130ft ↑ 50m/165ft 1km/½ mile

Travel NE through the depression and accompany the Roman road until it comes onto the crown, then veer half-right to the bouldery crest.

HIGH STREET ↓ 95m/310ft ↑ 130m/425ft 2km/1¼ miles

Head SW with the popular path that comes over Twopenny Crag into the narrow depression known as the Straits of Riggindale. Follow the wall, via the cairn on Short Stile, all the way up to the OS column.

KIDSTY PIKE ↓ 25m/80ft ↑ 10m/35ft 0.5km/¼ mile

A simple matter of walking E to the peak's outcrop-topping cairn.

REST DODD ↓ 200m/655ft ↑ 105m/345ft 1.8km/1 mile

Travel W to join the regular path which swings from N to W. Upon meeting the wall, retain its company in descent, stepping over Well Gill and passing through the damp depression, then climb to where the wall departs W. Here keep N to the cairn on the crown of the fell.

PANORAMA

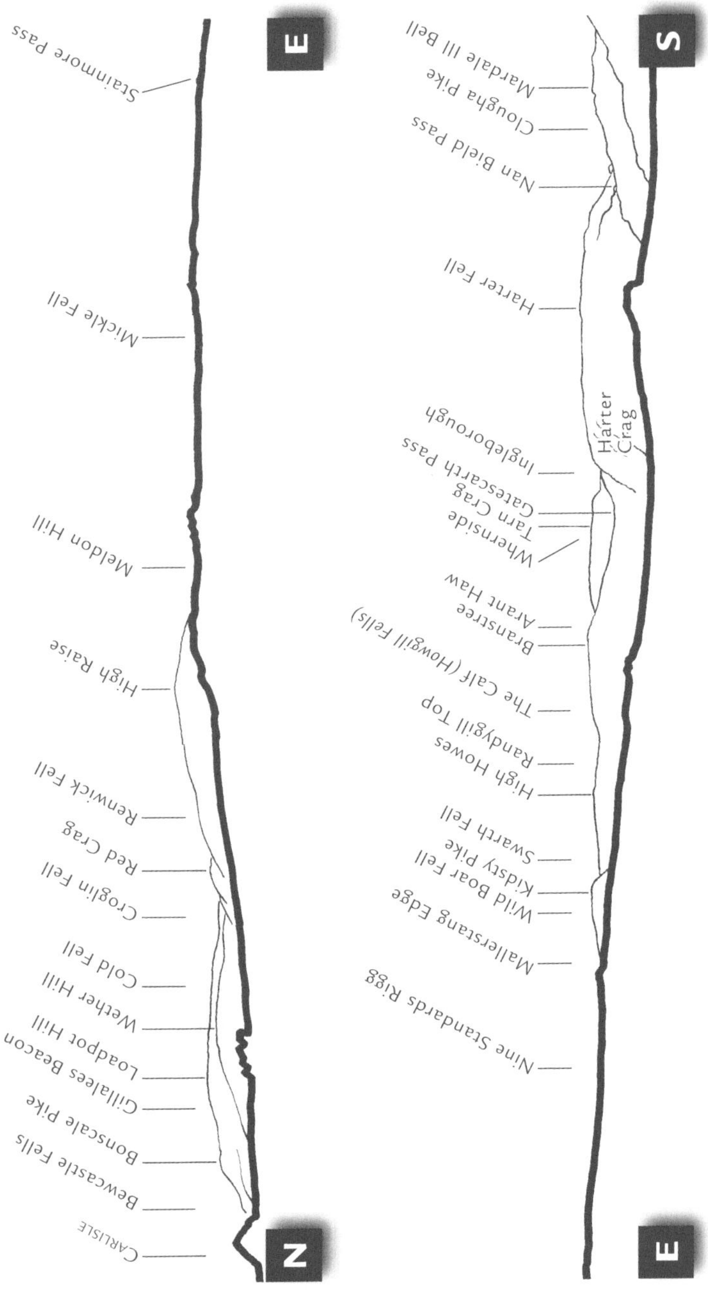

N

CARLISLE
Bewcastle Fells
Bonscale Pike
Gillalees Beacon
Loadpot Hill
Wether Hill
Cold Fell
Croglin Fell
Red Crag
Renwick Fell
High Raise
Meldon Hill
Mickle Fell
Stainmore Pass

E

E

Nine Standards Rigg
Mallerstang Edge
Wild Boar Fell
Kidsty Pike
Swarth Fell
High Howes
Randygill Top
The Calf (Howgill Fells)
Branstree
Arant Haw
Whernside
Tarn Crag
Gatescarth Pass
Ingleborough
Harter Crag
Harter Fell
Nan Bield Pass
Clougha Pike
Mardale Ill Bell

S

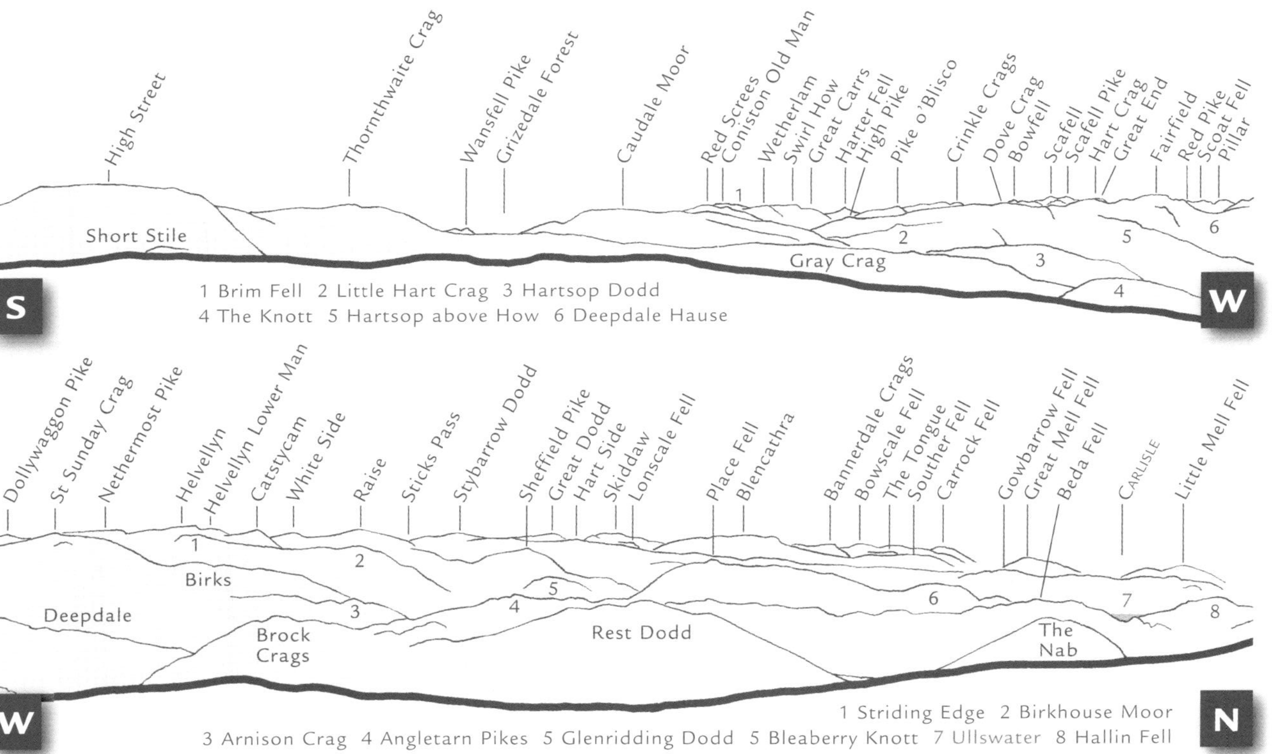
High Street
Thornthwaite Crag
Wansfell Pike
Grizedale Forest
Caudale Moor
Red Screes
Coniston Old Man
Wetherlam
Swirl How
Great Carrs
Harter Fell
High Pike
Pike o'Blisco
Crinkle Crags
Dove Crag
Bowfell
Scafell
Scafell Pike
Hart Crag
Great End
Fairfield
Red Pike
Scoat Fell
Pillar
Short Stile
Gray Crag
S
W
1 Brim Fell 2 Little Hart Crag 3 Hartsop Dodd
4 The Knott 5 Hartsop above How 6 Deepdale Hause
Dollywaggon Pike
St Sunday Crag
Nethermost Pike
Helvellyn
Helvellyn Lower Man
Catstycam
White Side
Raise
Sticks Pass
Stybarrow Dodd
Sheffield Pike
Great Dodd
Hart Side
Skiddaw
Lonscale Fell
Place Fell
Blencathra
Bannerdale Crags
Bowscale Fell
The Tongue
Souther Fell
Carrock Fell
Gowbarrow Fell
Great Mell Fell
Beda Fell
Carlisle
Little Mell Fell
Birks
Deepdale
Brock Crags
Rest Dodd
The Nab
W
N
1 Striding Edge 2 Birkhouse Moor
3 Arnison Crag 4 Angletarn Pikes 5 Glenridding Dodd 5 Bleaberry Knott 7 Ullswater 8 Hallin Fell

23 REST DODD *(697m/2287ft)*

The Nab and the sunlit Rest Dodd at the head of the Howe Grain valley

The name Rest Dodd is intriguing, and is perhaps an allusion to a regular resting place used during the ancient beating of the Martindale parish boundary. The fell is mentioned in the late 12th century as 'Restdode' and in the 13th as 'Rostdode' – this latter might imply a place where birds took roost, but either way it is a genuinely old name. Probably the majority of ridge walkers tend to give it the slip by using the connecting ridge above Satura Crag, thereby avoiding the big dip en route to Rampsgill Head. Yet no honest circuit of the Martindale skyline would be complete without visiting the summit, if only to marvel at the grand craggy prospect of Rampsgill Head.

↑ The Nab and Rest Dodd from Bannerdale

ASCENT FROM HARTSOP (3)

Via Satura Crag 515m/1690ft 4km/2½ miles

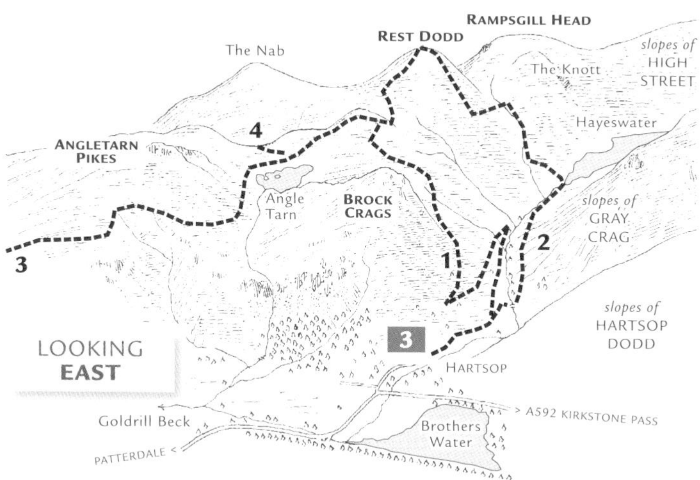

1 Head up the valley track, but after crossing the cattle grid bear up with the tarmac roadway, aiming for the waterworks building. On reaching the road-end, switch acutely back on the green-way overlaying the Hayeswater aqueduct. Coming above walled enclosures, watch for a path that turns acutely right up the fellside. This leads

Notch in the ridge path from Angle Tarn, looking to Fairfield

through a wall gateway and rises in a groove to the head of Calfgate Gill. Slip over a broken wall and through a gateway, and bear right beside the wall to meet up with the ridge path from Angle Tarn (Route 3). Step over the rocky top of Satura Crag, and as the path declines take the left-hand-fork path. This gains height on the swelling grassy ridge, rising right well before the wall (access line for The Nab). Climb irresistibly to the cairn on the north-eastern brow of the fell, with the summit cairn only a short stroll and a peat step away.

Via Hayeswater **530m/1740ft 3.5km/2¼ miles**

2 A variant, useful should you want to capture Rest Dodd in one fell swoop round, is the path that runs all the way up the track to the Hayeswater dam and then slants half-left easing up N. Coming by the rising wall join the regular trail at the head of Sulphury Gill. Follow this

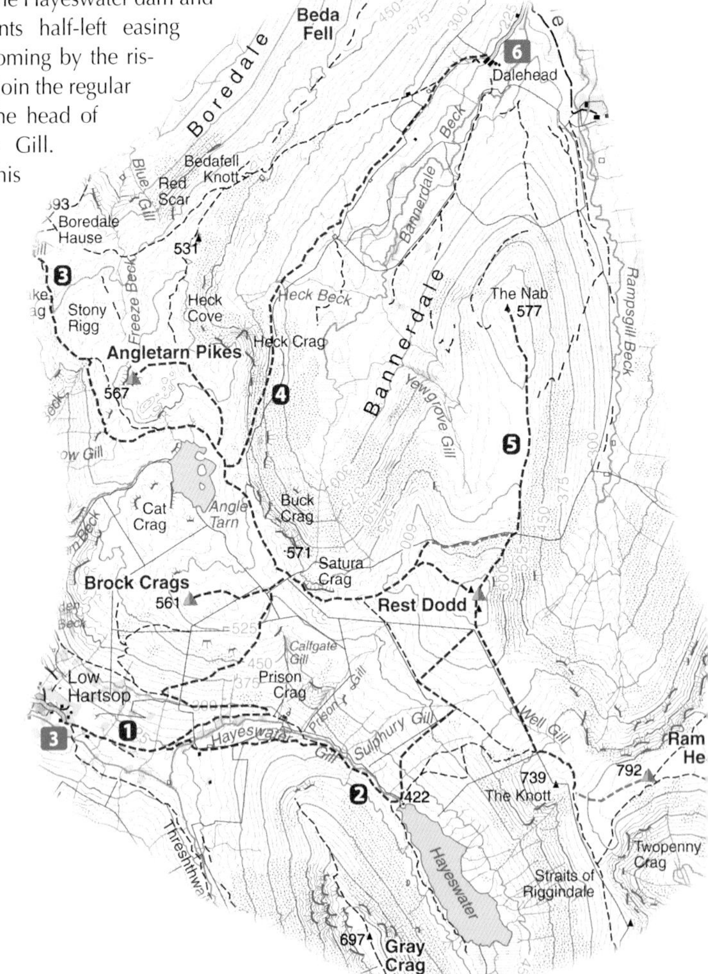

Helvellyn from Rest Dodd

left, then march up the steep fellside of Rest Dodd, avoiding peaty ground, to the wall angle at the top. From here continue to the summit cairn.

ASCENT FROM PATTERDALE (5 – off map NW)

Via Angle Tarn 590m/1935ft 5.8km/3½ miles

3 From the village street cross Goldrill Bridge with the cul-de-sac road, swinging left past the cottages to the road-end gate. Here find a slate sign directing right by a gate for 'Boredale Hause'. Climb the lower of the two rising paths to the hause, coming up by Stonebarrow Gill. Boredale Hause is a Piccadilly Circus interchange of paths and can be confusing in mist. This is the common route of the Coast to Coast Walk and has a few stone-pitched moments that lead on through a gully to come onto the scarp edge, with optional higher and lower paths contouring below the summit of Angletarn Pikes. Swing round the northern side of Angle Tarn and over the ridge top of Buck Crag onto Satura Crag's rocky top, now in unison with Route 1.

ASCENT FROM DALEHEAD, MARTINDALE (6)

Via Heck Cove 500m/1640ft 4.8km/3 miles

4 Follow ANGLETARN PIKES Route 8 to the head of Bannerdale, a great fellwalking ascent in a wild setting. Bannerdale means 'the valley where holly grows', although the

Narrow trod running up under Heck Crag

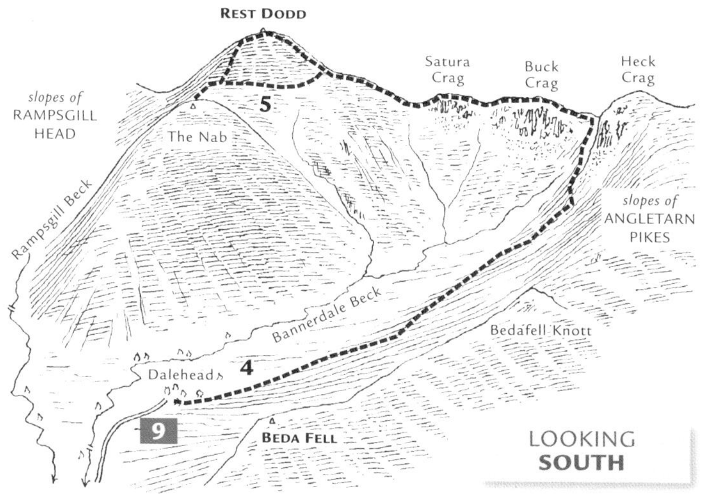

flanks of the vast marshy bowl have no residual evidence of this native shrub. The very narrow path clinging to the steep dale-side under Heck Crag draws into a skyline notch next to Buck Crag and joins the regular trail heading E. Partial reparation of the wear and tear caused by Coast to Coasters and Martindale skyline trekkers has been carried out, with stepping stones in peaty stretches. The more attractive, more energetic, strict skyline ridge is seldom followed over Buck and Satura Crags. Coming through a narrow gateway the path weaves through bedrock exposures to begin the climb onto Rest Dodd. Be careful not to be lured by the tempting path right, running across the southern flank of the fell to the Straits of Riggindale. The ascending path veers from E to NE onto the swelling grassy ridge. Walkers will notice a path-fork on the high shoulder of the north-west ridge, the left-hand path being the direct route for The Nab. However, the primary ascent swings SE to come upon a small cairn on the summit lip, and a short hollow and peat-grough step bring the large summit cairn underfoot.

SPUR PATH TO THE NAB

From Rest Dodd (descent) 120m/395ft 1.6km/1 mile

5 The fell's north ridge is far from conventional. It swells into the great protruding nose of The Nab (577m/1895ft), and but for Martindale Deer Reserve would be considered a separate fell in its own right. However, access is sensibly restricted to a there-and-back path from the parent fell. Nonetheless, many walkers will correctly consider their round of all the fells incomplete without visiting the summit, for all its unique characteristics. The spur path emanates from a stile at the base of the Rest Dodd north ridge (GR434140). This point can be reached either by descending

Access stile to spur path to The Nab

Summit cairn backed by High Raise and Rampsgill Head

from the summit of Rest Dodd due N, an uncomplicated path, or from off the high shoulder where a wall crosses the north-west ridge. Be mindful not to go through the open gateway – a fixed hurdle is presently thrown down enabling quad-bike access, but this does not imply recreational access. Follow the wall on the south side, dipping and then contouring, and ignore a fallen stretch of wall and an in-situ hurdle gateway partway along. Continue to the very end to find the stile, where the ground falls smartly away into the upper realms of the Rampsgill Beck valley. The summit lies 1.2km from the stile and is reached by crossing the intervening shallow depression, where eroding peat makes progress less pleasant in damp weather. One flat stone is all that is passed en route to the cairn, set upon a simple domed summit.

You might wander around the top a little to get a sense of the setting – and the rarified feeling of being aloof in a private world high above the secretive Bannerdale and Rampsgill Beck valleys. The view is inevitably confined by higher neighbouring ridges, but there is a fine view in the western arc from Red Screes round by Fairfield and the Helvellyn range overtopping the Angletarn Pikes ridge, where Heck Crag and Cove make a striking foreground to St Sunday Crag and Helvellyn. On a sunny day there is every excuse to dawdle on the summit and listen to the skylarks in a haven of peace far removed from the regular procession of casual walkers. As it is a fine little summit in its own right, with excellent views, albeit inaccessible from the base because of the deer reserve, I have included panoramas for the Nab as well as for Rest Dodd at the end of this fell chapter.

THE SUMMIT

Grass predominates, with a small exposure of blanket peat a reminder of the damp climate – if any reminder were necessary! The large cairn is a fine viewpoint, inevitably restricted by the bulk of High Raise and Rampsgill Head to the east, but to the north and, particularly, west there is a concentration of fells to study. Take pleasure in identifying Glaramara and Great Gable over Deepdale Hause.

SAFE DESCENTS

To the west and south routes gives confidence of journeys to safe dale havens, notably Hartsop by the Hayeswater Gill valley.

RIDGE ROUTES

ANGLETARN PIKES ↓ 220m/720ft ↑ 90m/295ft 3km/2 miles

A consistent path leads off the west brink of the summit dome and runs down to join the regular ridgeway on the skyline of Satura Crag. Pass through the wall-gap and skirt to the E of Angle Tarn, bearing off half-right as this swings to the north side. Reaching the brow, level with the knoll above Heck Crag. Bear left (W), skirting the peaty ground to find a narrow trod leading SW onto the rock ridge.

BROCK CRAGS ↓ 155m/510ft ↑ 20m/65ft 1.8km/1 mile

Leave the summit W, descending the ridge path which swings SW to a dip in the ridge to come over the bare rock crest of Satura Crag. Go through the gateway and bear left accompanying the wall SW, duly crossing the broken wall at its junction beyond a depression. Soon ushered right over the adjacent broken wall, negotiate a pooled hollow to reach the summit.

RAMPSGILL HEAD ↓ 105m/345ft ↑ 200m/655ft 1.8km/1 mile

Descend S, following the wall SSE down through a damp depression to climb by Well Gill. Where the heavily used path crosses, go left with this, rounding the north shoulder of The Knott. As this levels, take your whim in climbing left onto the domed summit.

PANORAMA from Rest Dodd

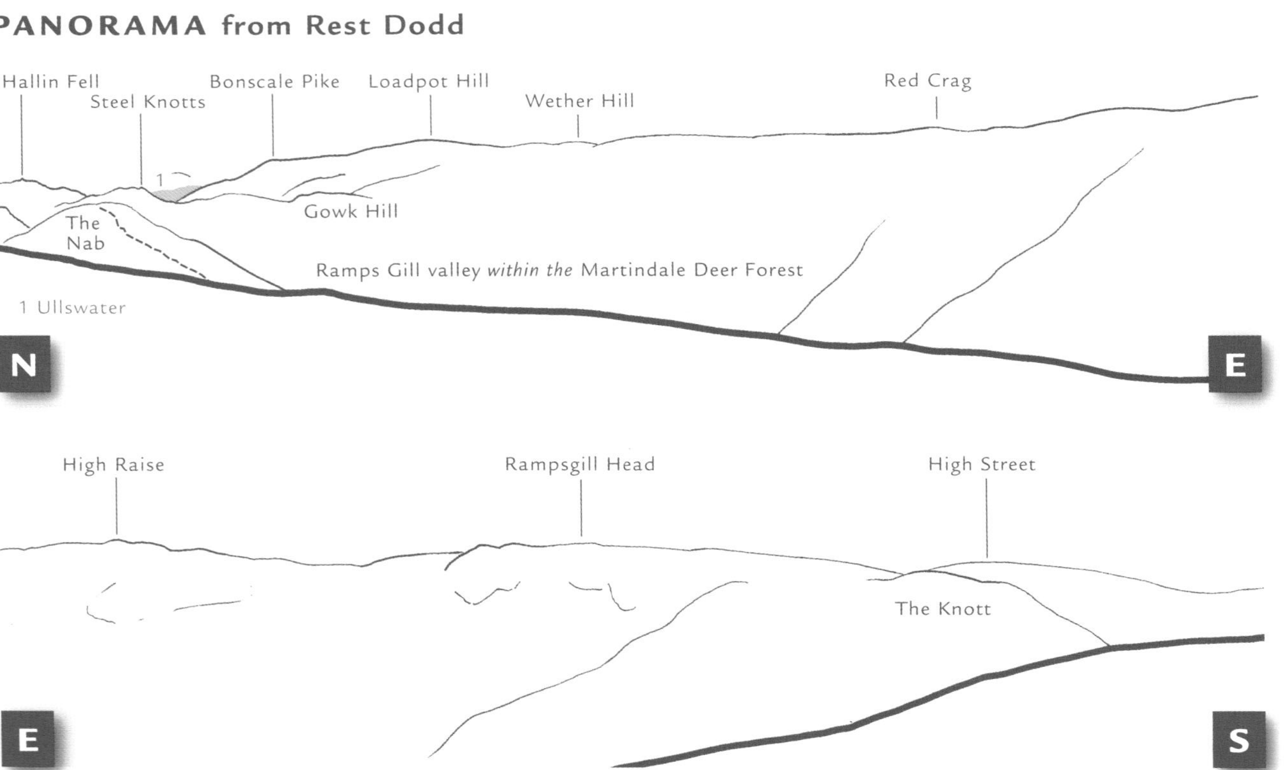

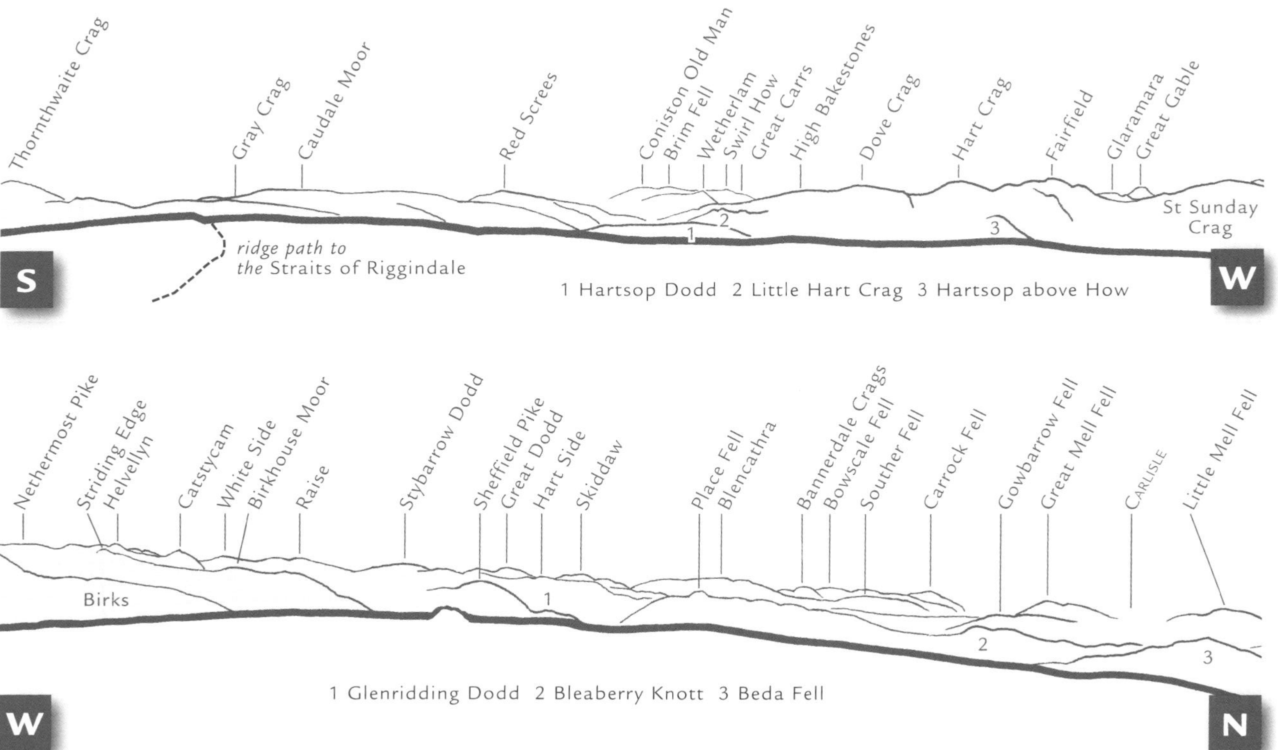
Thornthwaite Crag
Gray Crag
Caudale Moor
Red Screes
Coniston Old Man
Brim Fell
Wetherlam
Swirl How
Great Carrs
High Bakestones
Dove Crag
Hart Crag
Fairfield
Glaramara
Great Gable
St Sunday Crag
ridge path to the Straits of Riggindale
S
W
1 Hartsop Dodd 2 Little Hart Crag 3 Hartsop above How
Nethermost Pike
Striding Edge
Helvellyn
Catstycam
White Side
Birkhouse Moor
Raise
Stybarrow Dodd
Sheffield Pike
Great Dodd
Hart Side
Skiddaw
Place Fell
Blencathra
Bannerdale Crags
Bowscale Fell
Souther Fell
Carrock Fell
Gowbarrow Fell
Great Mell Fell
CARLISLE
Little Mell Fell
Birks
1 Glenridding Dodd 2 Bleaberry Knott 3 Beda Fell
W
N

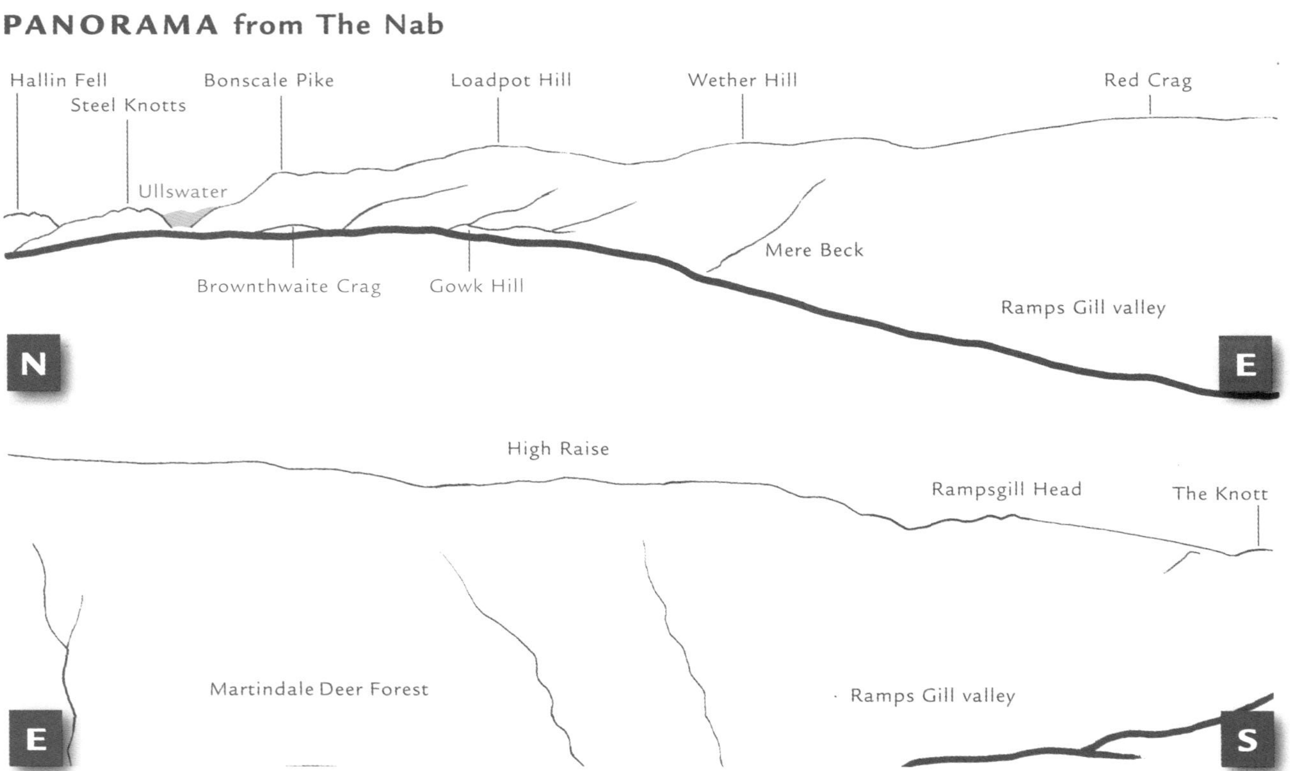
PANORAMA from The Nab
Hallin Fell
Steel Knotts
Bonscale Pike
Ullswater
Loadpot Hill
Wether Hill
Red Crag
Brownthwaite Crag
Gowk Hill
Mere Beck
Ramps Gill valley
N
E
High Raise
Rampsgill Head
The Knott
Martindale Deer Forest
Ramps Gill valley
E
S

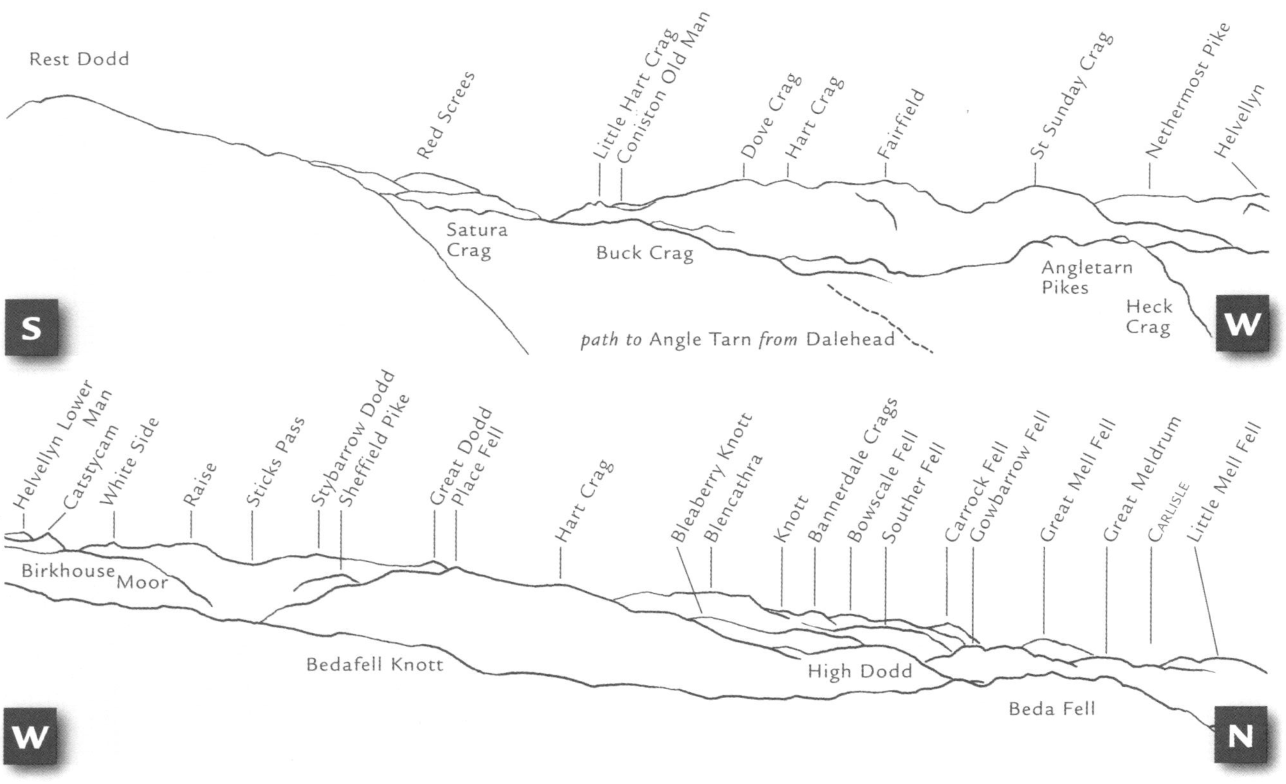
Rest Dodd
Red Screes
Little Hart Crag
Coniston Old Man
Dove Crag
Hart Crag
Fairfield
St Sunday Crag
Nethermost Pike
Helvellyn
Satura Crag
Buck Crag
Angletarn Pikes
Heck Crag
S
path to Angle Tarn from Dalehead
W
Helvellyn Lower Man
Catstycam
White Side
Raise
Sticks Pass
Stybarrow Dodd
Sheffield Pike
Great Dodd
Place Fell
Hart Crag
Bleaberry Knott
Blencathra
Knott
Bannerdale Crags
Bowscale Fell
Souther Fell
Carrock Fell
Gowbarrow Fell
Great Mell Fell
Great Meldrum
Carlisle
Little Mell Fell
Birkhouse Moor
Bedafell Knott
High Dodd
Beda Fell
W
N

24 SALLOWS *(516m/1693ft)*

Garburn Road

Sallows ('the place of dwarf willows'), together with its companion height Sour Howes (483m/1585ft), provides gentle exercise and scope for lovely round-rambles on the foothills of Lakeland, linking an array of pleasant tracks trending north from the low country between Kentmere and the Trout Beck valley. Bands of slate periodically outcrop in the area and were formerly exploited for local building purposes, notably at Applethwaite Quarry (a fascinating place to cautiously explore) on the western flank of Sour Howes.

Most summit-baggers content themselves with a smash-and-grab raid of Sallows from off Garburn Pass, but this approach misses the point of the fell's situation. Sallows is a distinguished high point in its own right, commanding green vales, its countenance being to the south. However, the best views are from the western brink of Sour Howes, gazing west across the Troutbeck valley beyond Wansfell Pike to the Langdale Pikes, backed by the serrated and momentous roof of England.

↑ Sallows from Green Quarter

ASCENT FROM KENTMERE (29)

Via Garburn Pass 355m/1165ft 3.2km/2 miles

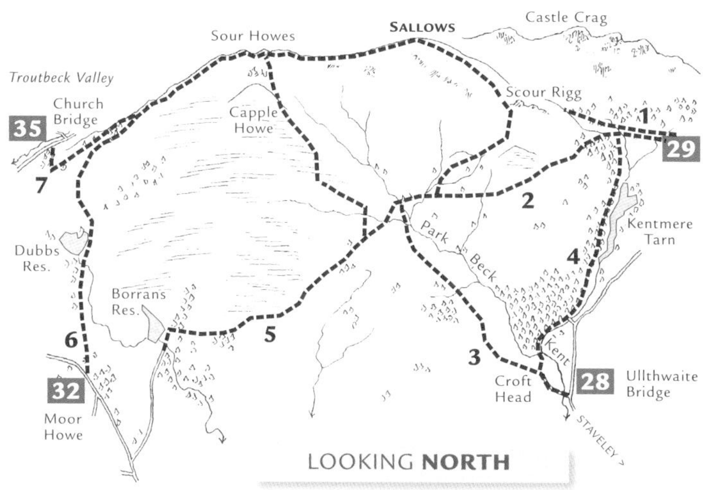

1 Follow the village road N from the church to The Nook, opposite which the Garburn Road (restricted bridleway to Troutbeck) is signed up right. Some new surfacing has been undertaken on this hugely popular route, both on the early gated lane approach towards the Brock Stone (Badger Rock) and higher, with pitching on the final zig-zag climb to the hause. However, heavy use in between, notably these days by bikers, has made some uncomfortable walking with loose stones. The Brock Stone must have been carried to its present location at the latter stage of the last Ice Age and is perfect for agile bouldering climbers.

As you wend on from here make a point of looking down on Kentmere Hall Farm with its pele tower (rare in Lakeland). The tower is a reminder of torrid times 400 years ago, when to farm these rough dales one had more than hostile weather to contend with. The glowering crags of Piked Howes, and Castle and Buck Crags, emphasise

Bouldering climber on the Brock Stone (Badger Rock)

the presence of igneous rock, formed as a volcanic island in a long-lost ocean south of the equator. Follow the track on through the gate and at once cross the stile left, marching up the blank damp fell bank onto the ridge.

Via Whiteside End 375m/1230ft 4km/2½ miles

2 Follow the metalled lane to Kentmere Hall Farm, passing on past the farmyard and over the Cowsty Beck bridge, keeping with the rising track. This gated lane, understandably popular with bikers, provides fine views back on Piked Howes and, in due course, excellent views down on Kentmere Tarn. Approaching the third gate swing up the pasture right, climbing to a stile to the right of a gate accessing the rough pasture of Kentmere Park, grazed by cattle and sheep. Trend part-right via the low ridge, aiming for the rocky peak of Scour Rigg. Skirting its base, swing up leftwards (W) with scant evidence of a quad track, then follow a grass path that passes a line of four old stone shooting butts as it climbs onto the summit ridge of Sallows. The grassy nature of the fell raises the question as to what were they shooting, as grouse would not have been immediately present.

ASCENT FROM ULLTHWAITE BRIDGE (28)

Via Park Beck 430m/1410ft 6km/3¾ miles

3 Park on the adjacent verge and follow the metalled lane over Ullthwaite Bridge. This leads to and between Ulthwaite Fold and white-washed Croft Head, a traditional Westmorland farmhouse tastefully renovated with a touch of aplomb. Pass on through, via the gate, and follow the confined lane. Ignore the footpath signed

Shooting butt on Sallows

right ('Kentmere Hall'). Stay with the main bridleway (also signed to Kentmere Hall). This drove-way winds up through bracken, passing a lone bothy to ford a gill. It now runs on via stepping stones and a ford spanning Park Beck to reach a gate at the junction with a second bridleway track. Don't go through the gate, but swing left over the stepping stones, following the open track over a culverted gill. With a thorn bush drawing near left and the remains of a dead tree right, branch acutely right on a narrow trod, a former shooters' track, which fords a gill at the site of a small bridge and comes to a wall-corner. Go left round this and follow the wall up to a gate. Go through and swing right, drifting slightly away from the right-hand wall and aiming for a small outcrop on the near brow, where the remains of a stone shooting butt are found.

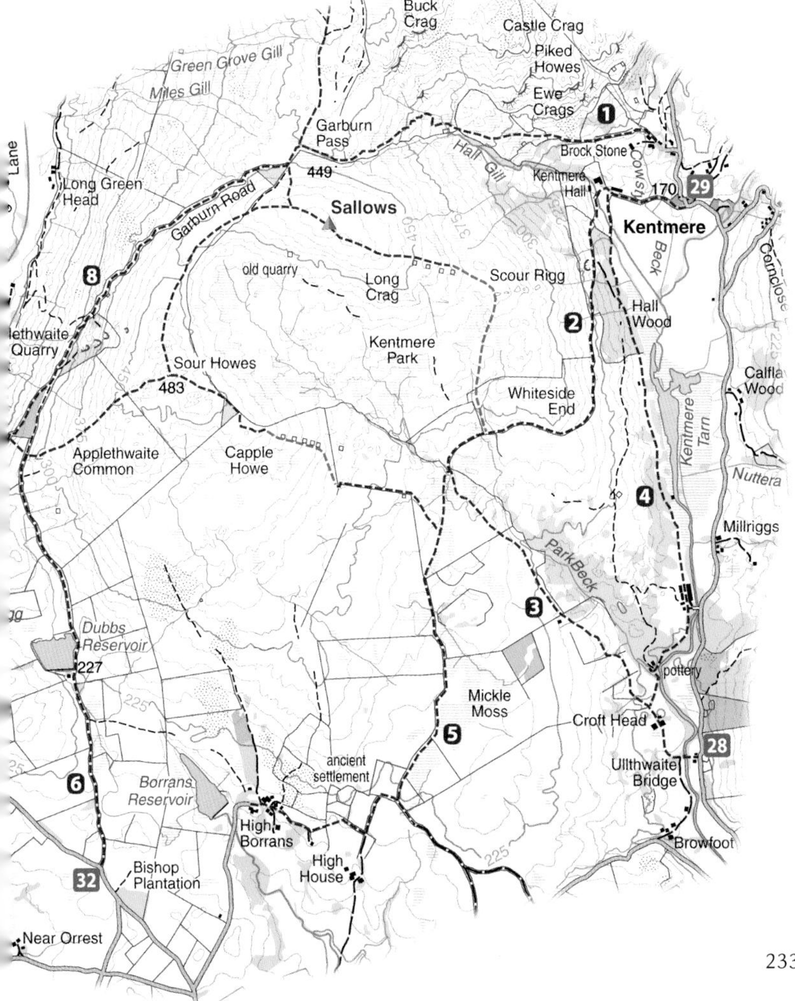

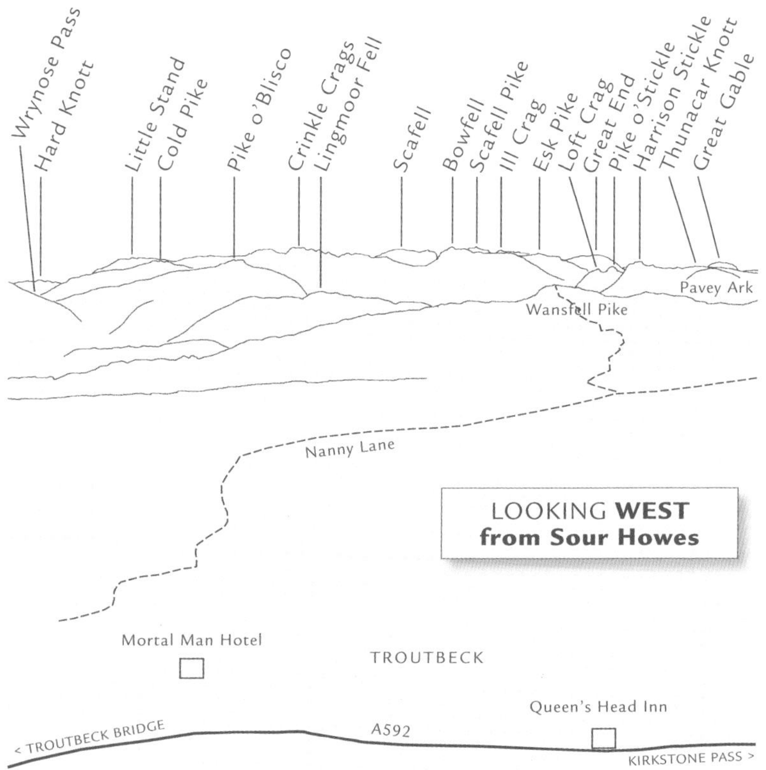

Head straight up the damp fell without a trace of a path via five butts to come by the right-hand wall on Capple Howe – which translates as 'the horse's high pasture'. Skirt a marshy pooled hollow to reach a stile to the right of a small conifer plantation. Follow the broken wall up beside the trees to a second stile and keep on with the open path onto the ribbed ridge that leads to the cairnless summit of Sour Howes. The continuing path dips and follows the ridge N, coming back into contact with the ridge wall to reach a stile. From here the ridge path climbs a little more to reach the bare summit.

Valley connection with Kentmere Hall **90m/295ft 3.4km/2 miles**

4 A lovely dale path – a particular asset in reverse, should you be considering a low-level return. It branches right as a footpath beyond Croft Head, signed 'Kentmere Hall 1¼', first as a walled lane to a footbridge over Park Beck, close to its confluence with the River Kent, and then as a confined path to Kentmere Pottery, after which follow the access roadway to the works of Hollingworth & Vose. The path is ushered

Kentmere Tarn

through by painted yellow men on the tarmac to become a gated green-way, largely screened from the irregular shores of Kentmere Tarn, that continues all the way to Kentmere Hall Farm, making a handy connection with Route 2.

ASCENT FROM MOOR HOWE (32)

Via Borrans Lane 370m/1215ft 7km/4½ miles

5 There is no convenient parking at the end of Borrans Lane, with the Dubbs Lane parking your only real option and the road-walk. The metalled Borrans Lane is signed 'High Borrans'. This wends down and then up by the entrance to the North Tyneside Outdoor Centre, passing through the farmyard of High Borrans, over the ineffectual cattle grid and along the twin-banded tarmac strip track as to Woodside. But short of this, where a green salting box stands by the roadway, go through the facing field-gate and join a bridleway beside a fence. This leads to a gate. Step over a gill and follow the track through two fields via another gate. Enter a fenced lane beside a wall, and where this ends go through a gate. With the open bridleway from High House converging from the right beside a gathering of field-stones all shaded by a sycamore, turn left through the gate signed 'Kentmere Hall'. Rise up a further fence/wall lane, and at the next gate swing right to go through a further gate into a walled lane. But ignore this lane, and turn immediately left through the adjacent gate upon a green track signed 'Kentmere' with a wall now to your left. After the next gate the track skirts the edge of an extensive marsh, Mickle Moss, sparsely colonised by spindly alder. Three gates further and, in passing a thorn bush, you may veer half-left following the narrow trod described in Route 3, should you wish to climb Sour Howes first.

Alternatively, continue to the stepping stones over Park Beck and go through the next gate, keeping to the track until immediately after the next gate. Here step up left as per Route 2, bound for Kentmere Park and Sallows direct.

Via Dubbs Lane 355m/1165ft 4.8km/3 miles

6 Follow Dubbs Lane, which is a BOAT (byway open to all traffic). The firm, basically level track provides a fine start to proceedings. Pass the actual 'dubb' (sheep washpool) only as the waterworks building of Dubbs Reservoir draws near. The beck flows from Dubbs via Borrans Reservoir en route to Ings as the River Gowan, a tributary of the Kent. The track deteriorates in passing the reservoir and particularly after a gate – your average car would end its days following this byway – although the track does improve. Enjoying fine views into the Trout Beck valley march on until, with a conifer copse in sight, facing stiles are found crossing the line of the lane. Here climb the high ladder-stile, glancing back down on Limefitt chalet park. The path ascends by an irregular rock ridge, giving entertainment to the climb en route to a stile, a definite point to pause and gaze back to a fine Lakeland scene. Head on with the path onto the wildly undulating pasture of Sour Howes, passing a tiny pool to reach the cairnless rock high point.

Rock-rib summit of Sour Howes

Drift down left following the ridge path and curving in harmony with the wall to a stile. Complete the ascent to Sallows's equally minimalist summit.

ASCENT FROM CHURCH BRIDGE, TROUTBECK (35)

Via Sour Howes 430m/1410ft 3.7km/2¼ miles

7 Cross the footbridge beside the main road and, following the footway a matter of metres, seek the narrow lane entry across the busy road. This marks the beginning of the Garburn Road, a narrow rough-surfaced way – although curving up via a gate there is an extremely well-pitched bend, turning the 'road' NE on a steady rise. Crossing the line of a bridleway, come up towards a conifer copse and find a stile right. Leave the lane and follow this footpath, which crosses Dubbs Lane by facing stiles and continues straight up the fell as per Route 6.

Via Garburn Pass 400m/1310ft 4km/2½ miles

8 The swift route to Sallows's summit follows Route 7 initially, but keeps faith with the Garburn Road on its steady climb, passing below the tree-decorated remnants

Stile onto Sour Howes

of Applethwaite Quarry – if you have time this is a fascinating place to (carefully) explore. Coming up to the gate at the top of the lane, defer to the adjacent stile right and climb straight up the fellside to the summit.

THE SUMMIT

A lateral rock spine of no more than 10m length defines the summit; no stones have been brought to manifest a cairn. The view is not the fell's greatest gift, being somewhat hampered by Sour Howes to the west, although keen eyes will be drawn towards the Langdales, and Yoke baulks the north. Elsewhere the view round the southern arc is far ranging – from the Howgills, via Ingleborough and Morecambe Bay to Black Combe.

SAFE DESCENTS

Stride back NW down to the stile onto the Garburn Road for sure guidance in mist for Kentmere (E) and Troutbeck (SW).

RIDGE ROUTE

YOKE (OFF MAP N) ↓ 70m/230ft ↑ 260m/855ft 3km/2 miles

Follow the ridge path NW but dip off NNW to the stile at the northern tip of the small plantation. Go right through the gate and follow the open track to the right-hand bend. Here step off onto the northward-running newly surfaced trail, which gives a sure guide up to a kissing-gate and beyond, with some valuable drained pitching on the one brief climb onto the plateau.

PANORAMA

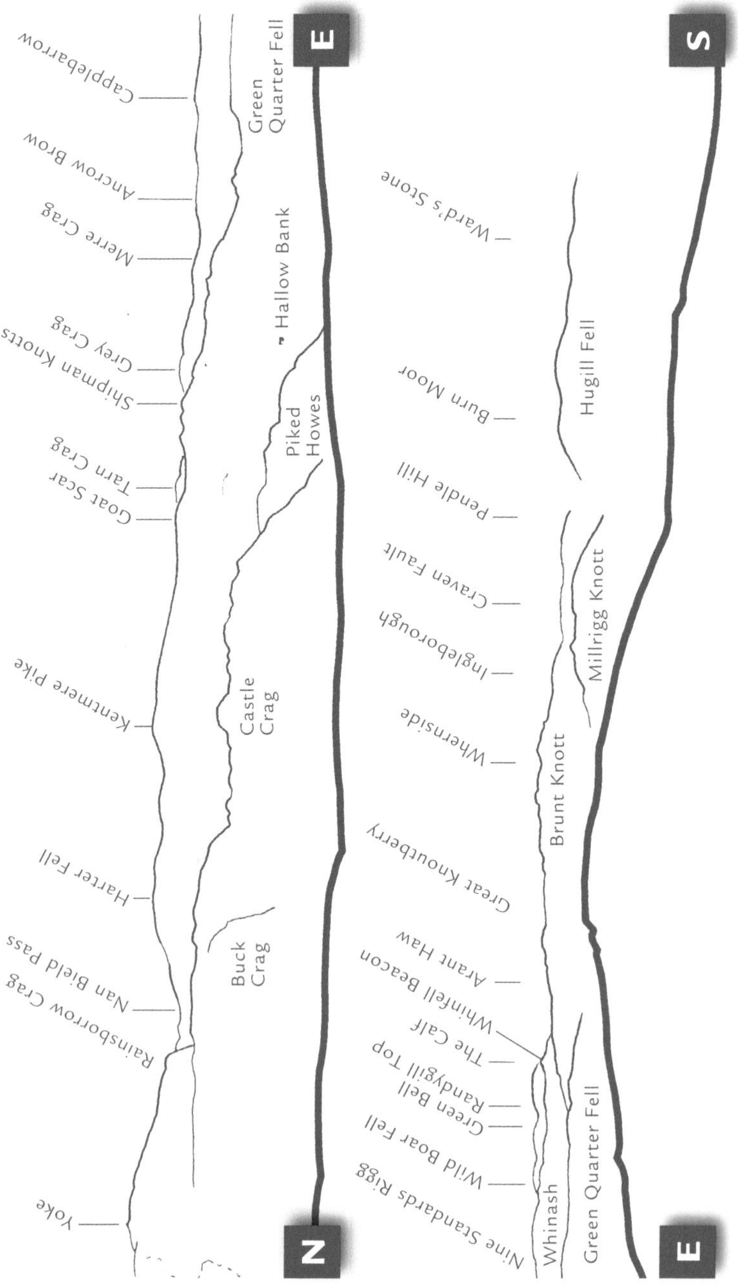

N
Yoke
Rainsborrow Crag
Nan Bield Pass
Buck Crag
Harter Fell
Castle Crag
Kentmere Pike
Goat Scar
Tarn Crag
Piked Howes
Shipman Knotts
Grey Crag
Hallow Bank
Merre Crag
Ancrow Brow
Green Quarter Fell
Capplebarrow
E

E
Green Quarter Fell
Whinash
Nine Standards Rigg
Wild Boar Fell
Green Bell
Randygill Top
The Calf
Whinfell Beacon
Arant Haw
Great Knoutberry
Brunt Knott
Whernside
Ingleborough
Millrigg Knott
Craven Fault
Pendle Hill
Burn Moor
Hugill Fell
Ward's Stone
S

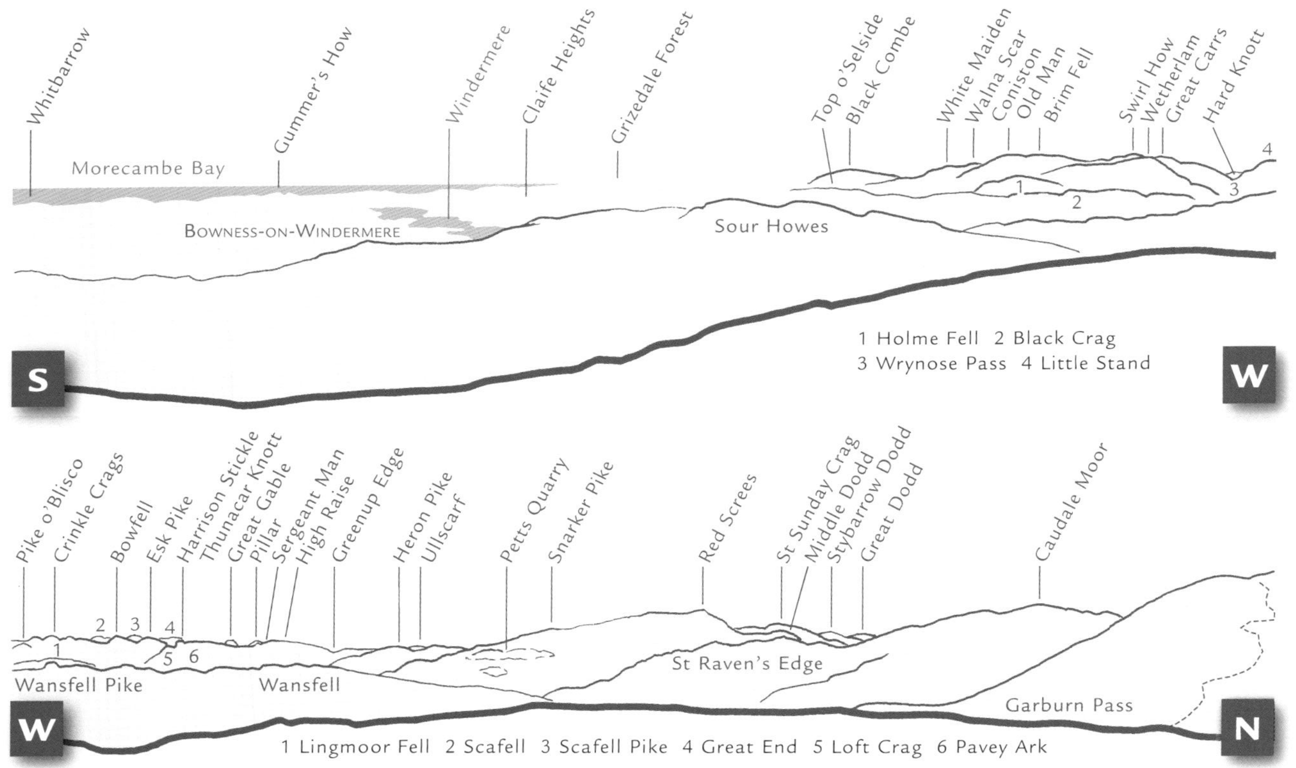
Whitbarrow
Gummer's How
Windermere
Claife Heights
Grizedale Forest
Top o'Selside
Black Combe
White Maiden
Walna Scar
Coniston
Old Man
Brim Fell
Swirl How
Wetherlam
Great Carrs
Hard Knott
Morecambe Bay
Bowness-on-Windermere
Sour Howes
1 Holme Fell 2 Black Crag
3 Wrynose Pass 4 Little Stand
S
W
Pike o'Blisco
Crinkle Crags
Bowfell
Esk Pike
Harrison Stickle
Thunacar Knott
Great Gable
Pillar
Sergeant Man
High Raise
Greenup Edge
Heron Pike
Ullscarf
Petts Quarry
Snarker Pike
Red Screes
St Sunday Crag
Middle Dodd
Stybarrow Dodd
Great Dodd
Caudale Moor
St Raven's Edge
Wansfell Pike
Wansfell
Garburn Pass
W
N
1 Lingmoor Fell 2 Scafell 3 Scafell Pike 4 Great End 5 Loft Crag 6 Pavey Ark

25 SELSIDE PIKE *(655m/2149ft)*

Selside Pike is the guardian height of Swindale, brooding down on this shy green strath. Step back in time and reflect on the unspoiled nature of Swindale. The valley name refers to the foraging place of pigs within a far more extensive native mixed woodland. Be thankful that this secretive valley did not succumb to the dammed fate of its two neighbours, Mardale and Wet Sleddale. The head of the dale is a remarkable textbook on the residual effects of glaciation – bring your geomorphological students here for the complete story. The fell is normally climbed from the Mardale Head road via the Old Corpse Road in a round trip that includes Branstree, but there is no doubt that the best expedition begins from Swindale, again starting by the Corpse Road, and concludes by Geordie Greathead, visiting the top of Hobgrumble and wild-watered environs of Forces Falls. Be mindful that there is no car parking beyond the first cattle grid on the approach, but the walk along the narrow dale road is a sheer joy – the peace of a little-known part of Lakeland is yours for the day.

 ↑ Selside Pike from Lady's Seat

ASCENT FROM MARDALE BANKS (19)

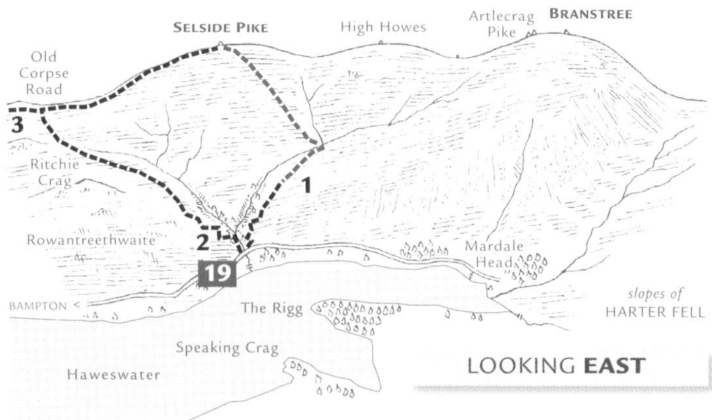

Use the shoreline path or the road from the Mardale Head car park. Notice how the steep fall of Woodfell Gill has brought massive quantities of stone spilling onto the road and, in fans, below. The shore path gives a good introduction to the setting, and enables you to find your fell-feet before hitting the fell. After crossing the little bridge spanning Hopegill Beck take the path climbing right to a kissing-gate onto the road. However, most walkers will be content to park up in the lay-by just to the north of the bridge above the hand-gate marking the start of the Old Corpse Road. This road once served as the means by which the deceased of Mardale were conveyed by horse pannier to consecrated ground at Shap.

Geordie Greathead Crag

Via Hopegill Beck 370m/1215ft 1.9km/1¼ miles

1 From the reservoir road turn right, and immediately after crossing the Hopegill Beck road bridge go through the hand-gate to be confronted by a chaos of cascades, boulders and tree growth. But the shepherd's way is at hand, so at once switch right to follow an obvious groove drove-path. This winds up to pass under the Hollow Stone, a large tilted boulder, and progresses steadily, with the roar of the ravine a constant accompaniment. When the bracken is thick, getting close to the waterfalls is impossible, but at other times it can be achieved, although the confines are ill suited to generous casual inspection. Higher up, as the slope eases, come by two ruins; the upper has the taller walls. See the tapered window-slot, which must have given a draughty view upon Mardale. The path becomes far less certain from here on, and damp tussocks herald arrival at a large sheepfold with fenced extension. Keep to the left, coming to the confluence with Captain Whelter Beck. The sheepfold had a double opening to the beck, which must have been dammed, for this was a sheep-wash. Clamber up the facing rigg and simply head SE up the plain grassy west ridge of Selside Pike. Early evidence of a path is lost as the slope steepens, with little in the way of rock to deflect a beeline ascent to the fence-corner and summit.

Via Old Corpse Road 370m/1215ft 3km/2 miles

2 Not a road to drive, but very much a way to wander, for its scenic attributes are quite exceptional, certainly on the early zig-zagging rise. The converging ravines of Hopegill Beck and, more shy, Rowantreethwaite Gill are tremendous sights and best avoided – not even sheep venture too close. The old way comes up by the ruins of sturdy stone peat-store bothies, although they have long since forfeited their roofs.

Sheep-wash fold complex Captain Whelter Beck

Burnbanks
Park Bridge
Gill Dubs
213
Naddle Bridge
213
Woodnook Gill
Naddle Farm
Scalebarrow Knott
339
Wallow Crag
Hugh's Laithes Pike
435
Naddle Beck
Reservoir
419
Harper Hills
Mere Sike
3
21
Guerness Wood
Naddle High Forest
Low Goat Gill
Haweswater Hotel
428
Pod Net
Guerness Wood Gill
Guerness Gill
Powley's Hill
Swindale Foot
Mullender
Swindale
Hare Shaw
503
Black Crag Gill
Truss Gap
260
Aaron's Bield
Woof Crag
Swear Gill
Waite Howes
4
Gouthercrag Gill
Swindale Beck
Mardale Banks
Brownhowe Crags
Swindale Head
Gouther Crag
Outlaw Crag
Ritchie Crag 529
Old Corpse Road
High Birkin Knott
Glede Howe
High Loup
2
Selside End
5
Haskew Beck
Rowantreethwaite Gill
The Knott
Simon Stone
509
Willy Winder Hill
Mardale Common
Dodd Bottom
Forces Falls
Swindale Common
Haskew Tarn
1
Selside Pike
Geordie Greathead Crag
Nabs Crag
Hobgrumble Gill
High Wether Howe
531
618
Hopegill Beck
Swirle Crag
Captain Whelter Bog
Mosedale Beck
Scam Matthew
673
High Howes
Howes
Survey Post
410
Branstree
Mosedale Quarry (dis)

Ruin beside Old Corpse Road above Mardale Banks

Although they were hardly built with the view in mind, you will be transfixed by the outlook from the bothies to the craggy faces of Harter Fell, Mardale Ill Bell and, most special of all, High Street and Kidsty Pike, flanking Riggindale. Invariably the diminutive Wood Howe island directly below is raucous with gulls or geese. The path eases onto the moor, and walkers stride on until a stake is found where a quad track crosses the old way a little over the marshy watershed. Here bear right and ascend the north-east ridge of Selside End. Take the opportunity to glance over the left-hand edge en route to admire the craggy surrounds of Dodd Bottom and the green strath of Swindale Head, a beautiful and largely forgotten corner of Lakeland. The quad track veers off half-left to a sheep-feeding box, but the ridge path continues, slipping through a peaty exposure and on to the summit.

ASCENT FROM SWINDALE (21)

At the point where the unenclosed approach road from Bampton via Bomby or Shap via Rosgill becomes enclosed, find the only proper car parking for the valley. There are, in effect, three rewarding lines of ascent from this point, either via Hare Shaw (Route 3) or from Swindale Head (Routes 4 and 5).

Via Hare Shaw 450m/1475ft 6.4km/4 miles

3 Step directly up from the parking space, the path forcing a line through the bracken immediately right of an invariably dry stony beck. The bridleway is quirkily signed by the wall on the far side of the beck. From that point it is practical to follow only if you hug the wall and go through a novel concrete stile above, and then clamber back over the galvanised ladders in the waterworks structure – an unnecessary

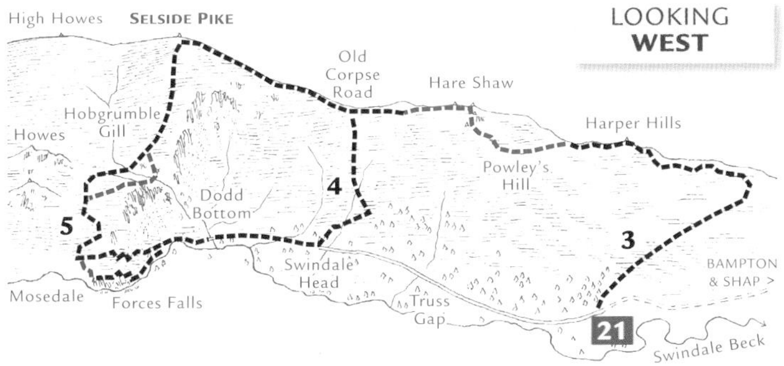

complication! The regular route quickly unites with the 'official' line of the bridleway and slants easily across the slope rising onto the moor. Keep forward, escaping the bracken to cross just one really damp patch in reaching the main track close to the ridge wall (opposite the bridleway gate from Naddle Farm). Turn left and follow the track's undulating course to come up onto Harper Hills, visiting the prominent cairn up to the left. A confession – this was originally built by the author in 1973!

A thin path continues S from here, although you can rejoin the track. By either means descend to a gate, ford the gill and pass the fenced enclosures. With the objective of tracing the main skyline ridge, veer left, avoiding the marshy hollow and bracken to climb the pathless slope onto the cairnless Powley's Hill. Evidence of a quad track may be found, leading to a cairn on a small fractured rock knoll. From here veer right to visit a cairn on a north-facing outcrop, a lovely spot to idle before trending S again, passing a cairn on a rise and then the smaller cairn on the actual summit of Hare Shaw. The author started both of the latter two cairns, too, on 10th March 1973, when out with Alfred and Betty Wainwright. AW commented that it was strange that the actual summit was bereft of a marking cairn – so I duly obliged there and then.

A faint sheep trod leads S, coping with various further marshy expanses and at least two small fenced bogs, showing what herbage would survive if sheep where excluded. Cross the line of one quad track more on the ridge to come down onto a more consistent quad track to reach the 'pass' cross-ways with Old Corpse Road at a cairn and stake. Continue S, climbing Selside End in harmony with Routes 2 and 4 onto Selside Pike.

Via the Old Corpse Road — **440m/1445ft 5.2km/3¼ miles**

4 As you wander up the sheltered green dale admire the serrated skyline to the south, focused upon the great buttresses of Gouther and Outlaw Crags bounding the damp upland leading to Seat Robert. Truss Gap Farm harbours interest as the name, present in the romantic-sounding Trusmadoor in the Northern Fells and Truss Lane at Troutbeck, embodies the British term meaning 'a cross-passage', present in Welsh

Gouther Crag, Swindale

names such as Trawsfynydd. The tarmac road ends at Swindale Head, a farmhouse that has never had the benefit of electricity and only recently gained a diesel generator. After a gate beside the farmhouse a bridle-path sign 'Mardale' directs right up the tapering enclosure to a gate. A groove leads up to a hand-gate and over a ford, beneath a pleasing cascade. Ascend beside the wall, avoiding the dense gorse, to a somewhat stunted but nonetheless great umbrella of a sycamore. Immediately above this find a path veering left away from the wall. A cairn guides walkers onto the shelf path of the Old Corpse Road. This crosses a gill and makes onto the open fell with the possibility of a stake to guide you (the ones the author saw are likely to have gone by the time you visit!). The odd old cairn on the damp, gently angled fell slope leads to a distinct cross-way at a stake, where Routes 2 and 3 converge. Turn S upon the easy grass slope to climb Selside End.

Via Dodd Bottom and Hobgrumble Gill 500m/1640ft 6.4km/4 miles

5 The gill name alone should be sufficiently intriguing to make you susceptible to this walk – Hobgrumble suggests 'a noisy goblin'. This is a grand little climb. Follow the gated drove-way beyond Swindale Head, passing the stone barns by an irregular walled lane. After a gate/wall-stile cross the plank-bridge over the out-flowing

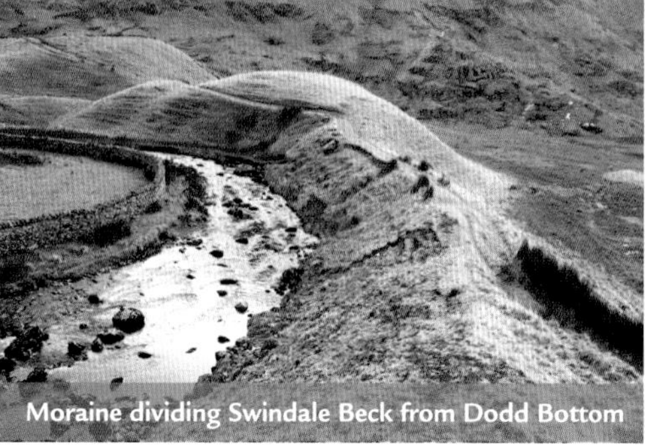
Moraine dividing Swindale Beck from Dodd Bottom

beck from Dodd Bottom and follow the moraine track. Soon walkers come along a narrow section between Swindale Beck and the great basin of Dodd Bottom, clearly once the receptacle of a tarn. The path swings up the rising moraine, sensing the drama of this wild sanctuary.

Many walkers come this way not with the intention of climbing Selside Pike nor venturing on up into the watery wastes of Mosedale. The majority come to witness one of the shy wonders of the Far Eastern Fells, Forces Falls. So while you may be content

Top falls, Forces Falls

to stick resolutely to the hairpin bends of the old bridle route climbing up the rough dale-head slope ahead into Mosedale direct, the more adventurous and thrilling course is to follow your instincts and explore Forces Falls. To visit them rise with the path on the moraine after the beck turns sharply left. Coming through a block of rushes veer left on a faint trod, which leads over marshy ground to the foot of the cascades. The sturdy footbridge installed in 1984 at the foot of the falls has been swept away, with little hope of replacement, so there is no easy means of viewing the falls from the east side, as extolled by Wainwright. Climb the bedrock banks to view higher instalments of this fabulous cataract, the sponge-like gathering ground of Mosedale ensuring a steady flow to give visual splendour to the falls at most seasons of the year. Note the colony of ant-hills early on the ascent. It is not practical to follow the ravine internally, but a faint path makes its way up the rocky shoulder and gives scope to view the noisy gorge at various points, with the final mare's-tail fall and swirling pool, definitely the highlight, simply accessed. Above this naturally reconnect with the bridleway by the broken wall. Above, walkers must cope with marshy ground, a portent for anyone contemplating the damp journey through Mosedale (pronounced 'mowsdil').

As a low broken wall comes into view veer right with the quad track, which weaves a nice grassy line up the slope above Nabs Crag to meet the fence. Follow the fence W, dipping through the basin of Hobgrumble Gill. For an attractive variant, as you come onto Nabs Moor drift right and come down along the brow of Nabs Crag to reach the impressive head of the Hobgrumble Gill ravine. Watch your footing in the dramatic setting, as you peer back down upon Dodd Bottom and Swindale Head. Angle left to reconnect with the fence and climb unhindered to the summit.

THE SUMMIT

The fact that the considerable wind-shelter rests a little distance from the precise summit will be an academic point in a storm. Close behind the shelter the ridge fence

Summit wind shelter

takes a right-angled turn – again useful for navigation in the said storm. The view is split between the Eden and the greater near mass of High Street, itself best viewed from the western edge of the plateau.

SAFE DESCENTS

Although the fence is a handy guide, the simplest recourse in atrocious weather is to head NE then N via Selside End. A clear path leads down to the pass traversed by the Old Corpse Road (moorland track). Go left for Mardale Head and right for Swindale Head.

RIDGE ROUTE

BRANSTREE ↓ 115m/375ft ↑ 55m/180ft 2km/1¼ miles

The continuous ridge fence is a mist-defying navigation aid, although it does not abide to the ridge. Captain Whelter Bog is a minor bare peat moment in the first depression, at which point the strict ridge can be adhered to by crossing carefully. A thin path is found leading over the gentle dome of High Howes, some 18m (60ft) higher than Selside Pike. This route enables you to pass a large pool and visit the survey post erected by the Haweswater engineers as alignment for their aqueduct down Longsleddale to Watchgate, bound for Mancunia (Greater Manchester). The two cairns on Artlecrag Pike provide the main foreground interest on the ridge connection, the vertically fractured bedrock underfoot reminiscent of Ill Bell.

PANORAMA

N

Gillalees Beacon
Penrith
Castle Carrock Fell
Cold Fell
Hare Shaw
Croglin Fell
Knipe Scar
The Three Battalions
Hartside Pass
Melmerby Fell
Cross Fell
Little Dun Fell
Great Dun Fell
Knock Fell
Shap
High Cup Nick
Appleby
Murton Pike
Mickle Fell
Roman Fell
Warcop Military Range
Brough
Seat Robert
Great Knipe
Stainmore Pass

E

E

Nine Standards Rigg
Scam Matthew
Mallerstang Edge
Wet Sleddale
Wild Boar Fell
Swarth Fell
Wasdale Pike
Green Bell
Randygill Top
The Calf
Arant Haw
Great Yarlside
Howes
Whernside
Ingleborough
Craven Fault
Pendle Hill
Hobgrumble Gill *combe*
Harrop Pike
Grey Crag

S

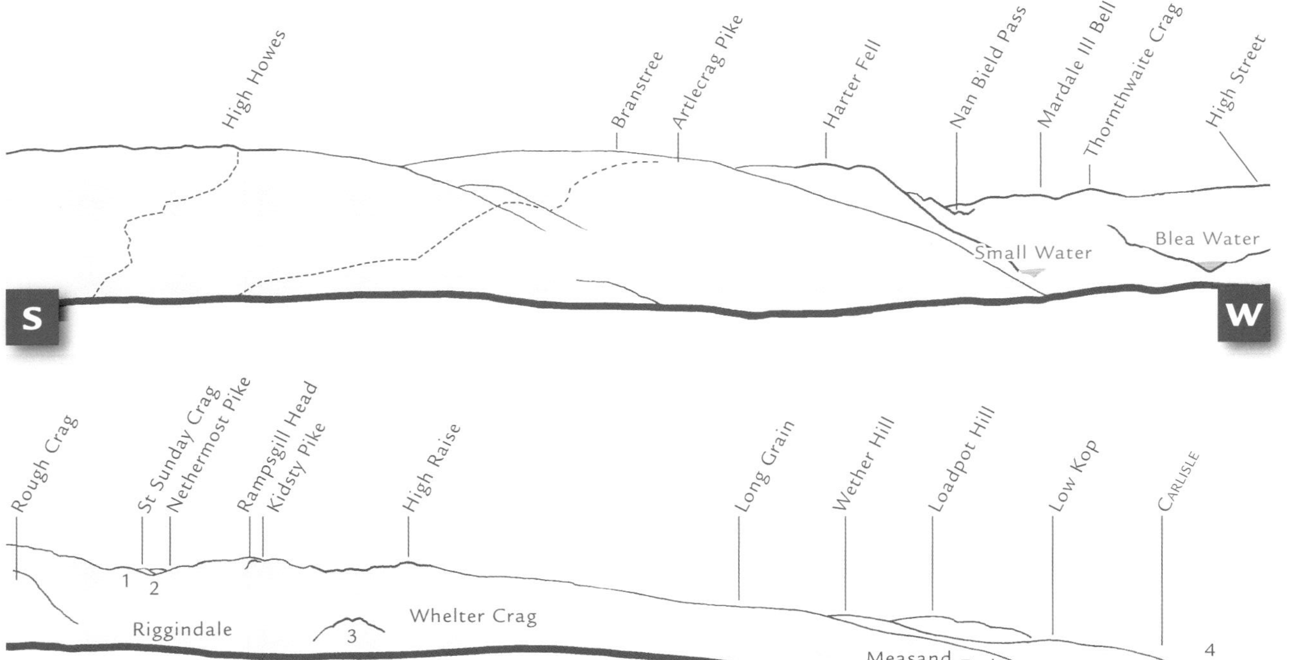
High Howes
Branstree
Artlecrag Pike
Harter Fell
Nan Bield Pass
Mardale Ill Bell
Thornthwaite Crag
High Street
Small Water
Blea Water
S
W
Rough Crag
St Sunday Crag
Nethermost Pike
Rampsgill Head
Kidsty Pike
High Raise
Long Grain
Wether Hill
Loadpot Hill
Low Kop
Carlisle
1
2
Riggindale
3
Whelter Crag
Measand End
4
W
N
1 Short Stile 2 Straits of Riggindale 3 Lady's Seat 4 Brunskill Pike

26 SHIPMAN KNOTTS *(587m/1926ft)*

The gradual fall of high pasture from Harter Fell over Kentmere Pike and Goat Scar is briefly held in check upon the knobbled top of Shipman Knotts. A comparatively narrow, final robust statement of fell-hood, it forms a craggy partition dividing upper Longsleddale from Kentmere. On either side of the fell are contrasting hamlets. The shaded bower of Sadgill is an enchanting place – to simply stand before the bridge and consider the scene, two traditional farmsteads set against the mighty backdrop of Goat Scar, is both thought-provoking and incredibly beautiful. It encapsulates human endeavour sustained and pitted against a wild, unforgiving terrain and climate. Contrast this with the residential community of Hallow Bank on the Kentmere flank, open to bask in the afternoon sun. The fell name, meaning 'Shipman's rocks', comes from a surname that evolved in the 14th century to describe a shepherd – although why it occurs just the once in Lakeland remains a mystery. A sturdy ridge wall snakes over the crest, denying walkers the chance to stand on the true summit. Appropriately, only shepherds and their sheep have that honour! Ways to the top are rather limited, too – confined to the south, from off the Stile End Pass, and the west, by Withered Howe.

 ↑ Shipman Knotts – not the true summit, but the accessible one

ASCENT FROM SADGILL (27)

Via Stile End Pass 390m/1280ft 3km/2 miles

At the point of obvious transition from rolling moorland to craggy mountains, from Silurian to Borrowdale volcanic rock, sandwiched by a thin band of Coniston limestone, there runs an old inter-dale connecting track which is the obvious springboard for an ascent. **1** Cross Sadgill Bridge, bear left to go through the gate right of the grand old Westmorland barn and enter a gated lane, the surface of which has been challenged by sudden wash-out events. Higher, beyond the walled lane, cobbling has been attempted in the bedrock; nonetheless the surface is less than pleasant for both walkers and bikers (many of whom come this way on their extended journeys). Levelling, go through a gate and break right from the farm track, stepping through marshy ground to embark on the ascent proper, guided by the rising wall.

The bad step leading to the first wall-side shoulder from the south

A rock-step adds interest (but is unpleasant during a wet-weather descent). Above Wray Crag (which means 'the corner cliff') the ridge takes a breather itself. This inevitably this means further marshy ground to cope with through the knolls, until the climb is resumed beside the snaking wall to the compensatory summit cairn (as the true summit, on the east side of the ridge wall, is not accessible).

Sadgill Bridge backed by Goat Scar

ASCENT FROM HALLOW BANK (31)

Via Stile End 320m/1050ft 2.3km/1½ miles

2 Turn E up the gated lane, passing the Stile End field barns, go through a third gate, and follow the open track round a curve. As a fenced sapling is passed on the right break onto a quad-bike green-way half-left through the early bracken. As the canny modern shepherd knows where he may drive his fell-bike, so walkers will find by deft design an unhampered way to climb the south-east slope avoiding outcropping. Coming onto the ridge to join forces with the regular recreational route from the top of the Stile End Pass, weave through the marshy hollows to connect with the ridge wall and complete the climb.

Via Withered Howe 330m/1085ft 2.3km/1½ miles

3 Follow the road into the hamlet of Hallow Bank, keep right, and below Brockstones take the green track up from the garage by Beald Head to a gate onto a fell path. A consistent path, sometimes in a stony groove, by trees and bushes ensures a steady plod up to and through a gateless wall-gap, from where the top of the bastion outcrop of Withered Howe is niftily gained for a brilliant view of the upper Kentmere valley. From here soft rushes cause the path to keep reasonably close order with the rising wall, but it does veer away N and NE before the wall falters. But take no heed of this; continue up the fell without the benefit of a path, curving onto the damp ridge unfettered, bound for the summit knoll.

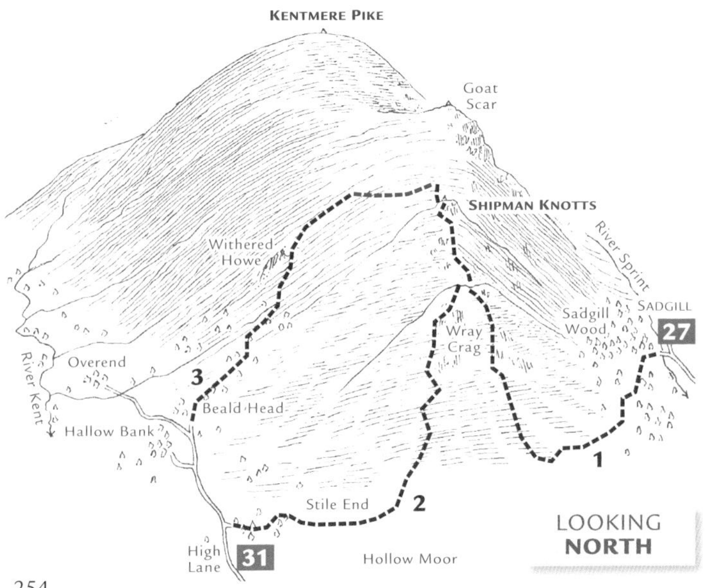

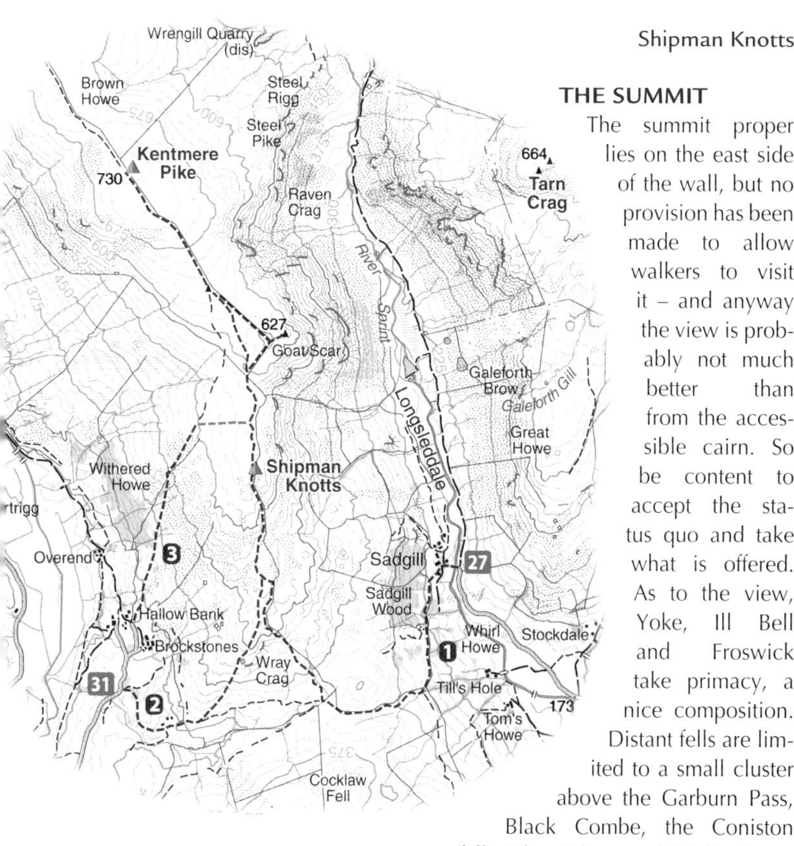

THE SUMMIT

The summit proper lies on the east side of the wall, but no provision has been made to allow walkers to visit it – and anyway the view is probably not much better than from the accessible cairn. So be content to accept the status quo and take what is offered. As to the view, Yoke, Ill Bell and Froswick take primacy, a nice composition. Distant fells are limited to a small cluster above the Garburn Pass, Black Combe, the Coniston fells, Pike o'Blisco and Crinkle Crags.

SAFE DESCENTS

Retrace Route 2, achieved by following the wall S onto the knolled shoulder and holding to the course of the quad-bike track down to the Stile End track. This angles off the south-east shoulder, avoiding Wray Crag and certainly avoiding the plague of the wall-side path, which has two uncomfortable rock-step moments.

RIDGE ROUTE

KENTMERE PIKE **↓ 165m/540ft** **↑ 20m/65ft** **2km/1¼ miles**

Walk N, passing to the left of a knoll and coping with marshy ground before crossing a high ladder-stile. Walkers may bear right with the fence to visit the top of Goat Scar, greatly recommended, or follow on NW with hasty hikers, coming up by the fence, and later a wall, to reach the summit.

PANORAMA

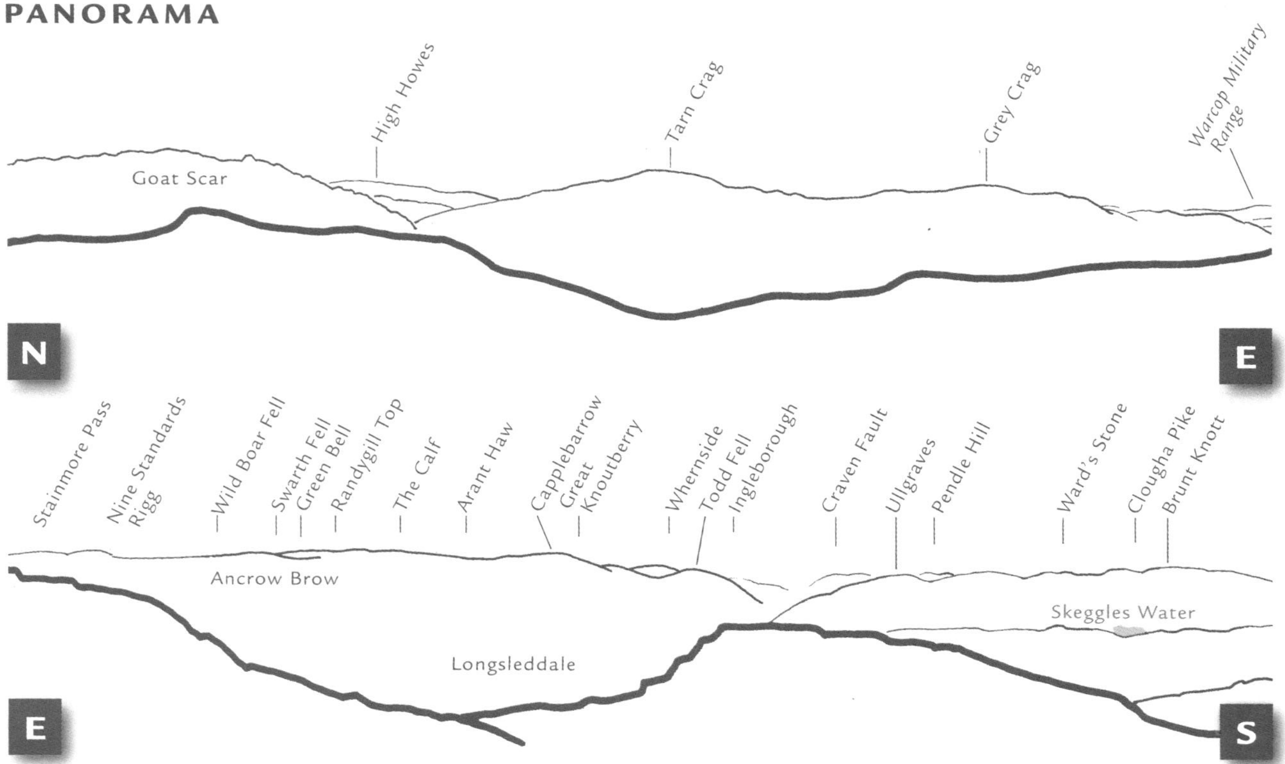
High Howes
Tarn Crag
Grey Crag
Warcop Military Range
Goat Scar
N
E
Stainmore Pass
Nine Standards Rigg
Wild Boar Fell
Swarth Fell
Green Bell
Randygill Top
The Calf
Arant Haw
Capplebarrow
Great Knoutberry
Whernside
Todd Fell
Ingleborough
Craven Fault
Ullgraves
Pendle Hill
Ward's Stone
Clougha Pike
Brunt Knott
Ancrow Brow
Skeggles Water
Longsleddale
E
S

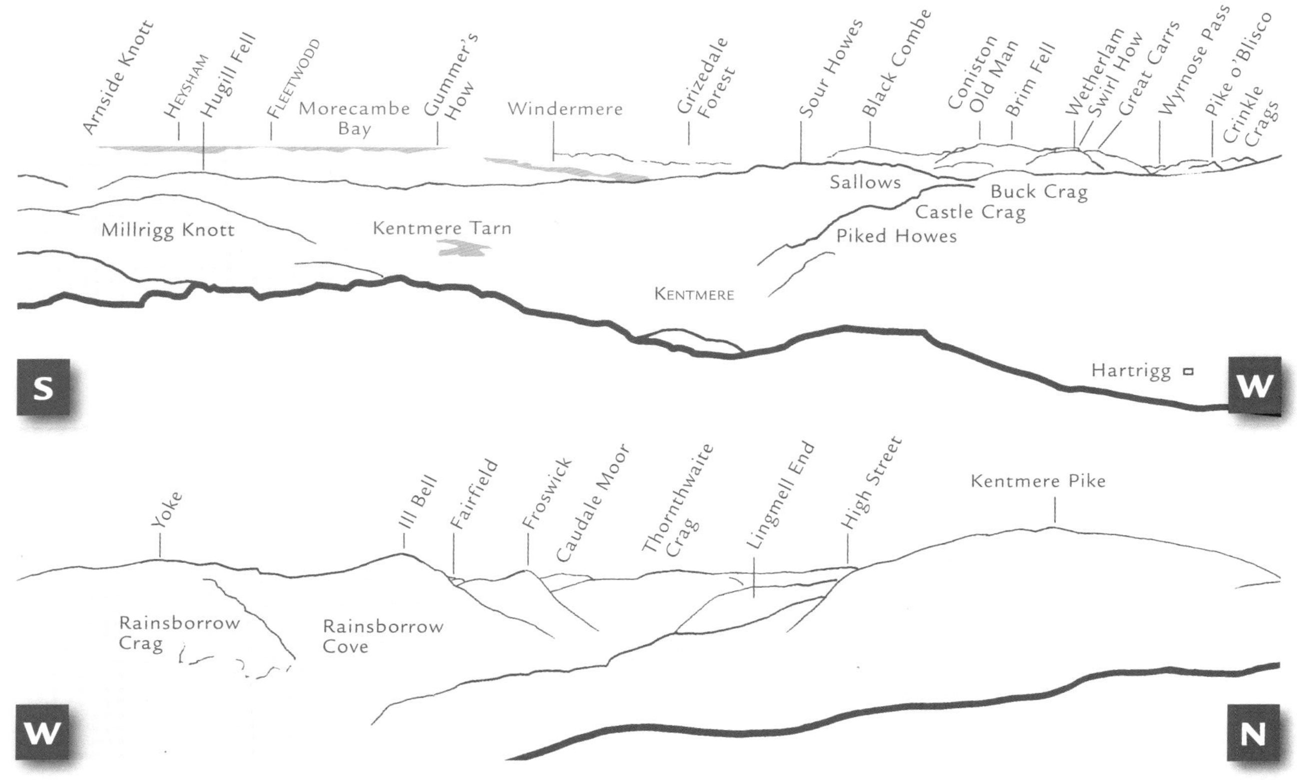
Arnside Knott
HEYSHAM
Hugill Fell
FLEETWOOD
Morecambe Bay
Gummer's How
Windermere
Grizedale Forest
Sour Howes
Black Combe
Coniston Old Man
Brim Fell
Wetherlam
Swirl How
Great Carrs
Wrynose Pass
Pike o'Blisco
Crinkle Crags
Sallows
Buck Crag
Castle Crag
Piked Howes
Millrigg Knott
Kentmere Tarn
KENTMERE
Hartrigg
S
W
Yoke
Ill Bell
Fairfield
Froswick
Caudale Moor
Thornthwaite Crag
Lingmell End
High Street
Kentmere Pike
Rainsborrow Crag
Rainsborrow Cove
W
N

27 STEEL KNOTTS *(433m/1421ft)*

This little rocky ridge with its impressive summit may lack the stature of many in the range, but will endear itself to all who pay it due attention. Many walkers are content to climb Steel Knotts as a solo event, in the same way that they tackle Hallin Fell across The Hause. However, from Steel Knotts there is a long, tenuous ridge connection with the high ground of Wether Hill and the High Street Roman road, via Brownthwaite Crag and Gowk Hill, to lure you to greater things (see WETHER HILL Route 1 for the route description). The fell forms the western side-wall to the quiet pastures of Fusedale, the 'dale of the cow-house', while to its west are the glories of Martindale in all its serenity, a landlocked world apart. The more natural lines of ascent come up from Martindale's new and old churches, with a lovely bonus up the north ridge from Howtown and one off-beat rear route out of Fusedale.

 ↑ Steel Knotts from across the southern entrance to Fusedale

ASCENT FROM FUSEDALE (10)

Via Fusedale 260m/855ft 2.4km/1½ miles

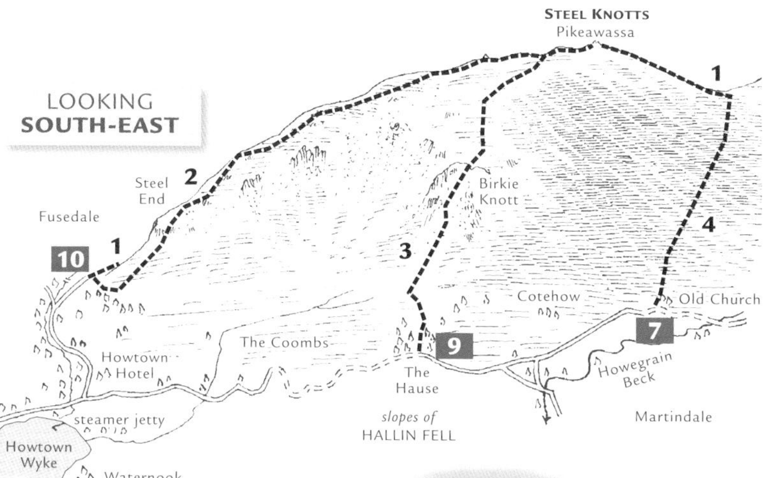

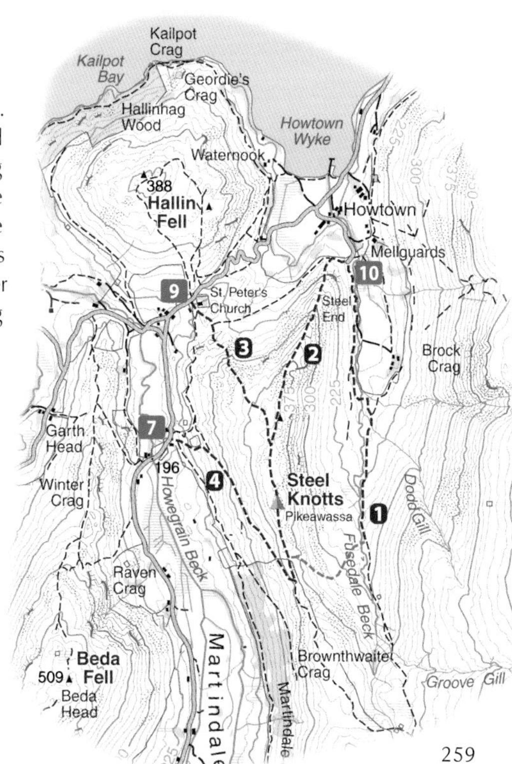

1 The nifty backdoor approach. Follow the concrete farm road S as for Cote Farm. Coming to a cattle grid, step over the footbridge right and follow the footpath that rises then declines to cross the footbridge over Fusedale Beck. The succeeding path angles right and crosses Dodd Gill via a smaller footbridge and heads up the valley. A lovely gorge is seen close beneath the path adorned with trees. As this section ends, and with stone heaps to the right excavated to create the original drove, step off down to the right and ford the beck. Angle half-left, avoiding the bracken, to a ruckle of stones and then switch up right to

Steel End

find an earthy path through the upper band of bracken and reach the saddle close to the wall-stile. Complete the ascent unfettered right, joining Route 4.

Via Steel End 255m/835ft 1.5km/1 mile

A joy every step of the way. **2** Follow the bridle track rising from the verge parking at the cattle grid. The bridle path comes up by the wall, passing an ash tree to reach a manhole cover and AV marker. Break left onto Steel End, with a tangible path mounting through the bracken and up a gap in the ridge-end outcropping. Ascend the north ridge by a sequence of pleasant stepped stages, with ample encouragement to stop and enjoy the surroundings. As well as the comings and goings of the Ullswater cruises in Howtown Wyke, there are views over Cote Farm in Fusedale to the great mass of Loadpot Hill (E) and over The Coombs to Hallin Fell (W). Higher, notice a line of stones mark a division of the ridge – presumably set in place to resolve an argument of grazing rights sometime in the past. Bracken keeps up appearances until the higher ridge is gained and the path switchbacks, easily passing an intermediate cairn en route to the summit outcrop.

ASCENT FROM THE HAUSE (9)

Via Birkie Knott 195m/640ft 1.2km/¾ mile

A route for anyone opting to start from The Hause at the entry to the landlocked Martindale valleys. **3** The blunt craggy ridge of Birkie Knott is a grand little challenge, best used as an ascent. From St Peter's Church the bridleway heads SE over the bracken-clad knoll to the left of Lanty Tarn. Depart the bridleway and set to work climbing the nose of the ridge ahead. As the slope abates, the path wends S onto a grassy ridge to unite with the ridge path south of the prominent cairn and undulates to the summit.

ASCENT FROM MARTINDALE OLD CHURCH (7)

Via the bridleway 230m/755ft 1.5km/1 mile

St Martin's Church in spring

4 From the open verge beside the humble 16th-century kirk, where in spring golden daffodils carpet the small church garth, walk up behind the ageing yew onto a bridleway that slants right up through the bracken and goes via a hand-gate in a downward wall onto the ridge. Cut back left to cross the ridge-wall stile after 100m and complete the climb up the open turf of the south ridge.

THE SUMMIT

An impressive blade of pale volcanic rock defines the summit, meriting a name – Pikeawassa. A well-balanced walker might place a foot on the precise summit, but such an act is tempting fate. Far more worthy is the pleasure of the view, particularly south into the secret world at the head of the Howegrain Beck valley, centred upon The Nab, intervening between the valleys of Rampsgill Beck and Bannerdale. More immediately Beda Fell is extremely well seen to the south-west. The summit lies at the southern end of a lovely ridge, which is best explored in a south–north expedition to Steel End.

Pikeawassa – a cairn would be superfluous

SAFE DESCENTS

Head S to cross the wall-stile and after 100m switch right for Martindale.

PANORAMA

Liddesdale
Bewcastle Fells
Gillalees Beacon
Cold Fell
Sharrow Bay
Croglin Fell
PENRITH
Renwick Fell
Bonscale Pike
course of High Street Roman road
Loadpot Hill
Ullswater
Mellguards
Croft Farm
Fusedale
Dodd Gill
N
E
Wether Hill
Red Crag
High Raise
Rampsgill Head
Dodd Gill
Gowk Hill
Fusedale
Brownthwaite Crag
E
S

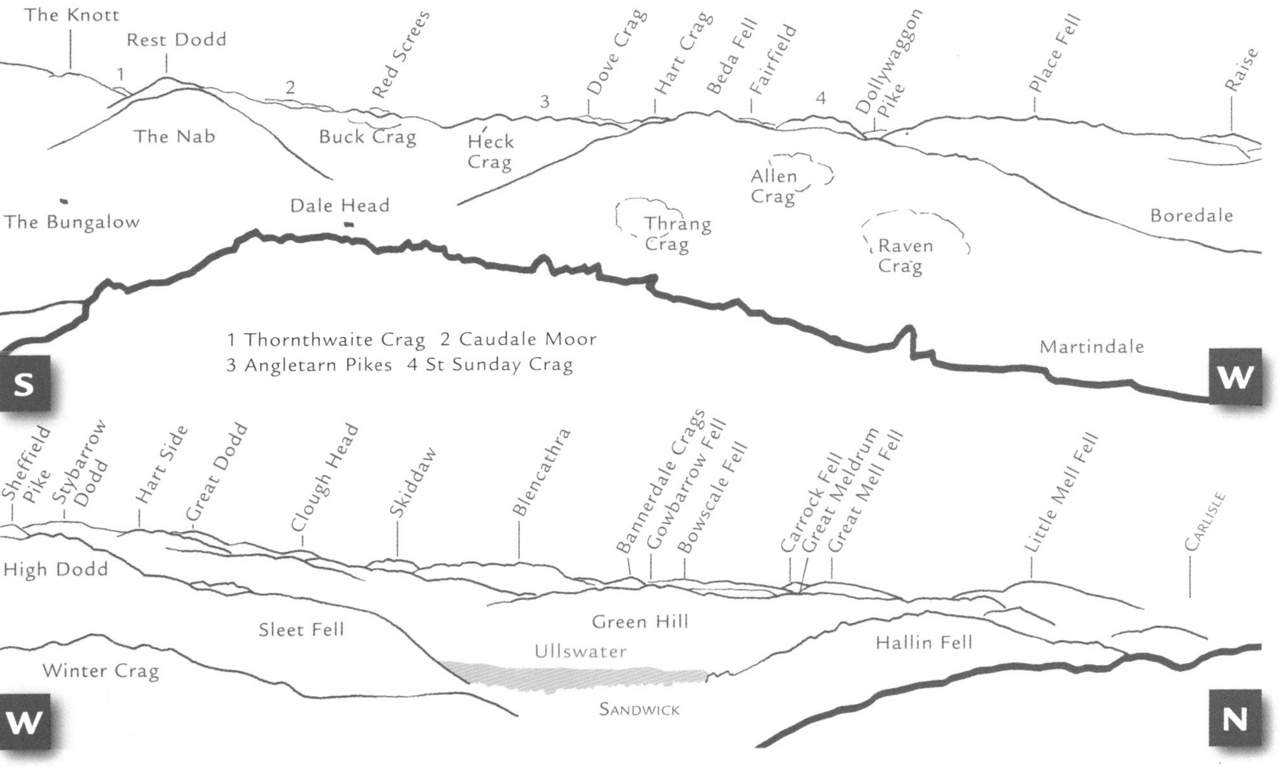
The Knott
Rest Dodd
1
2
Red Screes
3
Dove Crag
Hart Crag
Beda Fell
Fairfield
4
Dollywaggon Pike
Place Fell
Raise
The Nab
Buck Crag
Heck Crag
Allen Crag
The Bungalow
Dale Head
Thrang Crag
Raven Crag
Boredale
1 Thornthwaite Crag 2 Caudale Moor
3 Angletarn Pikes 4 St Sunday Crag
Martindale
S
W
Sheffield Pike
Stybarrow Dodd
Hart Side
Great Dodd
Clough Head
Skiddaw
Blencathra
Bannerdale Crags
Gowbarrow Fell
Bowscale Fell
Carrock Fell
Great Meldrum
Great Mell Fell
Little Mell Fell
Carlisle
High Dodd
Green Hill
Sleet Fell
Ullswater
Hallin Fell
Winter Crag
Sandwick
W
N

28 TARN CRAG *(664m/2179ft)*

Tarn Crag from Steel Pike

A soul mate of Grey Crag, Tarn Crag sits at the very edge of everything Lakeland and lovely. Being a beginning and an end carries responsibilities, a burden the fell carries with a dour charm. Its steep west wall, centred upon the fierce buttresses of Buckbarrow Crag, lends majesty to the head of Longsleddale and gives the fell sufficient dignity to claim its rightful place in the company of Cumbrian mountains. It is likely to be climbed, much as George Mallory climbed Everest, 'because it is there', rather than for its own intrinsic beauty. Only one route to the top can claim to be fun, that by Galeforth Brow. Walkers might also venture to the fell from Mosedale Cottage, a wet trek in any season, and from Wet Sleddale, aiming for Brunt Tongue moor, but both routes, though saturated, are drained of joy and not described here.

 ↑ Western aspect of Tarn Crag in winter clothes

ASCENT FROM SADGILL (27)

Via Galeforth Brow 470m/1540ft 2.8km/1¾ miles

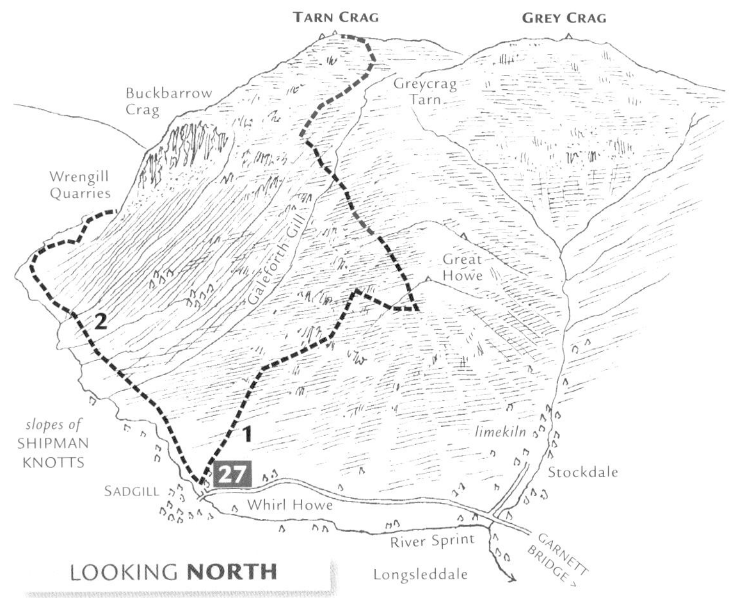

1 Embark as per GREY CRAG Route 1, and upon reaching the second stile with its dog-gate, where the wall converts to a fence, cross and switch back N alongside the wall. Keep with this, although the path rises slightly under a low crag and rowan tree to reconnect, until the wall abruptly and wantonly ends. The faint hint of a contouring path may be detected across the grassy slope, the trod becoming more evident as Galeforth Gill draws near and is forded. Beyond, accompany a fence rising easily to a fence-stile. Continue along Galeforth Brow and make a turn off right, at your inclination, contriving a pathless course onto the ridges and mossy slopes below the southern flank of the upper fell. Curve from NE to N by minor ribbed volcanic outcrops onto the summit plateau, bearing left to reach the summit cairn and the old aqueduct survey pillar.

Haweswater survey pillar

 ↑ Buckbarrow Crag from Goat Scar

Via the quarry lane-end 490m/1610ft 3.9km/2½ miles

The valley phase of this expedition, within the walled lane, contains all the scenic excitement of the next two routes. **2** Follow the drove and old quarry access lane N from Sadgill. As the broad valley floor squeezes down spot a new hand-gate on the right, inserted for the express use of rock-climbers intent on Buckbarrow Crag – it carries a seasonal notice. From the beginning of March to the end of May climbers are barred to permit the resident ravens to rear their annual brood. Walkers will keep within the lane, which becomes pitched as it steepens, with the lure of handsome waterfalls over the wall to the left in Cleft Ghyll. Come up to and go through a gate. Now turn to claim and climb your fell. Go right following the wall and then fence over the brow. Higher up cross a lateral plain fence (no stile) to ease onto the ridge, joining the edge path leading right to the summit.

Pitched quarry droveway above Cleft Ghyll

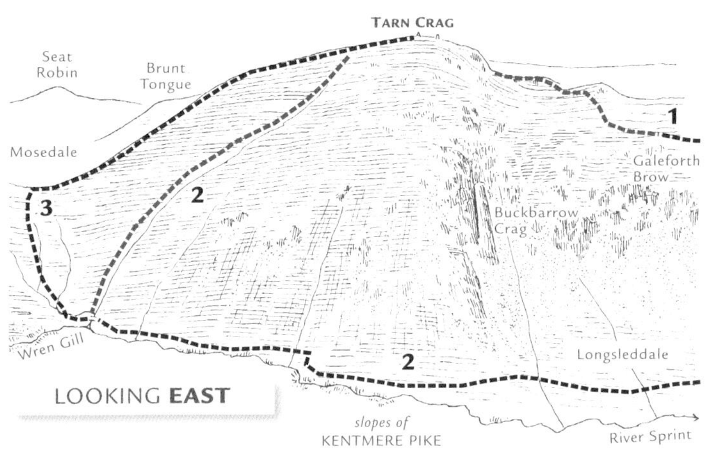

Via the north ridge 485m/1590ft 5km/3 miles

3 Walk on beyond the track gate, and on rounding a bend come to a three-way sign-post. Break right, signed 'Mosedale/Swindale', fording the beck draining Brownhowe Bottom. Keep to the more obvious path through damp ground, rising to a gate in the broad saddle, where Mosedale begins. But don't go through; instead turn right and follow the regular path beside the fence, easily evading a few early peat groughs. Higher up a lateral fence-stile is crossed to reach the summit plateau, with one consistent path all the way to the cairn.

THE SUMMIT

While it might be tempting to be disparaging about the general bearing of the fell, its dreary and far-ranging outlooks, the actual summit is worth its weight in salt. A small cairn sits on the highest point, but some 80 years ago Haweswater engineers built a survey pillar as a sighter for their south-flowing aqueduct and gave the southern brink a fascinating subject beside a rippling, reflective pool. Indeed, this southern scarp edge is a place to linger and reflect, taking a long perspective on Lakeland's bountiful fells, which may be said to have their beginnings here.

SAFE DESCENTS

Walk N, taking the early pathless line down a shallow hollow NNW to cross the plain fence. Follow on, descending on easy ground with a fence close left, and later a wall, to reach the gate at the top of the lane into Longsleddale.

Tarn Crag summit cairn

RIDGE ROUTES

BRANSTREE ↓ 155m/510ft ↑ 205m/675ft 2.6km/1½ miles

Head N to join the fence as it descends via a stile into the damp depression. Pass the gate and follow the continuing fence up as it bends and is replaced by a wall on Selside Brow. The path on grass rises steadily to a fence-stile on the summit.

GREY CRAG ↓ 65m/215ft ↑ 40m/130ft 1.4km/¾ mile

Track NE to join the ridge fence, with pools beyond. A sure and trusted companion, the fence comes down into a shallow basin of peat and soggy mosses. (For all its ankle-dipping moisture, this route is much better than following a compass bearing direct from Tarn Crag to Grey Crag, which would put the hapless navigator into waist-deep and worse water in traversing the bog of Greycrag Tarn.) Where the fence ends on a peaty waste bear S, with more clarity in the path, to the summit cairn.

PANORAMA

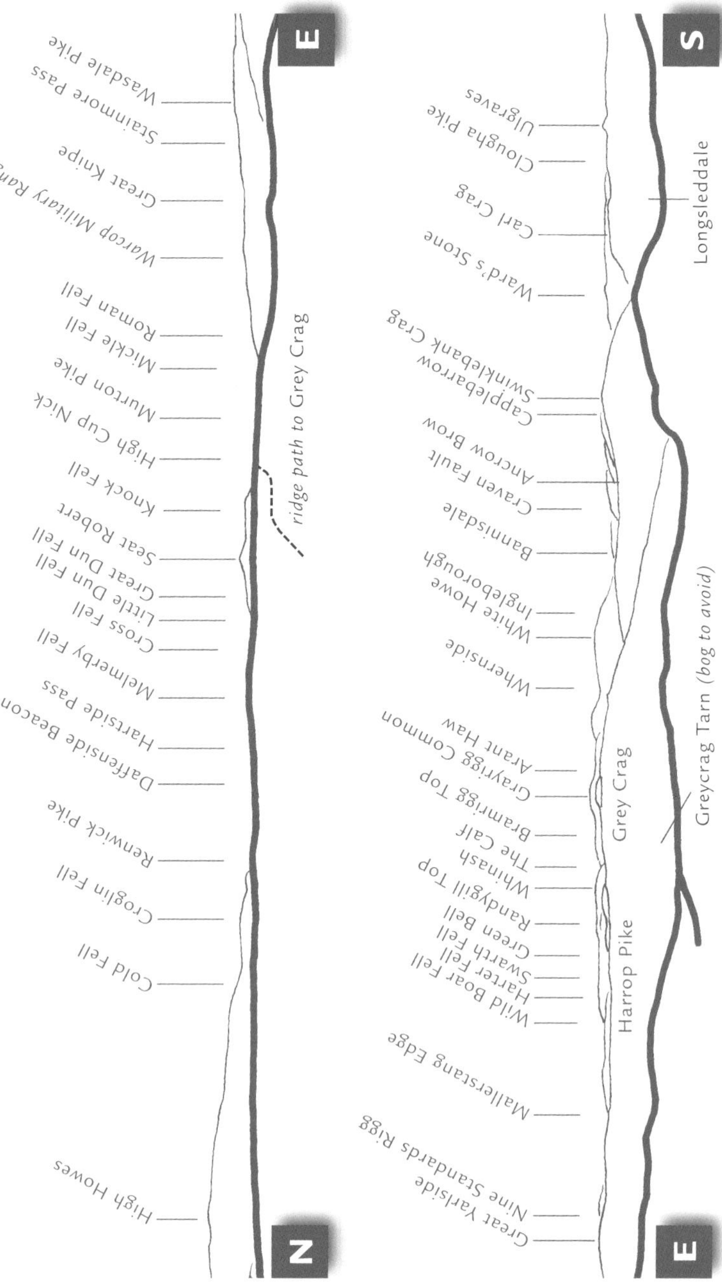

N – E

High Howes
Cold Fell
Croglin Fell
Renwick Pike
Daffenside Beacon
Hartside Pass
Melmerby Fell
Cross Fell
Little Dun Fell
Great Dun Fell
Seat Robert
Knock Fell
High Cup Nick
Murton Pike
Mickle Fell
Roman Fell
Warcop Military Range
Great Knipe
Stainmore Pass
Wasdale Pike

ridge path to Grey Crag

E – S

Great Yarlside
Nine Standards Rigg
Mallerstang Edge
Wild Boar Fell
Harter Fell
Swarth Fell
Green Bell
Randygill Top
Whinash
The Calf
Bramrigg Top
Grayrigg Common
Arant Haw
Whernside
White Howe
Ingleborough
Bannisdale
Craven Fault
Ancrow Brow
Capplebarrow
Swinklebank Crag
Ward's Stone
Carl Crag
Clougha Pike
Ulgraves

Harrop Pike
Grey Crag
Greycrag Tarn *(bog to avoid)*
Longsleddale

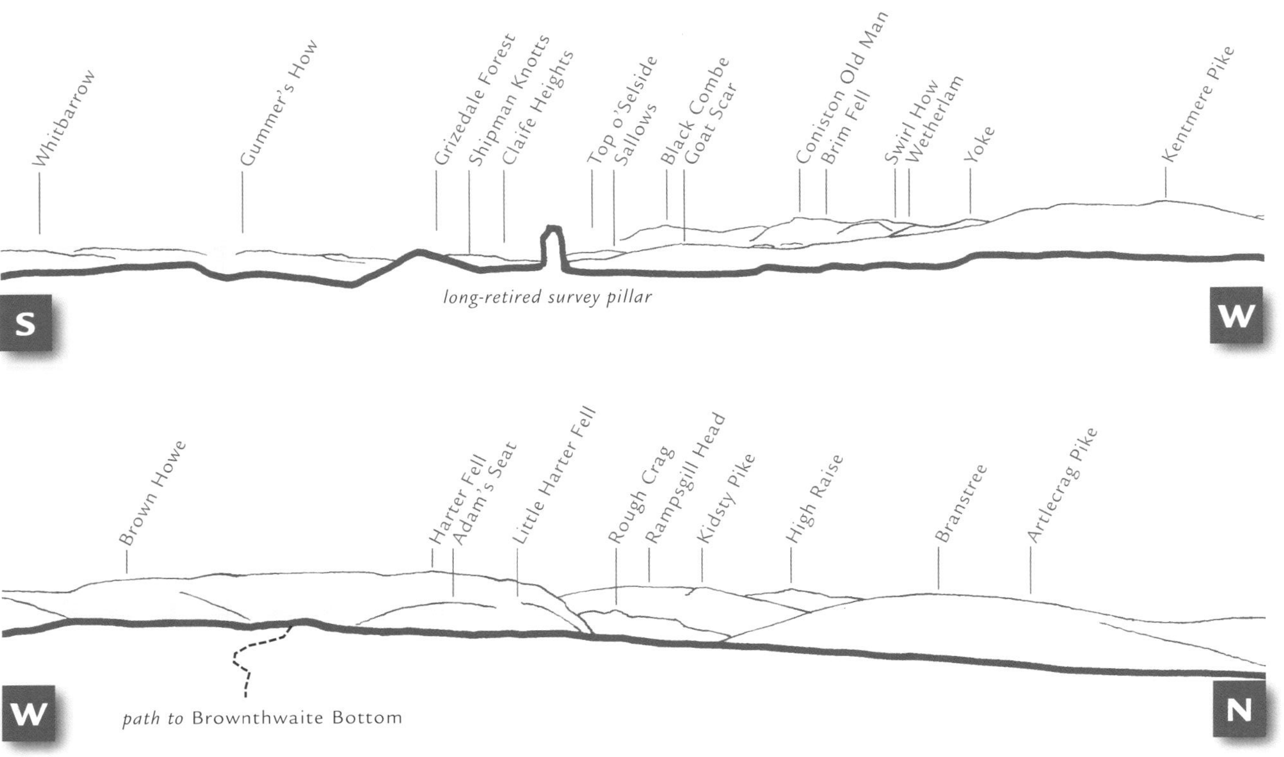
Whitbarrow
Gummer's How
Grizedale Forest
Shipman Knotts
Claife Heights
Top o'Selside
Sallows
Black Combe
Goat Scar
Coniston Old Man
Brim Fell
Swirl How
Wetherlam
Yoke
Kentmere Pike
long-retired survey pillar
S
W
Brown Howe
Harter Fell
Adam's Seat
Little Harter Fell
Rough Crag
Rampsgill Head
Kidsty Pike
High Raise
Branstree
Artlecrag Pike
W
path to Brownthwaite Bottom
N

29 THORNTHWAITE CRAG *(784m/2572ft)*

A landmark cairn and a nucleation of ridges and paths make this fell a popular target and the sure culmination of a great mountain day. With ridge routes to five fells practical, it is easy to see Thornthwaite Crag's radial appeal. The tall currick on the summit is known as a beacon, suggesting that a fire was lit on this prominent high point at important times in history. It would have been seen from many points in the south of the district and perhaps from some to the north, fixing this as a major horizon on the ancient highway. The Roman road glances just to the east of the beacon site, although walkers, bikers and horse-riders seldom fail to pay it homage.

WARNING: ROUTES 1 AND 4

The path climbing E beside the wall from Threshthwaite Mouth (Routes 1 and 4) is an abomination of loose stones. Avoid this horrible line of ascent by turning N on reaching the steepening slope, keeping below the rocks until matters improve. There is only a sheep trod on the grassy slope as the route comes over a lateral wall and works up onto the ridge from Gray Crag (and no path at all here), but the going is at least feasible and pleasant.

 ↑ Thornthwaite Crag from Caudale Moor

ASCENT FROM HARTSOP (3)

Via Threshthwaite Mouth 620m/2035ft 4.4km/2¾ miles

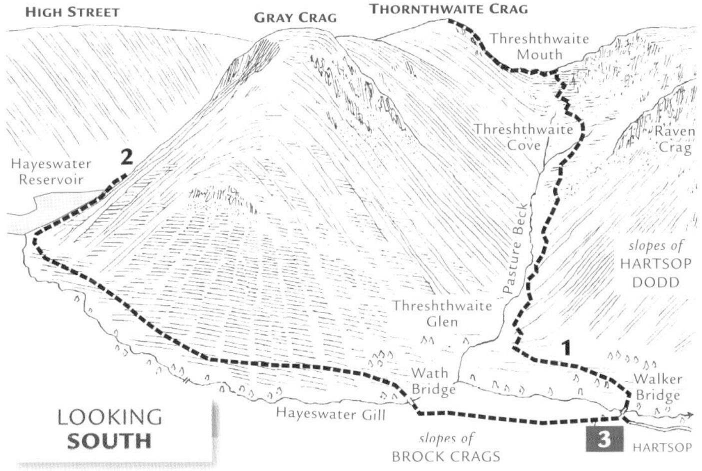

1 An impressive journey up the Threshthwaite Glen – the use of the Scottish term is appropriate, as walkers could well imagine that they were in some lonesome Highland mountain setting blinkered by mighty Munros. Cross Walker Bridge and follow the bridle track, which leads via gates into the Pasture Beck valley. This winds on merrily at an easy gradient until, with Raven Crag looming ahead, the path encounters rougher going via a wall-gap and passes up by great boulders. Much of the path from this point on has received sterling repair from Fix the Fells, with the headwall trod a sequence of stone steps by way of a couple of gill crossings. Coming onto the saddle, cross the broken wall and turn left. This is Threshthwaite Mouth (which translates as 'the threshold gap') – its disconnected 'tongue' protrudes, but not rudely, a long way to the south down the Trout Beck valley. Heed the route advice at the head of this chapter, and turn off the horrible stony ridge trail as the scree and outcropping intervene. Leave the mindless, head-down brigade to toil up the loose ribbon of stones onto the fell's eastern skyline. As the ridge wall becomes more solid, so arrives the handsome beacon cairn.

Via Hayeswater 620m/2035ft 5km/3 miles

2 Perhaps the bottom-rung choice, this is in effect a valley route almost to the summit. The early stage by the track up the Hayeswater Gill valley is a delight, the reservoir sombre, and the wild dale above rough underfoot and barren – although this may make the arrival of the Roman road all the more exciting! Follow the regular

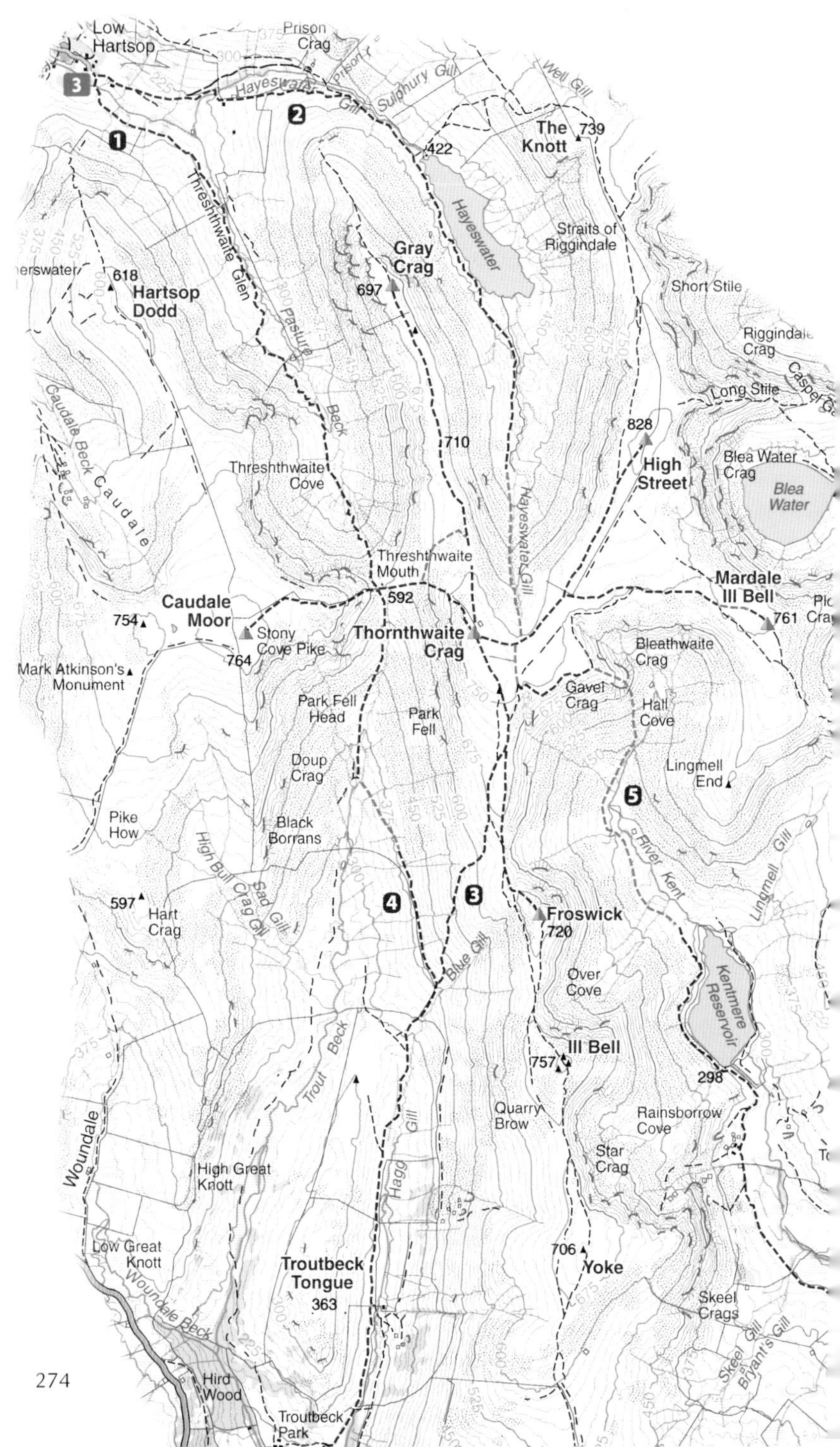
Low Hartsop
Prison Crag
Hayeswater Gill
Sulphury Gill
Well Gill
The Knott
739
422
Hayeswater
Threshthwaite Glen
Gray Crag
697
618
Hartsop Dodd
Pasture Beck
Straits of Riggindale
Short Stile
Riggindale Crag
Long Stile
Caudale Beck
Caudale
Threshthwaite Cove
710
828
High Street
Blea Water Crag
Blea Water
Hayeswater Gill
Threshthwaite Mouth
592
Mardale Ill Bell
761
Caudale Moor
754
Stony Cove Pike
764
Thornthwaite Crag
Bleathwaite Crag
Mark Atkinson's Monument
Park Fell Head
Park Fell
Gavel Crag
Hall Cove
Doup Crag
Lingmell End
Pike How
Black Borrans
River Kent
High Bull Crag Gill
Sad Gill
Lingmell Gill
597
Hart Crag
Froswick
720
Blue Gill
Over Cove
Kentmere Reservoir
Trout Beck
Ill Bell
757
298
Quarry Brow
Rainsborrow Cove
Woundale
Hagg Gill
Star Crag
High Great Knott
Low Great Knott
706
Yoke
Troutbeck Tongue
363
Woundale Beck
Skeel Crags
Skeel Gill
Bryant's Gill
Hird Wood
Troutbeck Park

track from the car park via gates, heading E, and pass the sheep pens. Avoid the inviting metalled waterworks roadway after the cattle grid. The track crosses Wath Bridge (where 'wath' means 'the fording place') and ascends by gates and a mossy-roofed laithe (field barn) to reach the reservoir. Hold to the near (western) shoreline. See the great landslip on the far fellside, an ancient event which created a massive gully at the top and gave some sense of isolation to The Knott from its parent, Rampsgill Head. Follow a dwindling path, which is lost on a rising rigg as the lake ends. Thereafter, with only moraine to catch the camera's lens, contour to find the easier ground until the boulders in the final phase at the gill birth cannot be avoided. The blessed relief of the Roman road, for all its worn bed, comes as salvation. Turn right to reach the beacon within 200m.

ASCENT FROM TOWN HEAD, TROUTBECK (34 – off map S)

Via Scot Rake 660m/2165ft 7.3km/4½ miles

3 Follow the navigation guidance in FROSWICK Route 1 from Troutbeck, via Ing Lane and the Hagg Gill valley, to embark on the grassy shelf of the old Roman way, Scot Rake. In effect stay with it through the grassy pasture, although walkers can bear off to join the modern substrate-inverted ridge path higher up. Yet the romance of continuity with travellers from an entirely different era has great appeal.

Scot Rake Roman road and modern ridge route climbing north

Water

Water

Hartrigg

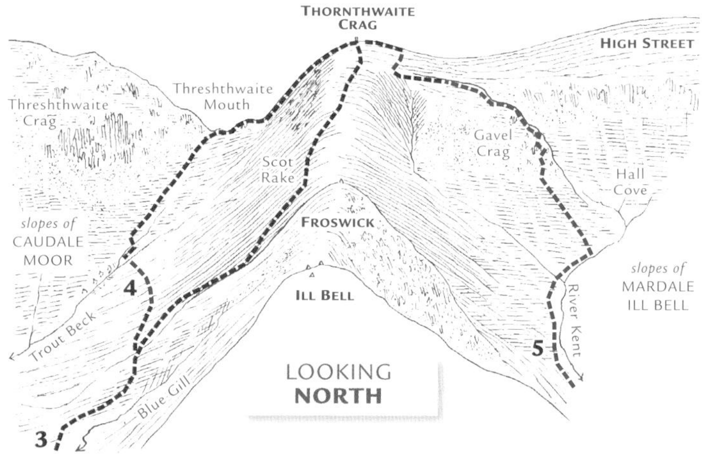

Via Threshthwaite Mouth 720m/2360ft 8.3km/5¼ miles

4 A little-considered variant breaks from the Roman way at the point where it climbs away from the wall adjacent to Blue Gill. Follow what is nothing more than a sheep path beside the wall, and as the wall drifts down left continue. The trod is quickly lost, but the going is straightforward, if rush-bound in places. Ford the headstream of Trout Beck immediately above the upper section of a rowan-filled ravine, where a waterfall spills excitedly into the dark channel. On top of the facing rigg find a path, created by descending walkers. Follow this narrow path in the grass up the valley, soon to be joined, acutely from the left, by the normal ascending path. The odd hoary cairn indicates the path's course, although it is never in doubt, coming under the scree slope beneath Threshthwaite Crag to reach the high threshold. At which point join the ridge route – or at least the route recommended at the start of the chapter!

Working up through small outcrops on the Gavel Crag route

ASCENT FROM KENTMERE (29 – off map S)

Via Kentmere Reservoir 630m/2065ft 7.3km/4½ miles

Thornthwaite Crag's lofty summit beacon in need of repair

5 This uncommonly tested route is described in HIGH STREET Route 4, a wild-country expedition demanding fair weather. Upon gaining the contouring path above Gavel Crag keep left (W) until a re-entrant gully intervenes. Here bear right (N) onto the plateau and join the Roman road to reach the summit.

THE SUMMIT

No shrinking violet of a cairn here – quite the contrary, a monumental pile, set up under purposeful instructions. Exposure to fierce winds and wild weather has inflicted damage to the beacon's crown. A scaffold would be needed to remedy affairs – and why not? There is history in those stones, or at least in the beacon's situation. The great cairn stands upon a fractured rock footing, the perfect situation to rest and partake of

High on Scot Rake looking south

Skyline cairn on ridge route from Froswick

refreshment. The panorama is spacious and rewarding. Of course the Helvellyn range serves up much of the fell fayre, but from Black Combe to Pillar the roof of Lakeland is there to be seen, with Mickledore set directly above Stony Cove Pike. Wansfell hides most of the upper reach of Windermere. A fine stretch of the Roman road is visible sweeping north along the western edge of High Street, apparently springing from beneath your feet.

SAFE DESCENTS

When in Rome do as the Romans – well, if you want to travel S then the Scot Rake path is as safe as they come. The ridge N to Gray Crag is preferable to skipping down to Threshthwaite Mouth and into the Threshthwaite Glen. Although be watchful of the crag at the northern tip of the ridge (keep right to avoid it) when joining the Hayeswater access track for Hartsop.

RIDGE ROUTES

CAUDALE MOOR ↓ 190m/625ft ↑ 170m/560ft 1.5km/1 mile

While it is possible to follow the wall and the ridge path NW, why suffer? This is meant to be a pleasure. Far better is to leave the summit on the east side of the ridge wall and stick to the ridge path (whose ultimate destination is Gray Crag). Watch for a lateral wall down to the left, aim down to it, cross it and come under the rough slope onto the ridge with its broken wall into Threshthwaite Mouth. Climb W from the notch, with several rock steps to entertain (or irritate) depending on prevailing conditions. Coming over the rock obstacle onto the grassy fell maintain company with the wall until the cairn of Stony Cove Pike lures you half-left.

FROSWICK	↓ 165m/540ft	↑ 95m/310ft	1.7km/1 mile

Follow the regular path S to a cairn on the brink, from where a modern trail ensues, leading down the ridge and through the saddle, and climbing on the path angling SE to the summit cairn.

GRAY CRAG	↓ 140m/460ft	↑ 50m/165ft	2km/1¼ miles

Walk N along the spine of the ridge, with handsome views on both hands. The chances of spotting a small herd of Martindale red deer is high, so be attentive. After a cairn, slip over a broken wall straddling the ridge to reach the solitary summit cairn.

HIGH STREET	↓ 30m/100ft	↑ 75m/245ft	1.6km/1 mile

Follow the worn trail E, which swings around the head of the Hayeswater valley and crosses over a broken wall in trending NE. Watch for a path breaking half-right which leads direct to the summit column.

MARDALE ILL BELL	↓ 60m/200ft	↑ 40m/130ft	1.8km/1 mile

Follow the Roman road until the broken wall. Here turn right (E), joining the edge path above Hall Cove, and veer off as the ground modestly rises onto the summit.

Ill Bell range from the ridge path to Mardale Ill Bell

PANORAMA

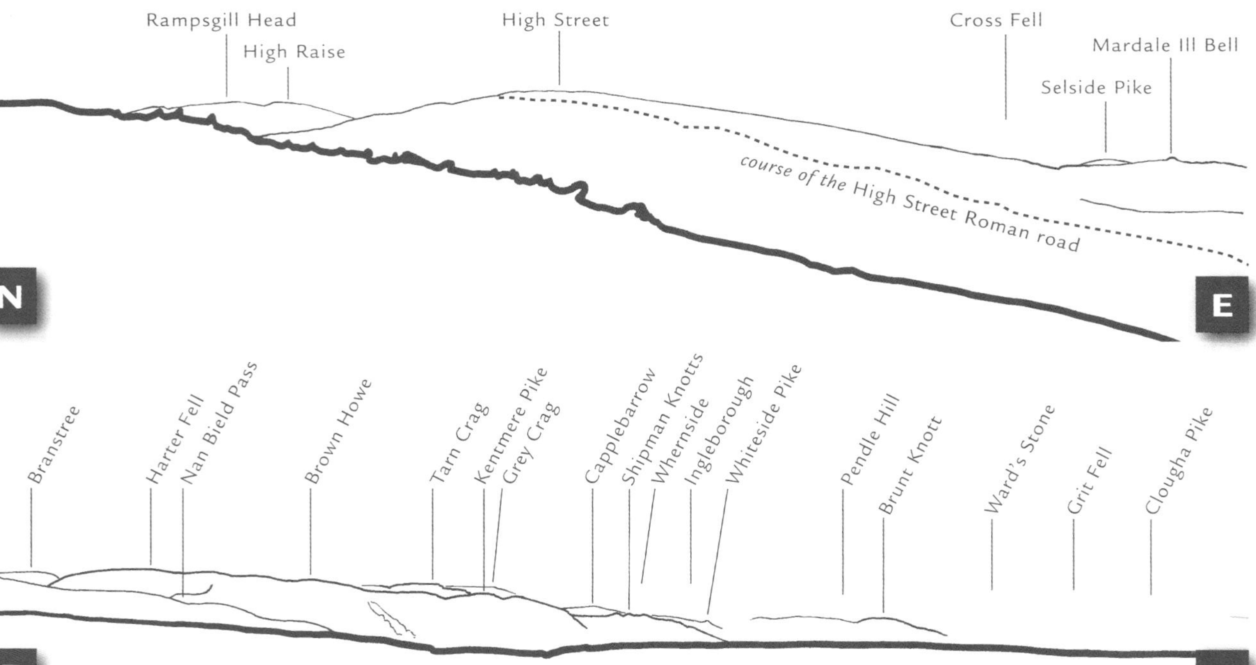
Rampsgill Head
High Raise
High Street
Cross Fell
Mardale Ill Bell
Selside Pike
course of the High Street Roman road
N
E
Branstree
Harter Fell
Nan Bield Pass
Brown Howe
Tarn Crag
Kentmere Pike
Grey Crag
Capplebarrow
Shipman Knotts
Whernside
Ingleborough
Whiteside Pike
Pendle Hill
Brunt Knott
Ward's Stone
Grit Fell
Clougha Pike
E
S

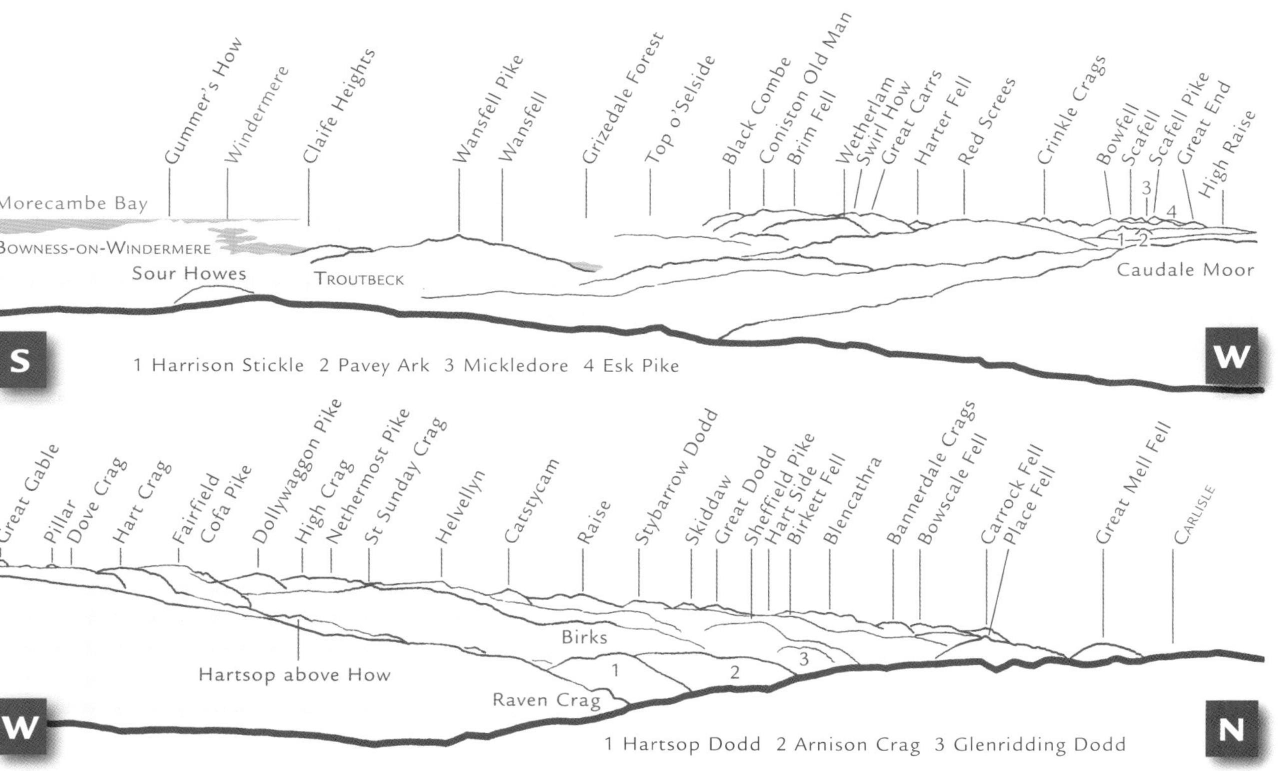

Gummer's How
Windermere
Claife Heights
Wansfell Pike
Wansfell
Grizedale Forest
Top o'Selside
Black Combe
Coniston Old Man
Brim Fell
Wetherlam
Swirl How
Great Carrs
Harter Fell
Red Screes
Crinkle Crags
Bowfell
Scafell
Scafell Pike
Great End
High Raise
Morecambe Bay
Bowness-on-Windermere
Sour Howes
Troutbeck
Caudale Moor
S
W
1 Harrison Stickle 2 Pavey Ark 3 Mickledore 4 Esk Pike
Great Gable
Pillar
Dove Crag
Hart Crag
Fairfield
Cofa Pike
Dollywaggon Pike
High Crag
Nethermost Pike
St Sunday Crag
Helvellyn
Catstycam
Raise
Stybarrow Dodd
Skiddaw
Great Dodd
Sheffield Pike
Hart Side
Birkett Fell
Blencathra
Bannerdale Crags
Bowscale Fell
Carrock Fell
Place Fell
Great Mell Fell
Carlisle
Birks
Hartsop above How
Raven Crag
W
N
1 Hartsop Dodd 2 Arnison Crag 3 Glenridding Dodd

30 TROUTBECK TONGUE *(363m/1191ft)*

Peering down upon the Troutbeck valley

By a quirk of nature this lowly wedge of rocky upland, which would feature only as a footnote elsewhere, provides nascent walkers with all they need to gain their first foothold in fellwalking. In combination with a stroll through the much admired village of Troutbeck and the dale pastures, it is superb. As the smallest fell in this guide, Troutbeck Tongue is proof that scale and size are not everything. Having no connection in any shape or form to another fell, it stands proud as punch in its own humble domain. While Trout Beck may seem to be a traditional hay meadow when viewed from Ing Lane, it turns wild and inhospitable upstream of Troutbeck Park Farm. 'Park' suggests the fell's former purpose as a red deer preserve. To the east of the fell runs a quiet side-valley drained by Hagg Gill, where ran the Roman High Street. The term 'hagg' tells of the former management of the valley as a coppiced woodland. Find here old slate quarries – the quantity of discarded stone seems either profligate or, more likely, suggests that the stone was not good enough. There is even a small slate quarry on the west side of the Tongue's summit ridge.

 ↑ Troutbeck Tongue from the Kirkstone Road

ASCENT FROM TOWN HEAD, TROUTBECK (34)

Via south ridge 240m/785ft 3.6km/2¼ miles

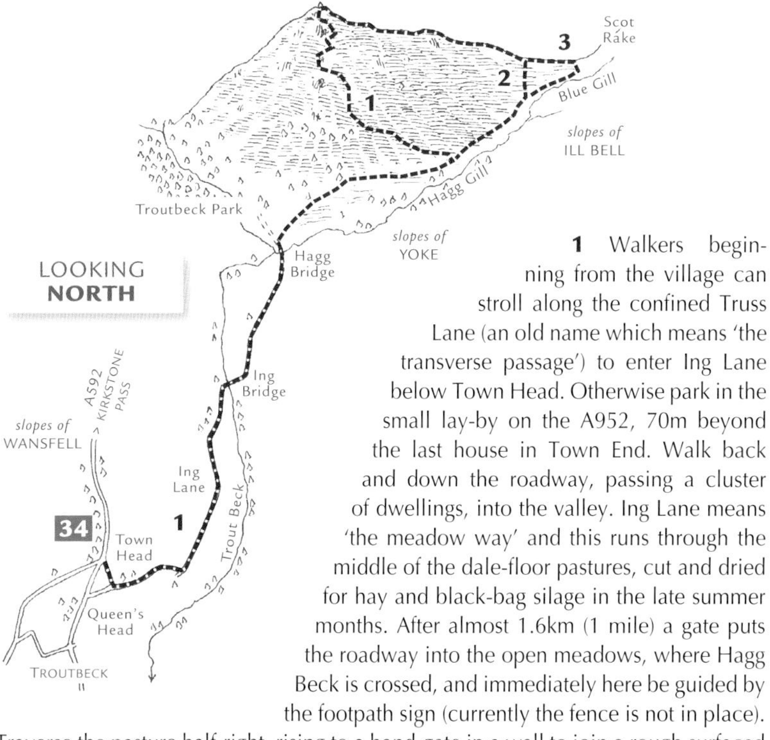

1 Walkers beginning from the village can stroll along the confined Truss Lane (an old name which means 'the transverse passage') to enter Ing Lane below Town Head. Otherwise park in the small lay-by on the A952, 70m beyond the last house in Town End. Walk back and down the roadway, passing a cluster of dwellings, into the valley. Ing Lane means 'the meadow way' and this runs through the middle of the dale-floor pastures, cut and dried for hay and black-bag silage in the late summer months. After almost 1.6km (1 mile) a gate puts the roadway into the open meadows, where Hagg Beck is crossed, and immediately here be guided by the footpath sign (currently the fence is not in place). Traverse the pasture half-right, rising to a hand-gate in a wall to join a rough surfaced track going right (there is no way left, for all the inference of a footpath on OS maps).

The track comes round into the Hagg Gill valley and leads through a gate. Here step up left, not tidily, nor with clear signs of a path, but be assured that a path exists once you are up beside the wall. Soon the path turns upwards, beating a way up the bracken slope onto the rocky spine of the south ridge. Cross a fence-stile and continue up the ridge by several turns to ultimately reach the summit cairn. It is a great ascent by any measure, excepting it is short – although new recruits to fellwalking will probably consider it sufficient for an initiation.

Via north ridge 250m/820ft 5.7km/3½ miles

2 Keep within the Hagg Gill valley on the bridle track via two further gates, and as the wall on the right dips away turn up onto the cut green way. This comes onto the ridge, at which point turn acutely left. Rough moor grass will slow the walker's eager stride up to a wonky stile located at an angle in the ridge-straddling fence. The ridge path thereafter comes by a rocky bank and heads on over a grassy knoll, which may in fact be a whisker higher than the following knoll, which is considered to be the summit. Well, at least this is where the conventional cairn is set.

Via the tumulus 250m/820ft 6.5km/4 miles

Ancient cairn

3 If you want to make a little more of the journey, continue with what is taken as the Roman road up the dale-floor of Hagg Gill. As this rises bear off left with a shepherd's track and cut back SW over the damp tussock pasture to find a Bronze Age tumulus. This has been tampered with in recent decades, creating both wind- and squat-shelters. It is in the way of man – he/she cannot resist handling stones and fashioning something new and meaningful from them, however inept and sacrilegious in hindsight. Evidence of a walkers' path can be detected weaving S through the tussock grass and duly uniting with Route 2 at the wonky stile. Let's hope it has been fixed by the time you use it!

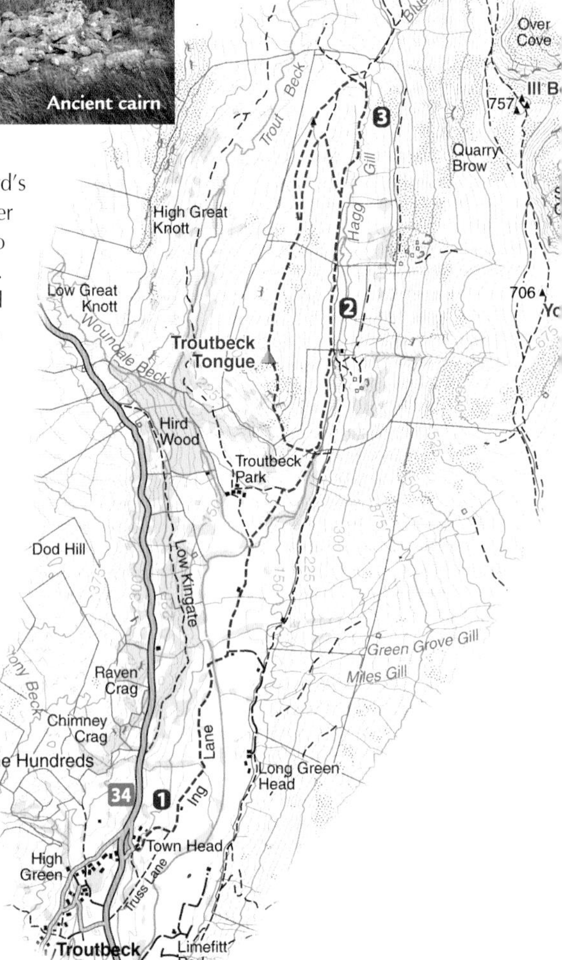

Troutbeck Tongue summit cairn

THE SUMMIT

They do say that if you want to enjoy a mountain you need to view it from mid-height. Well, sadly, little of what is in view looks better from this lowly station, although the wooded slopes leading up to and above the Kirkstone Road onto Dodd Hill look fine enough. As part compensation, you might have the fun of spotting Pike o'Blisco and Bowfell over the shoulder of Idle Hill, Wansfell's north ridge.

Troutbeck Tongue and the Hagg Gill valley from the foot of Blue Gill

SAFE DESCENTS

The regular way S is steep, so walkers new to the recreation should keep to the north ridge route and, after the wonky fence-stile, find the incline green way cutting back down into the Hagg Gill valley.

PANORAMA

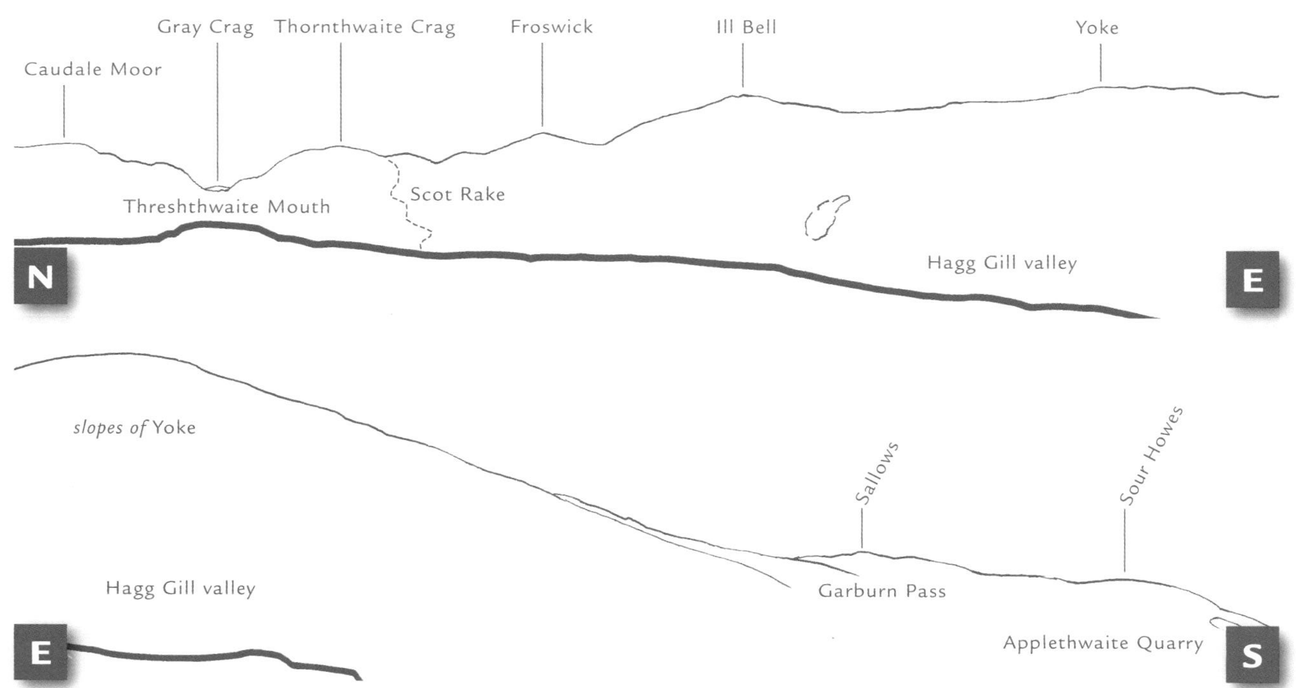
Caudale Moor
Gray Crag
Thornthwaite Crag
Froswick
Ill Bell
Yoke
Threshthwaite Mouth
Scot Rake
Hagg Gill valley
N
E
slopes of Yoke
Sallows
Sour Howes
Hagg Gill valley
Garburn Pass
Applethwaite Quarry
E
S

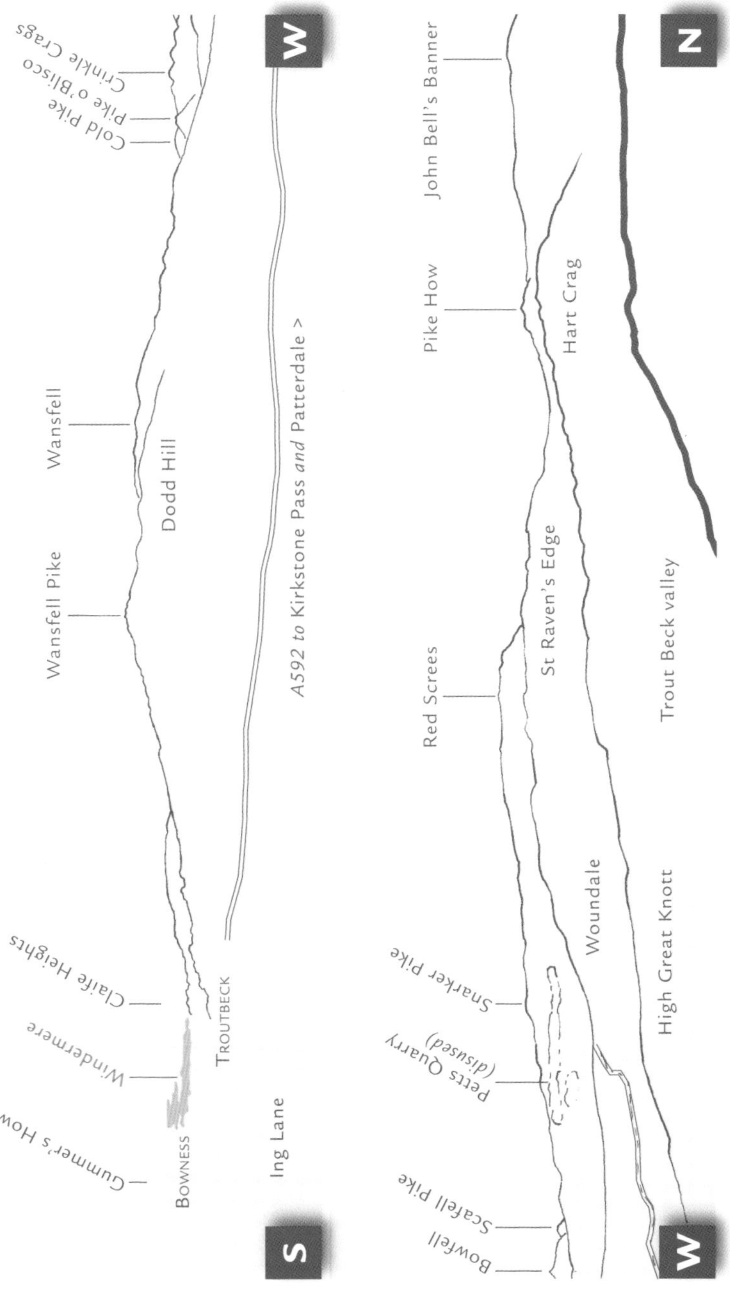
W
Crinkle Crags
Pike o'Blisco
Cold Pike
Wansfell
Dodd Hill
Wansfell Pike
A592 to Kirkstone Pass and Patterdale >
Claife Heights
Windermere
Troutbeck
Gummer's How
Bowness
Ing Lane
S
N
John Bell's Banner
Pike How
Hart Crag
St Raven's Edge
Red Screes
Trout Beck valley
Woundale
Snarker Pike
High Great Knott
Petts Quarry (disused)
Scafell Pike
Bowfell
W

31 WANSFELL *(489m/1604ft)*

Lying right in the midst of the Lakeland dream Wansfell pays host to two of its most popular paths, and yet much of its extent is quiet unfrequented pasture. Sandwiched between the Stock Ghyll and Trout Beck valleys, and isolated from the rest of the Far Eastern range by the straddling Kirkstone Road rising from Troutbeck Bridge, it is a fell apart. Troutbeck, strung along its eastern slope, is one of the village gems of Cumbria. Composed of a succession of traditional yeoman's steadings set along a mile-long lane, the village includes the National Trust's Town End, with its bank-barn still in use. Along the fell's southern apron, woods and pastures tumble to the shores of Windermere, lined with grand buildings. One, Brockhole, has been transformed into a dynamic inspiration centre for the Lake District National Park.

Of all the fell's virtues quite the best is the view from the summit of Wansfell Pike, even though this is not the summit of the fell. Windermere stretches south to the islands off Bowness, and round the arch from east to west is ranged such an amalgam of fantastic fell country that it may take the breath away. At the western foot of the fell lies the hub and hubbub of Ambleside, from where, since Roman times, walkers have made their way onto the slopes of the fell to marvel at its scenic setting.

 ↑ Summit cairn of Wansfell

ASCENT FROM AMBLESIDE (37) AND (38)

Via Stock Ghyll Force 465m/1525ft 3.7km/2¼ miles

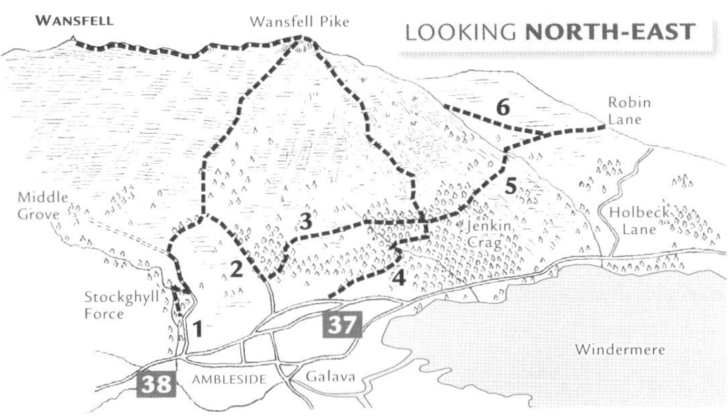

The popular route to Troutbeck via Wansfell Pike, invariably part of a circuit returning via Robin Lane and Skelghyll Woods. **1** From the Market Place, the busy shopping heart of the town, pass up by the Town Hall into Stockghyll Lane, above Cheapside. Either stay with the steep road or give yourself the early treat of visiting the impressive waterfall Stockghyll Force. For the latter, at gates enter the woodland park. Follow the eventually stepped pathway upstream to find the railed stance from where the elegant crashing falls can be admired. Veer right and rejoin Stockghyll Lane at a turnstile, then go left to emerge into pasture. The road advances to where the Wansfell Pike path is signed right, stepping up to a stile. The climb begins in earnest. At the

West to the head of Great Langdale from Wansfell Pike

Pitched path from Ambleside

next gate the path in a lane from Blue Hill Road joins from the right. Above this the fellside path climbs through light woodland via a plank-bridge and encounters some fine stepped pitching, an essential embellishment on a path that receives such constant footfall. Wansfell Pike itself is defended by a rugged boss of rock, and the path splits to achieve the headland viewpoint by a choice of steep ways. Pass through the metal hand-gate and settle upon the view for a few minutes – reward for all that effort. The common practice is to wend straight over on the path linking to either Nanny or Hundreds Lanes. Summiteers will follow the path by the wall NE, revelling in the ups and downs of the ridge, but maybe less so in the marshy hollows.

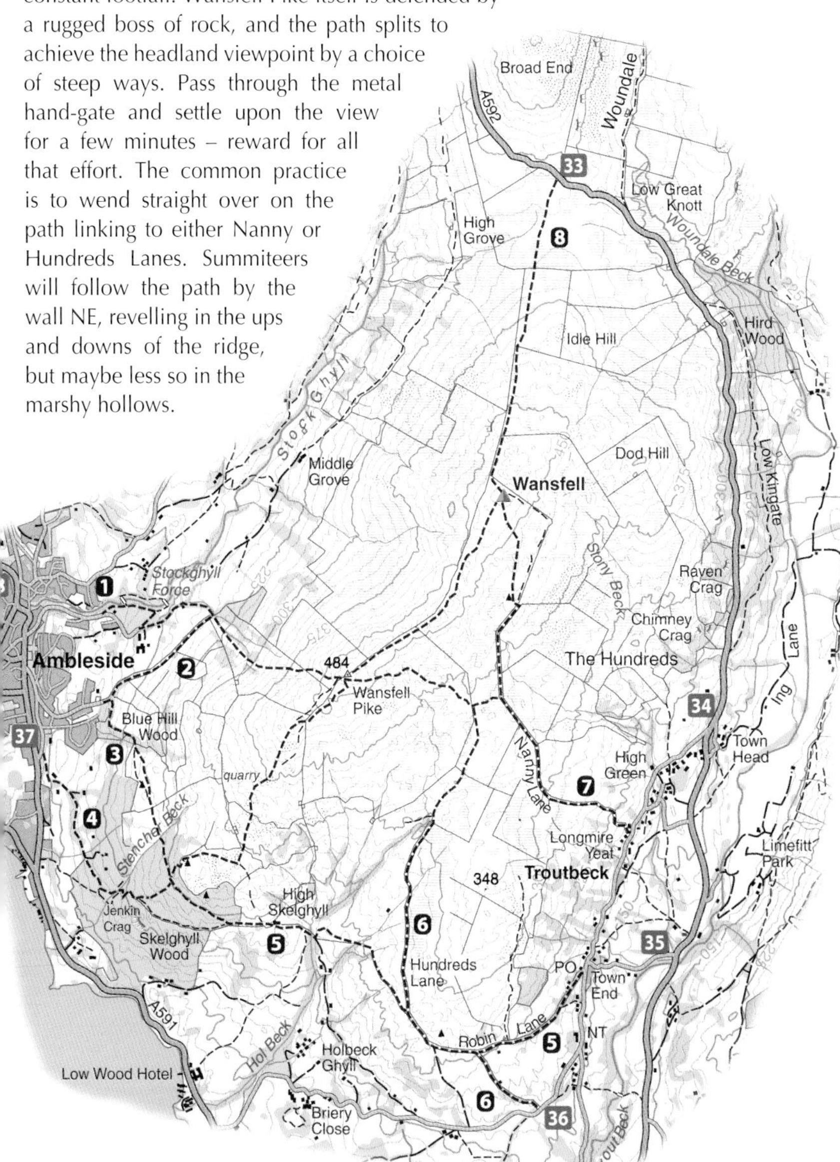

From Wansfell Pike, Ambleside and the great fell parade at the head of Great Langdale

Via Blue Hill Road 450m/1475ft 3.7km/2¼ miles

2 Off Old Lakes Road find the quiet suburban Blue Hill Road, which draws up into a lovely lane at the edge of woodland. Passing the interpretative board the lane leads by a ruin to meet up with the popular path at a kissing-gate and duly joins the endeavour by climbing SE steeply onto the rocky crest of Wansfell Pike.

Via Blue Hill Wood 420m/1380ft 3.3km/2 miles

A far more involved and fascinating route to the top of Wansfell Pike, with fewer walkers to disturb your solitary meanderings. **3** At the top of Blue Hill Road, a matter of 20m into the woodland way, veer right at the Blue Hill Wood National Park signboard, passing through the wooden gate. The path levels above a wall, and as a quarry nears veer left, ascending the rocky stepped path with the quarry-bounding fence right. This path leads up into the wood, passing on above the facing metal hand-gates (associated with a buried aqueduct) to go through a wooden gate up right. Enter a bracken-clad pasture. The path at once splits, although both paths have a common gateway goal. The lower comes by a woodland wall-corner to a beacon cairn that enjoys fine views over Ambleside to the backing fells of Langdale and Rydal.

As the paths converge at the gateway contour on to a metal hand-gate that leads into Skelghyll Wood. Here ford Stencher Beck and contour on. Watch for a small

National Trust waymark post indicating the key path to follow, turning up acutely left (if an obvious fork in the path is reached, you have just passed the turning). Rising to cross a ladder-stile out of the wood, climb on to pass a curious small fold with a tall wall-beacon inside – this, apparently, was an observatory for the aqueduct. The path mounts low outcropping, veering right. Consistently low wooden waymark posts indicate the way, and at the next rise turn left heading for a sequence of two gateways. Beyond these pass to the right of a tiny quarry defended by a fence, with a large cairn set on the fore-spoil. Weaving up, the path splits, with the main way being the left-hand option. The paths come together and split again – one aims for a ladder-stile, while the recommended option aims for a wall-stile half-right and from there on rises with the ridge wall to the left. There is a wall-stile at the foot of the ultimate headland that provides the option of climbing the gully on the left of the wall or slanting right and keeping to grass to the top of Wansfell Pike. The ongoing ridge accompanies the wall NE. A notable depression causes the path to veer away from the wall, sporadically coping with spongy hollows en route to the far-flung summit.

Via Skelghyll Wood 420m/1380ft 3.2km/2 miles

4 From Low Fold at the southern end of Old Lakes Road, directly behind the Mountain Rescue base and Hayes Garden Centre, find a narrow road signed 'Jenkins Crag – Skelghyll and Troutbeck (bridleway)'. This is the ever popular route to Troutbeck, in all probability founded upon the High Street Roman road from Galava. Follow this uphill, passing the entrance to Broad Ings to lose the tarmac road at Skelgarth. The continuing track leads into the National Trust's Skelghyll Wood by a laurel fence to come by Stencher Beck and climbs in zig-zags, with bedrock apparent, to cross a stone bridge and complete the climb with a wall right. Watch for the path branching half-left at a National Trust 'Kelsick Scar' sign – this leads past a rock recording the gift of this land by Alfred Illingworth in 1925. The path climbs up the woodland to merge with a path coming from the right and promptly veers up right at the next fork with a low post waymark (Route 3).

Illingworth memorial on Kelsick Scar in Skelghyll Wood

ASCENT FROM TROUTBECK, TOWN END (36)

Via High Skelghyll Farm 395m/1295ft 4.5km/2¾ miles

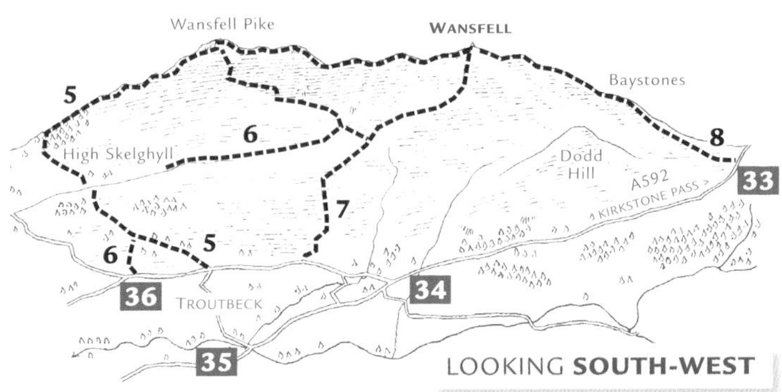

5 From the Post Office follow up Robin Lane, passing a group of cottages where the tarmac ends and a loose-surfaced trail ensues. The walled lane is joined by the lane from the lay-by parking (Route 6). Continue, perhaps paying a visit to the small

High Skelghyll Farm

Townend Farmhouse (NT)

beacon cairn in the knoll up from a wall-stile. Coming to a kissing-gate go through (ignoring Hundreds Lane), signed 'Skelghyll/Jenkins Crag'. Slip through the pen by the gate and follow the regular track via a further kissing-gate, fording Hol Beck, and, passing a low ruin, come down to hand-gates and a cattle grid to join a road. Rise with the fence right to High Skelghyll Farm, discreetly passing through the yard and sheep-handling pen via gates. Passing through a gate, come by a seat with a handsome view over Windermere, and 30m after the metal hand-gate in the fence on the left veer off the regular path angling into the woodland on a narrow path. This duly comes over a wall, and as a path merges from the left find the National Trust waymark post guiding up right (Route 3).

Via Hundreds Lane 325m/1065ft 4km/2½ miles

6 Directly opposite the lay-by parking follow the bridle lane rising to link with Robin Lane. Go left, rising to reach the kissing-gate/gate where the route leaves the bridleway to High Skelghyll. Instead keep within the rough-tracked Hundreds Lane, which offers fine views and less disturbance, being the road less travelled. Wansfell commands attention, although the far summit remains a mystery. After two gates the track opens, with an attractive cascade in Hol Beck close left. Head straight, on ignoring the track bridge, with the path rising easily to a wall-stile beside a gate. Continue skipping over several damp patches and hug the wall to reach the popular path from Nanny Lane. Here there are two option – either go through the kissing-gate and follow the oft-pitched path climbing onto Wansfell Pike, then traverse the ridge NE, or bear right with the path to a corresponding kissing-gate into Nanny Lane and join Route 7.

ASCENT FROM TROUTBECK, TOWN HEAD (34)

Via Nanny Lane 290m/950ft 2.3km/1½ miles

Nanny Lane

7 Nanny Lane begins from Lanefoot Farm, situated some 400m south along the village street from the lay-by. A gate gives access into the rough-track winding walled lane, which curves above the barns and sheep-handling pens. After the third bend briefly come over bedrock. The views back are well worth the occasional pause. There is one gate near a bend, otherwise the lane is unhindered, arriving by the kissing-gate for Wansfell Pike. Again, you may wish to follow this popular path and then the skyline ridge to Wansfell. But the more direct route keeps within the green lane to reach a ladder-stile at the lane's end. Climbing over, there are two choices – either maintain company with the wall right, useful in misty conditions, or step up onto the rigg and, passing a cairn, angle N to the summit, crossing marshy ground early on.

Wansfell Pike and Ambleside from Brow Head

ASCENT FROM THE KIRKSTONE ROAD, WOUNDALE (33)

Via the north ridge 150m/490ft 1.8km/1 mile

8 A wall-stile with mini-gate leaves the small lay-by GR406068 heading due S over rush-laden marshy terrain to a wall-stile. Now climb Idle Hill, naturally taking the occasional idle glance back to admire Caudale Moor and Red Screes on the rise to a further wall-stile. Now with the wall close right come onto the ridge at Baystones. Keep to the wall, and after the fence crossing-point bear left to complete the ascent.

THE SUMMIT

A small dishevelled cairn sits upon a grassy knoll. While the many traipse over Wansfell Pike, the few come to this less appreciated spot. This is a summit for the lover of the fells, as Wansfell Pike has the greater diversity of scenic subjects, with Windermere seen in near full extent.

SAFE DESCENTS

Nearby walls are the great asset in poor conditions. The securest line heads for Troutbeck. Follow the trace of a path ESE. This steps down in close order with the wall, passing a slate plaque recording the rebuilding of a 150m section of drystone wall in 2006 by M Simpson – a nice touch. If only there were plaques of this nature from the past elsewhere marking this beautiful product of solitary labour. The wall ushers walkers to the ladder-stile and so into Nanny Lane.

Windermere from Wansfell Pike

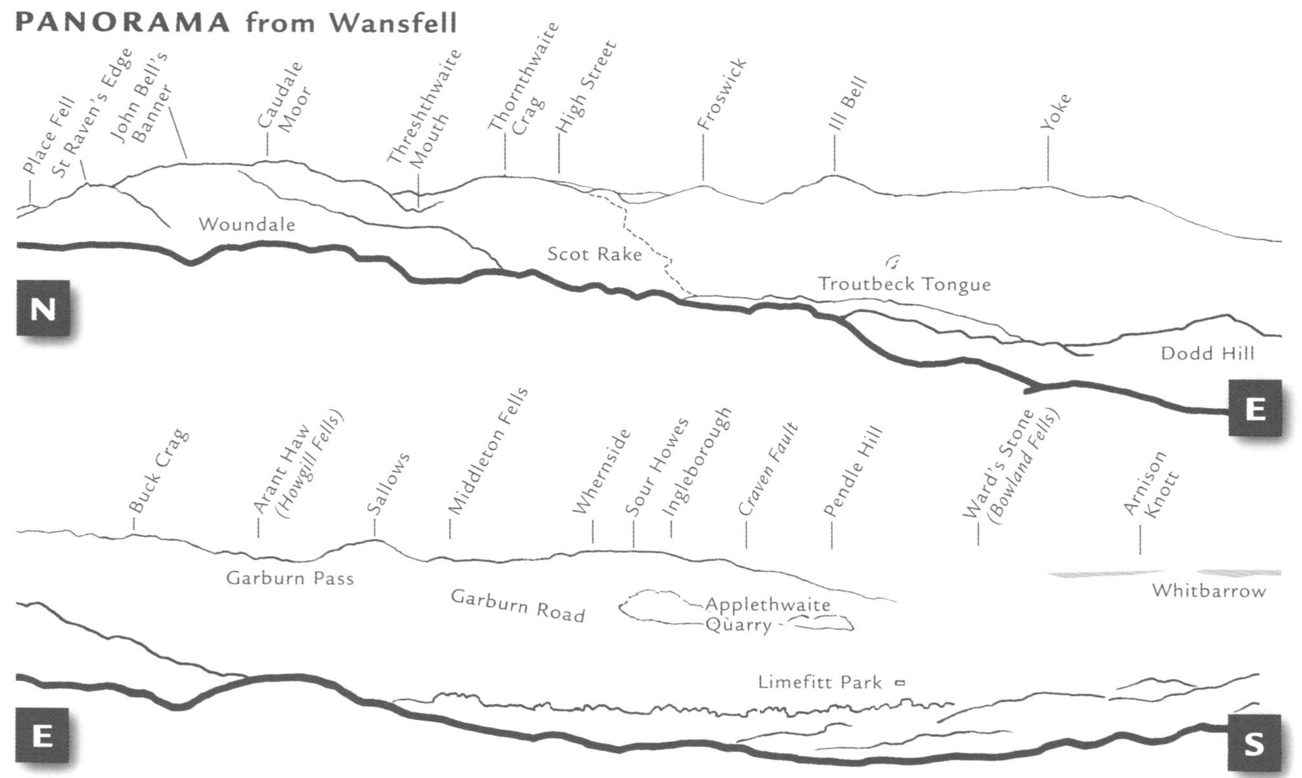
PANORAMA from Wansfell
Place Fell
St Raven's Edge
John Bell's Banner
Caudale Moor
Threshthwaite Mouth
Thornthwaite Crag
High Street
Froswick
Ill Bell
Yoke
Woundale
Scot Rake
Troutbeck Tongue
Dodd Hill
N
E
Buck Crag
Arant Haw (Howgill Fells)
Sallows
Middleton Fells
Whernside
Sour Howes
Ingleborough
Craven Fault
Pendle Hill
Ward's Stone (Bowland Fells)
Arnison Knott
Garburn Pass
Garburn Road
Applethwaite Quarry
Whitbarrow
Limefitt Park
E
S

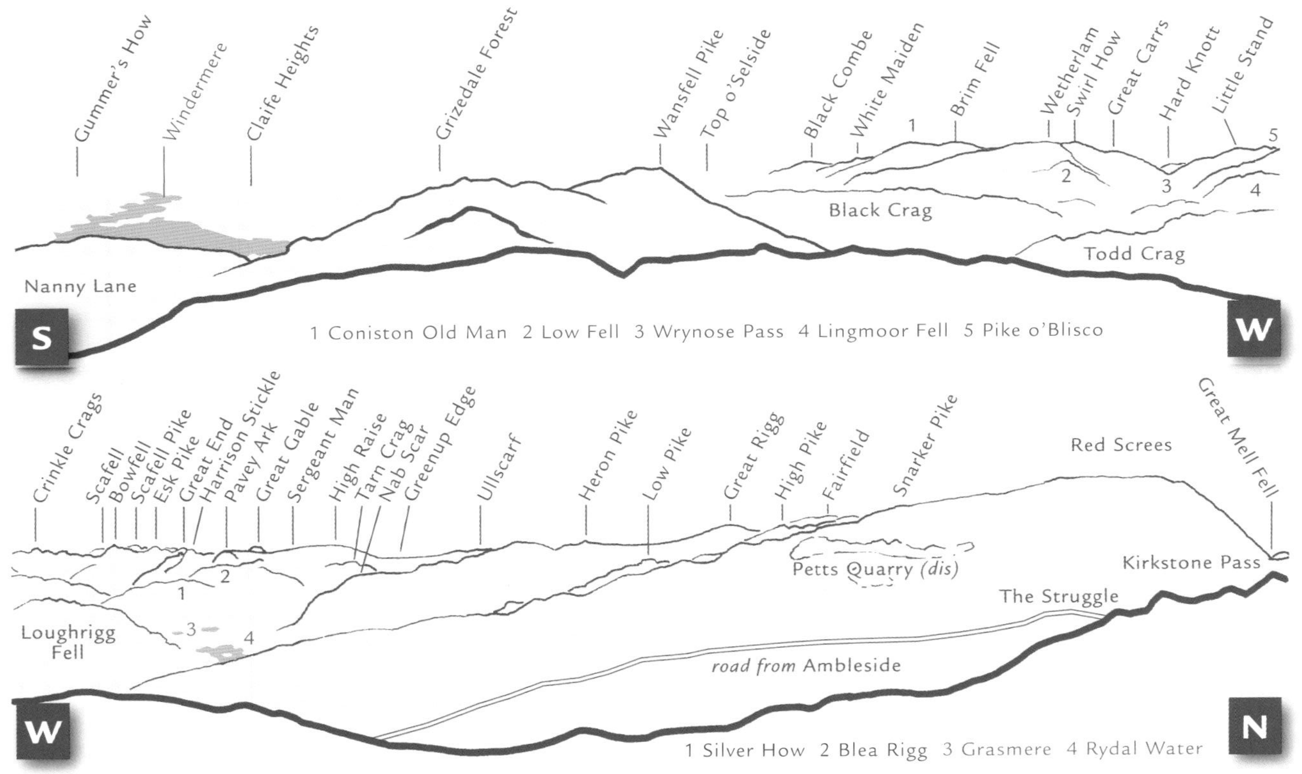
Gummer's How
Windermere
Claife Heights
Grizedale Forest
Wansfell Pike
Top o'Selside
Black Combe
White Maiden
1
Brim Fell
Wetherlam
Swirl How
Great Carrs
Hard Knott
Little Stand
Black Crag
Todd Crag
Nanny Lane
S
W
1 Coniston Old Man 2 Low Fell 3 Wrynose Pass 4 Lingmoor Fell 5 Pike o'Blisco
Crinkle Crags
Scafell
Bowfell
Scafell Pike
Esk Pike
Great End
Harrison Stickle
Pavey Ark
Great Gable
Sergeant Man
High Raise
Tarn Crag
Nab Scar
Greenup Edge
Ullscarf
Heron Pike
Low Pike
Great Rigg
High Pike
Fairfield
Snarker Pike
Red Screes
Great Mell Fell
Kirkstone Pass
Petts Quarry (dis)
The Struggle
Loughrigg Fell
road from Ambleside
W
N
1 Silver How 2 Blea Rigg 3 Grasmere 4 Rydal Water

PANORAMA from Wansfell Pike

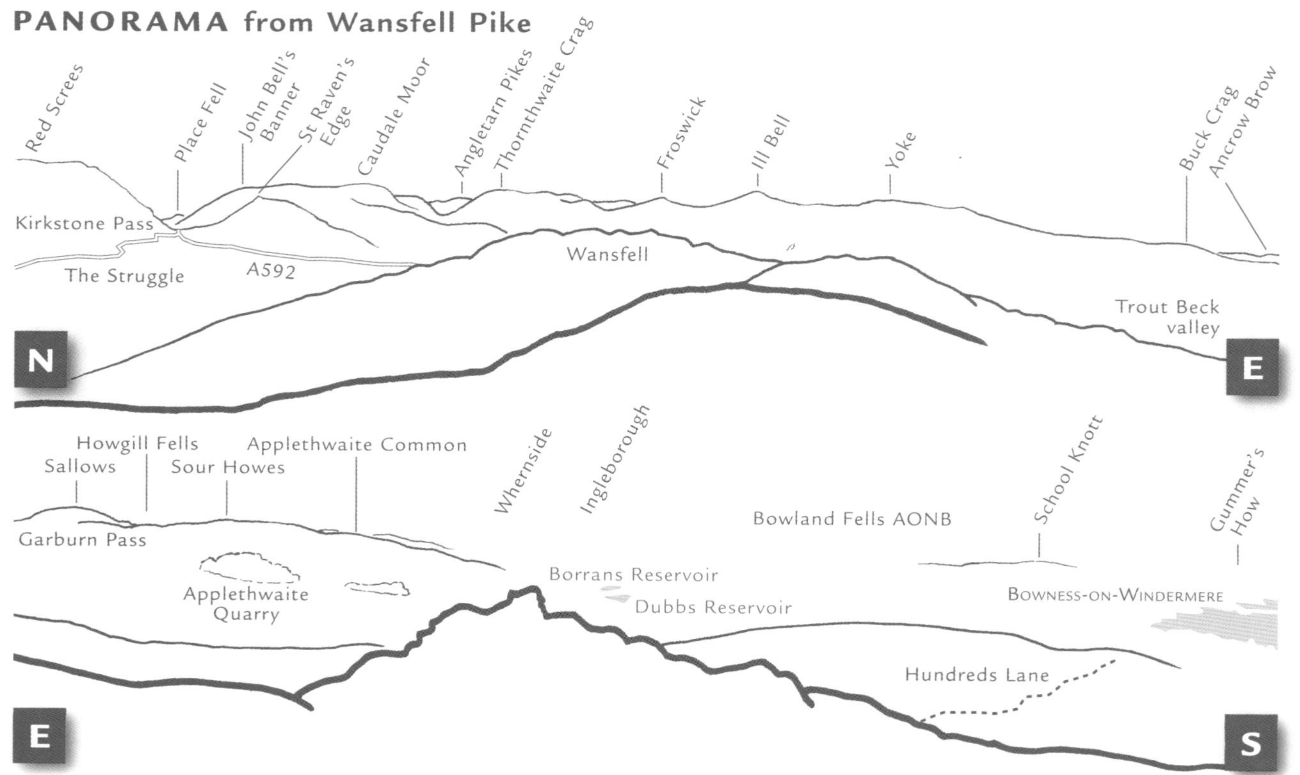

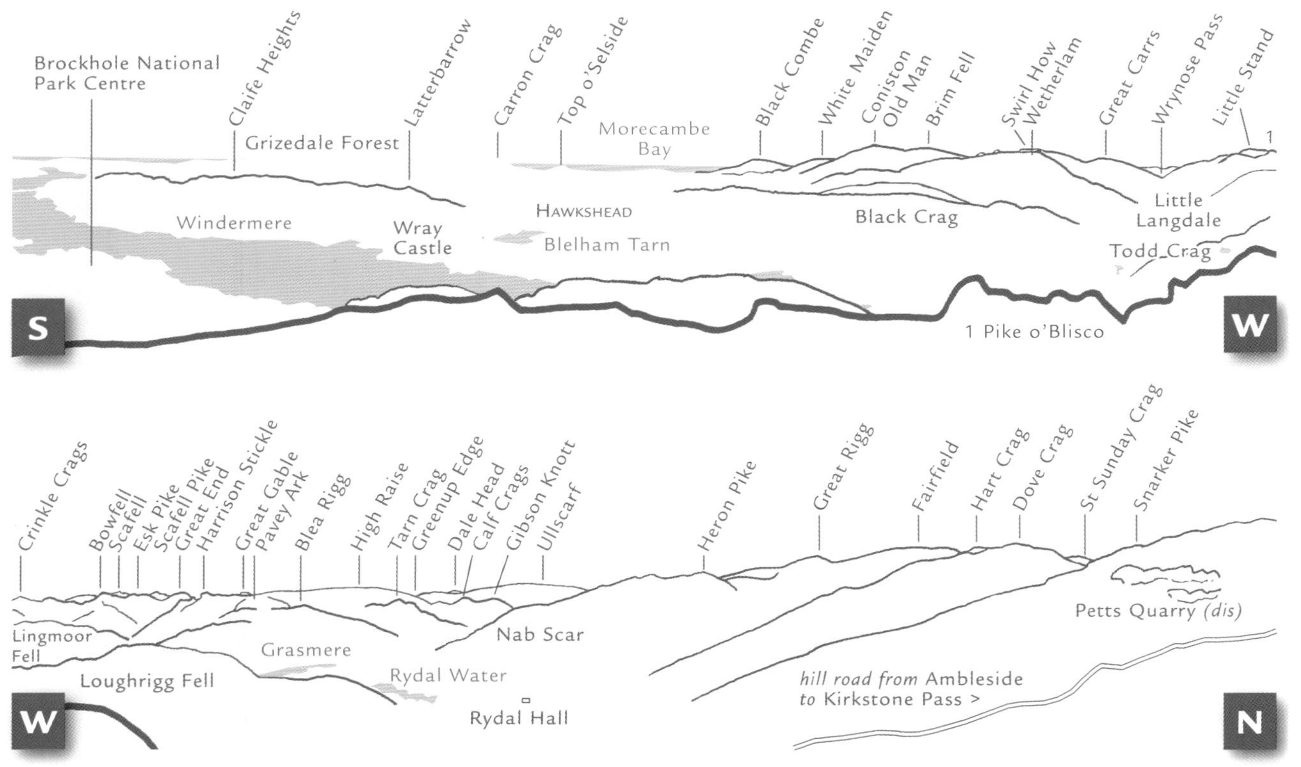
Brockhole National Park Centre
Claife Heights
Grizedale Forest
Latterbarrow
Carron Crag
Top o'Selside
Morecambe Bay
Black Combe
White Maiden
Coniston Old Man
Brim Fell
Swirl How
Wetherlam
Great Carrs
Wrynose Pass
Little Stand
1
Windermere
Wray Castle
HAWKSHEAD
Blelham Tarn
Black Crag
Little Langdale
Todd Crag
S
W
1 Pike o'Blisco
Crinkle Crags
Bowfell
Scafell
Esk Pike
Scafell Pike
Great End
Harrison Stickle
Great Gable
Pavey Ark
Blea Rigg
High Raise
Tarn Crag
Greenup Edge
Dale Head
Calf Crags
Gibson Knott
Ullscarf
Heron Pike
Great Rigg
Fairfield
Hart Crag
Dove Crag
St Sunday Crag
Snarker Pike
Petts Quarry (dis)
Lingmoor Fell
Grasmere
Nab Scar
Loughrigg Fell
Rydal Water
Rydal Hall
hill road from Ambleside to Kirkstone Pass >
W
N

32 WETHER HILL *(673m/2208ft)*

Wether Hill, the wild home of red deer and far-wandering sheep, means 'the upland pasture of yearly male lambs' – brave little souls being pitched to so remote a place. In turn this is the perfect place for walkers with an independent spirit seeking solace and energetic days. An integral piece of jigsaw in the High Street range, Wether Hill forms the eastern horizon to Martindale and grows out of the Lowther valley by billowing moorland ridges that flank the peaceful havens of Cawdale and Measand. The ridge sandwiched between these two valleys carries the names Low and High Kop, suggesting a watchful past. For many the best part of the fell is the little hills overlooking the foot of Haweswater. For an evening ramble or a place to practise navigation, the grassy hills south of Willdale are superb. Who would fault the view from Four Stones Hill, although only two standing stones remain from its naming? An old lead mine adit tucked in just below has the fanciful nick-name Goblin's Cave. There are several generous striding routes to the top from the east, or take your pick from shorter, more immediately scenic routes climbing out of Martindale and Fusedale.

 ↑ Wether Hill from Steel Knotts

ASCENT FROM MARTINDALE OLD CHURCH (7)

Via Brownthwaite Crag 510m/1675ft 4.4km/2¾ miles

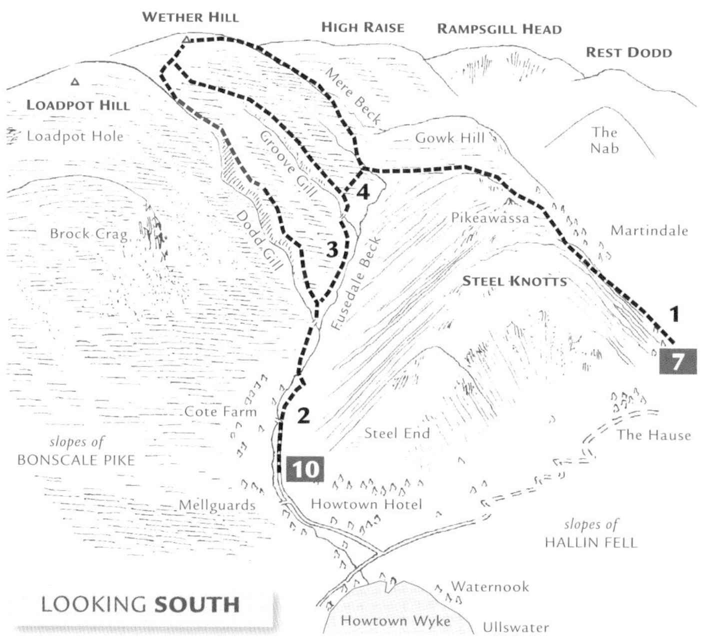

1 Follow the path rising directly behind the Old Church and slanting SE across the flanks of Steel Knotts. This leads through a hand-gate in a downward wall to reach the attractive ridge of Brownthwaite Crag, a wonderful parade giving the best of all views into Martindale. Heading S the path veers left under Gowk Hill (a reference to the cuckoo), crosses a marshy patch and slips through a gap in the wall to ford the headstream of Fusedale Beck between two ruined laithes (fell-barns). The drove-path drifts S to embark on a steady climb across the western slopes of Wether Hill and comes up beside the ravine of Mere Beck to reach the saddle, where the rising wall curves south amid the peat groughs. Turn N, accompanying the free-rein way of riders, ramblers and Romans along the gentlest of rising ridges to the summit cairn.

ASCENT FROM FUSEDALE (10)

There is a choice of three routes climbing out of the enclosed valley directly onto the plateau.

Path from Martindale Old Church looking north to Blencathra

Via Dodd Gill 505m/1655ft 3.2km/2 miles

2 Follow the concrete Cote Farm access road S from the verge parking above the cross-path signpost. Coming to the cattle grid break right over the simple stone-flag bridge and follow the footpath above the beck. This comes back down to cross a footbridge over Fusedale Beck and bears right. Cross the single plank-bridge over Dodd Gill. The route embarks on the climb left (there is an intermittent path) and higher up copes with some stony ground. Coming above the gill cross the lateral line of a strong sheep path and continue pathless to the join the ridge path. Bear right, passing the pool in the shallow saddle and heading up the ridge to the summit cairn.

Via Groove Gill 510m/1675ft 3.6km/2¼ miles

3 Start with Route 2, but continue pursuing the path above Fusedale Beck, which comes by a stone ruin. The bench encourages an early break to reflect back on the quiet world of Fusedale and consider the craggy peak of Pikeawassa (Steel Knotts) on the near west skyline. The path continues rising to a stone-flag crossing of Groove Gill. Climb on to reach a path junction and two choices. The primary option (for the other option see Route 4) keeps uphill in harmony with Groove Gill to reach the Roman road south of the broad saddle. Turn right to reach the summit cairn unhindered.

Via Mere Beck 520m/1705ft 4.6km/3 miles

4 Alternatively bear right at the junction, contouring to the meet up with the path from Martindale (Route 1) above the roofless stone bothy.

ASCENT FROM MOORAHILL (17)

Via The Pen 360m/1180ft 5km/3 miles

5 Follow the walled lane from the gate with 'Carhullan' affixed. Go to the left of the cottage and then the lovely old farmhouse (holiday let) along a walled passage between stone barns to a gate, and here enter the open fell. Green paths follow the walls right and left, but your intent is up the fell straight ahead westward. With a tenuous hint of a path, walkers should avoid the bracken and aim onto The Pen, well above Cawdale Edge, to unite with the regular path near the prominent cairn. Follow this path SW to pass beneath a bield wall. Bear off the more regular way after some 20m with the line of rushes that defines an old drove-path. This leads to the main ridge depression, with its large pool. Joining the Roman road, turn S to complete the ascent.

The remote Carhullan

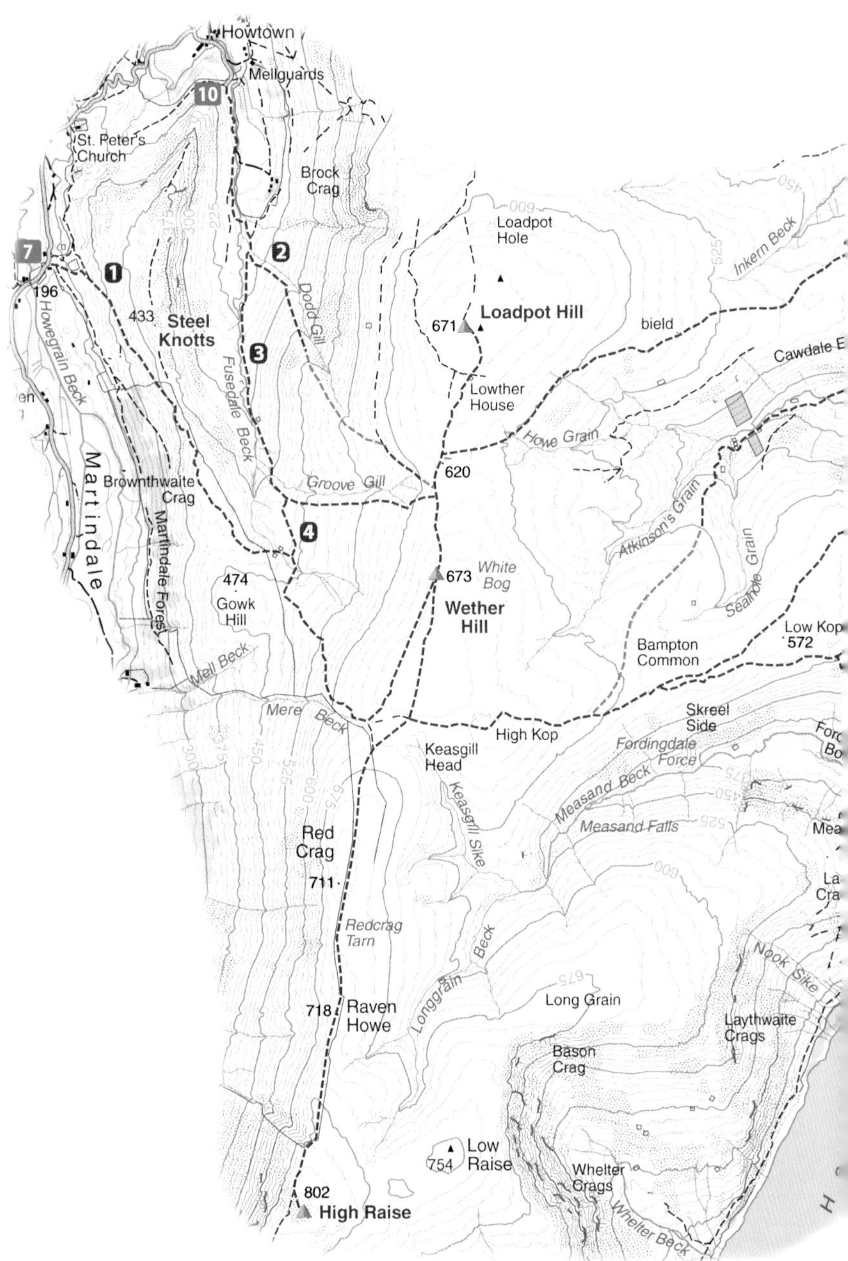
Howtown
Mellguards
10
St. Peter's Church
Brock Crag
Loadpot Hole
7
1
2
196
Howegrain Beck
433
Steel Knotts
Dodd Gill
671
Loadpot Hill
bield
Cawdale Beck
Inkern Beck
3
Fusedale Beck
Lowther House
Howe Grain
Martindale
Brownthwaite Crag
Groove Gill
620
Martindale Forest
4
Atkinson's Grain
474
Gowk Hill
673
White Bog
Wether Hill
Sealhole Grain
Low Kop
572
Bampton Common
Mell Beck
Mere Beck
High Kop
Skreel Side
Keasgill Head
Fordingdale Force
Measand Beck
Keasgill Sike
Measand Falls
Red Crag
711
Redcrag Tarn
Longgrain Beck
Nook Sike
Long Grain
718
Raven Howe
Laythwaite Crags
Bason Crag
Low Raise
754
Whelter Crags
802
High Raise
Whelter Beck

Via Cawdale 395m/1295ft 6km/3¾ miles

6 This leads off as per Route 5, although on passing beyond the confines of Carhullan keep forward alongside the wall. As the wall is lost the track begins to decline to gain the flat dale floor and advances to skip over Cawdale Beck at the conveniently narrow kink. The dale, a typical secluded haven of red deer, owes its name to it being the frequent of crows. The old quarry-approach track comes above a small ravine, with the

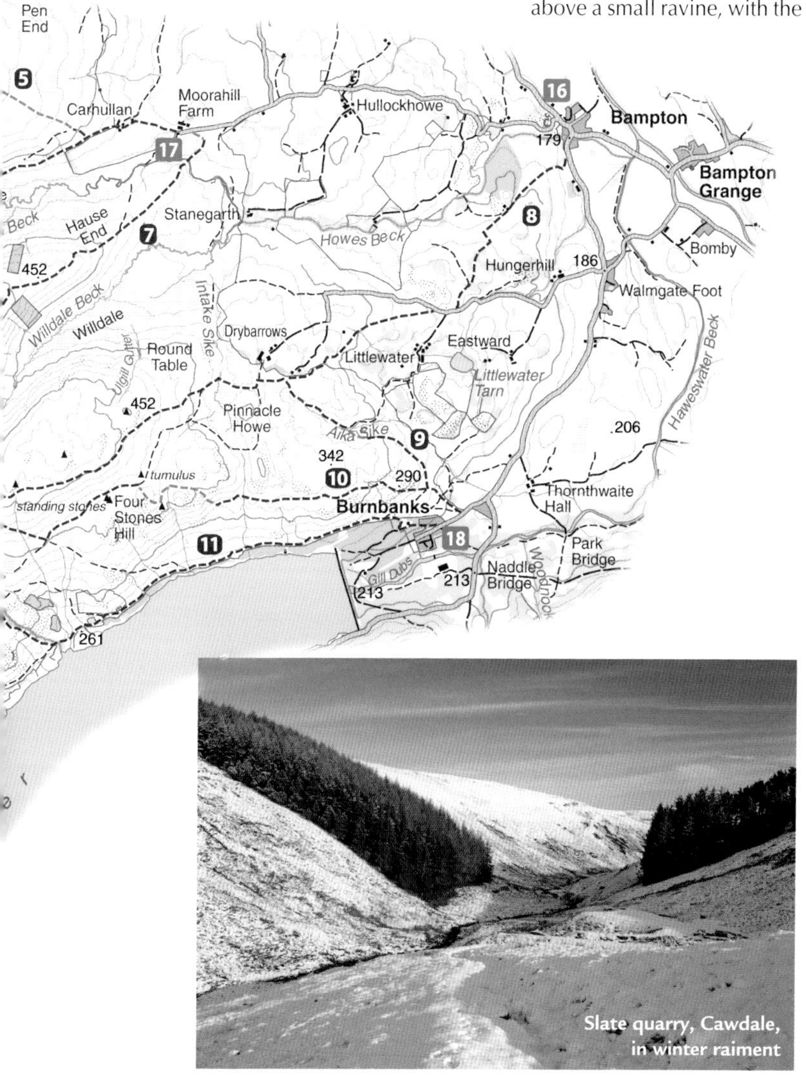

Slate quarry, Cawdale, in winter raiment

ruins of a tiny bothy just above, and leads to the slate spoil bank with several more roofless ruins, harking back to long-gone days of dour endeavour. Ford Sealhole Grain and follow the obvious path, which bends back and gains the higher portion of the quarry hollow. Take the opportunity to discover the old workings beyond a final ruin, and within a bay find an impressive cavern with a low cave to the left and ferns growing lush even in the depths of winter (the author visited this spot in January, with a half-metre of snow shrouding the quarry and the fell above). Backtrack and join the ascending drove, which climbs onto the ridge and is lost as the fell slope eases. Continue pathless, in a general SSW direction, to join the quad track leading onto High Kop. Seek out the crossing ridge path on the plateau and turn N to the summit.

Via The Hause 380m/1245ft 5.7km/3½ miles

7 It is possible to start in Bampton (starting point 16) and follow the road winding up via cattle grids by Hullockhowe ('the wolves' playground hill') to reach Moorahill, where there is suitable verge parking. The waymarked footpath 'The Hause' leading off down by the wall fords Cawdale Beck, but this can carry a strong flow. Hence the more appealing option is to bear left skirting the small fenced spring and the body of soft rushes to join a path that swings right to cross a flag-footbridge – an attractive rustic subject for the camera. Climb the bank and pass the mysterious low circular

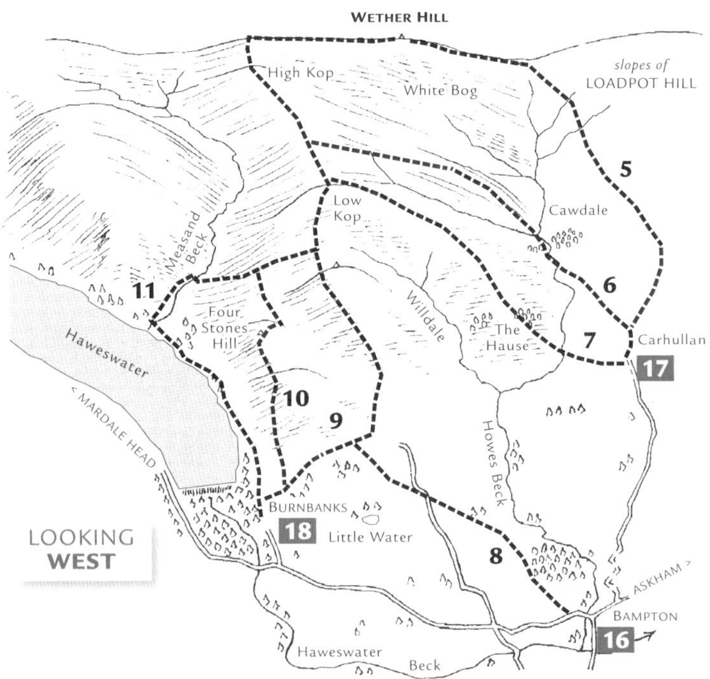

Looking over Low Kop to Cross Fell

enclosure called Towtop Kirk. The name suggests that the enclosure was thought to have religious origins, but it is the outline of an early Viking homestead. Towtop probably is the dialect phrase 't'howe top', for 'the hill top'.

The path marches on SW, gently rising to merge with the track from the ford. It climbs Hause End to level on the actual Hause, flanked by mature conifer belts, although the concept of a lateral pass seems far fetched. The walking is hardly exciting, but the gradient ensures a flowing stride on the old drove-path and a wonderful spacious feeling of being in a big country of far horizons. Coming onto Low Kop (which means 'the low viewpoint') the ridge levels again, the path merging with a heavily used quad track (half-left see High Raise at the head of the Measand Beck valley). As the path comes over the ridge find a narrow trod crossing. This gives a quiet line off the Roman road, although alternatively you may very well relish the sense of starting marching orders with the legionary way. To follow the Roman road, continue as towards the wall and bear right when the main ridge path is encountered. By either path draw up and head along the featureless ridge to the cairn on the northern extremity. There is a hint of higher ground to the right, but the greater view is from the cairn.

ASCENT FROM BAMPTON (16)

All too readily walkers head for fell-foot parking places, and in so doing miss many a lovely pastoral approach. The delightful little village of Bampton makes a thoroughly grand starting point. Find here a tearoom in the village shop and a lovely 'open all day' pub, the Mardale Inn; nearby Bampton Grange has choice walkers' accommodation in the Crown & Mitre – a strategic overnight on the perennially popular Coast to Coast Walk.

Via Low Kop 530m/1740ft 8km/5 miles

A great long-striding route up onto Bampton Common. **8** At the southern end of the village, beyond the Mardale Inn, find a footpath signposted right by a sheep pen that steps up an open track. This forms a very pleasant precursor stage to the open common and high fell. Where the adjacent fence ends, march on to go through the gate beside stone barns. Pass through the gateway and continue uphill with a field-wall close right, then go left at its corner to reach a hand-gate. Go through and traverse the open woodland pasture to a gate, and here join an open track to a gate onto a minor road. Turn right, soon finding a fence-stile left. Angle half-right through a shallow cutting to a sequence of four ladder-stiles advancing to a waymarked gap. Bear left to a hand-gate, where the open common is entered and walkers quickly join Route 7.

ASCENT FROM BURNBANKS (18)

All three routes converge at the head of Willdale (which means 'the wild valley') intent on Low Kop.

Via Aika Hill 490m/1610ft 7km/4½ miles

9 Walk back from the car park to a gate some 100m along the access lane. Go through and follow the path uphill beside the wall, and as the wall bears away right continue angling to the right on the hillside ahead. The path dwindles, but continue to join a more sure green track emerging from the gorse. This path leads along the flank of Aika Hill to link up with the field-path route from Bampton (Route 8) near the larch copse and barn. Veer left over a flag spanning a marsh to meet up with the muddy track rising from Drybarrows Farm. Crossing the brow decline to ford Intake Sike – the unlikely, but easy ford being to the right of the pool where quad bikes have churned up the peaty basin. The continuing green way angles half-left rising SW onto the fellside ahead. This promenades at an easy gradient to come into the broad saddle at the head of Willdale, linking up with Routes 8, 9, 10 and 11. Keep to the regular quad-bike track to come up the eastern flank of Low Kop by a small ruin. Soon in a grass groove leading along the plateau of Low Kop WSW, duly link up with Routes 6 and 7, en route to High Kop, where the ridge path is joined. Turn N to the summit.

Via Four Stones Hill 510m/1675ft 7km/4½ miles

10 The Four Stones Hill ridge deserves its own attention, and while prone to being cloaked with bracken in high summer is otherwise a fun place to navigate for its excellent views over Haweswater. The route described is but one option, as there is scope for inventive exploration. Begin from the gate identified in Route 9, but this time clamber up the rough path running up by the near scarp and leading ever westward. As this fades bear up onto the ridge and make for the sighter cairn, built by the reservoir engineers, perched on a forward ledge of Four Stones Hill. The view is superb across the waters to Hugh's Laithes Pike and features Wallow Crag

Two standing stones on Four Stones Hill

rising from the dense tree cover and mimicking its Keswick near namesake. Up the reservoir lavish attention on the inspiring mountainscape of Mardale Head. The top of Four Stones Hill has bedrock but no cairn. For rock interest venture down to stand by the two stones that presumably were once a stone circle quartet, to judge by the hill name, and go back some 150m to the E to find a circular gathering of stones, a remnant tumulus – both features were old even when the Romans strode their High Street. The ascent route heads W, then at a faint cross-ways branch right, rising to the head of Willdale to unite with Routes 8, 9 and 11.

Above The Forces ravine looking down on Haweswater

Via The Forces 520m/1705ft 7.4km/4½ miles

11 Follow the regular path along the eastern side of Haweswater to cross the footbridge spanning Measand Beck. Here veer immediately right, rising in harmony with The Forces ravine, an exciting and excited calamity of rock and water, a great place to watch the hydraulic energy of a mountain stream – although the best of the ravine is impossible to enter. Above, pass through the new deer-fence gate (defining the new woodland compound) and advance to cross the plank footbridge, putting you back on the east side of Measand Beck. Follow the path leading NE over several damp patches. At the first hint of a gill bear up left, thereby avoiding the rank bracken, on a clear path climbing onto the ridge. On the brow this meets up with the quad track of Routes 8 and 9.

THE SUMMIT

The plateau is extensive and undistinguished – the name White Bog provides a clue to its worst characteristic. The plain grassy setting of the cairn has no such hazard, and the view will not cause you to linger long – there are better stations in line along the ridge.

SAFE DESCENTS

All routes up are easily retraced. The best route westwards is by Groove Gill, while eastwards the main routes by High Kop and The Pen give confidence on a wild day.

Wether Hill summit cairn

Pool on the ridge between Loadpot and Wether Hills

RIDGE ROUTES

HIGH RAISE ↓ 30m/100ft ↑ 160m/525ft 3.5km/2¼ miles

Two paths, one above the other, venture S. By either course come onto the eroded peaty ground above Mere Beck to run over the broken wall and connect with the ridge fence on Red Crag. Pass its namesake tarn to go through a hand-gate and unite with the continuing wall. As this ends a fence-stile is crossed and the Roman highway maintained, but briefly, as the stony crown of High Raise draws you half-left.

LOADPOT HILL ↓ 55m/180ft ↑ 53m/175ft 1.4km/¾ mile

Head N, descending in peaty steps into the broad hollow, where languishes a lovely pool. The Roman way surges on, although you need to aim for the ruins of the old shooting box (Lowther House), from where the summit plateau comes readily to hand as you traverse to the OS column.

33 YOKE *(706m/2316ft)*

The fell name means 'the square-shouldered hill', from its likeness to the wooden beam that drew two hauling-oxen together or ran over the shoulders to aid carrying two buckets. Yoke's greatest attractions lie on its shady eastern side, notably Rainsborrow Cove and Crag. The latter has little of interest to a rock climber, but the cliff is hugely impressive and certainly attracted slate quarrymen, who picked and blasted a massive cavern and a vertical cutting at the foot of the cliff and also exploited seams of the best slate up in the cove. These are part of an eastward seam that runs over The Tongue and up onto the slopes of Kentmere Pike, where there is further evidence of the toils of these hardy men. Below the cove the old slate workshops have been tidily converted into an outdoor centre, known as Reservoir Cottage, inspiring new generations of young walkers and climbers! Almost to a man and woman, walkers traverse the fell upon the ridge path from Garburn Pass, but as this guide reveals, Rainsborrow Crag's northern edge awaits your mild scrambling delectation.

Yoke from Lingmell End

 ↑ Tongue House and Rainsborrow Crag

ASCENT FROM CHURCH BRIDGE, TROUTBECK (35)

Via Garburn Pass 600m/1970ft 6km/3¾ miles

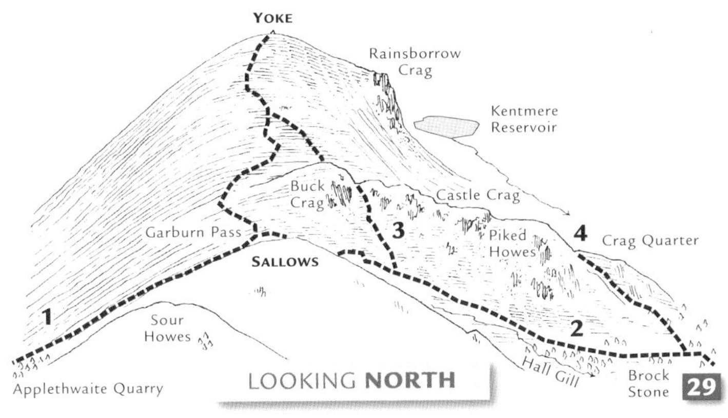

1 Cross the footbridge beside the road bridge and after 60m watchfully cross the A592 into the narrow walled lane. The lane rises by a gate and cobbled corner, marching up the slope below the old Applethwaite Quarry, with occasional evidence of wash-out in the stony track-bed. Eventually the track levels and goes through a gate by a small conifer spinney, then comes to a right-hand bend in the track at the summit of Garburn Pass. At this point a newly engineered path has been created, speeding your fleet feet across an otherwise damp moorland ridge and rising by a kissing-gate to come up a pitched rise onto the summit.

ASCENT FROM KENTMERE (29) OR HALLOW BANK (31)

Via Garburn Pass 545m/1790ft 5.2km/3¼ miles

2 Follow the road W from Kentmere church to reach The Nook, where the Garburn Pass bridleway is signed right. The loose trail has received recent improvement approaching the gate short of the Brock Stone. The walled lane leads on, providing lovely views back towards the church, passing on below a cluster of lesser boulders in the open woodland right and shortly offering an intriguing glimpse down upon the pele tower at Kentmere Hall. After the gate the surface condition of the track deteriorates, pressured by a range of recreational users – loose stones threaten a twisted ankle. The way leads up the combe, with volcanic outcropping up to the right, and the softer Silurian rocks to the left creating a gentler profile to Sallows. The track zig-zags up to the gate in the pass. Dismiss all thought of following the ridge wall right and instead advance to the sharp left turn, where a new 'made' path departs right, in

Raven Crag on the open road to Hartrigg

common with Route 1. This surfaced track provides a very comfortable way over the otherwise damp ridge, winding up to a kissing-gate. Beyond it the open track includes some fine pitched steps to a cairn, from where the summit hoves into view ahead.

Via Buck Crag 560m/1840ft 4.2km/2½ miles

3 Walkers with a desire to explore the volcanic curtain overbearing the track on Route 2 can follow a narrow trod which breaks from the pitched Garburn track at a ford with a fenced thorn bush right. Pass the thorn and follow the trod aiming for a weakness in the rocky façade. The grass gully leads to a peaty hollow, and the path marches on to cross a fence-stile and duly come beside the ridge wall. This is followed to the point where the regular improved path from the top of Garburn Pass is joined above a kissing-gate.

Via the secret drove 540m/1770ft 4km/2½ miles

4 The impressive craggy fellside overbearing the Garburn combe is unbreached by regular walkers' trods, except for one unsung drove-way that departs just short of Brock Stone. At the first left bend bear off right beside the tiny gill to go through a gate and ascend the irregular walled enclosure, climbing to a double barred hurdle across a rock-bed and slipping under it. Where the wall insinuates right keep up with a continuing wall to step over a gill and go through a hand-gate in the upper intake wall. From here on a palpable drove-way wends up, with hints of retaining stones and juniper shrubs. This opens onto a broad walled pasture corridor. Hold more to the left, picking up a quad track as it joins from the left and keep to its course.

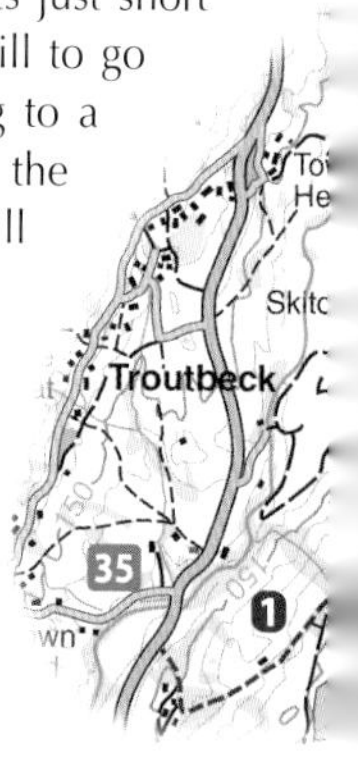

Alternatively, a far more adventurous mission lies in exploring the pathless volcanic headlands over to the left, Piked Howes and Castle Crag. This is a seldom visited mountain world to delight the roaming instinct of aficionado fellwanderers.

The primary route comes over a marsh, where the broken wall is replaced by a fence, and meets up with the Route 3 path converging from the left at a fence-stile.

Scales, with its handsome Westmorland barn

Via Rainsborrow Crag 590m/1935ft 5.5km/3½ miles

5 Unorthodoxy is a-calling. Here's your chance to join a select band of adventurous fellwanderers who have sampled the sensational ascent of Rainsborrow Crag's northern edge. There is nothing scary or unduly exposed about the route, but a nice dry day is a prerequisite in order to derive the fullest pleasure from it. However, even on a cloudy day the intimacy with easy rocks will reward your eager hands and feet.

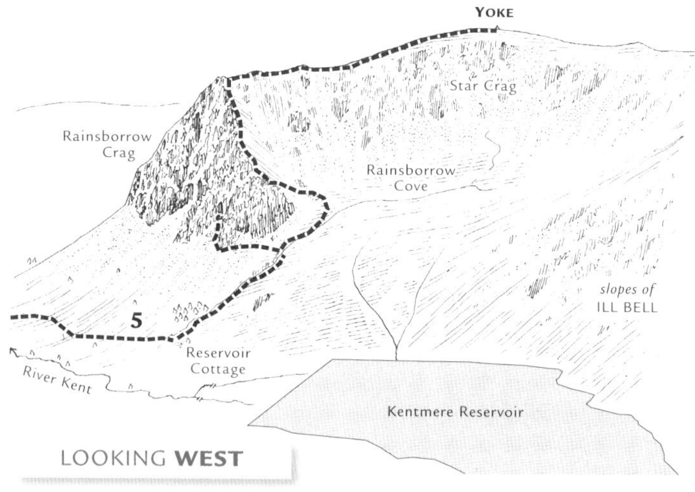

Great slate quarry cavern under Rainsborrow Crag

There are several optional routes up the dale to Reservoir Cottage, including from Green Quarter via Low Lane and Hallow Bank. The preferred route, however, follows the village road from Kentmere church and at the sharp left turn goes straight ahead from the metal road-gate with a slate sign 'Hartrigg'. The open road leads attractively on, passing below craggy headlands, via two cattle grids, by Scales to Hartrigg Farm. A rough surfaced track continues via gates to come under the mighty shadow of Rainsborrow Crag. With the readapted buildings of the old slate mine close ahead, bear up left beside the gill spilling from Rainsborrow Cove. A faint trod is discernible, rising increasingly steeply through the bracken on the north bank and leading above the copse to and above a lovely fall.

At this point a recommended indulgence is to ford the three strands of the gill and traverse into the slate spoil, where evidence of quarrymen's ruins are to be found below a massive quarry face. Continue, slipping down to cross a rising wall where it butts up to the foot of the cliff, then climb the grass and scree to enter the gaping mouth of a quarry cavern. There are two chambers – although, not wishing to risk being swallowed in the inner throat, the author did

Sharp edge high on the north ridge of Rainsborrow Crag

not test his luck threading through! However, there were Tibetan prayer flags draped within, so someone visits from time to time.

Backtrack and complete the easy ascent to the upper slate workings in the cove. After inspecting the ruins bear half-left, crossing the broken wall to encounter the ridge and making steady, if steep, progress up the north ridge. Nearing the top the ridge becomes an irregular arête, so choose to either take the sporting line or keep to grass on the right-hand side to ease yourself onto the crest. Throughout the ascent the views back over the reservoir to the head of the dale are a rich reward. Follow the ridge and come up by a lovely shelf tarn to then cross the ridge-straddling wall, completing the ascent entirely on grass.

THE SUMMIT

Nature endowed cairn builders with all they needed to make their statement – a low rock rib, a clear-cut summit and a choice spot to stop and admire a spacious panorama. As stop you should. The view in the south-western sector is quite brilliant, from Black Combe through to High Stile before Red Screes intervenes, while further north see Helvellyn in a host of huddled fells. Close by, like a fell-festival ribbon, the ridge path beckons you on to neighbouring Ill Bell.

Kentmere Reservoir and Mardale Ill Bell from the top of Rainsborrow Crag

Yoke summit cairn

SAFE DESCENTS

The one solid way S passes a small cairn on the plateau edge and then leads clearly down by the kissing-gate and consistent inverted substrate path to the open track at Garburn Pass – go right for Troutbeck and left for Kentmere.

RIDGE ROUTES

ILL BELL ↓ 50m/165ft ↑ 100m/330ft 1km/½ mile

The ridge path N has received modern effective mending. While hasty runners have made their own contouring routes along the western slopes of Yoke, Ill Bell and Froswick, the one true ridge path provides all the scenic inducement to stick to the spine of the ridge and climb to the triple-cairned summit, with fine views into Rainsborrow Cove a special pleasure en route.

SALLOWS ↓ 260m/855ft ↑ 70m/230ft 3km/2 miles

Head S following the clear trail via the kissing-gate and easy trail down to the Garburn Pass track. Go right to the gate by the conifer spinney. Go through, turn immediately left over the stile and climb the bank ahead onto the moorland ridge of Sallows.

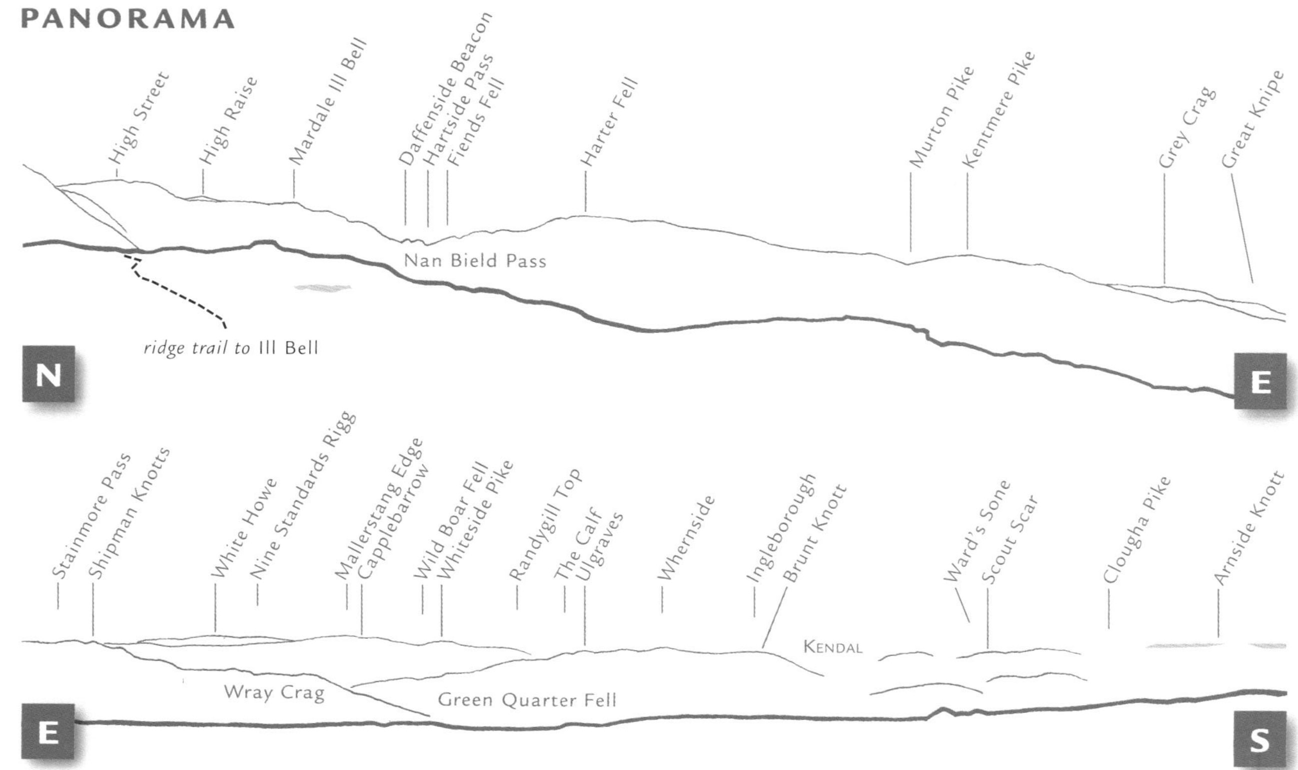
PANORAMA
High Street
High Raise
Mardale Ill Bell
Daffenside Beacon
Hartside Pass
Fiends Fell
Harter Fell
Murton Pike
Kentmere Pike
Grey Crag
Great Knipe
Nan Bield Pass
ridge trail to Ill Bell
N
E
Stainmore Pass
Shipman Knotts
White Howe
Nine Standards Rigg
Mallerstang Edge
Capplebarrow
Wild Boar Fell
Whiteside Pike
Randygill Top
The Calf
Ulgraves
Whernside
Ingleborough
Brunt Knott
Ward's Sone
Scout Scar
Clougha Pike
Arnside Knott
Kendal
Wray Crag
Green Quarter Fell
E
S

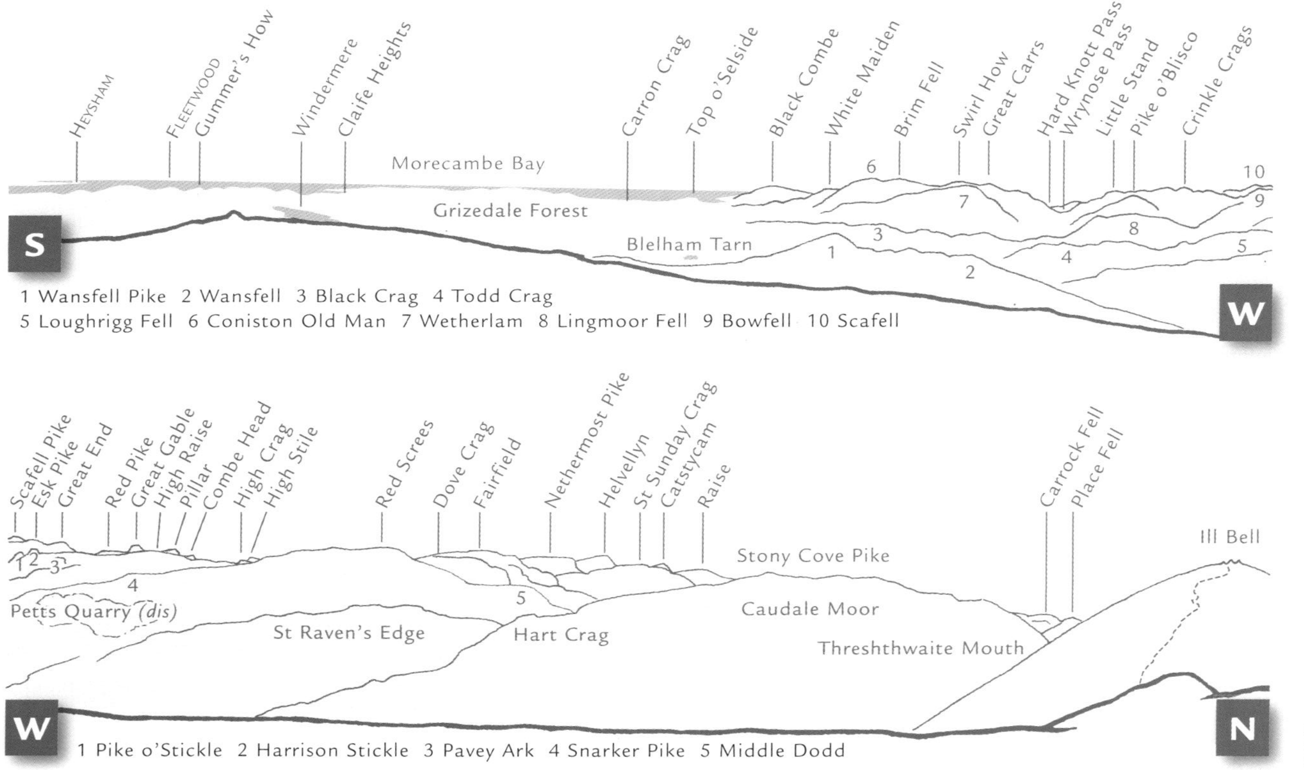
HEYSHAM
FLEETWOOD
Gummer's How
Windermere
Claife Heights
Carron Crag
Top o'Selside
Black Combe
White Maiden
Brim Fell
Swirl How
Great Carrs
Hard Knott Pass
Wrynose Pass
Little Stand
Pike o'Blisco
Crinkle Crags
Morecambe Bay
Grizedale Forest
Blelham Tarn
S
W
1 Wansfell Pike 2 Wansfell 3 Black Crag 4 Todd Crag
5 Loughrigg Fell 6 Coniston Old Man 7 Wetherlam 8 Lingmoor Fell 9 Bowfell 10 Scafell
Scafell Pike
Esk Pike
Great End
Red Pike
Great Gable
High Raise
Pillar
Combe Head
High Crag
High Stile
Red Screes
Dove Crag
Fairfield
Nethermost Pike
Helvellyn
St Sunday Crag
Catstycam
Raise
Carrock Fell
Place Fell
Ill Bell
Stony Cove Pike
Petts Quarry (dis)
Caudale Moor
St Raven's Edge
Hart Crag
Threshthwaite Mouth
W
N
1 Pike o'Stickle 2 Harrison Stickle 3 Pavey Ark 4 Snarker Pike 5 Middle Dodd

Helicopter delivering path-building rock on the steep slopes of Dollywaggon Pike

FIXING THE FELLS FOR THE FUTURE

In preparing this guide I am ever more keenly aware of the work being done to secure the fell paths, making the whole fell environment visually a better place. The National Park Authority in conjunction with the National Trust are playing crucial roles within the structure of the Fix the Fells Project (visit: www.fixthefells.co.uk).

A huge amount of work has been devoted to stabilising paths, including intelligent pre-emptive work. Capital projects too, have seen mechanical diggers carried high onto the fells at key points to heal sorely worn paths. Huge quantities of path-pitching stone is carried most economically by helicopter. Sadly worn paths of Wainwright's day have been given a new lease of life. While some walkers may gripe that the hard pitching is tough on the ankles and knees, at least it's not so tough on the mountains themselves. All of which has to be good.

See the difference – 'before and after' on the path above Comb Crags on the upper slopes of Nethermost Pike

In common with so many countryside projects Fix the Fells faces a 'strapped for cash' future, and for its work to continue unabated it looks to Nurture Lakeland for assistance. As an associate member I am committed to supporting its work. The charity actively encourages businesses, particularly those that benefit from tourism, to pay into environmental-project funding through 'Payback' schemes that sustain the beautiful landscape so many visitors and locals adore.

Visit: www.ourstolookafter.co.uk.

INDEX

Bold indicates Fell Chapters

LISTING OF CICERONE GUIDES

BRITISH ISLES CHALLENGES, COLLECTIONS AND ACTIVITIES
The End to End Trail
The Mountains of England and Wales
1 Wales & 2 England
The National Trails
The Relative Hills of Britain
The Ridges of England, Wales and Ireland
The UK Trailwalker's Handbook
The UK's County Tops
Three Peaks, Ten Tors

MOUNTAIN LITERATURE
Unjustifiable Risk?

UK CYCLING
Border Country Cycle Routes
Cycling in the Hebrides
Cycling in the Peak District
Cycling the Pennine Bridleway
Mountain Biking in the Lake District
Mountain Biking in the Yorkshire Dales
Mountain Biking on the South Downs
The C2C Cycle Route
The End to End Cycle Route
The Lancashire Cycleway

SCOTLAND
Backpacker's Britain
Central and Southern Scottish Highlands
Northern Scotland
Ben Nevis and Glen Coe
Great Mountain Days in Scotland
North to the Cape
Not the West Highland Way
Scotland's Best Small Mountains
Scotland's Far West
Scotland's Mountain Ridges
Scrambles in Lochaber
The Ayrshire and Arran Coastal Paths
The Border Country
The Cape Wrath Trail
The Great Glen Way
The Isle of Mull
The Isle of Skye
The Pentland Hills
The Southern Upland Way
The Speyside Way
The West Highland Way
Walking Highland Perthshire
Walking in Scotland's Far North
Walking in the Angus Glens
Walking in the Cairngorms
Walking in the Ochils, Campsie Fells and Lomond Hills
Walking in Torridon
Walking Loch Lomond and the Trossachs
Walking on Harris and Lewis
Walking on Jura, Islay and Colonsay
Walking on Rum and the Small Isles
Walking on the Isle of Arran
Walking on the Orkney and Shetland Isles
Walking on Uist and Barra
Walking the Corbetts
1 South of the Great Glen
Walking the Galloway Hills
Walking the Lowther Hills
Walking the Munros
1 Southern, Central and Western Highlands
2 Northern Highlands and the Cairngorms
Winter Climbs Ben Nevis and Glen Coe
Winter Climbs in the Cairngorms
World Mountain Ranges: Scotland

NORTHERN ENGLAND TRAILS
A Northern Coast to Coast Walk
Backpacker's Britain
Northern England
Hadrian's Wall Path
The Dales Way
The Pennine Way
The Spirit of Hadrian's Wall

NORTH EAST ENGLAND, YORKSHIRE DALES AND PENNINES
Great Mountain Days in the Pennines
Historic Walks in North Yorkshire
South Pennine Walks
St Oswald's Way and St Cuthbert's Way
The Cleveland Way and the Yorkshire Wolds Way
The North York Moors
The Reivers Way
The Teesdale Way
The Yorkshire Dales
North and East
South and West
Walking in County Durham
Walking in Northumberland
Walking in the North Pennines
Walks in Dales Country
Walks in the Yorkshire Dales
Walks on the North York Moors – Books 1 & 2

NORTH WEST ENGLAND AND THE ISLE OF MAN
Historic Walks in Cheshire
Isle of Man Coastal Path
The Isle of Man
The Lune Valley and Howgills
The Ribble Way
Walking in Cumbria's Eden Valley
Walking in Lancashire
Walking in the Forest of Bowland and Pendle
Walking on the West Pennine Moors
Walks in Lancashire Witch Country
Walks in Ribble Country
Walks in Silverdale and Arnside
Walks in the Forest of Bowland

LAKE DISTRICT
Coniston Copper Mines
Great Mountain Days in the Lake District
Lake District Winter Climbs

Lakeland Fellranger
The Central Fells
The Mid-Western Fells
The Near Eastern Fells
The Northern Fells
The North-Western Fells
The Southern Fells
The Western Fells
Roads and Tracks of the Lake District
Rocky Rambler's Wild Walks
Scrambles in the Lake District North & South
Short Walks in Lakeland
1 South Lakeland
2 North Lakeland
3 West Lakeland
The Cumbria Coastal Way
The Cumbria Way and the Allerdale Ramble
Tour of the Lake District

DERBYSHIRE, PEAK DISTRICT AND MIDLANDS

High Peak Walks
Scrambles in the Dark Peak
The Star Family Walks
Walking in Derbyshire
White Peak Walks
The Northern Dales
The Southern Dales

SOUTHERN ENGLAND

A Walker's Guide to the Isle of Wight
Suffolk Coast & Heaths Walks
The Cotswold Way
The North Downs Way
The Peddars Way and Norfolk Coast Path
The Ridgeway National Trail
The South Downs Way
The South West Coast Path
The Thames Path
Walking in Berkshire
Walking in Kent
Walking in Sussex
Walking in the Isles of Scilly
Walking in the New Forest
Walking in the Thames Valley
Walking on Dartmoor
Walking on Guernsey
Walking on Jersey
Walking on the Isle of Wight
Walks in the South Downs National Park

WALES AND WELSH BORDERS

Backpacker's Britain – Wales
Glyndwr's Way
Great Mountain Days in Snowdonia
Hillwalking in Snowdonia
Hillwalking in Wales Vols 1 & 2
Offa's Dyke Path
Ridges of Snowdonia
Scrambles in Snowdonia
The Ascent of Snowdon
Lleyn Peninsula Coastal Path
Pembrokeshire Coastal Path
The Shropshire Hills
The Wye Valley Walk
Walking in Pembrokeshire
Walking in the Forest of Dean
Walking in the South Wales Valleys
Walking on Gower
Walking on the Brecon Beacons
Welsh Winter Climbs

INTERNATIONAL CHALLENGES, COLLECTIONS AND ACTIVITIES

Canyoning
Europe's High Points
The Via Francigena (Canterbury to Rome): Part 1

EUROPEAN CYCLING

Cycle Touring in France
Cycle Touring in Ireland
Cycle Touring in Spain
Cycle Touring in Switzerland
Cycling in the French Alps
Cycling the Canal du Midi
Cycling the River Loire
The Danube Cycleway
The Grand Traverse of the Massif Central
The Rhine Cycle Route
The Way of St James

AFRICA

Climbing in the Moroccan Anti-Atlas
Kilimanjaro
Mountaineering in the Moroccan High Atlas
The High Atlas
Trekking in the Atlas Mountains
Walking in the Drakensberg

ALPS – CROSS-BORDER ROUTES

100 Hut Walks in the Alps
Across the Eastern Alps: E5
Alpine Points of View
Alpine Ski Mountaineering
1 Western Alps
2 Central and Eastern Alps
Chamonix to Zermatt
Snowshoeing
Tour of Mont Blanc
Tour of Monte Rosa
Tour of the Matterhorn
Trekking in the Alps
Walking in the Alps
Walks and Treks in the Maritime Alps

PYRENEES AND FRANCE/SPAIN CROSS-BORDER ROUTES

Rock Climbs in The Pyrenees
The GR10 Trail
The Mountains of Andorra
The Pyrenean Haute Route
The Pyrenees
The Way of St James France & Spain
Through the Spanish Pyrenees: GR11
Walks and Climbs in the Pyrenees

AUSTRIA

The Adlerweg
Trekking in Austria's Hohe Tauern
Trekking in the Stubai Alps
Trekking in the Zillertal Alps
Walking in Austria

EASTERN EUROPE

The High Tatras
The Mountains of Romania
Walking in Bulgaria's National Parks
Walking in Hungary

FRANCE

Chamonix Mountain Adventures
Ecrins National Park
GR20: Corsica
Mont Blanc Walks
Mountain Adventures in the Maurienne
The Cathar Way

The GR5 Trail
The Robert Louis Stevenson Trail
Tour of the Oisans: The GR54
Tour of the Queyras
Tour of the Vanoise
Trekking in the Vosges and Jura
Vanoise Ski Touring
Walking in the Auvergne
Walking in the Cathar Region
Walking in the Cevennes
Walking in the Dordogne
Walking in the Haute Savoie North & South
Walking in the Languedoc
Walking in the Tarentaise and Beaufortain Alps
Walking on Corsica

GERMANY

Germany's Romantic Road
Walking in the Bavarian Alps
Walking in the Harz Mountains
Walking the River Rhine Trail

HIMALAYA

Annapurna
Bhutan
Everest: A Trekker's Guide
Garhwal and Kumaon: A Trekker's and Visitor's Guide
Kangchenjunga: A Trekker's Guide
Langtang with Gosainkund and Helambu: A Trekker's Guide
Manaslu: A Trekker's Guide
The Mount Kailash Trek
Trekking in Ladakh

ICELAND & GREENLAND

Trekking in Greenland
Walking and Trekking in Iceland

IRELAND

Irish Coastal Walks
The Irish Coast to Coast Walk
The Mountains of Ireland

ITALY

Gran Paradiso
Sibillini National Park
Stelvio National Park
Shorter Walks in the Dolomites
Through the Italian Alps
Trekking in the Apennines
Trekking in the Dolomites
Via Ferratas of the Italian Dolomites: Vols 1 & 2
Walking in Abruzzo
Walking in Sardinia
Walking in Sicily
Walking in the Central Italian Alps
Walking in the Dolomites
Walking in Tuscany
Walking on the Amalfi Coast
Walking the Italian Lakes

MEDITERRANEAN

Jordan – Walks, Treks, Caves, Climbs and Canyons
The Ala Dag
The High Mountains of Crete
The Mountains of Greece
Treks and Climbs in Wadi Rum, Jordan
Walking in Malta
Western Crete

NORTH AMERICA

British Columbia
The Grand Canyon
The John Muir Trail
The Pacific Crest Trail

SOUTH AMERICA

Aconcagua and the Southern Andes
Torres del Paine

SCANDINAVIA

Walking in Norway

SLOVENIA, CROATIA AND MONTENEGRO

The Julian Alps of Slovenia
The Mountains of Montenegro
Trekking in Slovenia
Walking in Croatia
Walking in Slovenia: The Karavanke

SPAIN AND PORTUGAL

Costa Blanca: West
Mountain Walking in Southern Catalunya
The Mountains of Central Spain
The Northern Caminos
Trekking through Mallorca
Walking in Madeira
Walking in Mallorca
Walking in the Algarve
Walking in the Cordillera Cantabrica
Walking in the Sierra Nevada
Walking on La Gomera and El Hierro
Walking on La Palma
Walking on Tenerife
Walks and Climbs in the Picos de Europa

SWITZERLAND

Alpine Pass Route
Canyoning in the Alps
Central Switzerland
The Bernese Alps
The Swiss Alps
Tour of the Jungfrau Region
Walking in the Valais
Walking in Ticino
Walks in the Engadine

TECHNIQUES

Geocaching in the UK
Indoor Climbing
Lightweight Camping
Map and Compass
Mountain Weather
Moveable Feasts
Outdoor Photography
Polar Exploration
Rock Climbing
Sport Climbing
The Book of the Bivvy
The Hillwalker's Guide to Mountaineering
The Hillwalker's Manual

MINI GUIDES

Avalanche!
Navigating with a GPS
Navigation
Pocket First Aid and Wilderness Medicine
Snow